$V_6 2$

DATE DUE

HIS
EMINENCE
of Los Angeles

HIS EMINENCE
of Los Angeles

James Francis Cardinal McIntyre

VOLUME TWO

Msgr. Francis J. Weber

Saint Francis Historical Society
Mission Hills, California 1997

The author wishes to gratefully acknowledge the William R. and Virginia Hayden Foundation, the Ernest and Helen Chacon Trust, the Cardinal McIntyre Fund for Charity and Cardinal Roger Mahony for their generous financial support in the publication of this book.

Designed and printed by Kimberly Press
Santa Barbara, California
in a press run of 1,500 copies

Library of Congress Cataloging-in-Publication Data

Weber, Francis J.
    His Eminence of Los Angeles : James Francis Cardinal McIntyre/Francis J. Weber.
        p.   cm.
    Includes bibliographical reference and index.
    ISBN 0-87461-921-1
    1. McIntyre, J. Francis A. (James Francis Aloysius), 1886-1979.
2. Cardinals – California – Los Angeles Region – Biography.
3. Catholic church – California – Los Angeles Region – History – 20th century.
4. Los Angeles Region (Calif.) – Church history – 20th century. I. Title.
BX4705.M4763W43 1996
282'.092 – dc20
[B]
                                        96-32975
                                          CIP

Table of Contents

Appendices

16. Ethnic Ministry

HISPANIC-AMERICANS

Soon after his canonical installation at Saint Vibiana's Cathedral, McIntyre set out to develop a comprehensive program for dealing with what others called the Mexican-American "problem," but what he referred to as the Hispanic "challenge." Enlisting the assistance of Father Augustine O'Dea, the archbishop felt that by defining the scope of the "challenge," he could thereby come up with the best methodology for dealing spiritually with what was even then the largest foreign language group in Southern California.

At that time, Hispanics were the fastest growing group in the area, with a birth rate of forty two per one thousand, a factor complicated by an ongoing emigration from Mexico. McIntyre estimated that 40% of the Catholics in the archdiocese were Mexican-American by birth or origin and fully half of the baptisms were accounted for by Mexican babies.

While 80% of the Mexican-Americans claimed to be Roman Catholic, only 30% practiced their faith, with the women more committed than their spouses. The largest concentration of them had come from Chihuahua, Sonora, Sinaloa and Baja California where they had little if any educational opportunities or association with the Church. For that reason, the archbishop felt that religious instruction programs for the children were imperative. Most observers felt that there was very little discrimination against them such as is found in other regions of the Southwest. Those living in and around Los Angeles were "better off here not only socially and economically," but also had better opportunities for religious worship and religious instruction than they had experienced in the parts of Mexico from which they came.

McIntyre was puzzled and upset by Protestant proselytization among the Mexican-Americans. Available figures indicated that most Protestant denominations admitted that their largest proportional increases came from converts from among the Latin American people. At the same time, when the Church had been able to give them adequate religious instruction, as well as church facilities, Protestants inroads were minimal. Most of the Protestant successes were occurring in colonies where there was no Catholic church or religious educational center.

Assessing the goals of the Church among these people, McIntyre saw "the greatest need" as being the erection of more parochial schools. Next was the need for more Religious men and women and catechists to work among public school children. Also necessary were more Settlement Houses in Mexican-American districts and boarding homes to accommodate court wards. He noted that juvenile delinquency among the Mexicans was high and he thought that a trade school for boys would greatly alleviate that problem. He viewed the average Mexican-American colony as being "entirely disorganized." There was very little responsible leadership and he felt that the Church should take measures to develop that quality by offering, where possible, "greater opportunities for higher education." He advocated scholarships in Catholic colleges, as well as training courses preparatory for civil service jobs.

Already the archdiocese was at work. In particular McIntyre told about his envisioned drive for funds with which to build two high schools on the east side, as well as five grammar schools, two of which had already been inaugurated. He mentioned the work being done by the Catholic Youth Organization as providing "a healthy outlet for their energies in those districts where there is a second generation." Young people were often confused by the old fashioned culture of their parents and the manners of the United States which were frequently "presented to them under the worst possible auspices. We need to give archdiocesan support to the associations of Mexican youths - for boys and girls - encouraging pastors to develop such organization in their parishes." Of particular benefit was the renewed emphasis on teaching Spanish in the archdiocesan seminaries. Perfunctory courses had given way to new and more appealing programs. Courses in Hispanic culture, history of proselytism and pastoral methods were being offered. Seminarians were encouraged to speak Spanish at meals, during their recreation periods and on walks. More gifted students were given the opportunity of a visit to Mexico City. McIntyre concluded by calling for greater cooperation with the Bishops' Committee for the Spanish speaking, suggesting that Archbishop Robert E. Lucey's "tendency to overemphasize the social side at the expense of the religious" might need to be re-examined. He noted that "some of the older bishops of the southwest, who had long lived with the Mexican-Americans had suggested privately that the committee would be on more solid foundation if in time it were headed by a prelate more universally acceptable."[1]

In the recent past it has been fashionable, if not historically correct, to criticize members of the Catholic hierarchy in the United States for not doing enough for Mexican Americans. One writer, in an essay entitled "Chicano and Catholic," complained and declared that "simple honesty demands that high tribute" be paid to people like James Francis Cardinal McIntyre for the pioneering work he did "in training and assigning priests specifically to this work" within his jurisdiction.[2] Speaking only for Los Angeles, the Church was indeed very active in looking after Mexican-Americans in many ways. The first obvious example would be that of supporting and partially financing the apostolate of the Bishops' Committee for the Spanish Speaking which had its headquarters in San Antonio, Texas. At a time when priests were at a high premium number-wise, McIntyre released two of them to act as directors of the Committee, Fathers John J. Birch and Matthew Kelly. The publication for that Committee, published quarterly and entitled *Our Catholic Southwest* together with the minutes of the meetings of the Committee, indicate widespread concern and action on behalf of Mexican-Americans in the Archdiocese of Los Angeles.

BRACEROS - MIGRANT WORKERS

One area in which Los Angeles excelled all other areas of the southwest was its outreach to migrant workers, generally referred to as *braceros*. McIntyre never liked the law that allowed them to work in the United States because he felt that it attracted persons into an unknown and often unfriendly land. In the late 1950s, when labor camps were set up in Orange and Ventura counties, the cardinal endeavored to provide chaplains to visit the camps and look after their spiritual needs. In Orange county, there were camps at Fullerton, Anaheim, Irvine, Villa Park and Tustin employing about 3,000 citrus workers. Father Raphael Toner, M.S.Ss.T., administrator at La Purisima Mission at El Modena coordinated Masses, confessions and other sacraments for those contract workers. He also distributed rosaries, pamphlets and other religious articles, along with the Catholic weekly newspaper *La Frontera* from Tijuana. Toner and the other priests assisting in the program were paid directly from the Chancery Office. In 1960, the annual report on the spiritual care of *braceros* in Orange county indicated that upwards of 5,000 men were active in the program. Television programs in Spanish were shown as were visual aids in Catholic doctrine. As the years progressed and the number of *braceros* escalated, the ministrations of local clergy kept pace.[3]

330

In mid-1955, provisions were made to care for the approximately 4,000 *braceros* in Ventura county who were located in fifteen different camps. The largest concentrations were at camps in Oxnard, Saticoy and Camarillo. A priest was acquired from Mexico and, with the assistance of seminarians from Saint John's Seminary, he made periodic visits to the various camps on a weekly basis. McIntyre wrote to Rome for faculties to allow priests to offer evening Mass more than once a day, a provision that was then given only rarely.[4] Missions were preached and a series of radio messages was beamed out to the county weekly over stations KASA and KVEN. In later years, additional *bracero* camps were opened in Santa Barbara and Los Angeles counties. It was an ambitious apostolate and one which has received little or no recognition in the annals.

A feature story in *The Tidings* told about spiritual ministrations at the Somis Labor Camp, home for "250 *braceros*, Mexican nationals, brought into the U.S. for field work under terms of an agreement between the two nations." Noting that their contract carried no provisions for "spiritual care," the article explained how Father Harold Beutler, C.M., journeyed to the camp twice weekly for Mass and the other sacraments. Camp manager Frank Gill had acquired a former barracks building which the workers had renovated for a chapel dedicated to Our Lady of Guadalupe. After the celebration of Mass, seminarians would recite the rosary, teach catechism and write letters to families back in Mexico. Located in a picturesque eucalyptus grove, the chapel was looked after by Legion of Mary members from nearby Camarillo. "To the men, the chapel makes this corner of a strange land less alien."[5]

Among the reports contained in a publication for the Bishops' Committee for Spanish Speaking was one in 1958 in which Father F. A. Alvarez told about his ministry in Ventura County. He said that "only this last year I gave 1,018 lectures by radio. I preached daily at Mass and on Sunday I celebrated three Masses. I celebrated Mass daily at night among the twenty-five camps. We also had fifty-two Sunday Holy Hour devotions. It was difficult to hear their Confessions because of the large numbers. As I was sick three months I could only preach twelve missions in twelve camps, but I expect to do more in 1959. The *braceros* in this region of California received very good treatment from Mrs. Herky and Fidel Villaseñor. This last year they had the largest *bracero* camp in the United States. An enormous salon was turned into a chapel where Mass was said each Sunday. There was a special playground which was kept orderly and clean. One day we had a solemn High Mass in the open at this camp for more than 3,000 *braceros* who all sang together and then marched in a solemn procession in groups of four carrying candles. I ministered to some 6,000 *braceros* in Ventura County."[6]

In mid-1955, Archbishop Amleto Cicognani, the Apostolic Delegate to the Church in the United States, wrote to McIntyre asking about the conditions of Mexican workers who had crossed the border "secretly" and were obliged to live hidden lives. He wondered what was being done for them spiritually.[7] McIntyre replied that the subject had "been the occasion of much concern in the Southwest." He explained the migratory worker program and how they were provided for in various labor camps. But he noted that the so-called "wet-back" situation was a totally different problem. Such "enter illegally and of course without family. They mix with their Mexican confreres. In many instances, they continue without difficulty until by some means or other, they come in contact with the law. Meanwhile they live with Mexican families and do not constitute a particular group to be served. In fact, anonymity is an advantage. Besides, many of them wish to return as soon as their purpose is served and rejoin their families. Our Catholic Welfare Agency tries to help them whenever difficulties arise."[8]

McIntyre was an effective administrator who anticipated problems. For example, in 1950, he asked the editor of *The Tidings* to reprint an essay by Louis Budenz on "How Reds Lure L.A. Workers," wherein the author attempted to alert readers about the dangers of communist exploitation of Mexican-American grievances. Budenz expressed alarm that "the Reds were able to attract almost 10,000 Mexican-Americans to hear Henry Wallace speak in Spanish at Los Angeles during the 1948[9] presidential election campaign." The communist movement was seen by Budenz as a threat to Catholic allegiance and loyalties. Barrio dwellers did not need social reforms but ministers of the Gospel.

McIntyre's greatest success on behalf of Mexican-Americans was in the area of education. Parochial schools, he felt, would provide a "safeguard in their tradition" and preserve them "from an American brand of liberalism." By 1957, twenty-two parochial schools had been constructed, at a cost of over $4,700,000 in predominantly Mexican-American areas and with the passage of three more years almost every parish in East Los Angeles had its own school.

The Americanization theme was a further motive in the archbishop's promotion of parochial schools for Mexican Americans. In a 1949 address to a largely Mexican-American audience, he said: "We look to the Mexican people to take leadership in American ideals, to take their places in the government." The Church, he assured them, would do all it could "to further their opportunity."[10]

In a dedication ceremony for a parochial school in a Mexican area, the Spanish-born pastor in 1953 echoed the archbishop in proclaiming the patriotic value of the parochial school. "Apart from being a true protection against juvenile delinquency," he said, the school "has opened . . . the doors to genuine American life with its integral sense of the human person as a child of God, Christian and democratic."[11]

The school building program, then, was an important manifestation of a twofold strategy adopted by McIntyre and by other Church officials in the Southwest: 1) to preserve and defend the Catholic faith of Mexican-Americans and their offspring against Protestant influence and, later, against communism, moral "liberalism" and "secularism"; 2) to exhibit the Church to the larger society as an institution instilling American ideals into its laity of Mexican background, i.e., only under Catholic auspices and supervision could Mexicans be made into good, loyal Americans.[12]

In a report submitted to the archdiocesan Board of Consultors in 1961, Msgr. Patrick Languille said that of the approximately 3,500,000 Americans of Mexican ancestry then living in the United States, nearly 90% resided in the western states with Los Angeles county accounting for 700,000. The heaviest concentration of Mexican-Americans lived in the Boyle-Heights, Belvedere, East Los Angeles and Pico Rivera areas. He found that there was an increased interest in education, political ascendance and stronger social life. There was "little, if any, anti-clericalism among the average Mexican-American families." He reported that the close identification of Mexican-Americans with their parish was not being lost as they advanced socially and economically. The Church and Church-related organizations, such as the C.Y.O., were the most influential institutions among the Mexican-American people. Surveys had shown that between 82 and 85% of the Mexican-Americans listed the Catholic Church as the most influential and important institution in their lives. Practically all were interested in getting a better education and the "drop-out" rate in Catholic high schools was considerably less than in public schools. Newspapers had some influence, but radio and television were the "most influential" forms of the media among Mexican-Americans.[13]

CURSILLO MOVEMENT

The contribution made by Mallorca to California did not end in 1856 with the death of Fray Juan Cabot, the last of the island's friars. Indeed, there is much of that same missionary enthusiasm evident almost two centuries after the arrival of the first missionaries from that Mediterranean paradise. In 1944, Eduardo Bonnin, a convert from Judaism, invited about thirty priests and laymen to join him in counteracting the personal immorality and religious indifference then creeping into Spanish society. His aim was to transform the small group into militant Catholics whose lifestyles would revolve about the sacraments.[14] Shortly thereafter, Bonnin approached the Right Reverend Juan Hervas y Benet, and asked the Bishop of Mallorca for guidance and approval of the movement. Bishop Hervas heartily endorsed the proposals and personally assumed direction of what would later be known as the *Cursillos de Cristianidad*. From the very outset, the prelate insisted that the retreat like movement be carefully structured.

The Cursillo, as envisioned by Hervas, was to be "a short, intensive course, in which priest and lay leaders, in close collaboration, develop a particular method, the aim of which is the Christian renewal of the Cursillistas and their apostolic projection into society, so that they will extend the Kingdom of Christ."[15] In May, 1957, two flyers from the Spanish air force, Agustin Palomino and Bernardo Vadell, while on a training program in Waco, Texas, joined with Father Gabriel Fernandez, to launch the Cursillo program in the United States. The initial Cursillo was held in Los Angeles under the direction of the Claretian Fathers in 1962. Within four years, thirty-three Cursillos had been conducted and, by 1967, nearly 1,200 persons, 600 with Spanish surnames, had made the Cursillo.[16]

The unsubstantiated charge by former Jesuit Patrick H. McNamara that the Cursillo movement was "just tolerated" in the Archdiocese of Los Angeles, an allegation he attributed to a prominent churchman interviewed,"[17] is patently untrue and calumnious. McIntyre was not overly enthusiastic about certain elements in the movement, namely its pledge of secrecy and the practice of recruiting first men and then women, something which he felt was basically sexist. On the other hand, he was deeply impressed by the fact that the Cursillo appealed to and attracted action orientated Catholics who were then motivated toward social involvement. That was something he always advocated, namely lay not clerical involvement in social issues. He also was enamored by the lifetime commitment made by Cursillistas.

Involvement of the Church in social action took on a new and more dramatic form in the mid 1960s with the famous Delano grape strikes in Central California. Though he didn't favor the notion of priests getting actively involved, he was among the signatories to a statement issued by all the California bishops reaffirming the right of farm laborers "not to be looked down upon as outside agitators." Their organizations "must be protected by law." It would be "unjust for . . . grower organizations to strive to prevent by reprisal the legitimate efforts of farm laborers to form worker associations or unions."[18]

The late 1960s witnessed a breaking down of the traditional affection exhibited by Mexican-Americans for the Church and its clergy. In 1969, Msgr. William Johnson reported on the East Los Angeles Parish Program which clergyman in that area of the city had organized. He noted that many "priests are concerned about the growing militancy in the Mexican-American community. The leadership which promotes this antagonistic spirit is often disassociated from the Church, but their activities do have an impact on our parishes, schools and other institutional activities."[19]

The new and often self-proclaimed leadership that began speaking for Mexican-Americans in the mid-1960s disliked McIntyre and the "father figure" he had become in the barrios. An editorial in the Phoenix *Evening American* wondered why none of the many wire stories had pointed out that Cardinal McIntyre "is regarded as the great friend of the Spanish-American groups in the United States." The writer noted that he had "devoted lengthy time and service to helping the groups who are numbered in the hundreds of thousands in his overseeing of 1.6 million parishioners" in Los Angeles. Astutely it was observed that McIntyre's conservative philosophy is well known and "it is for this reason that the liberal press has criticized him whenever possible."[20]

McIntyre was never discouraged by the unpleasant things he read about himself in the press, probably because he didn't place much credence in its validity, especially on such occasions as that which took place on May 15, 1965, after he had dedicated the new church for Resurrection Parish in East Los Angeles. A surprise *fiesta* was staged honoring the cardinal by the parish which served 15,000 Catholics, most of them Americans of Mexican descent. The *fiesta* was staged to express gratitude for McIntyre's work on behalf of parishioners and others in the area. Mrs. Jennie Reyes presented a plaque on behalf of *Las Damas Catolicas* thanking him for his "cooperation and consideration in providing East Los Angeles with more educational institutions for the betterment of our youth and our community."[21]

In 1972 when the patriarch of Mexican-American Catholics in the Archdiocese of Los Angeles, Msgr. Michael Sheahan, celebrated his golden priestly jubilee, the Catholic paper published an interview which portrayed the way things really were in East Los Angeles. About the Mexican-Americans, Sheahan said that "they will possess the land because they have children, because they have the faith and the faith gives them fortitude and an outlook on life." Then he observed that "the Church is the great center and focus of their lives and they become integrated into the community through the Church. People should not be misled by those who now shout loudly against the Church, because this is not the common feeling among the Mexican people I know and come in contact with." When asked about charges that the Church had neglected Mexican-Americans, Sheahan said that to him "Cardinal McIntyre is one of the greatest benefactors the Mexican people here have had, because he tried to raise them up economically and socially through education. He set aside everything, Cathedral and all, when he came here and saw what had to be done. He gave them the best that he could."[22]

When McIntyre retired in 1970, Richard Cruz, leader of the militant Mexican-American *Catolicos por la Raza*, sent a message wishing the cardinal "good health and happiness in all sincerity." Mrs. Paul Leininger, local President of the Southern California branch of the National Federation of Laymen, said that it would "be a long time before his record is equalled in the areas of education, social welfare and work in the minority communities of Los Angeles. They will crucify him because he isn't marching out in the streets . . . but the work he has done is very little known because he is very modest and humble."[23]

ETHNIC MIGRATIONS

Like most of his contemporaries in the California episcopate, McIntyre did not like, encourage or allow the formation of "national" parishes in Los Angeles. His experience in New York convinced him that such groupings caused far more problems than they solved. He often pointed to downtown Chicago, where earlier generations had built three or four Catholic national churches within blocks of one another. Invariably, as youngsters grew up speaking English, the need and usefulness of such parishes and churches disappeared and neighborhoods were left with empty houses-of-worship. While he encouraged retention of the best old world traditions and lingual diversities, the cardinal felt that the sooner immigrants became Americanized, the sooner they would start moving up the economic ladder.

During the mid years of his tenure, McIntyre was confronted with the beginnings of sizable ethnic immigrations by peoples who brought with them many of the same problems and challenges that earlier faced Catholic leadership on the eastern seaboard. In addition, immigration from the Orient began in the 1970s. In every case, McIntyre endeavored to obtain lingually and culturally sensitive and qualified priests to look after their spiritual needs, all the while insisting that, eventually, the new immigrants should take their place alongside those whose parents or grandparents had come to the United States and/or California in earlier times. While a whole treatise could be written about this fascinating phase of McIntyre's archiepiscopate, there is only room in these pages to cursorily mention the larger groupings.

LITHUANIANS

There was great love and affection for the Lithuanian colony in Los Angeles and each year McIntyre or one of his delegates would attend a Mass in August for the liberation of Lithuania and the other suppressed nations. In 1957, McIntyre himself presiding at the ceremonies, said "it was our hope and prayer that your noble contributions to American life will ever be sustained." He joined "in expressing sympathy to your brothers and sisters in the homeland as we ask God's bountiful blessings upon them."[24]

While Saint Casimir parish in Los Angeles was always referred to as a Lithuanian parish, it was canonically a territorial parish and remains so even today. When asked by the Lithuanian R.C. Priests' League of America in February of 1960 to allow "a salaried Lithuanian priest" to come to Los Angeles and to engage in work among the Lithuanians exclusively,[25] the cardinal politely demurred, noting that the parish where most of them worshipped was already presided over by a Lithuanian pastor. He felt the archdiocese would "not welcome the injection of a greater and perhaps predominate national spirit" in their lives in Los Angeles.[26]

When a new church was in preparation, in 1961, the archdiocesan newspaper observed that Saint Casimir's parish had "more displaced persons than any other parish in the archdiocese." It also noted that the parish had become "an orientation center to help former Lithuanians in their adjustment to American life."[27]

HUNGARIANS

Primary beneficiaries of the Catholic Resettlement Committee, established by McIntyre under the watchful eye of Father Mathias Lani, were Hungarians. A report for 1951 indicates that upwards of 3,000 persons were processed, located and employed through this agency. Lani reported to McIntyre that "most of the new arrivals are fine, religious and church-going people."[28] Volunteers were organized to teach the new immigrants language skills, along with the other amenities needed by candidates for American citizenship.

Stories were run in *The Tidings* about the immigrants at least monthly. In June of 1956, for example, an essay appeared about an ethnic German family who spent more than three years in a miserable and overcrowded refugee camp in Linz, Austria.[29] Most of the Hungarian refugees were initially affiliated with Saint Stephen's parish, where Lani was pastor, until they could be relocated.

In one of his *El Rodeo* columns, Alphonse Antczak recalled how "displaced persons from refugee camps in Europe were arriving here regularly in long trains. They were met, always at dawn, at Union Station by Fr. Matthias Lani, pastor of St. Stephen's, 37th and Woodlawn, and volunteers of Catholic Resettlement. St. Stephen's was a gateway to America and a new life for thousands of European refugees. Fr. Lani was one of the great priests of the Church of Los Angeles. By sheer energy and force of personality he resettled thousands - got them homes, got them jobs."[30]

CZECHOSLOVAKIANS

In 1950, estimates placed the number of Czechs and Slovaks living in Los Angeles at 2,498 and double that number of offspring living in the archdiocese. By 1964, the number exceeded 10,000 due partly to the fact that a large number of their families moved to California from the east for health reasons and also because of the country's favorable immigration policies. A report to Cardinal McIntyre indicated that there were twelve organizations comprised of about 1,500 members who met at the Sokol Hall on North Western Avenue. They attended Mass at Blessed Sacrament church in Hollywood where they were cared for by Father Adolph Pelikan, S.J.[31]

McIntyre followed their progress closely. At a Mass celebrated for the 1100th anniversary of the death of Saint Cyril, the cardinal referred to exiled Czechoslovakians as "living martyrs of the Church of Silence." At that time, Bohumil Smutnik, secretary of the Czech Mission, was awarded the *Benemerenti* Medal personally by McIntyre. The cardinal said he was "proud to have so many Czechoslovakians living in this archdiocese" and he welcomed them, observing they had "demonstrated love of the faith and love of the Church. They have suffered and it has made them stronger." Thinking back to his New York days, McIntyre said he had "lived a long time, long enough to see much history made. When I was Chancellor in New York I had to provide priests for many groups of immigrants driven from their lands or who came here to make a new life. I know how they feel, and I know how they have enriched these United States with their arts and crafts and hard work."[32]

ITALIANS

The parish of Saint Peter in downtown Los Angeles had always been an umbrella for the Italian community of the archdiocese, embodying the religious and cultural roots cherished by every Italian. Of the many programs existing for the Italian people, none surpassed the Italian Catholic Federation whose avowed purpose was "to bring back people to the Body of Christ."[33] Cardinal McIntyre was an enthusiastic backer of the ICF and, in 1959, told his priests that it was "a group of adults, of Italian origin or extraction" with a purely spiritual orientation. He noted that the ICF was already functioning in twenty-five parishes "and the results have been very gratifying, so much so that we recommend the establishment of a group in any parish where there are Italian residents."[34] Throughout McIntyre's time, the ICF prospered and became the most active and effective organization in the archdiocese, fulfilling its objective of being "an ideological, beautiful expression of Catholic Action."[35]

CUBANS

McIntyre's work with the Cuban refugees is among the most memorable and significant of any parallel program anywhere in the world. In 1962, he organized the Cuban Refugee Resettlement Committee and, within two years, that organization had relocated the second largest number of refugees outside the New York area. John F. Thomas, an official in the United States Department of Health, Education and Welfare, issued a statement commending the program, saying that "we would like to express the deep appreciation of the Federal government for the work accomplished by the Cuban Resettlement Committee of the Archdiocese of Los Angeles."[36]

The cardinal took an active part in the various outreach activities of the committee. On one occasion, after a group of children gave him a statue of Our Lady of Charity of Cobre, the patroness of Cuba, he took the occasion to encourage youngsters to learn

English. He told them about having traveled to Cuba in the days when he was stationed in New York and he spoke about the large Cuban colony that he knew in Manhattan.[37] McIntyre received many signs of affection from the Cuban refugees, including a plaque which assured him they would "be forever grateful for the fatherly spirit with which he has taken care of all our needs during our stay in the archdiocese."[38]

Even as late as 1967, an average of 200 Cubans a month were still coming to Los Angeles.[39] In 1968, "the 10,000th Cuban refugee arrived, just five days after being airlifted from his homeland. It was estimated that about half the total number of Cuban refugees coming to California had been located under Catholic auspices.[40]

NATIVE AMERICANS

The esteem for McIntyre among Native Americans was amply demonstrated by a feature story that ran across the wires of the NCWC News Service in April, 1958. It proclaimed that "the Apaches of Arizona have a new chief. His name is Red Robe Friend. In his own territory, he is better known as His Eminence James Francis Cardinal McIntyre." The investiture took place at the Statler Hilton hotel, before 1,000 members of the 144 Lay Mission Circles. The Apaches had come from Saint John's Mission, Komatke Village, to "express their appreciation for the Cardinal's aid to Indian missions. They said it in actions by their spirited dancing and in words by making Cardinal McIntyre a chief of their tribe."[41]

By 1969, the archdiocesan newspaper estimated that there were about 45,000 Indians in the county, about ten percent of whom were Catholic. Widely scattered, they were affiliated with fifteen tribes. The article noted that the native Americans no longer fought off the white man's gun fire with bow and arrow. "Instead, he fights the white man's indifference with calmness, patience and a courtesy that ought to be the envy of older Christian civilizations. He is not angry with the white man's rush to affluence. To curse the darkness is the one luxury the American Indian knows he cannot afford. He is too busy trying to reach the American dream."[42]

Cardinal McIntyre and his two auxiliary bishops visit a booth at the Holy Childhood meeting in 1966.

"Chief Red Robe Friend" was inaugurated into the Apaches of Arizona, 1958.

KOREANS

Though the first Koreans moved to Los Angeles in 1905, there were only a handful living in the area prior to the late 1960s. When the *Korea Weekly* was established in 1969, Cardinal McIntyre sent a letter to the editor saying that he was "happy to learn that the Korean community in Los Angeles is establishing a medium of expression." He predicted that the reception of the newspaper would "be warm and gracious."[43] A short article in *The Tidings*, the following year, noted that the Korean Catholic Association had grown "from thirty to more than 400 members in two years."[44] McIntyre gave every encouragement to the Koreans, asking Father Lawrence J. Lee, a Korean priest, to offer Masses for them at Saint Vincent's Church each week. Perhaps even McIntyre did not foresee that by the early 1990s, the City of Los Angeles would boast of the largest Korean Catholic population outside the Orient.

JAPANESE

After World War II, a number of the Japanese interned during the hostilities returned to Los Angeles. Only a small number of them were Catholic. A report sent to the clergy of the archdiocese in 1954 said that "out of a total Japanese population of almost 40,000 in Los Angeles County, Catholics number scarcely 1,200."[45] Father Everett Briggs, a Maryknoller, looked after the Japanese Catholics. With McIntyre's endorsement and encouragement, Father Briggs served as editor, publisher and treasurer of three Japanese Catholic newspapers, all of which were printed and distributed mostly in Japan. All three tabloids were devoted to giving the Catholic answers to social problems of the day, an important task in Japan where communist propaganda was then prevalent.[46] Saint Francis Xavier Chapel, which was operated under the auspices of Maryknoll, also sponsored a fifteen minute program each Sunday on KBLA. Those programs, in both English and Japanese, were widely circulated.[47] Cardinal McIntyre personally participated as often as he could in all the outreach activities for the Japanese people.

FILIPINOS

In mid-1956, Bishop Alejandro Olalia of Lipa, in the Philippines, apparently complained to the Apostolic Delegate in the United

States that the Filipino people in Los Angeles and other areas were not receiving adequate religious attention. The charge irritated McIntyre who said he had received no complaints. While acknowledging that it wasn't always possible to obtain Filipino priests, "the fact is that all services are available to the Filipino people throughout the archdiocese in both English and Spanish." He told the delegate that the 35,000 Filipinos in the greater Los Angeles area were widely scattered and did not live in clusters, as was the case with other nationalities. He noted that there was a Filipino parish conducted by the Columbian Fathers which serves its people effectively. That church also served as a "social center and a national gathering point for the Filipino people." Inasmuch as most spoke English and/or Spanish, there was no reason why the couldn't also attend other parishes in the archdiocese. McIntyre felt that "they are better Americans and better Catholics by attending the parish church of the area in which they live," noting that they "are received everywhere with equality."[48]

Notes to the Text

1. AALA, Brief Report on the Condition of Mexicans in the Archdiocese of Los Angeles, Los Angeles, 1948.
2. Charles Dollen, "Pastoral Reflection" in the *Homiletic and Pastoral Review* LXXI (March, 1971), 415.
3. AALA, Annual Report on the Spiritual Care of *Braceros*, Los Angeles, 1960.
4. AALA, James Francis Cardinal McIntyre to Alfonso Carinci, Los Angeles, July 26, 1956.
5. *The Tidings*, July 15, 1955.
6. AALA, Progress Report 1958. Regional Office, Bishops' Committee on the Spanish Speaking (San Antonio, 1958), Pp. 4-5.
7. AALA, Amleto Cicognani to James Francis Cardinal McIntyre, Washington, D.C., June 2, 1955.
8. AALA, James Francis Cardinal McIntyre to Amleto Cicognani, Los Angeles, June 7, 1955.
9. *The Tidings*, August 4, 1950.
10. *Ibid.*, November 4, 1949.
11. *Ibid.*, May 22, 1953.
12. Patrick McNamara, S.J., *The Mexican-American People* (New York, 1970), p. 460.
13. AALA, Memo to James Francis Cardinal McIntyre, Los Angeles, September 7, 1961.
14. *The Tidings*, September 22, 1961.
15. *Utreya* III (November, 1961), 8.
16. AALA, James Francis Cardinal McIntyre - Memo, Los Angeles, April 14, 1962.
17. *The Mexican-American People* (New York, 1970), p. 484.
18. *Central California Register*, March 17, 1966.
19. AALA, William R. Johnson to James Francis Cardinal McIntyre, Los Angeles, December 9, 1969.
20. AALA, Undated editorial, c. 1965.
21. *The Tidings*, May 21, 1965.
22. *Ibid.*, June 16, 1972.
23. Los Angeles *Times*, January 22, 1970.
24. *The Tidings*, August 9, 1957.
25. AALA, Joseph G. Cepukaitis to James Francis Cardinal McIntyre, Philadelphia, February 8, 1960.
26. AALA, James Francis Cardinal McIntyre to Joseph G. Cepukaitis, Los Angeles, February 23, 1960.

27. *The Tidings*, January 9, 1961.
28. AALA, Mathias Lani to J. Francis A. McIntyre, Los Angeles, April 21, 1952.
29. *The Tidings*, June 22, 1956.
30. *Ibid.*, May 13, 1988.
31. AALA, Bohumil Smutnik to James Francis Cardinal McIntyre, Los Angeles, February 26, 1964.
32. *The Tidings*, June 27, 1969.
33. Francis J. Weber, *California Catholicity* (Los Angeles, 1979), p. 187.
34. AALA, James Francis Cardinal McIntyre to Priests, Los Angeles, January 20, 1959.
35. Robert Brennan quoted in *The First Fifty Years* (San Francisco, 1974), p. 69.
36. *The Tidings*, December 11, 1964.
37. *Ibid.*, December 25, 1964.
38. *Ibid.*, May 21, 1965.
39. *Ibid.*, October 13, 1967.
40. *Ibid.*, March 22, 1968.
41. AALA, NCWC News Service, Los Angeles Release for April 21, 1958.
42. *The Tidings*, June 13, 1969.
43. AALA, James Francis Cardinal McIntyre to Peter M. Park, Los Angeles, February 6, 1969.
44. *The Tidings*, March 20, 1970.
45. AALA, Timothy Manning to Priests, Los Angeles, July 29, 1954.
46. *The Tidings*, November 2, 1956.
47. *Ibid.*, February 1, 1957.
48. AALA, James Francis Cardinal McIntyre to Amleto Cicognani, Los Angeles, August 4, 1956.

17. Pope-Pourri

THE HOLY SEE

To James Francis Cardinal McIntyre, the Holy Father truly was the Vicar of Christ. McIntyre esteemed the office of Pius XII as well as the person of Eugenio Pacelli whom he had known since the 1930s. That affection was evident in his correspondence, addresses and references to the pontiff in casual conversation.

Each year, he wrote a lengthy letter to the priests, seeking their assistance in the annual collection for the Holy Father known as Peter's Pence. In 1948, for example, he reminded them that "the Holy Father leads the universe in thought, and is a living example to the world in the expression of truth and the practice of charity. He is the direct successor of St. Peter to whom our Divine Savior spoke, Thou art Peter, and upon this Rock I shall build My Church and the gates of Hell shall not prevail against it. That promise Christ has fulfilled throughout the centuries."

He went on to say that "The power of Peter, the voice of Peter, the charity of Peter expressing the power, the voice and the charity of Christ - are proclaimed by the white-robed figure of Pius XII as he speaks words of advice and admonition; words of gentleness and kindliness; words of encouragement and exhortation; words of blessing and benediction to Catholic and non-Catholic throughout the known world. His plea is always for the poor, the afflicted, the persecuted, the lame, the halt, the oppressed, the underprivileged. His charities are world-wide and constant. They are hidden and known to few. They are real and magnanimous.

"As he is the representative of Christ on earth, so is he our representative before the world, our leader. In this leadership he needs our support, moral and material, as well as spiritual; that he may continue to supply the aid he is constantly giving to the most needy of a suffering world. They constantly beseech the Father of Christendom for crumbs from the table of Catholics throughout the world. On next Sunday, we shall gather up these crumbs which constitute what is called Peter's Pence, or the offerings of the faithful to the works of the Universal Church. May we ask that your generous offering be a crust rather than a crumb."[1]

When the pontiff observed his golden jubilee of priesthood, McIntyre asked that the anniversary be a jubilee on which "in all the churches of this archdiocese, there be held a triduum for the intentions of the Holy Father." For that year, he transferred the Peter's Pence collection to Pentecost Sunday, so that Catholics could make a sacrifice, in honor of the Pope, "to help the stricken of suffering lands."[2] He said that "those places where God's sunshine has been the most productive . . . must look to the fields that have been ravaged in battle."[3]

In his appeal for 1951, McIntyre said that Pius XII "manifests the unchanging truths of God, the Father, Son and Holy Ghost, as they apply to the wayward world." He went on to observe that "because these truths are the bases for world peace, thinking men listen in reverence to the utterances of His Holiness. He has implored the all-powerful God for the shielding of our warring soldiers; he has pleaded to the merciful Father in heaven to move the hearts of men in charity toward the hungry. His hand is stretched out to the homeless and the harassed peoples without freedom, despoiled of the fruits of the soil their labor has produced. His voice is a voice crying in the wilderness of war: Make straight the pathways of the Lord."[4] On yet another occasion, he said that "our offerings are small, but given with grace and generosity, the Holy Father will be a wise and discerning almoner in our behalf. Our contribution shall be an expression of our gratitude to God and of our love for our fellowmen. For all those who love God all things work together unto good."[5]

In 1954, the Marian Year, the cardinal wrote that "Our Sovereign Pontiff is constantly manifesting this solicitude in our times. The wandering and weary peoples of the earth, regardless of their creed, plead to him as to the Father of Christendom. His arms are outstretched and his lips are ever in prayer. Through the agencies of his mercy, his meager resources are distributed to the hungry and the naked the world over. From these resources, too, may he alone sustain the ministrations of the Church in its mission among men. It is the generosity of the faithful that enables Our Holy Father to dispense, as their almoner, this benign charity. We of the United States who have been spared the chastisement of the times and who are so generous to every cause, we are the prime source from which he may receive."[6]

Pope Pius XII celebrated his eightieth birthday in 1956 and, once again, a series of novenas were inaugurated in every parish of the archdiocese. This time, McIntyre urged that the faithful read one or more of the many encyclicals issued by the Holy Father, preferably in a parochial setting.[7] In one of his last letters about the Holy Father, McIntyre said the pontiff "is so frequently reported in the daily press, and his magnificent comments on world conditions are so strikingly outstanding, that they command attention at all levels. Amidst the trials and difficulties of the faithful throughout the countries of Europe and the East, His Holiness is the one source of consolation, comfort and relief. His charity has been boundless, and he has used with the greatest of efficiency the means supplied to him by Catholics who are fortunate to be spared the tribulations of many afflicted peoples."[8]

When Pope Pius XII died on October 9, 1958, McIntyre issued a statement which read:

> Our hearts are strained with the pangs of grief as the radio announces that His Holiness, Pope Pius XII, has been called to his eternal reward in the Bosom of the Eternal Father.
>
> The trumpet summoning his separation from earthly bonds has sounded. He is relieved of the super-human burdens of the Vicarship of his Eternal Lord, Christ Our Saviour.
>
> After a protracted tenure of phenomenal dedication to the highest ideals of religious and social accomplishment in government, science and education, all with a wisdom partaking of the Divine, the recording angel has spoken and opened the heavenly gates to a welcome repose from earthly strife and struggle with the forces of worldly evil.
>
> He had a burning love for his fellow man which was eloquent in his daily speech and shining in his countenance and gesture. The resounding tributes from the hearts of mankind are but the echo of that love which consumed him, heart and mind, in imitation of Our Redeemer.
>
> Our grief can find consolation only as we reflect on the thanksgiving due to Almighty God for this prodigious career that has brought to our era such supreme consolation and blessings.[9]

At McIntyre's suggestion, a whole edition of *The Tidings* was devoted to the Holy Father. Featured were some of the bold initiatives inaugurated by the Holy Father, including liberalization of the Eucharistic fast, mitigation of the Lenten rules, battle against communism, proclamation of a Holy Year in 1950, a Marian Year in 1954 and a series of encyclicals on pivotal issues facing the modern Church. In a statement released by the cardinal, His Eminence of Los Angeles said that "people the world over, of every

McIntyre blesses the vault holding the remains of Pope Pius XII.

Cardinal McIntyre prays at the tomb of Pope John XXIII.

Cardinals gathered in the Sistine Chapel following the conclave at which Angelo Roncalli was chosen as Pope John XXIII.

View from the Tribune for the celebration of Holy Mass with the cardinals and other members of the Roman Curia.

VOTA SCRUTINII

Vespere   die   Mensis Octobris   Anno 1958

EPISCOPI VI

E.mus Tisserant
E.mus Micara
E.mus Pizzardo
E.mus Aloisi Masella
E.mus Tedeschini
E.mus Mimmi

PRESBYTERI XLVI

E.mus van Roey
E.mus Cerejeira
E.mus Liénart
E.mus Fumasoni Biondi
E.mus Fossati
E.mus Dalla Costa
E.mus Tappouni
E.mus Copello
E.mus Gerlier
E.mus Agagianian
E.mus Mooney
E.mus McGuigan
E.mus Roques
E.mus Motta
E.mus Gilroy
E.mus Spellman
E.mus Caro Rodriguez
E.mus de Gouveia
E.mus Câmara
E.mus Pla y Deniel

E.mus Arteaga y Betancourt
E.mus Frings
E.mus Mindszenty
E.mus Ruffini
E.mus Caggiano
E.mus Tienchensin
E.mus Alvaro da Silva
E.mus Cicognani
E.mus Roncalli
E.mus Valeri
E.mus Ciriaci
E.mus Feltin
E.mus de la Torre
E.mus Stepinac
E.mus Grente
E.mus Siri
E.mus D'Alton
E.mus McIntyre
E.mus Lercaro
E.mus Wyszyński
E.mus de Arriba
E.mus Quiroga
E.mus Léger
E.mus Luque
E.mus Gracias
E.mus Wendel

DIACONI II

E.mus Canali
E.mus Ottaviani

Infirmarii	Scrutatores	Recognitores	Praesentes in Conclavi num.		Nemini
			Aegroti absentes a Scrutinio num.		
			Absentes a Conclavi		
			Omnes num.	LIV	

351

Eligo in Summum Pontificem Rev.mum

D. meum D. Card.

Blank ballot for the 1958 papal conclave.

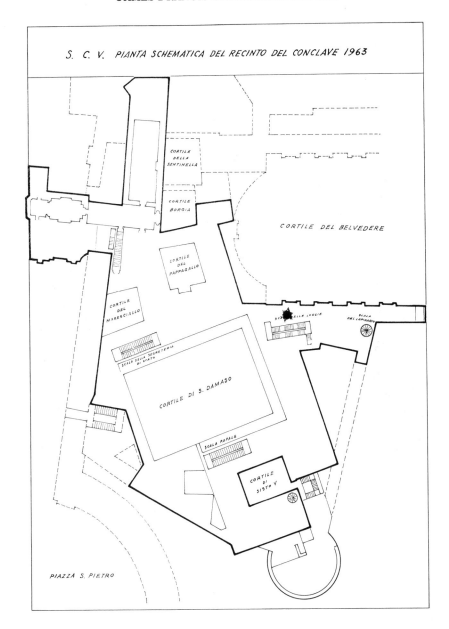

Papal elector McIntyre lived in Cell #80, on the second loggia, in a place normally reserved for the security police of the Holy See.

353

Cardinal McIntyre and his entourage, Msgrs. Bernard Dolan, Benjamin Hawkes and Thomas Aiken meet with the newly elected Pope John XXIII.

Cardinal McIntyre enters conclave on June 19, 1963.

Pope John XXIII greets one of his electors at an audience following the conclave.

persuasion, have with love and affection accepted his teachings because they were of Divine Wisdom. In them, they recognized the depth and sincerity of a spokesman possessing a supreme love for his fellowmen, surmounted only by his love for the Redeemer Himself."[10]

The first "prerogative" of cardinals and, in fact, the chief rationale for their very existence, is that of electing the Roman Pontiff. During his years as a member of the Sacred College of Cardinals, McIntyre exercised that role on two occasions.

JOHN XXIII

McIntyre left for Rome on the evening on October 10th, accompanied by Msgrs. Vincent Lloyd-Russell and Benjamin Hawkes, both of whom were to enter the conclave with McIntyre as his personal assistants. After viewing the pontiff's remains, laid in state at Saint Peter's Basilica, McIntyre and the other cardinals prepared for the funeral of the man who for nearly nineteen years had guided the destinies of the Church. The Archbishop of Los Angeles was not alone in wondering how best to provide for the Church after one whose influence stretched back to the early years of the century.

Conclaves are supposed to be closed to speculation and measures taken by modern popes have made them even more secret than they used to be, even in Rome, the city of inspired rumor. There was, of course, considerable speculation in the press as to whether the ultimate choice of a successor to Pius XII would be a pastoral or political candidate. Among the leading conservative *papabili* were Cardinals Alfredo Ottaviani, Benedetto Aloisi Masella and Ernesto Ruffini. The liberal contenders were Cardinals Giacomo Lercaro and Giuseppe Siri. The American newspapers publicized the chances of Francis Cardinal Spellman who had both a brilliant record in New York and a list of solid accomplishments during his days in the Vatican Secretariate of State. Giovanni Battista Montini, long regarded by Spellman and McIntyre as the logical successor to Pius XII, was not yet a cardinal and so the electors had to look elsewhere for someone to restore the working machinery of the Vatican which Pius XII had allowed to stagnate. McIntyre was among those feeling that a "caretaker" pope, one who could expand membership in the Sacred College and name new members to that body, made good sense. Angelo Cardinal Roncalli, the seventy-seven year old Patriarch of Venice, a man with long diplomatic and wide pastoral experience, was the logical choice for those sharing

McIntyre's point of view. For one of the few times in their lives, McIntyre and Spellman did not agree.

There were fifty-two members of the Sacred College of Cardinals gathered for the opening of the conclave on October 25th, a number tragically reduced by one with the sudden death of McIntyre's friend, Edward Cardinal Mooney of Detroit, who succumbed shortly after the pontiff's funeral. By ancient custom, the conclave took place in the Sistine Chapel, with the cardinals sequestered in a secluded and walled-off part of the Apostolic Palace. For two days, as the cardinals voted twice each morning and twice each afternoon, the smoke emitting from the iron stove in which the ballots were burned, was black. On the third afternoon of the conclave, the weary cardinals gathered for what was the eleventh and final ballot. When the last vote had been recorded, a delegation of cardinals walked solemnly to the place where Angelo Roncalli was seated. There, the Cardinal-Dean asked, "Do you accept your election, made canonically, as Supreme Pontiff?" The affirmative response inaugurated the pontificate of Pope John XXIII.

McIntyre left no diary of the conclave, nor would he ever speak about its inner workings. He did address the Catholic Press Council on November 20th, telling his listeners that "our journey commenced in sorrow and grief." He told the details about Cardinal Mooney's demise and the general setting of the conclave. He thought it was amusing "to observe the positive expressions of those who attempted to inform the public of the detailed action of the participants", most of which was totally spurious. McIntyre likened the conclave to a "United Nations gathering" except that participants had a common denominator of faith in the one true religion and the common denominator of the Latin language. Saying that "the joy of Catholic people throughout the world was universal" when the name of the new pontiff was announced, he said that the end result confirmed that "universality and unity can prevail despite the variance that accompany time, climate, race, color and disposition." He concluded his address by observing that the recent days had "been filled with emotion, and the climax came," in Saint Peter's Basilica, "amid the splendor of brilliance and decoration - when the shrill notes of the silver trumpets" announced the formal enthronement of John XXIII as the Vicar of Christ.[11]

Though there were those at the Vatican who were less than enthusiastic with Pope John XXIII, McIntyre was not among them. He genuinely liked the Holy Father and identified with him in many ways, much to the annoyance of Francis Cardinal Spellman who openly expressed disdain for the elderly but agile "Angelo." McIntyre was especially pleased when Pope John, during his first consistory, took occasion to speak about the "sad circumstances prevailing among the clergy and laity in many regions of Europe and Asia by virtue of religious persecutions." The Holy Father was especially upset about China "which had exceeded the usual form of civil and religious antipathy." McIntyre asked his people to join with the Holy Father in a prayer crusade "imploring God's mercy and blessings upon our suffering brothers and sisters in Christ."[12]

The Johannine papacy lasted only five years, but they were momentous years, marked by innovative and lasting accomplishments. Surely the most lasting of his many works for the Church was his call for Vatican Council II which convened at Rome in the fall of 1962. John XXIII was indeed a "caretaker" pope, but one who planted his imprint deeply in the annals of Christendom. When the Holy Father's illness was disclosed to the world, McIntyre asked the people of the archdiocese to pray for his recovery. And, shortly thereafter, he issued a lengthy letter about the role of the papacy as reflected in the Holy Father:

A well known theologian has said that today - as in the days of the Council of Chalcedon (451) - it is still Peter who speaks, whether it be through the mouth of a Pope Leo, a Pope Pius, or today, a Pope John. It is still the Lord Jesus who is speaking, but through the mouth of the Vicar of Christ.

Thus, our beloved and respected Holy Father, Pope John XXIII, has in current days addressed the people of the entire world. In words of sublime simplicity and sincere love and affection, he has spoken in the words of Christ Himself, and he has spoken not to any one group, but to all people in all lands. He has reminded men that God is their creator, and of the consequent obligation to serve God in right thinking and in right conduct, and in avoidance of what is contrary to God's wishes. Furthermore, he exhorts man to reciprocally cultivate the love and devotion manifested by their Divine Creator and Redeemer. The fundamental truths he has expounded have staggered the world by their simplicity and reasonableness. Thinking men recognize the mercy extended by God to the frailty of human nature. The Holy Father implores the love of man for God that is comparable to the love of God for man, and for which He died on the cross.[13]

Pope John XXIII died on June 3, 1963. In his statement issued on that occasion, McIntyre said:

Life is mysterious yet strictly according to an established order. The Creator gives life, and takes it to Eternity, in His Divine Wisdom. God the Creator gives to time and circumstance men and minds and talents to meet every situation.

The coming and the passing of the world-beloved Pontiff, John XXIII, manifests God's goodness and mercy upon our times.

In his simplicity and firmness of purpose, John XXIII has been a true father to all men, a loving father and a gracious friend and benefactor to men of all races and climes. He has inspired us in a way of life, and has been a model in the acceptance of death.

Thus are our souls grieved as his mission on earth is terminated. We are consoled in the expectation that his greeting into heaven will be the reward for a "good and faithful servant" -- as he is accompanied by the earnest prayers of loving people.[14]

POPE PAUL VI

Until the minutes of the 1963 conclave are made public, and that may never happen, there can only be an informed guess as to precisely how events unfolded. The secrets have been well kept, perhaps due to the stern insistence of Pope John XXIII. McIntyre and his confreres in the Sacred College of Cardinals only spoke in vague generalities, something that has frustrated more than one keeper of the records.

By the time Pope John died, after a long illness, election fever had been in the Roman air for months. The atmosphere was further charged by the realization that, for the first time in history, the non-Roman cardinals could and probably would affect the outcome of a conclave, a factor not lost on electors like James Francis Cardinal McIntyre. It was the biggest conclave ever, with eighty-one cardinals eligible to vote, including seven from North America.

The pro-Montini faction, shared by McIntyre, was headed by Julius Dopfner (Munich), Giacomo Lercaro (Bologna) and Paul-Emile Leger (Montreal). Interestingly, the curia cardinals, under the leadership of Arcadio Larraona, were not enamored of Montini, even though he had worked among them for most of his priestly life. When the conclave assembled on June 20, there were two options: continue Vatican Council II in the spirit of John XXIII which pointed to Montini, or conclude it swiftly and harmlessly as possible with Giuseppe Cardinal Siri of Genoa. There were other fringe candidates, but these two stood out as the ones to be elected or defeated.

Suenens, McIntyre, Spellman and others supporting Montini argued that all his life had been a preparation for the papacy and he possessed the balance that others, like Lercaro, lacked. Montini would move ahead slowly and gradually, despite his acknowledged reputation for indecisiveness. Because there was never any real chance to block Montini, the curia cardinals eventually threw their support to Montini, most of whom liked him as a person and felt easy with him, if not with his policies. The conclave must have been a spirited gathering. Montini finally got the votes he needed but did not seek or really want on the sixth ballot. Throughout his pontificate, however, he was troubled by the memory that over twenty cardinals declined to vote for him, even when his election was assured.

Peter Hebblethwaite set the record straight when, in his masterful treatise on *Paul VI. The First Modern Pope*, he stated that when the new pontiff embarked on his reign, "Pius XII was his model of how to be Pope, not John XXIII,"[15] something that surely must have pleased his supporter from Los Angeles, James Francis Cardinal McIntyre.

Upon his arrival home from the conclave, McIntyre described the new pontiff as "a most affable man. Basically, he is a thinker with the people, sympathetic to their needs." He told how, after his election, the cardinals came up to extend their felicitations. "When the older cardinals came along, the Holy Father got up and came down from the throne to them. He was younger than they and he thoughtfully and kindly came to them." He further said that "in the long view, he was encouraged by the awareness and interest of the world in the life of the Church. " He viewed it as a recognition that "in an age where great natural mysteries are being probed, the Church deals with mysteries of the spirit that are just as real and forceful and with a commanding objective -- the salvation of souls."[16]

McIntyre signed on early as a strong advocate of the Holy Father's visit to the 1,374th meeting of the United Nations on October 4, 1965. Though he was never an enthusiastic supporter of the United Nations, McIntyre applauded the notion of the pontiff's appearance there, fittingly enough on the Feast of Saint Francis of Assisi. He was sent an advance copy of the message delivered there by the Holy Father and several of the notes he scribbled were incorporated into the final text. He was especially pleased by the words: "No more war, never again war. Peace, it is peace which must guide the destinies of peoples and of all mankind."[17]

During the rest of his years as Archbishop of Los Angeles and those he spent in retirement, Cardinal McIntyre enjoyed an exceedingly close and cordial relationship with Pope Paul VI. The two had been friends for many years and their affection was obvious in the many times they met.

Notes to the Text

1. AALA, J. Francis A. McIntyre to Priests, Los Angeles, August 4, 1948.
2. *Ibid.*, J. Francis A. McIntyre to Priests, Los Angeles, March 25, 1949.
3. *Ibid.*, J. Francis A. McIntyre to Priests, Los Angeles, May 24, 1949.
4. *Ibid.*, J. Francis A. McIntyre to Faithful, Los Angeles, April 25, 1951.
5. *Ibid.*, James Francis Cardinal McIntyre to Faithful, Los Angeles, April 18, 1953.
6. *Ibid.*, James Francis Cardinal McIntyre to Los Angeles, May 25, 1954.
7. *Ibid.*, James Francis Cardinal McIntyre to Sisters, Los Angeles, February 21, 1956.
8. *Ibid.*, James Francis Cardinal McIntyre to Priests, Los Angeles, May 28, 1957.
9. *The Tidings*, October 10, 1958.
10. *Ibid.*
11. AALA, "Catholic Press Council," Beverly Hills Hotel, November 20, 1958.
12. *Ibid.*, James Francis Cardinal McIntyre to Priests, Los Angeles, February 11, 1959.
13. *Ibid.*, James Francis Cardinal McIntyre to Faithful, Los Angeles, May 17, 1963.
14. *The Tidings*, June 7, 1963.
15. (New York, 1993), p. 332.
16. *The Tidings*, July 5, 1963.
17. *The Pope's Visit* (New York, 1965), p. 28.

18. The Episcopal College

THE HOLY SEE

Catholics believe that by divine institution bishops are the canonical pastors of the Church, teachers of doctrine, priests of sacred worship and ministers of governance. Indeed bishops belong to the most exclusive college or club in all the world and their relationship to one another knows of no parallel. The structure of the bishopric that has evolved since apostolic times is carefully spelled out in canon law and universal practice.

As the second incumbent of the Metropolitan Province of Los Angeles, J. Francis A. McIntyre was charged with presiding over an area comprising the Archdiocese of Los Angeles and the Dioceses of Monterey-Fresno, San Diego and Tucson. In his role as metropolitan, he was to see that Catholic faith and ecclesial discipline were carefully observed and to conduct canonical visitations if and when needed. Though he had no power of governance outside his own archdiocese, McIntyre was expected to act as an overseer of the suffragan bishops in the province, a position that he took seriously.

MONTEREY-FRESNO

McIntyre knew Bishop Aloysius J. Willinger before he came to Los Angeles and the two prelates were soul mates in many ways. In 1954, when the Bishop of Monterey-Fresno was preparing to celebrate the twenty-fifth anniversary of his episcopal ordination, McIntyre was approached about seeking a titular archbishopric for Willinger. In a letter to the Apostolic Delegate, the cardinal agreed that Willinger was exceedingly worthy of such a distinction. He hesitated only because his senior suffragan, Bishop Daniel J. Gercke of Tucson, lacked that honor and he was considerably older in seniority. In its place, McIntyre suggested that Willinger be named an Assistant at the Pontifical Throne which the Holy See would happily confer.[1] The cardinal journeyed to Fresno on many occasions and was there when the bishop observed his golden sacerdotal jubilee in 1961. A week earlier, at Willinger's invitation, he went to Carmel for services at which San Carlos Borromeo Mission was designated a minor basilica.[2]

In May of 1961, McIntyre was asked by the Apostolic Delegate about complaints from the Diocese of Monterey-Fresno claiming that Willinger "treats his Auxiliary Bishop in an un-Christian manner and is openly critical of him." Moreover, it was alleged that "Mexican Catholics are not receiving proper attention and there is imminent danger that many of them will be lost to the Church." The delegate wondered if McIntyre "might have any suggestion as to how this situation might be approached."[3] There's no record of McIntyre's response, though he likely explained that Willinger had been a missionary for most of his life and often overlooked the niceties of ecclesial decorum. It was known widely that Willinger had no affection for his auxiliary, Bishop Harry Clinch, who was not his first choice for that position.

There had long been a clamor for dividing the Diocese of Monterey-Fresno. In February of 1967, the Apostolic Delegate met with the bishops of the Metropolitan Province of Los Angeles at Fremont Place. Archbishop Egidio Vagnozzi announced that Willinger had submitted his resignation and that it was appropriate to discuss the question of dividing the diocese. McIntyre deferred any comment to Willinger who felt that the subject should be delayed for five years. When the cardinal was asked for his personal view, he responded that it would "be better for the development and growth of the diocese to be concomitant with it rather than resulting from it." Bishop Timothy Manning favored the division and Clinch suggested that Santa Barbara and San Luis Obispo be added to the division, with the resultant division being known as Monterey-Santa Barbara. The proposal appeared to meet with general favor and McIntyre "expressed no objection to the withdrawal of Santa Barbara from Los Angeles."[4]

For reasons unknown, the subsequent division, which took place on October 6, omitted consideration of Santa Barbara. McIntyre concurred in the ultimate decision, and attended events at both Monterey and Fresno when the new bishoprics were formally established with Bishop Clinch being named to Monterey and Timothy Manning to Fresno.

SAN DIEGO

In 1936, Giuseppe Cardinal Pizzardo, a close confidant of Popes Pius XI and Pius XII, suggested to Archbishop John J. Cantwell that the rector of the Cathedral in Saint Joseph, Missouri, Father Charles Francis Buddy, was uniquely qualified to serve as the proto bishop for the newly created Diocese of San Diego. Buddy was subsequently appointed to the vacancy and was consecrated on December 21st.

Though Buddy eventually became one of the nation's most celebrated ecclesial "characters," he proved to be a hard-working and dedicated churchman, one whom James Francis Cardinal McIntyre highly esteemed and respected. Buddy served his people well and the correspondence between him and his metropolitan archbishop was always cordial on both sides. Unhappily, as the years unfolded, the Bishop of San Diego ran afoul of some who complained about his manner of funding the University of San Diego, arguing that it impacted negatively on the overall economical well-being of the diocese. Nothing so alarms Roman officials as the suggestion of financial impropriety at any level, and there were those in high places who felt obliged to look into the charges.

Late in 1956, McIntyre was told by the Apostolic Delegate about a letter he had received, outlining the details of financial problems in San Diego. Cicognani asked the cardinal to visit Buddy and ascertain what if any action should be taken.[5] After the meeting, Buddy wrote directly to Cicognani, telling him that "the report you received is in error. In fact, last week officials of the Bank of America, after carefully weighing our annual fiscal statement, notified me officially that they were making available three and one-half million dollars for loan purposes in this diocese during the coming year. In view of the current wave of inflation pressure which has made borrowing of money more difficult, with correspondingly higher rates of interest, this allocation by the Bank is, in itself, a recognition of credit and sound financial standing."[6] Actually, things were not all that serene. At the Holy See's suggestion, McIntyre stepped in and was able to apply a tourniquet on the hemorrhage of funds, after which be renegotiated Buddy's loan schedule in a manner that assured the survival of both the diocese and the university.

Two years later, new charges were made and again McIntyre was asked to visit San Diego. This time, the Apostolic Delegate hoped that "the very fact of your visit will cause His Excellency to reflect" on the complaints raised in certain quarters.[7] Late in 1961, Cicognani asked McIntyre if he would speak with Buddy about the advisability of accepting a coadjutor, a delicate task that the cardinal performed reluctantly. Buddy asked that he be allowed "to pray over and study your wise and prudent suggestion for a couple of months," after which he would journey to Washington for "a personal conference" with the Apostolic Delegate. He explained that he really didn't need any assistance because of the close proximity of Bishop Alfredo Galindo of Baja California who lived only seventeen miles away and who was exceedingly willing to help. Galindo spoke English fluently and was often asked to assist with confirmations.[8]

Finally, in July of 1963, Pope Paul VI abruptly and without consulting Buddy named Francis J. Furey, Auxiliary Bishop of Philadelphia, coadjutor of San Diego with the right of succession. Since Buddy resolutely refused to relinquish his title as Bishop of San Diego, Archbishop Egidio Vagnozzi notified McIntyre that it would be announced, on the day of the installation, that Furey would also be Apostolic Administrator, so that "the new coadjutor will give firm and prudent direction to the diocese so that many good results may eventuate."[9]

It is not clear, at this juncture, who Buddy's detractors were, what evidence they presented or why they wanted him out of office. True, he had grown old and crotchety, but no more so than many of his episcopal confreres. That McIntyre was not overly concerned about the financial affairs in the Diocese of San Diego lends credence to the view that the charges were exaggerated.

Bishop Buddy clung to his title until the very end. Not infrequently, his displeasure about the manner in which he was retired came to the surface. One such occasion was a talk he gave to Friendly Sons of Saint Patrick in which he said that "in the interest of justice" he needed to "refute a vicious calumny whispered throughout the United States" about the financial condition of the diocese: "The banks knew that we have never defaulted in a payment, never deferred an account due. The banks as well as certified public accountants, employed by us from time to time, point to our financial stability. Dun & Bradstreet rate the value of our property at 40 times what we started with in 1936. In this vast expansion program of 27 years, you could reasonably expect some debt." He said further that "this accurate record of our finances and corresponding high credit refutes the false assertions made by frustrated and irresponsible persons. The gossip mongers, 'broods of vipers and whitened sepulchers' who fabricated and promoted this calumny are the illegitimate descendants of Judas Iscariot. They can never claim the glorious heritage of St. Patrick and his sons, who stand for the truth consistently and firmly 'four square to all the winds that blow."[10]

That McIntyre retained his affection for Buddy explains his suggestion to the Holy See that Bishop Buddy be named an Assistant at the Pontifical Throne when he celebrated his golden jubilee. Shortly after Buddy's death, in March of 1966, the cardinal urged his friend, Daniel Donohue, to one day erect a statue of the bishop on the grounds of the University of San Diego, as a monument to a man whose foresight far surpassed that of his detractors.

FRANCIS FUREY

The tenure of Bishop Francis J. Furey in San Diego lasted only three relatively uneventful years. As an incentive for accepting the difficult challenge at San Diego, Furey had been given to believe that he would soon move on to an archbishopric. With the appointment of Timothy Manning as coadjutor to McIntyre, and the closing of any opportunity for moving north, Furey happily accepted an appointment to the Archdiocese of San Antonio. Cardinal McIntyre went to San Diego for a civic luncheon honoring Furey prior to his departure and there lauded him as a "highly esteemed and revered bishop," suggesting that Furey's "well-known and superlative qualities" had been recognized with his promotion to San Antonio where he would continue "under the patronage of famous saints in his place of departure and destination - San Diego and San Antonio."[11]

TUCSON

Daniel James Gercke came to Tucson as bishop in 1923, where he labored for forty-one years, becoming a legendary figure in the Catholic annals of the United States.

Shortly after his arrival in California, McIntyre petitioned the Holy See for the pallium, the liturgical symbol of his role as metropolitan Archbishop for the Province of Los Angeles and of unity with the See of Peter in Rome.[12] The archbishop asked Gercke, his senior suffragan, to preach for the occasion which was scheduled to take place at Saint Vibiana's Cathedral on a Sunday "for the benefit of the people who were unable to attend the installation ceremonies."[13] In his typical form, Gercke delivered a stirring panegyric, recalling how he had bestowed the pallium on Archbishop John J. Cantwell just a dozen years earlier.

Two months later, on one of his first treks outside of the Archdiocese of Los Angeles, McIntyre journeyed to Tucson where, on November 7th, he preached for Gercke's silver episcopal jubilee, paying tribute to a bishop who had "remained the true shepherd and pastor, serving daily in his cathedral, responding to the needs of the people as would the most humble of souls."[14] Three years afterwards, McIntyre attended celebrations honoring Gercke's golden sacerdotal anniversary and, in l953,[15] McIntyre was again in Tucson, this time blessing the new hospital opened by the Sisters of Mercy.[16]

After McIntyre became a cardinal, his ties with Gercke were strengthened and the two were in frequent communication, either by phone or letter. McIntyre happily rubber stamped Gercke's nomination of Francis J. Green as his auxiliary and eventual successor in 1953. The cardinal made a number of other visits to Tucson, each time expressing his affection for Gercke. When the bishop observed his fortieth anniversary of episcopal consecration, McIntyre wrote that he and the entire Church "recognized and appreciated deeply the abundant harvest that your pioneer years of sowing has brought, not only to the people of Arizona, but in the development of a splendid diocese and priesthood."[17] When Gercke retired in 1960, the cardinal recommended that he be named a titular archbishop. McIntyre presided at his funeral, along with Auxiliary Bishop Timothy Manning who delivered a memorable homily, recalling and applying to Gercke the words of Willa Cather.[18] McIntyre remained close to the Church in Arizona during the administration of Bishop Francis J. Green. In 1967, the cardinal bowed to the wishes of the Holy See that the Diocese of Tucson be transferred from his jurisdiction to that of the Metropolitan Province of Santa Fe.[19]

Because of the prominence of his position as Archbishop of Los Angeles and, later, in his role as cardinal, McIntyre exercised an honorary leadership role beyond the confines of his metropolitan province, especially for areas of the west coast. A strong leader on the local scene, he never exhibited any interest in becoming a powerbroker on the national level. Though often accused, at least by innuendo, of using his influence in the appointment of bishops, there is no archival evidence that McIntyre ever did any more than respond to occasional queries from the Apostolic Delegate about matters occurring in extra-territorial areas. An example would be the Diocese of Sacramento which had a long and pleasant relationship with Los Angeles that dated back to Eugene O'Connell who became Vicar Apostolic of Marysville in 1861.

SACRAMENTO

Robert J. Armstrong had been Bishop of Sacramento since 1929. He was a highly-beloved figure whose shadow was deeply imbedded along California's Gold Dust Trails. He and McIntyre became close friends and the bishop always stayed at Fremont Place on his visits to Los Angeles. In 1954, the cardinal journeyed to Sacramento for the bishop's silver jubilee ceremonies which were observed as a holiday by most residents of the state's capital city.[20]

During the early months of 1955, Bishop Armstrong fell ill and was absent from his office for several weeks. He had regained his strength by late June and informed the Apostolic Delegate that he had "recovered my health," noting that he "would not object to an Auxiliary."[21] Archbishop Amleto Cicognani then wrote to McIntyre and said he would be grateful for any information he could provide "relative to the details of the condition and health of the bishop." He also asked McIntyre for "suggestions as to what should be done at Sacramento."[22] Since McIntyre had the annoying habit of responding to the delegate at home on his personal stationery, without carbons, there is no record of his response. However, early in August, Cicognani thanked McIntyre for visiting Armstrong and telling him about his operation. The delegate said that "since the Holy See will wish to provide for the diocese, I am preparing a report and would like to include a *terna* from which a bishop will be chosen to conduct the affairs of the diocese." He acknowledged McIntyre's recommendation about appointing Auxiliary Bishop Joseph T. McGucken to the position of coadjutor.[23]

McIntyre felt a special kinship for Bishop Joseph T. McGucken that dated back to 1947, when the then auxiliary had been named Apostolic Administrator for the vacant Archdiocese of Los Angeles. Cardinal Spellman was also an admirer of McGucken and, in August of 1947, Spellman asked Archbishop John J. Cantwell if McGucken could be his representative and that of the American hierarchy at Marian observance in Argentina, noting that "Bishop McGucken would certainly do us all honor because of his person, his personality and his ability to represent us ably and his fluency in Spanish."[24] Three years later, again at the suggestion of Spellman, McGucken's name was proposed for a vacancy in the papal Secretariate of State caused by the death of Msgr. Walter Carroll. McIntyre had enthusiastically endorsed that proposal which never took place because Vatican authorities decided against naming an American to the post.[25]

McIntyre had observed firsthand the efficiency and administrative ability of his auxiliary and felt it was time for him to assume an expanded role in the service of the Church. He felt that McGucken's experience and administrative talent would be well utilized at Sacramento. On October 18, Cicognani informed McIntyre that the Holy Father had appointed McGucken Coadjutor Bishop of Sacramento with the right of succession.[26] The cardinal went to Sacramento for the installation and reported back to the delegate that Armstrong was able to attend part of the installation ceremonies but that he was "somewhat pitiful since he had to be helped on each side by priests." He noted that "in spirit, he was splendid and cheerful" and seemingly pleased with the appointment of McGucken.[27]

Bishop Armstrong lived for some months, during which time McGucken measured up to all expectations in his ministry. McIntyre was unable to attend Armstrong's funeral, but he did issue a statement describing the prelate as "distinctly a man of God, a staunch churchman and noble character. His charm and personality breathed the spirit of infused virtues and captivated the hearts of all."[28]

During the five years that McGucken served as Bishop of Sacramento, he maintained a close relationship with McIntyre. He was especially adept at dealing with the governmental officials in the state capital and setting up the machinery which eventually led to the establishment of the California Catholic Conference in 1971. McGucken was succeeded in Sacramento by another Southern Californian, Alden J. Bell, an appointment proposed by McGucken and enthusiastically endorsed by McIntyre.

SAN FRANCISCO

With the death of Archbishop John J. Mitty of San Francisco, in October of 1961, the Holy See decided to implement a plan for dividing that jurisdiction which had been in the planning stages for some years. There would be three additional episcopal seats taken from the existing archdiocese, with bishoprics established at Santa Rosa, Oakland and Stockton, along with an adjustment of the boundaries for the Diocese of Sacramento.

Originally, it had been Mitty's idea that his two auxiliary bishops (Hugh A. Donohoe and Merlin J. Guilfoyle) and secretary (Leo T. Maher) would be named to the newly-created dioceses. Bishop

Edward Francis Hoban of Cleveland, a close friend of Amleto Cardinal Cicognani had importuned that his auxiliary, Floyd L. Begin, would fill the vacancy at San Francisco.

Out of courtesy, the list of the candidates was shown to Cardinal McIntyre, along with a request for his observations. He had no objection to either the formation of the new dioceses or the list of proposed candidates, though he pointed out that Bishop Joseph T. McGucken of Sacramento, a classmate of Begin in Rome, outranked Begin in episcopal seniority and administrative experience. McIntyre thought that McGucken would be the more logical candidate for San Francisco, and Begin for Oakland. Roman officials apparently saw the wisdom of McIntyre's observations and made the changes he recommended.

At the luncheon held for McGucken, at the time of his installation as Archbishop of San Francisco, McIntyre ventured the comment "that Southern California shares in this joy and jubilation for Saint Francis and the angels were always companions of mutual consolation and comfort."[29] McIntyre returned to the Bay area on May 16th and invested the new archbishop with the pallium at Saint Patrick's Seminary in Menlo Park.[30]

SELECTION OF AUXILIARY BISHOPS

The normal procedure for selecting and appointing bishops involves a detailed and complicated process that is the envy of the Federal Bureau of Investigation and the Central Intelligence Agency. A secrecy pledge goes with the process that is comparable to the confessional seal and it can be dispensed only by the Holy Father.[31] Unlike his great mentor, Francis Cardinal Spellman, McIntyre never tried to short circuit the established channels or in any way diminish the effectiveness of a system that worked fairly well.

During his twenty-two years in Los Angeles, McIntyre had only three auxiliary bishops. He followed religiously the outlined procedure, even the recommended but not obligatory suggestion that he widen the process to allow for nominations from the senior clergy. In February of 1953, for example, he wrote to fifty-eight priests, telling them that the biennial meeting of the bishops of the province would be held after Easter. He asked that, "after prayerful consideration," they submit two or possibly three names of those in the archdiocese whom they considered "qualified" for the position of bishop. The names were to be sent to him directly and marked "*sub-secreto Sancti Officii.*"[32] He repeated that process every two years of his incumbency. To what extent the names were scrutinized by him is unknown, but at least it gave him an indication who the clergy considered for leadership positions.

The first *terna* sent through the Apostolic Delegate to the Holy See was dispatched in late 1955 and dealt with candidates to succeed Bishop Joseph T. McGucken who had departed for Sacramento. Listed in the order of preference, the list comprised the names of Monsignors Benjamin G. Hawkes, William E. North and Alden J. Bell. As was the usual practice, the delegation sent out a series of questionnaires on each candidate. McIntyre was later told that Hawkes was too young, lacked pastoral experience and was often brash with his fellow clergymen and North asked to be excused because of poor health. On April 11, 1956, Bell was named to the titular See of Rhodopolis and appointed Auxiliary to the Archbishop of Los Angeles. Consecrated by McIntyre on June 4th, Bell was named chancellor, a position he held for the following six years.

With Bell's transfer to the residential bishopric of Sacramento in 1962, another vacancy developed in the Archdiocese of Los Angeles. This time, the *terna* consisted of Monsignor Benjamin G. Hawkes, Patrick Roche and John J. Ward. For a second time, Hawkes was rejected for being too abrupt and not always gracious in his relations with priests. Roche, the editor of *The Tidings*, asked that his name be removed from consideration without mentioning specifics. John J. Ward, director of the matrimonial curia, was named to the titular See of Bria and named auxiliary on October 10, 1963.

Finally there was the unusual case of Joseph Dougherty, who had resigned his position as Bishop of Yakima, following a series of financial reverses. Bishop Dougherty who, at sixty-three years of age, was willing and anxious to continue some sort of pastoral work, asked the Holy Father if it would be possible to continue his ministry in another part of the vineyard. Pope Paul VI replied in the affirmative, suggesting that he look for what was then called a "benevolent ordinary." Archbishop Luigi Raimondi, the Apostolic Delegate, told Cardinal McIntyre that Dougherty would be "willing and indeed happy to serve in whatever capacity would suit the needs of the Archdiocese (of Los Angeles), provided Your Eminence judges this would be useful."[33] McIntyre was indeed pleased at the thought of having Dougherty, whom he personally admired, reside in Los Angeles and to "function as an Auxiliary Bishop." He discussed the matter with Dougherty and offered him a parish.[34] McIntyre was then told to make a formal request to the Holy See that Dougherty be named auxiliary, a distinction rarely then or now given to a retired residential bishop.

JURISDICTIONAL ALTERATIONS

Discussions about a possible diocese for Orange County predated by many years the actual erection of an episcopal seat that took place on March 24, 1976. Though most of the negotiations were oral, there is documentation for actions that were contemplated in the mid-1950s. In November of 1956, the Apostolic Delegate, Archbishop Amleto Cicognani, asked Cardinal McIntyre to consider a division of the Archdiocese of Los Angeles. In his reply, the cardinal admitted that he would welcome a diminution of his responsibilities, but pointed out that any division should proceed along county lines. Where that had not been done in the United States, all kinds of legal problems had later developed. McIntyre observed that almost 90% of the Catholic population resided in Los Angeles County.

To the north, Catholics in Santa Barbara and Ventura   Counties constituted about 4.5% of the total number of overall Catholic population. He noted that "were Ventura and Santa Barbara larger in population, they would make a splendid diocese," but at that time, such a jurisdiction would have only twenty-six parishes. Orange County was also a relatively small geographical area though, as the cardinal pointed out, "its development in recent years has been rapid and we would rather expect that it will require a total of forty or fifty parishes within the next three or four years." He already had property for nine or ten contemplated parishes which would be commenced as soon as priests were available. McIntyre thought that "Orange County would be self supporting and is already in itself a well established unit."[35]

Included with his observations were some charts that gave statistical data about the question:

Los Angeles County	5,250,000,	or	89.7 per cent
Ventura County	148,200,	or	2.5 per cent
Santa Barbara County	111,000,	or	1.9 per cent
Orange County	340,000,	or	5.9 per cent

These four Counties are divided into parishes, as follows:

Los Angeles County	215 Parishes
Ventura County	13 Parishes
Santa Barbara County	12 Parishes
Orange County	29 Parishes

McIntyre noted that, in gross income, practically the same proportion prevailed. The gross income of Orange County was less than 6% of that in Los Angeles. School expenses were relatively higher in Los Angeles County. Orange County, because of its recent development, had a little higher debt, about 8% of that of Los Angeles, as against a population of 6%. Ventura and Santa Barbara were relatively low in debt, each being less than 2% of Los Angeles County. The percentages of their assets followed closely the population proportions.

The financial income for the entire archdiocese was broken down in the following chart:

Counties	Los Angeles	Orange	Santa Barbara	Ventura	Total
Ordinary Income	12,364,052.18	737,199.48	301,400.95	238,832.38	13,641,484.99
Ordinary Expenes	5,009,747.00	348,460.47	173,505.21	125,195.96	5,656,908.64
School Income	3,421,665.10	150,493.28	60,309.32	62,732.08	3,695,199.78
School Expenses	4,363,511.75	209,101.09	68,592.84	74,058.19	4,715,200.87
Advance from Parish for School	1,018,550.18	64,567.45	12,513.05	11,995.81	1,107,626.49
Total Amt. of Debt	12,269,374.91	1,087,100.63	207,474.43	218,991.97	13,782,941.94
Paid on Debt during Year	2,557,678.83	188,189.00	15,000.00		2,760,867.83
Parish Money Invested	7,707,969.99	901,212.10	274,615.73	90,000.00	8,973,797.82
Cash on Hand, End of Year	22,970,329.19	214,617.41	93,374.29	128,834.39	2,407,155.78

Archbishop Cicognani thanked McIntyre for his lengthy and extensive report and noted that "as things stand, I can see that there are great difficulties involved." He concluded by assuring the cardinal "that I have deep appreciation for your evaluation of the situation and your conclusions will be mine."[36] Except for a statistical update in May of 1961, no further official discussion was made about splitting the archdiocese in McIntyre's time.[37]

EPISCOPAL MEETINGS

Between 1919 and 1966, the National Catholic Welfare Conference was the executive agency of the Catholic bishops in the United States. Organized with the approbation of the Holy See, its purpose was that of representing the hierarchy in matters of common interest on the national level. For many years, the bishops customarily gathered annually in Washington, D.C. on a Wednesday, Thursday and Friday in mid-November.

As bishop, archbishop and cardinal, McIntyre considered it a top priority to attend the annual meetings of the N.C.W.C., where he played an active role in its deliberations. As the published minutes of the general meetings plainly indicate, he was outspoken, blunt and frequent in his observations from the floor. McIntyre served for many years on the administrative board and there, too, he was known for doing his homework and having and expressing an opinion on every issue discussed.

As stated in the *normae* of the N.C.W.C., the resolutions passed by the bishops at their annual meetings did not have the force of law and McIntyre often reminded his confreres of that, even though he always implemented them in Los Angeles. He shied away from episcopal groupings that wanted to legislate or influence for particular regions of the country. He was conscious that the Church "beyond the Mississippi" was little regarded among the eastern block of bishops, a fact that irritated him immensely.

As the years progressed, the cardinal felt that the N.C.W.C. had gradually evolved into a costly and often inefficient bureaucracy, controlled on a day-to-day basis by staffers who endeavored to set policy rather than implement it. He was critical of many conference expenditures, especially those involved in the printing of endless brochures and pamphlets. He observed to Bishop Thomas J. Gorman that his confreres spoke too long, listened too sparcely, published too much and did too little, a statement that Gorman said was probably more right than wrong. During the deliberations at Vatican Council II about bishops' conferences, McIntyre said that "any proposal to decentralize authority in the Catholic Church is a radical change which might endanger the unity of the Church." He was firmly opposed to giving legislative powers to conferences, something which was advocated by many conciliar fathers.[38]

When the N.C.W.C. was re-organized, late in 1966, McIntyre wrote a lengthy intervention, spelling out his concept of how the two new agencies, the National Conference of Catholic Bishops and the United States Catholic Conference, should function as the organizations for insuring coordination, cooperation and assistance in the public educational and social concerns of the Catholic Church at the national and inter-diocesan level.[39]

Notes to the Text

1. AALA, James Francis Cardinal McIntyre to Amleto Cicognani, Los Angeles, September 1, 1954
2. *Central California Register*, April 28, 1961.
3. AALA, Egidio Vagnozzi to James Francis Cardinal McIntyre, Washington, D.C., May 23, 1966.
4. *Ibid.*, "Memorandum of the Visit of the Apostolic Delegate," Los Angeles, February 9, 1967.
5. *Ibid.*, Amleto Cicognani to James Francis Cardinal McIntyre, Washington, D.C., December 26, 1956.
6. *Ibid.*, Charles F. Buddy to Amleto Cicognani, San Diego, December 20, 1958.
7. *Ibid.*, Amleto Cicognani to James Francis Cardinal McIntyre, Washington, D.C., March 10, 1958.
8. *Ibid.*, Charles F. Buddy to Egidio Vagnozzi, San Diego, November 27, 1961.
9. *Ibid.*, Egidio Vagnozzi to James Francis Cardinal McIntyre, Washington, D.C., July 22, 1963.
10. San Diego *Union*, March 18, 1964.
11. *Southern Cross*, August 7, 1969. Furey later told Msgr. George Kelly, that after McIntyre had refinanced the Diocese of San Diego, he had thanked the cardinal for his intervention. McIntyre's only response was, "think nothing of it, Frank; but remember that forty years down the road, no one will ever know either of us was here. They'll only say what a man of great vision Bishop Buddy was!" See George A. Kelly, *The Battle for the American Church Revisited* (San Francisco, 1995), p. 70.
12. AALA, Thomas J. McDonnell to J. Francis A. McIntyre, New York, July 8, 1948.
13. *Ibid.*, J. Francis A. McIntyre to Priests, Los Angeles, September 2, 1948.
14. *Ibid.*, "Jubilee of His Excellency. Most Reverend Daniel J. Gercke," November 7, 1948.
15. *Ibid.*, Daniel J. Gercke to J. Francis A. McIntyre, Tucson, May 11, 1951.
16. *Ibid.*, March 25, 1953.
17. Arizona *Register*, September 13, 1963.
18. *The Tidings*, March 20, 1964.
19. AALA, James Francis Cardinal McIntyre to Egidio Vagnozzi, Los Angeles, March 27, 1967.
20. *The Tidings*, March 12, 1954.

21. AALA, Robert Armstrong to Amleto Cicognani, Sacramento, June 23, 1955.
22. *Ibid.*, Amleto Cicognani to James Francis Cardinal McIntyre, Washington, D.C., June 25, 1955.
23. *Ibid.*, Amleto Cicognani to James Francis Cardinal McIntyre, Washington, D.C., August 8, 1955.
24. *Ibid.*, Francis Cardinal Spellman to John J. Cantwell, New York, August 13, 1947.
25. *Ibid.*, Francis Cardinal Spellman to J. Francis A. McIntyre, New York, May 12, 1950.
26. *Ibid.*, Amleto Cicognani to James Francis Cardinal McIntyre, Washington, D.C., October 18, 1955.
27. AALA, James Francis Cardinal McIntyre to Amleto Cicognani, Los Angeles, December 16, 1955.
28. *The Tidings*, January 25, 1957.
29. *The Monitor*, April 6, 1962.
30. *Ibid.*, May 18, 1962.
31. For a description of the process used in McIntyre's time, see Francis J. Weber, "Episcopal Appointments in the U.S.A.," *American Ecclesiastical Review* CLV (September, 1966), 178-191.
32. AALA, James Francis Cardinal McIntyre to Priests, Los Angeles, February 24, 1953.
33. *Ibid.*, Luigi Raimondi to James Francis Cardinal McIntyre, Washington, D.C., December 14, 1968.
34. *Ibid.*, James Francis Cardinal McIntyre to Luigi Raimondi, Los Angeles, March 3, 1969.
35. *Ibid.*, James Francis Cardinal McIntyre to Amleto Cicognani, Los Angeles, February 27, 1957
36. *Ibid.*, Amleto Cicognani to James Francis Cardinal McIntyre, Washington, D.C., March 2, 1957.
37. *Ibid.*, "Orange County Statistics," May 20, 1961.
38. *The Register*, November 5, 1963.
39. AALA, "*Coetus*", Los Angeles, November, 1966.

19. *Vatican Council II*

Historically, the opening of Vatican Council II was the culmination of plans begun forty years earlier. In an encyclical letter of December 23, 1922, Pope Pius XI first proposed reconvening Vatican Council I, which had been unable to complete its agenda because of unsettled political conditions of Europe. Though the Pontiff wanted such a gathering from his earliest days, he never received the "manifest sign" for summoning the world's hierarchy into session.

Pope Pius XII discussed the possibility of a new council with Archbishop Francis J. Spellman and members of the Roman curia as early as 1939.[1] Ernesto Cardinal Ruffini, Secretary of the Congregation for Seminaries and Universities and later Archbishop of Palermo, encouraged the newly-elected Eugenio Pacelli along those lines, noting that the issues for such a convocation were "as abundant as they were at the Council of Trent."[2] Ruffini subsequently recalled that the Pope was favorably inclined towards the proposal and promised to examine it further.[3]

The question was actively considered again by Pope Pius after World War II and it was among the matters discussed by the Pontiff with the then Auxiliary Bishop of New York, J. Francis A. McIntyre, during his 1945 visit to the Vatican. The next year "commissions met to prepare the subjects to be discussed by the conciliar Fathers, including biblical studies, ecclesiastical celibacy, the use of the vernacular in liturgy and the re-establishment of the permanent diaconate for use in mission countries."[4] For reasons not yet disclosed, but very probably related to his always-precarious health, the Pope apparently took no steps to implement the proposals.

The Pontiff's long-time confidant in the papal Secretariate of State, Domenico Tardini, revealed that in 1956, with the partial recovery of his physical stamina, Pope Pius once again turned his thoughts to a council for which "certain studies had been undertaken by a small number of learned churchmen whose efforts would be utilized."[5] It was subsequently discovered from other

Cardinal McIntyre is flanked by his secretary Msgr. John A. Rawden, and Bishop Miguel Gonzalez Ibarra.

Procession into Saint Peter's Basilica for the opening of Vatican Council II.

Pope John XXIII is carried into the Vatican Basilica for the opening of Vatican Council II.

Daily Mass was offered at the council in a variety of rites.

sources that the envisioned council would have had five commissions, one each for dogmatic and speculative theology; practical and moral theology; the missions; canonical discipline and liturgy and culture; and Christian action. A list of thirty-six names was drafted for a preparatory commission, including representatives of eighteen countries. A tentative list of sixty-five bishops from all parts of the world, including the Archbishop of Los Angeles, was drawn up to solicit ideas and suggestions for an agenda.[6] Among the concrete accomplishments of this planning was a 200 page schema written by Celso Cardinal Costanini on ecumenism which reached the Pope's desk shortly before his death in 1958.[7]

Though no further action was taken, it is known that among the documents Pope John XXIII found at the time of his elevation to the papacy was his predecessor's detailed masterplan for dealing with the world's manifold problems along with an elaborate prognosis. Written into the text were the words: "concilio ecumenico."[8]

How and to what extent these preliminary activities influenced Pius XII's successor to convene Vatican Council II is a question that must await the opening of Eugenio Pacelli's files to researchers. In any event, no less an authority than Augustin Cardinal Bea repeatedly stressed the more basic theme that "in many ways the Second Vatican Council would not have been possible without the long and faithful doctrinal preparation provided by Pope Pius XII."[9]

It was Pope John XXIII who finally proclaimed "the Ecumenical Council in obedience to an inspiration which we felt given in the humility of our heart as a sudden, unexpected motion" during an address to seventeen cardinals, at the Basilica of Saint Paul Outside-the-Walls, on January 25, 1959.[10] Ironically, for the second time in history, a general council of the Church had been summoned by a John XXIII.[11]

In response to a request from Domenico Cardinal Tardini in mid-1959 for suggested topics to be discussed at the council, the Archbishop of Los Angeles submitted a number of proposals: he called for a mitigation of the rules for the Eucharistic fast in order that "more and more faithful can approach Holy Communion," a simplification of the Roman Breviary for those engaged in the parochial ministry, a retention of Latin in the Church's liturgy, alterations in canonical procedure for certain marriage cases, issuance of guidelines for determining validity of baptisms conferred by non-Catholic ministers and a requirement that dioceses be made to submit annual or bi-annual financial reports to the Holy See. To that list, James Francis Cardinal McIntyre appended a lengthy essay on economic inflation and deficit spending, both of which he looked upon as potential pitfalls to ecclesial expansion throughout the world. He concluded his observations by noting that the Catholic people in the United States had long lived in a pluralistic society and were competent to deal with non-believers at the local level, without the often meaningless and empty gestures of a superficial ecumenism.[12]

Shortly after the Council's convocation, Pope John XXIII named the Archbishop of Los Angeles to the fifty member board of the Council's Central Preparatory Commission. The more than 9,000 responses to questionnaires received from the world's hierarchy had been gathered into twelve bound volumes, and then distributed to various sub-committees for analysis and discussion. Drafts were prepared and submitted to the Central Preparatory Commission for a final determination before being placed on the agenda of the full conciliar gathering. Cardinal McIntyre attended his first meeting of the Commission in late 1961, and later told Archbishop Egidio Vagnozzi, the Apostolic Delegate to the United States, that the experience had been "a source of inexpressible edification and stimulation."[13] On November 10th, McIntyre met privately with Pope John XXIII for a lengthy conversation about matters related to the forthcoming council.

Upon his return to Los Angeles, the cardinal asked the clergy of California's southland to carefully explain the purpose and scope of the envisioned Council to their parishioners, either through a series of homilies or in parochial meetings called specifically for that reason. A portfolio of relevant historical and theological materials was distributed, along with a recommended prayer for daily recitation in the churches and classrooms of the archdiocese.[14] During the ensuing months, a series of informative articles on the subject appeared in *The Tidings*, the local Catholic newspaper.

Cardinal McIntyre later returned to Rome for another meeting of the Central Preparatory Commission. He subsequently elaborated on that nine-day meeting in an interview with the press, pointing out that the universal character, the democracy of procedure and the talent of participants augured well for the coming Vatican Council II. He foresaw that the impending gathering "could bring about untold changes: the possibility of world unity, a unity that has got to be spiritual."[15]

McIntyre and Auxiliary Bishop Timothy Manning left Los Angeles for the opening session on October 7th. Before his departure, he called upon the faithful of Los Angeles "to observe a triduum of prayer" for the Council's success, saying that "the Holy Father, through this Council, stands at the door of the hearts of all men, and knocks in the name of Christ. He places at that door a gift, the gift of God's love and His sacrifice for the redemption of souls."[16]

There was much of the past evident in the Eternal City on October 11th, 1962. Gone was the thunder of cannon on the Aventine which greeted the 744 prelates of Vatican Council I. Also missing were the Papal States, once thought to be an integral part of ecclesial machinery. Rome, itself, had suffered a transformation beyond that of any other ancient center in Christendom. And yet, as the bells of the city's churches pealed forth, Rome seemed to possess that mysterious continuity which no disaster, not even the lapse of time, had been able to interrupt, change or diminish.

From early morning, the six tribunes behind the tiers of the episcopal benches erected in Saint Peter's Basilica had been filled with theologians and canonists, together with a few fortunate outsiders. At precisely eight-thirty, the throngs outside the Vatican Basilica glimpsed the first of the solemn procession as it moved down the Scala Regia, through the Portone di Bronzo, onto the vast square of Saint Peter's. In front walked the Sistine Choir, followed by generals of religious orders, abbots, bishops, archbishops, metropolitans, patriarchs and cardinals, arrayed in silver copes and white linen mitres. Finally came the eighty-one year old Pontiff, John XXIII, led down the Bernini stairwell by his attendants and then surrounded on his *sedia gestatoria* by the picturesque Swiss guard.

When the Pope arrived at the papal altar, he intoned the *Veni Creator Spiritus* and the ancient hymn of Urbanus Maurus was taken up by the assembled prelates. On the altar, the four Gospels were opened in keeping with an ancient custom observed at all great synods from the earliest of times.

In 1962, the governing body of the Church was far larger numerically than it had been only ninety-two years earlier. The alignment of its members greatly differed from that of 1869. Roughly 37% of the Fathers at the Council represented Europe (whose total Catholic population was 210,000,000), about 33% hailed from the Americas (with a total Catholic population of 220,000,000), more than 11% came from Africa and 8% from Asia and Oceania. The center of influence had visibly shifted from the European world, a factor due not only to the notable increase in representation at the council, but also to the composition of that representation.

The last century witnessed an unprecedented expansion of the Church in English-speaking countries, as well as the newly-emerging nation of Africa, all of which brought with it, in the words of the late President John F. Kennedy, "staggering problems which, from the human point of view, seem at times to be almost insoluble." And yet, as the nation's first Catholic Chief Executive continued, it was "very heartening to know that the Council ... will strive to deepen the fellowship and love which are the 'natural needs of man' and 'are imposed on the Christian as rules for his relationship between man and man, and between people and people.'"[17] Cardinal McIntyre addressed the conciliar gathering, for the first time, during the Fifth General Congregation, October 23, 1962. Speaking to an assemblage of 2,363 about the draft of the Constitution on the Liturgy, the Archbishop of Los Angeles noted that:

In the United States of America, the Holy Sacrifice of the Mass is offered with great fidelity and devotion according to the Roman rite and the rubrics of the Roman missal.

By dogmatic and catechetical instruction, the distinction between the Mass of the Catechumens and the "preparatory part" of the Canon and the Consecration are clearly shown and well understood by the faithful. Very many of the faithful read the whole Mass assiduously and privately with the help of missals. These missals are written either in the vernacular or with the Latin on the same page.

The integrity of the Mass in Latin is kept. The vernacular used is separated from the action of the Mass, and it is not employed in all Masses. The schema on the Liturgy proposes confusion and complication. If it is adopted, it would be an immediate scandal for our people. The continuity of the Mass must be kept. The tradition of the sacred ceremonies must be preserved. The instructions on Sacred Scripture, dogma and on the catechism can be kept in the vernacular without offense to Latin. All these are kept in the present system; changes are not needed.

The Instructions of the Sacred Congregation of Rites, given in September, 1958, state that the primary attention in hearing the Mass is internal, the contemplation of the mystery of the Eucharist. Therefore, it seems to me, in these discussions active participation is receiving more consideration than needed.

This internal attention is frequently practiced by those whose intellectual capacity is not great. Furthermore, active participation is frequently a distraction.[18]

The concluding phrase of McIntyre's intervention caused some "*admiratio.*" Apparently the phrase about "active participation" being "frequently a distraction" had been taken from an article by

The five American cardinals present for the opening of Vatican Council II: Joseph Ritter (Saint Louis), James Francis McIntyre (Los Angeles), Francis Spellman (New York), Richard Cushing (Boston) and Albert Meyer (Chicago).

Albert Cardinal Meyer and James Francis Cardinal McIntyre greet Pope John XXIII. Bishop Fulton Sheen is in the background.

Plenary session of Vatican Council II.

Cardinal McIntyre and Cardinal Giacomo Lercaro at their place in the tribune of the Vatican Basilica as they registered their votes.

Holy Father offers Mass during a session of Vatican Council II.

Jacques Maritain which the famed philosopher later repudiated. That notion, according to one source, "had been combatted by the early fathers of the Church and, in particular, by St. Ambrose and St. Augustine, who demonstrated that the Platonic notion of contemplation of the good as the final end of man, even when supplemented by the Stoic and Ciceronian modification in favor of participation in the common welfare of one's fellowmen, was not the Christian idea of religion."[19]

What bothered the same observer more than the quotation was the impression "that the Cardinal of Los Angeles had paid little attention to the heart of the discussion which turned around the mysteries of the faith as they were to be made actual in the lives of both priests and faithful through the liturgy."[20] The editor of the Catholic newspaper for the Diocese of Camden criticized McIntyre for taking "the astounding position that we should not have a Mass in which people take an active part,"[21] an observation that was most probably the farthest thing from the cardinal's mind.

In his address on November 5th, Cardinal McIntyre was among the first of the conciliar Fathers to acknowledge and salute the observer-delegates, whom he referred to as *"Fratres Observatores."* Once again, the Archbishop of Los Angeles "in halting Latin, painfully defended the ancient language,"[22] stressing the unity, tradition and precision it provides:

> With the growth of the Roman Empire, the universal use of the Latin language in the Holy Church's liturgy was correctly ascribed to human and more than human wisdom. Divine Providence showed a clear path in that matter. In the fourth century, the Councils of the Church formulated doctrines and dogmas of the Church in precise Latin terminology. The events of the fourth century show a very serious reason for retaining the use of the Latin language in the holy liturgy and in sacred theology. The consideration of historical facts is very worthwhile at the present time. Attempts at weakening the solidity of the tradition of the Latin language in these matters involves catastrophe. Fundamentally, the Latin language was adopted because our fathers understood well the truly apostolic nature of Holy Mother Church and her universality as extending itself to all nations. They correctly believed that such a universality would be best served by a common means of communication. Certainly the Latin language wonderfully showed itself useful for such a common medium. Therefore, the doctrines of the Church were made precise through the

events of the fourth century. Doctrines so defined required formulation in an exact, clear, immutable, easily understood language which could at least be grasped by many and understood by all when it was interpreted to them.

The Latin language showed itself as just such a medium of communication. It gave rise to wonderful effects. Its severity overcame nationalities. In politics, it was neutral. With great constancy, its efficiency perdured into our epoch.

Once adopted, Latin became truly universal, especially among educated and literary men. Having a mathematical rather than vulgar structure, Latin attained a continuous primacy and perdured through the centuries. It is very outstanding in intellectual, literary and scientific matters.

The Councils of the first centuries formulated dogmas of the Church in Latin even to the point of accommodating and transcribing in Latin disputed Greek vocabulary. Latin was always the vehicle of dogma because it was an apt means of thinking and establishing principles accurately, definitively and in a determined fashion. It served faithfully not only ecclesiastical disciplines, but also civil law and philosophy. If this instrument, so fit for restraining and fixing, is removed from the sacred liturgy, the stability of dogma is jeopardized. Protestant sects turned to the vernacular and dissolved into numerous factions.

Throughout many centuries Latin showed a magnificent stability under the guidance of the Church. It is the basis of immutability and offers educated men a precious means of speaking and writing.

By the fact that Latin never evolved into a vulgar language, its stability and immutability grew. Clearly at all times it is the classical language, especially of erudite men.[23]

After recalling the predominance of Latin in earlier centuries, McIntyre admitted to being perplexed about the rationale for doing away with Latin as the official language of the Church. He certainly didn't take that stance because of his own facility in the language, but because he felt that few languages offered the preciseness of Latin, which was not an insignificant consideration in matters of doctrine and prayer. To say that "from the very outset of the council, (McIntyre) declared his opposition to liturgical reform, especially to the introduction of the vernacular,"[24] is simplistic. In this area, as in almost everything he did throughout his life, James Francis

McIntyre simply wanted assurances that "a new way would be better than the old." When that could be demonstrated to his satisfaction, he cheerfully acquiesced.

In any event, McIntyre went on to say that:

> In recent times, even in materialistic North America, the growth of the Church was magnificent with the liturgy being kept in Latin. The attempts of Protestants have failed, and Protestantism uses the vernacular. We ask again: Why the change, especially since changes in this matter involve many difficulties and great dangers? All of us here at the Council can recall the fundamental changes in the meaning of words in common use. Thus it follows that if the sacred liturgy were in the vernacular, the immutability of doctrine would be endangered. Finally, in recent years, unknown nations have come to the fore and many new languages, both of nations and of tribes, have become known through the United Nations.
>
> If the vernacular is introduced, we foresee many interpretations of sacred dogmas. To express the eternal truth of doctrine, let sacred dogmas immutably retain their pristine meaning and form! The introduction of the vernacular should be separated from the action of the Mass. The Mass must remain as it is. Grave changes in the liturgy introduce grave changes in dogmas.[25]

McIntyre's presentation dramatically underscored the divergent viewpoints held by members of the American hierarchy on the question of a vernacular liturgy. The cardinal's statement that "introduction of the vernacular should be separated from the action of the Mass" was widely and correctly interpreted as indicating his endorsement of local languages for the breviary. An Italian archbishop reportedly sighed aloud to that implication: "*Ah! Questi Americani!* Now, they want the priest to pray in English and the people to pray in Latin!"[26]

On November 16, on the second day of debate about divine revelation, ten cardinals, nine archbishops, one bishop and an abbot voiced opposition to the proposed schema, none of them favoring it as it was presented. Cardinal McIntyre, relying on notes supplied to him by the rector of Saint John's Seminary,[27] strongly defended that portion dealing with the biblical movement. He launched into a discussion on the value of faith, stressing its nature and importance for the Christian theologian and philosopher.

This schema has given to the modern world a summary and explicit confirmation of the truths relating to the sources of revelation. In a special way, our attention is drawn to the points which deal with present-day scientific investigations and theories. Allow me to indicate some things of major importance concerning these points:

On page ten, paragraph five, it is clearly indicated: "No one should dare make little of tradition or deny fidelity to it." On page twelve, paragraph eight, is given the definition of biblical inspiration: "Namely, that certain special charism for writing by which God, operating in and through the writer, speaks to men in writing, and consequently He is said to be and truly is the principal author of the entire sacred text." The Church unrestrictedly objects to any effort at reducing the nature of inspiration in any way to a merely natural impulse. In paragraph nine, it is stated: "Of each and every book of the Old and New Testament written in any period, there is only one primary author, namely, God."

On page thirteen, paragraph ten, it is declared: "... the charism of sacred inspiration was for the writers elected and led by God proper and personal, it was not a charism common or communicated to the assembly of the faithful."

On page seventeen, paragraph nineteen, ecclesiastical tradition is definitively confirmed: "The Church of God ... has constantly held and holds that the human authors were those who in the canon of the Sacred Books are called Matthew, Mark, Luke and John."

In paragraph twenty-one, the following errors are condemned: "Those who deny or extenuate in any way or for any reason the genuine historical and objective truth of the facts of life of Our Lord Jesus Christ as they are narrated in those Gospels." Today, we find many pernicious errors against this historical truth.

In paragraph twenty-two is condemned the error which asserts that the words attributed to Our Lord by the Gospels, at least regarding the very thing signified by the words, are most often not those of Christ himself, but rather refer to the mind of the Evangelist. The words "at least regarding the very thing signified by the words" ought to be examined with care.

Therefore, it seems to me that this schema really contains positive action aimed at correcting new theories which are not acceptable - and action against scientific theories, and against scientific theories *which should be considered only as theories*. Therefore, the schema should be accepted. The intention of the Council certainly is not to introduce new theology. Not only are (new theories) numerous, but they also exceed the present state of human understanding which is extremely limited in things divine. The necessity of faith must be admitted and professed.

The knowledge of God, the knowledge of man's relation to God, and the knowledge of the wonderful ordering of human things is near at hand for men inasmuch as they are able and have need of it; but our knowledge always remains within the limits of natural intellect when we consider the perception and assimilation of truth.

Gradually and at diverse historical moments, God granted to men's minds other and transcendent truths concerning himself and the order of nature. Man, when he became aware that these truths were divinely revealed, according to his ability and need gave his assent because of the authority of God revealing. This assent is called faith, which faith is the most precious human treasure.

Human reason, by reason of rational speculation and simultaneous illumination of the Holy Spirit, seeks and reaches some understanding of divine mysteries. These human speculations, inasmuch as they had been accepted in the course of centuries, also received the approval of Holy Mother Church. The Christian faithful recognize this understanding of mysteries as the valid expression of the dogmas of faith.

Nevertheless, it is at the same time evident that God has not given to men the possibility in this life - in our days - of reaching perfect and comprehensive understanding of the divine mysteries and of the nature of things.

God granted to His theologians and philosophers the faculty of exercising their more excellent rational powers in investigating all intelligible things, even in the order of possible things; but many things remain unknown. The acceptance in faith of truths not understood by us is rewarded by God.

Therefore, faith must hold some place in our investigation of truth. Gladly, with patience and serenity, we must accept in faith divinely revealed mysteries and dogmas of the Church.

It is also necessary in this Ecumenical Council that we should be contented - accepting in faith and confirming the truths which God revealed to us. We must expect, with anticipation and trust, progress in the understanding of dogmas. But it is not the purpose of this Council to solve every current problem.[28]

One commentator said that McIntyre's presentation was, "as were all his interventions at the Council, an honest statement. His Eminence casts a long shadow over the West Coast, but it is owing more to his financial than intellectual stature. Theological discussion does confuse him."[29] If, in fact, the cardinal were confused, it was mostly because of his lack of competent on-the-scene advisors. A written intervention by the cardinal on the same schema, according to one reliable observer, "brilliantly summarized the Church's teaching on the two sources of revelation as contained in most of the manuals of the seventeenth, eighteenth and nineteenth centuries."[30] He argued for the preservation of the two sources by giving an historical synopsis of their development in the apostolic Church.

Interestingly, McIntyre and his mentor, Francis Cardinal Spellman of New York, approached biblical exegetics from differing vantage points. In one of their few letters (they preferred daily telephone contact), McIntyre told Spellman "that you seem to be impressed with this thinking," is "I must be frank, somewhat shocking to me." McIntyre claimed that his Dunwoodie education inclined him to reject many of the notions that Spellman found acceptable, noting that his professors, Francis Gigot and Joseph Nelson, "in a scientific way refuted much of present-day contentions."[31]

McIntyre's own deep respect for the law is reflected in the following words he penned concerning the relationship between the two sources and the natural law:

> Let us recognize that Tradition and the written word contain some principles of the natural law. The law itself prescribed and instituted the order of nature. Law and order of nature were instituted by God for the common good of men. The basis or font of the order of nature is the natural law - the law according to which God created nature. By this law or order we, in turn, distinguish good from evil, that is, conformity or nonconformity with the divine will. Obedient to this law, we fulfill the obligation of grace due to God and conform our mind to the law of the natural order. Therefore, it follows that the divine disposition, that is, the antecedents of Tradition and Scripture in the natural law, constitute a law binding all men, even the mental errors and the voluntary faults which history has incited.[32]

McIntyre spoke to the conciliar fathers again on December 3rd, during discussions on the schema *De Ecclesia*, pointing out, among other things, its obvious omission of the delicate problem of infants who die without Baptism:

> In chapter two, paragraph nine of the schema on the Church, mention is made of those who are members of the Church in the proper sense.
>
> There does not seem to be complete separation among the orders of persons. There is a gap because infants dying without Baptism are not included in these classes. Since these infants are persons, it seems to me both reasonable and useful for the Holy Vatican Council, in this place, to concern itself with the eternal lot of these infants. This is most certainly an involved question, one that has been disputed for a long time among theologians.
>
> Perhaps the question does not pertain directly to this schema; but there is no treatment of this thing in any place of the schemas. Therefore, I propose that the consideration of this question be added to paragraph nine, at least in an implicit manner, because there seems to be some connection with the material treated in this paragraph.
>
> The solution of the question may, nevertheless, be a thing hidden in the eternal plan of the providence of God.[33]

On December 10th, the cardinal returned to Los Angeles, where he spoke publicly about his reactions to the first session of the Council. Expressing his gratitude at being able to share "in a tremendous epoch in the history of God's relationship with mankind," McIntyre said he was eagerly looking "forward to resuming our deliberations in September." He explained briefly the mechanical operations of the deliberations, noting that "the Council supplied a magnificent example of freedom of speech effectively carried out with complete justice and opportunity for all." He then remarked that the composition of this attendance was made of all races, of all cultures, of all countries. They were all bishops enjoying the fullness of the priestly office. Some possessed even higher dignity in rank and in administration.

"Thus, they were men of more than ordinary classical education. Most of them had academic degrees gained from advanced and scientific studies. They were all men of linguistic accomplishment." The cardinal went on to note that "these bishops were from all parts of the world. A large number of them were missionary

Cardinal McIntyre pauses before statue of Our Lady of the Angels which he commissioned for Santa Anastasia Church in Rome.

Cardinal McIntyre welcomes President Richard M. Nixon to San Juan Capistrano Mission in March, 1969.

C O A T - O F - A R M S

for

James Francis Cardinal McIntyre
Archbishop of Los Angeles

The heraldry of the Cardinal Archbishop is quartered with the coat-of-arms of the Archdiocese of Los Angeles. The left side of the shield represents the archdiocese and the right half bears cardinal's personal arms.

The archdiocesan half of the shield contains three sets of golden angels' wings on a field of azure, each guarding a golden rose. The golden rose is one of the Virgin Mary's livery badges and the angels' wings are symbolic of Los Angeles.

The cardinal's shield is blazoned thus: Gold, an eagle displayed in red and, on a breast, a silver crescent. A red eagle with wings extended on a gold field or background was the ancient original coat of the McIntyre clan. The crescent, symbolic of the Immaculate Conception of our Blessed Lady, is a personal detail. This symbol was selected from the many symbols of Mary in heraldry because, under her title of the Immaculate Conception, she is the patroness of the United States.

The motto *"Miserere Mei Deus"* is taken from Psalm 56:

> "Have mercy on me, O God,
> Have mercy on me;
> For my soul trusts You."

The external ornaments of rank are a golden cross with a double traverse indicating the jurisdiction of a metropolitan archbishop, and the red pontifical hat with fifteen scarlet tassels denoting the cardinalatial office.

bishops. They were all pastors of souls, and represented large groups of Catholic people in their respective dioceses. Thus, they were leaders of men.

"Many came from the areas of early Christianity. They placed in proximate focus the present day with the times of Our Lord Himself. All of these bishops were leaders, not in political matters, but primarily in matters of religion, and they were concerned only with the salvation of the souls and the relations of man with God." McIntyre pointed out that "they were interested in the social problems and conditions of their peoples insofar as these found reflection in their spiritual lives."

Noting that the Council had as its business no commercial or political objectives, McIntyre emphasized that its purpose was solely that of bringing the knowledge of God to the people, and being of assistance in the salvation of their souls. "This is God's business, and the Council was preeminently a work of God." Finally, McIntyre said that "the Council will stand out in history as a great accomplishment. In our time, the world has witnessed many conferences, discussions and summit meetings of varying degree and quality. Often the results of these have been frustrating. We are convinced that, unlike these, this Council will bear much fruit."[34]

Confounding those commentators who said or intimated that McIntyre's view of the council was negative were such articles as those of Leo J. Wollemborg who interviewed His Eminence of Los Angeles for the Washington *Post*. The cardinal was quoted as saying the Council had been a "truly worldwide gathering of shepherds, assembled in order to help bring their flocks closer to God and to each other." He told his interviewer that Vatican II gave "evidence of a growing emphasis on the unity of all people in God, despite their external differences of language, customs and traditions." McIntyre went out of his way to say that the "evidence of unity definitely applies to the relations with the representatives of various Christian denominations who attended the Council as observers." He said that there was a "splendid disposition on all sides" which gave "further, concrete meaning to that basic unity."[35]

Shortly after the conclusion of the first session, Robert Blair Kaiser, the Rome correspondent for *Time* and a former Jesuit teacher at Loyola High School, published his version of the proceedings under the title *Pope, Council and World*.[36] Though classified by the author among the "ecclesiastical bureaucrats," the cardinal agreed with Kaiser about the secrecy "foolishness" of the conciliar proceedings. On his own initiative, McIntyre sent a copy of the book to the Papal Secretary of State, Amleto Cardinal Cicognani, along with his observations that the press had been "invited to dinner but given nothing to eat." He pointed out that "there was no provision made for supplying them with material that could be published" without violating the *sub secreto* provision. Consequently, the cardinal noted, "they were forced to search for stray, unofficial comments and were obliged to enlarge upon passing remarks of a gossipy nature. The result was distressing to them and disturbing to many of the hierarchy because of the inaccuracy of many deductions." McIntyre strongly urged Cicognani to have "a well qualified priest or newspaperman" appointed "to give what constitutes news in a manner that would not infringe on the privacy of utterances made in the Council. This would not necessarily be a stupendous task," McIntyre noted, "but it would call for a man of prudence and intelligence, plus a little authority."[37]

Shortly thereafter, the cardinal submitted his written observations on the question of ecumenism, noting that:

> We have always dealt with great charity toward our truly Christian brothers who are not united to us in full faith or in the unity of obedience, and have shown these same brothers, without doubt or ambiguity, the objective and genuine doctrine which the Catholic Church has always held, knowing that they disagree among themselves in many areas. Neither have I accepted from them all the new things which are taught by some modern Catholic theologians. We strive to elevate and perfect the edifice of the Church which has been handed down to us by our spiritual and temporal fathers without destroying or weakening those things which are solid and remain apt for solving contemporary problems. Allow us to recall the words of St. Paul, "Do not be misled by various and passing doctrines," as well as the words read in St. Vincent of Lerins: "We must have great care to hold that which has been believed everywhere, always, and by all, for this is properly catholic.[38]

Before leaving for the second session of the Council in the fall of 1963, McIntyre implored the faithful of the archdiocese to pray that the deliberations "may be always truly wise and that the hierarchy may rejoice in the consolation and direction that comes with the presence and assistance of the Holy Spirit." He noted that the "Council has assumed a unique status in the reflections and considerations of all people throughout the world." The meetings had "exerted an unusual influence in the hearts and minds of peoples of all nations," a factor the cardinal attributed to a "realization that all life has its origin in a Supreme Being."[39]

McIntyre addressed the 60th general assembly of the Council, on November 5th, about the role of "Bishops and the Government of Dioceses." He strongly opposed the granting of legislative power to national conferences and said that "a proposal to decentralize authority in the Catholic Church is a radical change which might endanger its unity."[40] He went on to say that:

> The proposed plan to institute national or regional conferences is nothing new. Benefits increase when the circumstances of time and place are coordinated. The intention of these conferences is a reasonable and coordinated operation. They pertain to human activities as applied to the administration of the Church. Thus, they are useful and desirable especially in growing communities.
>
> But the question arises: Why should juridical status be given to them? It is said in the relation of this schema that these conferences which are to be instituted are not identified with plenary or provincial councils which are treated in Canon Law.
>
> The practical end of these conferences is to treat of the necessities and advantages of the circumstances which are peculiar to a certain region or a number of dioceses. The decisions of such conferences generally do not have, nor should they have, universal application. They should be applied only in a particular and definite region and according to the judgment of many bishops, with the approbation of the Holy See.
>
> The introduction of a juridical effect excepting the power of the ordinary of the place is neither necessary nor desirable in any way. The bishop has the power of jurisdiction in his own diocese; if many bishops decide to act in unity in a certain way, the same effect is obtained and a juridical sanction is not required. Thus a local *coetus* is a purely *voluntary* gathering among many dioceses with the same problems. If the problems require regulations besides the general law, permission can be obtained by petitioning the Holy See, and with apparent satisfaction.
>
> Therefore, it is better to give these conferences recognition, but without juridical status. A juridical status can introduce and create psychological consequences which could greatly disturb some bishops and some dioceses. It is clear from history that the unity of the Church often has been impeded because of juridical impositions which were not for the convenience of the local community.[41]

McIntyre reiterated his viewpoint on November 12th, when he noted to the conciliar gathering that:

> Regional conferences of bishops are good and must be advocated! However, the introduction of a juridical element is not necessary; in fact, it is also useless! The goal of the conferences can be reached in the same manner without the introduction of a juridical element.
>
> The jurisdiction of the regional conferences is restricted to the members and the territories of the conference. All in the region are obliged to keep the laws and regulations which they have determined. If there are some who do not agree, it would be better if the obligation were moral rather than juridical.[42]

Later that month, His Eminence addressed a message to the faithful of the Archdiocese of Los Angeles, in which he dwelt, to considerable length, on the proceedings of Vatican Council II:

> With the coming of the Holy Season of Advent, the Ecumenical Council concluded its second session.
>
> The work of the Council proceeded well and with much satisfaction. The definite decisions made and promulgated have established a very promising relationship between religion and the media of communications that can well have a universal effect for good.
>
> The discussions on the Liturgy will introduce, in some measure, a greater participation of the English language in some parts of the Mass. However, the details of this introduction will not be definitely determined - nor will they be put into effect - for perhaps another year.
>
> These will then be announced and employed gradually after ample notification. Some minor features have already been in use on special occasions.
>
> The discussions during the Council have been an exchange of opinions involving variances in practice during the years in different parts of the world and reflecting local conditions and traditions. These will be coordinated by sub-commissions and presented for action at the next session.
>
> The universal newspaper, periodical, radio and television coverage of the Council has been a spiritual stimulant to the religious spirit of people of all convictions throughout the world.
>
> The fact that the Council reviewed and confirmed the fundamental facts of the creation of man by God as given to

us in the Sacred Scriptures and in the unfailing traditions of time has been manifested in document and speech and even more in the very presence and liturgies of the peoples through whom these traditions have been transmitted in the annals and practices of history.

McIntyre went on to observe that "the council has renewed the convictions of religion - as manifest throughout time - even in profane history." He rejoiced that the conciliar fathers had "reaffirmed the obligation of all people to observe religious practice" and though "the errors of humanity in ignoring and misrepresenting the facts of redemption by dissenting groups in intervening centuries" were pointed out, the conciliar fathers treated those aberrations "with charity and love."

> The council has looked to the amendment of these differences and expressed hopefully and prayerfully that the stimulation occasioned by the discussions of the council awaken in the hearts and minds of all men a renewal of the spirit of God.
> The frank analysis of these vital and somewhat discarded questions will, it is hoped and prayed for, revive in all people the recognition of the obligations that come with the fact of creation. The obligation consequent to being created by God is the doing of what is right and the avoidance of what is wrong. This is the primary consideration of human relations and constitutes the basis of the natural law.

Concluding his remarks, His Eminence of Los Angeles said that "if the council stimulates the thinking of the world to greater reflection on these truths, we may expect consequent prayerful obedience to God's will in all human relations and the purpose of the council will have been blessed with great success."[43]

Shortly after returning to Los Angeles, the cardinal gave an interview to Robert T. Hartmann in which he cautioned against expecting too much from the council immediately, pointing out that "a council is not a convention. It requires time." He said that the conciliar fathers were "closer perhaps to the peoples of the world than any other group of men." Their purpose was that "of bringing about a closer relationship between God and each particular" person. When asked whether the council had been divided into "conservatives and liberals," he replied that he had been impressed and even "surprised at the seeming absence of factions." He said "our arguments were not just about right versus wrong, but about greater understanding and modern methods of applying eternal truths." He concluded by saying that "what we are doing is reaffirming the principles of religion in an age dominated by materialism and irreligious living."[44]

A little over a month later the cardinal spoke to the Archdiocesan Council of Catholic Women on "The Ecumenical Council," noting that its deliberations had given a spiritual stimulation to the whole world. "The impulses of religion that had become dormant have been revived and revivified. The thinking of people has been awakened to a renewed realization that all are creatures of God - that we owe our being to God - that we all depend upon God for our life and our sustenance and furthermore," the Cardinal said, "that we are and we shall be accountable to God on judgment day for the manner in which we have used, or abused, His providence and His sustenance."[45]

In a memorandum, the cardinal expressed his view that "the effect of the Ecumenical Council is world-wide and timely. It is world-wide because the newspapers and media of communication have publicized the Council in a very unusual manner." He went on to observe that "this great publicity has stimulated, from a marked degree of lethargy, the spiritual impulses of all people in the world. Many have come to the realization that spiritual motives and holy ideals have become somewhat atrophied. The Council has stimulated thinking to the point of seeking basic reasons for religion, and the human mind has discovered how barren are the bones of a glorified past."[46]

In his role as a member of the Commission on Bishops and the Government of Dioceses, the cardinal was obliged to return to Rome early in March to take part in interim meetings preparatory to the third session of the Council. Upon arriving back in Los Angeles, McIntyre wrote to the Apostolic Delegate, saying that he was "definitely hopeful that the coming session of the Ecumenical Council will be the final session." McIntyre felt that "the element of general good in the effect from the Ecumenical Council has been accomplished in a world-wide revival of recognition of the need of the spiritual life." He considered it "likely that the extension of these discussions beyond the coming session will invoke the mathematical principle of diminishing returns."[47]

On the following September 12th, McIntyre once again set out for the Eternal City, accompanied by Auxiliary Bishop John J. Ward. Prior to departing, he noted to the press that "the Council itself has been a great inspiration to all people" and hoped the faithful of Los Angeles would continue to support the conciliar gatherings with their prayers.[48]

Upon arriving in Rome, the cardinal rushed from the airport to Saint Peter's Basilica for the opening session of the council. Just after the Consecration of the Mass, he collapsed. Attendants wheeled him from the chamber on a stretcher and then took him by ambulance to the Blue Sisters Clinic. "Reports of this death ... spread rapidly through the Holy See," but his condition stabilized quite rapidly. "Doctors said the combination of fatigue and the heat of St. Peter's Basilica, filled with 2,500 conciliar fathers and several thousand spectators, caused him to lose consciousness."[49] Though he was able to return to the *aula* after a few days hospitalization, it was the judgment of physicians that a "prolonged attendance at the council might induce further fatigue."[50] The cardinal was received by Pope Paul VI who encouraged him to return home for the remainder of the third session. During McIntyre's absence from the Eternal City, Auxiliary Bishop Timothy Manning acted as his agent and kept him informed of developments on the various schemes. Each morning, a digest of happenings was sent by express mail to Los Angeles.

Interviewed shortly before departing for the fourth and final session of Vatican Council II, the seventy-nine year old Archbishop of Los Angeles said that "the Church has examined her conscience before the world. It is a brave act ... It has awakened man to the fact of the need of religion." The cardinal viewed the ecumenical council as "less revolutionary than many newspapers and magazine articles have proclaimed," noting that the Church had "demonstrated to the world that its doctrines were subject to analysis and discussion and dissection is the greatest manifestation of liberty that's happened in many, many years."[51]

McIntyre delayed his departure in order to be on hand for the arrival of Pope Paul VI at the United Nations. From New York, the cardinal proceeded on to the Eternal City where he arrived on October 7th.

The cardinal returned to Los Angeles for surgery before the final session had concluded. On December 10th, he called for a triduum of prayer in a pastoral letter to the People of God in Los Angeles.[52]

It was indeed an impressive Council that concluded on December 8th. One hundred sixty-eight general meetings and ten plenary ones were held. During the general or "open" sessions, 4,229 oral and 2,205 written interventions were recorded. Of that number, there were only 118 spoken interventions delivered by fifty-six American bishops. Though they constituted 10% of the total number of conciliar Fathers, Americans represented only about 5% of the total interventions. Despite the fact that illness negated his attendance at almost two complete sessions, Cardinal McIntyre spoke six times on the floor of the *aula* and submitted another dozen written interventions.

There were those who believed that "the Cardinal of Los Angeles arrived in Rome with a number of prejudices on his mind which he did not hesitate to ventilate."[53] Indeed, the simple, forthright and fearless McIntyre spoke and voted as his conscience dictated. Though his viewpoint was not always appreciated and occasionally rejected, especially in regard to the question of a vernacular Liturgy, the Archbishop of Los Angeles followed the example of his predecessor at Vatican Council I, Bishop Thaddeus Amat of Monterey-Los Angeles. That Vincentian prelate fought hard to block the definition of papal infallibility, was overridden and then set about writing a forceful pastoral in its defense.[54]

So too, "Cardinal McIntyre and a handful of others left their fight in Rome." They returned to America to implement the Council's decisions. They were churchmen who gave their obedience in the same measure that they demanded it. They may not have liked certain changes, but they accepted them.[55]

In an address to the students at Saint John's Seminary, on December 16, 1965, Cardinal McIntyre reflected on the influence that existentialism had upon the deliberations of Vatican Council II. He concluded that its overall effect was minimal and that the Thomistic Synthesis "is still valid and will continue to be."[56]

Early in February, 1966, Pope Paul VI named McIntyre Vice President of the post conciliar Commission dealing with the Pastoral Duties of Bishops. The purpose of that commission was to oversee the implementation of the principles contained in the conciliar document promulgated on October 28, 1965.[57]

A national survey about the degree of implementation given to the documents of Vatican Council II, published in June, 1966, revealed that the Archdiocese of Los Angeles was far ahead of other American jurisdictions in heeding the suggestions and spirit of the recent ecumenical gathering:

- Lectures on decrees and constitutions of Vatican Council prescribed in all parishes; extensive arrangements made for celebration of Council Jubilee.
- Commission on Liturgy in existence and intensely active since decree on liturgy was published; all directives regarding liturgy channeled through this commission.
- Commission on Ecumenism established; has sponsored Clergy Conferences in three counties of archdiocese, attended convention of the Episcopal Church, and sponsored talks within framework of the Council decree.

- Communications Department established in chancery office with own priest director, to coordinate principles of Decree on Communications and supervise breakthrough of Church into communications media.
- Intensified study given to requests for suggestions on revision of Code of Canon Law; representative of Curia sent to New York meetings, and lengthy studies of local canonists submitted.
- Vicar for Religious sent to Rome for four months to make contacts at Congregation for Religious and attend lectures at principal universities, in order to be fully informed on mind of Church regarding religious and to observe modern trends.
- Meetings held with Provincials of all religious communities in State to further intent of Constitution on Religious Life.
- In updating of seminary routine, the rule and course of studies have been revised; four years of college, housed in very modern structures, provide complete college-level education.
- Several priests released for work in Latin-American missionary countries.
- Prominent laymen form substantial membership in various organizations of diocese: Seminary Boards, diocesan paper, Welfare Bureau. Youth Organizations, etc.[58]

A writer from Torrance, California, thanked the editor of *America* for conducting the survey, noting that "without it, I would never have known about all the wonderful things Cardinal McIntyre and the Los Angeles diocese have been doing for us." The correspondent was especially grateful, for she had erroneously been made to think that "we were living in the Dark Ages" in Los Angeles![59]

Described by one writer as "the most visible Dunwoodie alumnus at Vatican II," the "irrepressible Cardinal McIntyre"[60] was indeed an active participant at the conciliar sessions who never hesitated to ask for assistance when the speaker's Latin was confusing or pedantic.

While openly admitting that his viewpoints on many of the issues were out of the mainstream of contemporary thought, McIntyre unhesitatingly expressed his opinions forcibly, content to have exercised his role as a member of the College of Bishops. In actuality, he sided with the majority on well over 95% of the roll calls and, when outvoted, he readily and graciously acquiesced.[61]

There were those who suggested and even proposed that Vatican Council II discuss issues other than those which ultimately comprised the sixteen conciliar documents. Had there been a discussion on stewardship, or how best to manage the temporal assets entrusted by God to His Church, then surely James Francis

Cardinal McIntyre would have emerged as one of the chief architects of the twenty-first of the ecumenical councils.

Notes to the Text

1. For the background, see Francis J. Weber, "Pope Pius XII and the Vatican Council," *American Benedictine Review* XXI (September, 1970), 421-424.
2. Ernesto Ruffini to John XXIII, *Acta et Documenta Concilio Oecumenico Vaticano II Apparando* (Rome, 1960), I, 124. See also Antoine Wenger, *Vatican II* (Westminster, 1966), I, 15, and Henri Daniel-Rops, *The Second Vatican Council* (New York, 1962), p. 58.
3. *Osservatore Romano*, November 1, 1959.
4. Francis J. Connell, C.Ss.R., "In Review," *American Ecclesiastical Review* CLVI (February, 1967), 127.
5. *Osservatore Romano*, November 1, 1959. See also Domenico Tardini, *Memories of Pius XII* (Westminster, 1961), p. 82.
6. See Giovanni Captrile, S.J., "Pio XII e un Nuovo Progetto di Concilio Ecumenico," *Civilta Cattolica* CXVII (August 6-20, 1966), 209-227.
7. See *Irenikon* XXXII (1959), 309 and *Unitas* XLVIII-XLIX (1959-1960),
8. Reported by Vincent A. Yzermans, *A New Pentecost* (Westminster, 1963), p. 298.
9. "Foreword" to *The Jerome Biblical Commentary* (Englewood Cliffs, N.J., 1968), p. viii.
10. For the complete text, see Floyd Anderson (ed.), *Council Daybook Vatican II* (Washington, 1965), pp. 1-2.
11. The earlier council had been called in 1414, by the pseudo-Pope, an action subsequently validated when the other two papal claimants endorsed the proposal.
12. AALA, *Acta et Documenta*, pp 254-268.
13. AALA, James Francis Cardinal McIntyre to Egidio Vagnozzi, Los Angeles, January 31, 1962.
14. AALA, Circular Letter, Los Angeles, February 6, 1962.
15. *The Tidings*, March 19, 1962.
16. *Ibid.*, October 5, 1962.
17. See Francis J. Weber, *"Tempora Mutantur et Non Mutamur in Illis," The Evangelist* XXV (Fall, 1962), 14-15, 25.
18. On September 8, 1965, this writer was asked by Msgr. Vincent A. Yzermans to provide the text of Cardinal McIntyre's interventions at Vatican Council II. The various materials were

gathered and subsequently submitted in their original Latin form on October 20, 1965. Yzermans then translated the interventions into English for incorporation in his informative and useful volume, *American Participation in the Second Vatican Council* (New York, 1967). Inasmuch as that book will likely become the accepted source for future researchers, this writer has decided to utilize the Yzermans' renditions throughout this section of the text. In every case, the Latin original is in the AALA. For this particular reference, see AALA, James Francis Cardinal McIntyre, Intervention, October 23, 1962.

19. Xavier Rynne, *Letters from Vatican City* (New York, 1963), p. 124. For this writer's appraisal of that book, see the *Homiletic and Pastoral Review* LXIII (September, 1963), 1071-1072.
20. *Ibid.*
21. S. J. Adamo, *While the Winds Blew* (Wilkes-Barre, 1968), pp. 44-45.
22. *Time* LXXX (November 9, 1962).
23. AALA, James Francis Cardinal McIntyre, Intervention, November 5, 1962.
24. Thomas J. Shelley, *Dunwoodie. The History of St. Joseph's Seminary* (Westminster, 1993), p. 228.
25. AALA, James Francis Cardinal McIntyre, Intervention, November 5, 1962.
26. Xavier Rynne, op. cit., p. 125.
27. Father William J. Kenneally, C.M., was also Professor of Sacred Scripture at Saint John's Seminary at Camarillo.
28. AALA, James Francis Cardinal McIntyre, Intervention, November 16, 1962.
29. Robert Blair Kaiser, *Pope, Council and World* (New York, 1963), p. 171.
30. Vincent A. Yzermans, *op. cit.*, p. 98.
31. Quoted by Thomas J. Shelley, "Francis Cardinal Spellman and His Seminary at Dunwoodie," *Catholic Historical Review* LXXX (April, 1994), 288. McIntyre joined eighteen other cardinals in addressing a letter of concern to the Holy Father about the manner in which scripture was being used or misused by certain conciliar interventions. Spellman would not sign the letter. See AALA, Amleto Cardinal Cicognani to Alfredo Cardinal Ottaviani, Rome, December 4, 1962.
32. AALA, James Francis Cardinal McIntyre, Intervention, November 16, 1962.
33. *Ibid.*, December 3, 1962.
34. *The Tidings*, December 14, 1962.
35. Los Angeles *Times*, December 8, 1962.

36. For this writer's appraisal of the book, see *Homiletic and Pastoral Review* LXIV (October, 1963), 85-87.
37. AALA, James Francis Cardinal McIntyre to Amleto Cardinal Cicognani, Los Angeles, August 20, 1963. McIntyre was also a strong and outspoken supporter of Richard Cardinal Cushing's offer to install simultaneous translation devices for the conciliar fathers, a factor that would have facilitated more lively and widespread discussions by bishops who lacked easy understanding of Latin. For some unintelligible reason, the offer was rejected.
38. AALA, James Francis Cardinal McIntyre, Intervention, n.d.
39. AALA, Circular Letter, Los Angeles, September 24, 1963.
40. Los Angeles *Times*, November 6, 1963.
41. AALA, James Francis Cardinal McIntyre, Intervention, November 5, 1963.
42. *Ibid.*, November 12, 1963.
43. *The Tidings*, December 6, 1963.
44. Los Angeles *Times*, December 1, 1963.
45. AALA, James Francis Cardinal McIntyre, Address delivered January 10, 1964.
46. AALA, James Francis Cardinal McIntyre, Memorandum, Los Angeles, April 30, 1964.
47. AALA, James Francis Cardinal McIntyre to Egidio Vagnozzi, Los Angeles, July 6, 1964.
48. *The Tidings*, September 11, 1964.
49. Los Angeles *Herald-Examiner*, September 14, 1964.
50. *The Tidings*, October 9, 1964.
51. John Bryan in the Los Angeles *Herald-Examiner*, September 12, 1965.
52. *The Tidings*, December 24, 1965.
53. Xavier Rynne, *op. cit.*, p. 124.
54. See Francis J. Weber, *California's Reluctant Prelate* (Los Angeles 1964), pp. 171ff.
55. S. J. Adamo, *op. cit.*, p. 45.
56. "Nova et Vetera," *The Evangelist* XXVIII (Winter, 1966), 9.
57. *The Tidings*, February 4, 1966.
58. "Post Conciliar Programs," *America* CXIV (June 11, 1966), 826.
59. *Ibid.*, CXV (July 23, 1966), 84. Others had the same, erroneous expression. A prime example was James Gollin who reported that McIntyre "reportedly" said that "none of the improvements of Vatican II will be promulgated here during my lifetime." See *Worldly Goods* (New York, 1971), p. 97.
60. Shelley, *Dunwoodie*, p. 238.
61. This statistic is all the more significant in view of Ellwood Kaiser's scurrilous remark that McIntyre "had voted with the

arch-conservative majority against most of the conciliar documents because he liked the Church of his boyhood and saw no reason to change it." See *Hollywood Priest* (New York, 1991), p. 176.

20. *Immaculate Heart Sisters*

T he election of Anita Caspary[1] to the superiorship of the
California Institute of the Sisters of the Most Holy and
Immaculate Heart of the Blessed Virgin Mary[2] in 1963 opened the
penultimate chapter in the life of a religious community founded at
Olot, Spain in 1848, one which marked "the first time in America
that nuns ever tried to bully a cardinal."[3] For almost a century, the
Immaculate Heart Sisters were among the most precious
adornments of the Catholic Church in California. Founded in
Catalonia's small town of Olot by Canon Joaquin Masmitja, the
congregation was brought to the Diocese of Monterey-Los Angeles in
1871 by Bishop Thaddeus Amat. From their humble beginnings,
the Sisters prospered and expanded until they found themselves
scattered over the entire Pacific Coast. Given canonical autonomy in
1924, the community ultimately became the largest single
component in the educational system operated by the Archdiocese of
Los Angeles. No fewer than 197 nuns taught and/or staffed twenty-
eight elementary and eight secondary schools throughout the four
county jurisdiction.

Taking over a community which John Cogley said was "stuck with
a pietistic name, an outmoded rule and a tradition that no longer
served their purpose,"[4] Sister Anita brought a wholly new concept of
leadership to the community, much of it based on interpretations
from a book by the late Leon Joseph Cardinal Suenens on *The Nun
in the World*. Interestingly, Suenens repeatedly refused to endorse
"renewal" efforts based on his book, noting that it was primarily
intended for religious women in Europe where most Sisters had
little or no participation in the apostolate. He stressed "the true
message of my book ... (was) an invitation to religious in active
orders and congregations to become more deeply involved in the
evangelization of the world, without letting the world take over
their lives."[5] His Eminence of Malines regretted that his book was
credited (or blamed) for ideas never advocated or even intimated.
Like the conciliar documents themselves, the Suenens book was
used as a source to justify a wide range of actions and activities

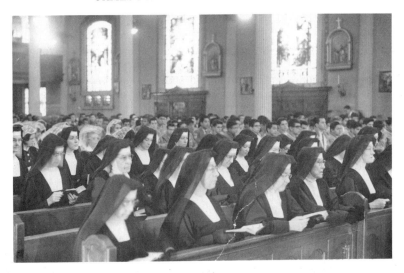

The Immaculate Heart of Mary Sisters, shown here in a memorial Mass for the Right Reverend Francis Mora at Saint Vibiana's Cathedral on December 5, 1962, were a vibrant force in the archdiocesan educational ministry.

Prior to Vatican Council II, the Sisters of the Immaculate Heart of Mary were a strong influence in the archdiocesan school system for Los Angeles.

totally foreign to what he considered the basic concept of religious life.

The new Mother General inherited some major problems, among them a movement begun in the early 1960s by Sister Aloyse, a psychologist on the faculty of Immaculate Heart College, who spent much of her time ministering to the mental health of the community. Aloyse and others were actively promoting an experimental program known as sensitivity training.[6] She had convinced the former superior general, Mother Regina, to allow the sessions among the sisters, an action fraught with dangers obvious only in retrospect.

In an extensive interview given early in 1994, Dr. William Coulson, a co-practitioner for many years with American psychologist Carl Rogers, recalled how his cadre of fifty-eight facilitators "invaded the IHM community" in 1966 with their notions of nondirective psychotherapy. The Sisters were preparing for a general chapter in which they wanted to re-evaluate their mode of living in order "to bring it more in line with the charisms of their founder."

Coulson and Rogers met with nearly the whole community at Immaculate Heart High School in Hollywood during April of 1967. With the pilot study already completed, they wanted "to get everybody in the system involved in nondirective self-exploration."

Coulson acknowledged that Rogers, "the brains behind the project," was "probably anti-Catholic," something that Coulson hadn't recognized at the time. He later admitted that "we both had a bias against hierarchy. I was flush with Vatican II and I thought, I am the Church; I am as Catholic as the Pope. Didn't Pope John XXIII want us to open the windows and let in the fresh air? Here. we come! And we did and, within a year, those nuns wanted out of their vows!"

As part of their program, they created a miniature utopian society, known as the encounter group. "As long as Rogers and those who feared Rogers' judgment were present, it was okay, because nobody fooled around in his presence. He kept people in line; he was a moral force. People did in fact consult their consciences, and it looked like good things were happening." But once the nuns were broken down into encounter groups, it didn't take long for trouble to erupt. "They were ready for an intensive look at themselves with the help of a humanistic psychologist. We overcame their traditions; we overcame their faith."

Coulson recalled that "it took about a year and a half" to destroy the order. He also admitted that Immaculate Heart College eventually "ceased to function, because of our good offices." He recalled how one mother pulled her daughter out of class, saying:

"Listen, she can lose her faith for free at the state college." The program was halted by Coulson after two years "because we were alarmed about the results. We thought we could make the IHMs better than they were; and we destroyed them."[7]

In all fairness, Coulson doesn't deserve all the credit. In her memoirs, Midge Turk, the former Sister Agnes Marie, recalls that in the early 1960s, Sister Aloyse brought the Dutch theologian-psychologist Father Adrian van Kamp to Montecito for several group encounters during which "all community rules were suspended." According to Turk, "this team of professionals, some Catholic and some not, revealed to us how dictatorial superiors were and in turn how dependent, submissive and helpless nuns were when it came to working with the outside world." She further recalled that as news of these sessions traveled the convent grapevine, "many of the sisters thought that this was the beginning of the end and that it could only lead to a breakdown of our community religious life as it had been lived."[8]

With the perspective of thirty years, her assessment appears to have been correct. In his fascinating book on *The Cult of Self-Worship*, Paul C. Vitz traces the "hostility of most psychologists to Christianity," pointing out that "psychology as religion" has for years been destroying individuals, families and communities. The humanist psychologists make no place for Christian, Jewish and other faith traditions to intrude into their mindset.[9]

In the spring of 1965, James Francis Cardinal McIntyre became concerned over the abnormally large number of applications being made by Immaculate Heart Sisters for dispensations from their vows. Because of complaints from certain members of the community and from pastors of parishes whose schools were staffed by the Sisters, McIntyre authorized several canonical visitations, the results of which he submitted to Ildebrando Cardinal Antoniutti, Prefect for the Sacred Congregation of Religious.

Though he was deeply troubled about the trend of the community's internal activities, McIntyre's primary concern was about their role as teachers in the archdiocesan schools. Even after it became evident that Anita Caspary and others advocated substantial alterations in the basic structure of the community, the Archbishop of Los Angeles, outspoken as he was privately to Anita Caspary, preferred that the extent and direction of the changes be arbitrated by Roman authorities.

Though it was the first ecumenical council in history not called to address a heresy or correct some major ecclesial problem, Vatican Council II had a greater effect on the Church of its time than any other such gathering in recorded annals. Especially is that true for

419

those men and women committed to God's service by private, simple or perpetual vows.

The conciliar decree on *The Appropriate Renewal of the Religious Life* was issued on October 25, 1965. The Most Reverend John J. McEleney, Jesuit Bishop of Kingston, Jamaica, noted in his commentary on the decree that the "legitimate need of renewal or any adaptation" should always be "carried out in a responsible and efficient manner," but he warned that "doubtlessly some daring experiments and perhaps even drastic changes will have to be made by competent authorities and we should not be afraid of engaging in them, even though some initial difficulties and failings may have to be overcome."[10] A prophetic statement indeed.

Among the religious women in the United States, and maybe in the whole world, no community was more anxious than the Immaculate Heart Sisters to begin the renewal authorized and encouraged by Vatican Council II. Little did anyone think then that the Sisters would be the first corporate victims of what became known as "post conciliar trauma."

On September 2, 1966, Pope Paul VI implemented the earlier conciliar decree by issuing a *Motu Proprio* in which he urged all religious "to examine and renew their way of life and, towards that end, to engage in wide-ranging experimentation."[11] The IHM sisters were among the first to respond and, within six weeks, the pontiff's letter had been circulated among the 560 members of the community. A number of commissions were appointed to study carefully all aspects of their religious commitment.

By the time the forty-three elected chapter members met at Montecito in July of 1967, for their 9th General Chapter, they had before them the results of several surveys circulated among community members. Throughout the remaining weeks of the summer, the chapter poured over the reports which ultimately resulted in a series of innovative documents, one each for Apostolic Works, Persons in Community, Authority and Government, Life of Prayer and Preparation for Life in the Community. The chapter authorized a large scale experimentation on the basis of those documents and called for another chapter meeting in the summer of 1968 to evaluate progress.

Of special interest to Catholics in California's southland was the document on Apostolic Works which dealt with the status of education in the Archdiocese of Los Angeles. A section on education was drawn up, discussed, and then passed without any consultation with the school department for the archdiocese, where the greatest majority of Immaculate Heart Sisters taught. One of the nuns noted that "It could have been taken from a primer on the ideal school system for it had little relevancy to parochial reality."[12]

Noting that "the goal of education" is not only to impart information, but to "develop flexible, adaptive individuals open to change and willing to learn continuously," the decree began by affirming the community's proposed move of Immaculate Heart College, Claremont to "because of the ecumenical dimension and the emphasis on excellence in education which this move implies." It encouraged the Sisters to "become involved as soon as possible in the needed and urgent apostolate of Adult Religious Education."

The Sisters were reminded that "financial realities will impose restrictions on the relative size of the Catholic school system and will suggest a reorientation toward a smaller system of more distinguished quality." Then the document spelled out some particulars which "although drastic in their short term implications, are essential for achieving the excellence in elementary and secondary education which alone justifies our involvement in it." Among those measures were:

a) Reasonable class sizes (ideally between thirty-five and forty);
b) Full time principals with authority to exercise responsibilities as administrator, supervisor, initiator (of new programs) and communicator with the pastor, parishioners, school staff, students and her professional peers;
c) Sufficient financial resources to facilitate the employment of a full staff of adequately prepared teaching personnel and to provide for instructional materials, adequate maintenance and clerical assistance.

Further, to ensure that these and other elements would be implemented and "to avoid any misunderstandings" the directives called for "a carefully prepared annual agreement" to be signed by all parties no later than June, 1968. The Immaculate Heart Sisters would agree to assign to such schools only those members of the community duly qualified to engage in such an important work for the Church. "If the community is to be a party to the agreement, the terms must be accepted by a committee on which representatives of the diocese and of the Sisters of the Immaculate Heart shall sit. The immediate ecclesiastical authority over the school (pastor, administrator, board chairman) should be a party to these committee deliberations. On the side of the sisters, the committee should include the principal of the school in question, a community supervisor, a representative of the General Government of the community, and legal counsel." At the end of this section, it was noted that "the community will withdraw from schools for which such agreements cannot be made."

Among the elements which would characterize an adequate teacher was the stipulation that he or she have "regular certification", a feature that had occasionally been waived in earlier hiring procedures, especially for persons already enrolled in classes for that purpose. It was stated, however, that effective in June of 1968, "no Sister of the Immaculate Heart will be assigned to a teaching position who does not have certification."[13] The stage was set for what *Newsweek* magazine declared would be "a joyous revolution in the making." A revolution it was, but how "joyous" would be open to question.[14]

Though admitting that "some sisters in the community of 560 are not in agreement with the decisions made by their elected delegates," Caspary felt that the "enthusiastic reception of the decrees" by most of the nuns indicated "an overwhelming consensus in favor of them."[15]

Immediately after the conclusion of the Chapter, in early August, Sister Anita Caspary left for Rome, where she met with Cardinal Suenens who discreetly advised her not to be seen in the Eternal City without her habit. Suenens suggested that upon her return home, she immediately inform Cardinal McIntyre about the results of the chapter. On October 16th, she and members of her council met with McIntyre who, up until that time, had heard nothing except rumors about the proceedings. He had only received his copy of the decrees the previous day.

While much and perhaps most of the provisions outlined in the education decree paralleled programs already envisioned and partially underway in the archdiocesan school system, the introduction of the arbitrary and mandatory deadline was seen as a totally unrealistic condition. McIntyre felt that the decree amounted to "an ultimatum that does not even admit to discussion or negotiation." He felt that such an ultimatum, with all its ramifications, was simply "not acceptable to the Archdiocese of Los Angeles and its Ordinary." That being the case, he saw "no other alternative than to accept the threat of the community that they withdraw from the teaching staffs of our parochial schools."[16]

At his meeting with the Sisters, the cardinal formally stated his "unwillingness to accept the ultimatum as contained in the Chapter" and repeated that if that is the mind of the community "they were perfectly free to withdraw" from the archdiocese. Though he noted that the arbitrary date of June, 1968 had been set for the compliance with their demands, he was willing to extend the deadline for another year. When Sister Anita said that she would reconvene the chapter for another vote, the cardinal was amenable, but told her bluntly that he would not "have a community teaching in one of our schools that did not have and practice a rule of life more rigid than that proposed."[17]

Anita Caspary released a letter in which she announced that the Immaculate Heart Community was involved in a "redefinition of goals, a reaffirmation of values and a reassessment of our resources and our ability to respond to the needs of the Church and the world today."[18] She then outlined parts of the Decree on Apostolic Works as indicative of what the community had in mind.

On the same day, the New York *Times* told its readers that the Immaculate Heart Sisters would soon inaugurate what it termed "liberal changes" in its rule, aimed at providing "more meaningful service to the complex changing world of 1967." It said that the reforms adopted by the Sisters "are also designed to provide the members with better opportunities to develop individual interests and talents, and an option either to elect the superior of their convent or govern it by group authority." Caspary had told the newspaper that "Sister Corita is the perfect example of what could be done in our Order," noting that "we have many other sisters like her, and we hope to have even more diversity and freedom."[19]

In an extensive interview with John Dart of the Los Angeles *Times*, Sister Anita spoke of the chapter's actions as a "major breakthrough" for Roman Catholic nuns in America. She said the "renewal will be more profound than any thus far announced for any American religious society of Catholic women." While noting that "all the new measures are experimental in nature," she saw little reason to suppose that those innovations which prove beneficial will not then be made permanent." As for religious garb, Caspary said that no style would be adopted as normative, "but sisters engaged in varying occupations may wear varying habits, suitable for their work."[20] Noting that the Immaculate Heart Sisters have in mind nothing less than a profound redirection of their communal lifestyle, *Commonweal* magazine labeled their "proposals as landmarks."[21]

In another interview, Caspary explained that she had not informed Cardinal McIntyre about any of the proceedings at Montecito until after the fact. She felt that he did not have to be consulted because the Order was a pontifical institute and under Rome's jurisdiction.[22]

Shortly after his meeting with Caspary, McIntyre wrote a long letter to Ildebrando Cardinal Antoniutti in which he described his encounter with Sister Anita in considerable detail. He told how "rumor had it that the community had employed great strategy in the presentation of the decrees of the Chapter" and that this methodology was adapted to "force the Archbishop to accede to the results of the Chapter." McIntyre said that while the educational proposals were subject to discussion, there appeared to be no elasticity in their original demands. More importantly, he felt that the whole notion of education was intertwined in the religious status, training and living of the community. It was his contention that "the community and the convent they live in should be subject to a determined and definite rule of life and a spirit of religion, not a secular spirit." He had no intention of allowing "our convents to become hotels or boarding houses for women."[23]

Sister Anita Caspary re-convened the chapter and, on October 23rd, she told McIntyre that "after serious deliberation, we unanimously reaffirmed by secret ballot the content of the total document." She believed that the rule of life adopted was "deeply Christian and expressive of the kind of religious life in the community to which we are committed." While remaining firm, Caspary held out an olive branch by saying that "we sincerely wish to continue serving the people of Los Angeles and we trust that our lives will give testimony to the worth of the direction we have taken."[24]

That same day, Caspary wrote to the entire community, telling them that the "reaction of His Eminence was generally negative not only on the issue of schools but also on the documents on prayer and local government as a way of life for religious." It was in this letter that Anita first accused the cardinal of "firing" the sisters. "His Eminence is in a position to discontinue our work in the archdiocesan schools."[25] This is a pivotal issue because at no time did McIntyre do anything more than acknowledge the decision of the Immaculate Heart Sisters to withdraw unless certain conditions were met. He didn't fire them. They withdrew.[26] One sister, who didn't want her name used but was later identified as Sister Francis Borgia,[27] stated unequivocally to a reporter from the Los Angeles *Times* that "we were not fired." She regretted that "the cardinal is made to take the blame for everything."[28]

There is ample reason to believe that Anita Caspary and her advisors felt there would eventually be some sort of accommodation with the archbishop "because of the large number of schools" then being serviced by the Immaculate Heart Sisters. When it became obvious that personal negotiations were not working, Sister Anita turned up the pressure by telling the press directly or at least intimating that the Sisters had been "fired" from their positions.[29] Though that statement was unfounded, it struck a responsive cord among journalists, many of whom portrayed McIntyre as a Catholic curmudgeon. By insisting that the purpose of the chapter was not to withdraw from the parochial schools of the archdiocese, Caspary fueled the "firing" notion.

The first major newspaper to use that terminology was the *National Catholic Reporter* which carried a headline on the first page of its issue for November 15th: "McIntyre to oust 200 updating nuns." In the accompanying essay, Sister Anita was quoted as saying that "the key issue between the sisters and the cardinal is the changes they are making in their living patterns."[30] McIntyre responded by noting that "the nature and structure of religious life is a subject which has profound roots in Canon Law, as well as in moral, pastoral and ascetical theology." And he doubted "whether such a subject can be competently discussed in the public forum."[31]

Though he personally disagreed with and opposed many of the experimental changes proposed by the sisters in their religious life, McIntyre was content to leave that aspect to the Sacred Congregation for Religious "which has jurisdiction in such matters." What primarily concerned McIntyre was the impact those changes would have on the archdiocesan school system.[32]

Meanwhile, others had taken up the "firing" torch, including *Newsweek* who erroneously reported that "the cardinal has quietly instructed pastors of diocesan elementary and secondary schools to fire all Immaculate Heart teachers by June 1."[33] John Cogley, who described the IHMs as having long been "a liberal light shining in the ultra-conservative darkness of the Los Angeles archdiocese," said that McIntyre's efforts to hold back change struck him "as being as foolish as trying to hold back the dawn."[34] S. J. Adamo entered the fray with the charge that the cardinal had taken "steps to ease them (the Sisters) out of his archdiocese."[35] Finally, Andrew Greeley, who had fallen in love with Immaculate Heart College in 1965 when he and some colleagues toured the "somewhat battered collection of buildings... where Francis of Assisi, Philip Neri and the Lord Himself would have felt at home," said that the new chapter documents were "sensible and balanced, and represent the path all religious orders are going to have to follow if they are to survive."[36]

One commentator who didn't go along with McIntyre bashing was Ed Grant of the Newark *Advocate*. He pointed out "some disquieting factors" in the controversy, among which was the practice followed by the Sisters of releasing their reports to the press at least no later than they were given to the cardinal. He thought that made them "at least guilty of bad taste."[37] Another privately-owned Catholic newspaper, tired of the bickering, said that "the cardinal virtues are: justice, prudence, temperance and fortitude. In Los Angeles, patience should be added to the list."[38]

Caspary made a final plea to McIntyre on December 18th by saying that the decrees on education were negotiable and that the Sisters would like to avoid the eventuality of withdrawing.[39] Unhappily for both sides, she did not offer to budge on the major problem in the whole discussion, the timetable. Coached by her own canonist, Caspary made every effort to clothe the chapter's decrees in conciliar language. She told the *Saint Anthony's Messenger*, for example, that "the key issue in the dispute... is our initiation of experimentation with a new mode of religious life as authorized by the directives of Pope Paul VI after Vatican II."[40]

Early in January, the cardinal and his advisors began preparing for the departure of the Sisters. He wrote to Caspary saying that "if there be any of the sisters of the community who would wish to remain on the staffs of our schools under the same conditions that have prevailed in recent years, we shall make provisions for them."[41] Later, some thirty accepted that invitation.

A few days later, Caspary wrote to all the pastors whose schools were staffed by the IHMs. "As you probably know, His Eminence, James Francis Cardinal McIntyre has asked the sisters of the Immaculate Heart to withdraw from the parochial and diocesan schools of the Archdiocese of Los Angeles."[42] She sent a similar letter to the parents of their 7,500 students, again repeating the entirely unfounded charge that "after 82 years in the Archdiocese of Los Angeles, the Sisters of the Immaculate Heart are being asked to stop teaching your children in the parochial schools of the archdiocese."[43] When the contents of the letter appeared in the columns of the Los Angeles *Times* the following day, McIntyre once again denied it by categorically repeating that "the archdiocese has not dismissed the Sisters of the Immaculate Heart of Mary."[44] The editor of *The Tidings* spoke to the "firing" charge even more forcefully when he pointed out that "the decision as to whether they will withdraw from the schools is in the hands of the Sisters themselves. It was they who took the initiative; it was they who laid down the conditions; it was they who issued the ultimatum."[45] Even the editors of the *National Catholic Reporter* quoted McIntyre as saying that "the final decision on the future steps to be taken by the Immaculate Heart Sisters resides with the Sisters themselves."[46]

Whether intended or not, Sister Anita's letter of January 8 brought a third party into the dispute, namely the parents, many of whom were understandably concerned about the future of their parochial schools. In most cases, the parents only knew what they had read in the local newspapers or heard from the Sisters, neither of which sources was unbiased or totally accurate. Home and school committees in such diverse places as Long Beach, Goleta and San Pedro went on record as supporting the continuance of Catholic education as if that were threatened. Throughout the whole controversy, McIntyre kept repeating that "we will undertake to keep in operation the schools in which they are presently engaged."[47] And he kept that promise.

In December of 1967, the Los Angeles Association of Laymen was organized and almost immediately "jumped into the smoldering dispute."[48] Claiming a membership of 700, the association "defended the nuns' right to experiment and make their own rules." They complained that "the great tragedy is that those people most effected by the decisions are the laity, who have not been consulted in any manner."[49] John Dart reported in the Los Angeles *Times* that another group of Catholics, "spurred on by what they consider the disobedience of the Immaculate Heart nuns," had formed a "militant organization" to call attention to those defying church authority.[50]

Reporting from Long Beach that "leaders of parents' groups stand with the sisters" in his area, Les Rodney noted that reaction by others "to this paper's stories indicates widespread rank-and-file support for Cardinal McIntyre." He noted that "few articles in this reporter's memory stirred as many reader phone calls to discuss the issues involved." "Some readers," he said, "while quite ready to grant that the sisters are entitled to liberalizing changes in their mode of life, feel that the matter is too complex for the press to present fairly and accurately, and that the public airing of the dispute is a mistake which can only confuse the youngsters and harm the educational fabric."[51]

Though she had been "asked by the Apostolic Delegate to the Church in the United States to refrain from discussing the matter publicly,"[52] Anita Caspary took to the lecture circuit. In Piedmont, California, she explained how the nuns had come to their decision about renewal "after a full year of careful study." She even got into the "semantic argument as to who was responsible for starting the controversy," admitting that "the matter is not yet resolved" and is "still very serious."[53]

The superior general also encouraged a letter writing campaign by those supporting the Immaculate Heart Sisters. Hundreds of missives were sent to the Los Angeles chancery, among them a plea from Mr. and Mrs. Barton P. Miller of Santa Barbara who felt that their "only recourse now is to the power of public opinion." They urged "all parents who have children in IHM schools to express their appreciation for the work of the Sisters,"[54] a ploy that elicited the comment from Msgr. Patrick Roche that "spokesmen for the Sisters have succeeded in creating an atmosphere of confusion and unhappiness which baffles understanding."[55]

Then came a series of public "endorsements" which dominated the headlines for a few weeks and only served to further confuse onlookers. The first was a group of thirteen theology professors at the Jesuit's Alma College who issued a letter praising the nuns for their "splendid response to the call for renewal and adaptation of religious life."[56] Next came twenty-nine members of the Society of Jesus, most of them faculty members at Loyola University who signed an "open" letter to Cardinal McIntyre strongly supporting the Immaculate Heart Sisters.[57] Several days later, twenty-eight other Jesuits associated with Loyola sent a memorandum to His Eminence disavowing themselves from the "open" letter[58] which they said "does not represent that of the entire religious community at Loyola University, or even a majority of it."[59] Finally a cadre of Franciscan priests and brothers of the Theological Seminary at Santa Barbara joined in publicly supporting the nuns.[60]

There was no shortage of inflammatory rhetoric on the wires. *Time* magazine, for example, consistently characterized Cardinal McIntyre as "an arch foe of Catholic renewal."[61] The editors of *America* were no less patronizing, noting that the nuns should have the "freedom to shape their own lives of service."[62]

Though he disagreed with anything bearing the McIntyre imprint, S. J. Adamo defended the cardinal's good intentions, saying that "after all, what prelate wants to go down in history as the man who forced 200 nuns to leave his archdiocese."[63] After interviewing the cardinal, Father Richard Ginder shot himself in the foot by presuming to speak for the 4,390 other Sisters in the archdiocese who "have their own opinion of the 200 little noisy IHMs and what they are doing to tarnish the image of God's Church in Los Angeles."[64] Martin J. Snelus of San Mateo suggested that Ginder should be nominated for "Man of the Year - of 1568."[65]

From his vantage point at Notre Dame University, Father Theodore Hesburgh cautioned patience, pointing out that "there always will be tension between those who want to go one way fast and those who want to go slow."[66] Another commentator counseled a slower pace at the modernizing process, noting that "if history shows anything, it shows that there are usually excesses in sudden change."[67] Finally, Father Sean Quinlan of Oakland observed that "we are witnessing here a conflict between very sincere principals," pointing out that "anyone who knows Cardinal McIntyre recognizes him as a man devoid of all pomp and cant."[68] Despite his deep misgivings about the direction and extent of the internal "renewal" of the Immaculate Heart Sisters, Cardinal McIntyre consistently avoided getting personally involved in any other than the educational pursuits of the community. The cardinal agreed with his counterpart in San Francisco, Archbishop Joseph T. McGucken, that it seemed obvious that the Sisters "will not listen to local authority and that peremptory commands will only stiffen their resistance." Even in retrospect, McGucken's advice "to await the action of the Holy See"[69] was sound.

On November 4th, Father Thomas R. Gallagher, a Dominican priest attached to the Apostolic Delegate in Washington, informed McIntyre that he had been appointed Apostolic Visitator for the California Institute of the Sisters of the Immaculate Heart of Mary by the Sacred Congregation for Religious. He asked if he could meet with the state's bishops before beginning interviews with the Sisters.[70] After lengthy discussions with all the parties involved, Gallagher, for the first time, disclosed that the majority of the nuns appeared "committed to the establishment of themselves as a secular institute,"[71] an arrangement that would require determining the status of those not wishing to follow that path.

Gallagher worked diligently for three months interviewing sisters, priests, laity and anyone expressing a willingness to testify. A canonist, he touched all the bases and he did it in a manner acceptable to all parties of the controversy. The delicate assignment was done quickly in response to Archbishop McGucken's suggestion that there be "speedy action" in order to allow preparation for the following academic year.[72]

In what was unprecedented rapidity for curial bureaucracy, the Sacred Congregation for Religious, after studying the extensive report made by Father Gallagher, handed down its decision on February 21, 1968. Gallagher was asked to inform the Sisters of the decision:

1) The members of the Institute have to adopt a uniform habit, which will be in conformity with the prescriptions of the Decree *"Perfectae Caritatis"*. The use of lay clothes is not only against the above-mentioned Decree, but violates Canon Law and the prescriptions of the *Motu Proprio "Ecclesiae Sanctae II"* which states that: "The General Chapter is empowered to modify on an experimental basis certain prescriptions of the Constitutions ... provided that the purpose, *nature and characteristics of the Institute are preserved intact*." The habit pertains to the nature and characteristics of any Institute for which it has been approved, and the interpretations given to the Sisters in this regard by certain so-called "competent Theologians" have absolutely no foundation, either doctrinal or juridical.

2) Every community of the Sisters of the Immaculate Heart should meet daily for some religious exercises in common. They should at least attend the Holy Sacrifice of the Mass together every day.

3) The Sisters should keep in mind their commitment to education as specified in their Constitutions: "The specific end is to labor for the salvation of souls through the work of Catholic education in schools and colleges..." Here, too, the above quotation from the *Motu Proprio* *"Ecclesiae Sanctae"* is applicable, namely that the purpose of the Institute must be kept intact.

4) The Sisters must observe the prescriptions of the Conciliar Decree *"Christus Dominus"* and of the *Motu Proprio "Ecclesiae Sanctae I"* in regard to collaboration with the Local ordinaries in the works of the Apostolate in the various dioceses. These prescriptions hold for all Religious, especially for those of Pontifical Right.

Idlebrando Cardinal Antoniutti noted that "the above decisions are taken with particular concern for the common good of the Church and for the religious education of the children which are so precious to her."[73]

In a letter to Cardinal McIntyre the following day, Antoniutti expressed his "firm hope that the Sisters will have the Grace and the virtue to accept these decisions in the proper spirit, and that peace and order will be restored to their Community and to the Institutions of the archdiocese in which they have been serving."[74]

There was a time lag of almost two weeks between reception of the Roman decision and any public reaction from the Sisters, probably because they had to meet, discuss and agree upon a unified response. On March 9th, the Pasadena *Independent Star-News* quoted "sources" close to the community as saying that "about 525 of the 600 members of the order will resign and form a loose confederation of religious women." Dorothy Townsend, a staff writer for the Los Angeles *Times* said that the nuns "refused to confirm or deny reports that more than 500 sisters planned to resign from the order *en masse* rather than halt their modernization program." It was reported that a decision would be made "at a chapter meeting scheduled today."[75]

In order to allow themselves more time, the "embattled" Sisters avoided an immediate crisis by appealing to Pope Paul VI. Sister Mary Mark, their spokesperson, said that "if we're stopped, then we and the other orders have been wasting our time." Apparently unacquainted with canonical procedures, she told John Dart of the Los Angeles *Times* that "the recent intercession in the matter by the Sacred Congregation for Religious was unprecedented."[76] She pointed out that the community hadn't definitively decided on a new rule, but was only experimenting with it. Meanwhile, Sister Anita Caspary, who was unavailable to reporters, let it be known that the "unfounded reports" about her resignation were totally false.[77]

One of the Sisters present for the community meetings reported to Father Gallagher that Sister Anita wasn't really in favor of either a secular institute or a pious federation, because both would fall under "ecclesiastical jurisdiction." She also expressed the fear that much of the community assets would be transferred over to lay boards "before the present crisis is settled."[78]

Not surprisingly, the press generally sided with the nuns. The *National Catholic Reporter* said that "guiding principle of the Congregation is to preserve intact a set of inherited definitions of the meaning, purpose, spirit of religious life" and that "any effort to enrich that tradition, to explore the world for new work to be done, to make us of new energies in new ways, conflicts automatically with the instincts of the aged male ecclesiastics who run the Congregation." The paper concluded that "if the decision is not surprising, it is no less disastrous. The IHM sisters are among the most creative, intelligent, inspiring nuns in the country, in the world."[79]

Jim Newsom wrote a series of essays about the nuns in which he hinted that "it was apparent" that Cardinal McIntyre had succeeded in "pulling strings" in Rome to force the congregation to rule in his favor.[80] Andrew Greeley said that the decision "to support the reactionary Los Angeles chancery office in its battle with the Immaculate Heart Sisters is one of the greatest tragedies in the history of American Catholicism."[81] John L. Reedy, editor of *Ave Maria*, weighed in to say that the decision was "insensitive" and "unfortunate" and predicted that it would result in unnecessary departures from religious life."[82] In another context, and not without humor, he admitted that his "personal opinion" about the controversy is not terribly important.[83]

A. V. Krebs complained that the decision from the Sacred Congregation of Religious "appears to have been written before the investigation was completed," a charge which he didn't substantiate. Krebs also took note of the fact that Leon Joseph Cardinal Suenens had been asked recently after a press conference at Berkeley what "world-wide ramifications he expected to see come out of the current efforts by Immaculate Heart nuns to modernize against the wishes of the Archbishop of Los Angeles" and he had refused "to comment on a specific situation."[84]

Bishop Remi De Roo of Victoria, British Columbia, entered the controversy by announcing that the thirteen IHM nuns working in his missionary diocese would "continue their experimentation in renewal with his complete support and approval." He went on to say that "the Vatican congregation should think more positively about the updating that needs to be done in the sisterhoods."[85]

The Vatican decree was not without its supporters. Msgr. Clement Bastnagal, Dean of the School of Canon Law at the Catholic University, said that "he could see nothing in the ruling that would do any harm to the essentials of Religious renewal," noting that "renewal is surely not threatened by this."[86] Father John Doran, an old friend of the community, pointed out that "the ruling did not say what the habit of the nuns must be, but simply that it must be uniform, that is that the Sisters must give indication in their dress that they belong to a particular group." After a lengthy commentary on the decision he said that "Rome's decree in favor of the local Bishop should cause people like those who run the *National Catholic Reporter* to rejoice, not complain." The liberals at the Vatican Council wanted things done at the local level. When that happened in Los Angeles, the IHMs were not satisfied.[87]

Mother Mary Omer, national chair for the Conference of Major Superiors of Women's Institutes, opined that "some Sisters have erroneously interpreted the document which grants them the right to introduce certain experiments in their renewal of Religious Life." She did not agree that the Congregation's decision "intends in any way to hamper or discourage the good work that is being accomplished in the renewal of religious communities."[88]

Finally, the Holy Father himself, addressing the first Assembly of the International Union of Superiors General touched upon the provisions mentioned in the decision given to the Immaculate Heart Sisters, observing that "members of any religious institute must seek God alone and above all else." Members should "combine contemplation with apostolic love through which they strive to join in the work of redemption and spread of the kingdom of God." He said that every congregation must see to it that "times and places are set aside for silence." The Pontiff noted that "community life provides dedicated souls with an enduring opportunity for developing their love, and it disposes them to contemplation." Finally, agreeing with his predecessor, Pope Pius XII, he advised Sisters to adopt "a habit that is dignified, suitably hygenic and adopted to modern living." Such attire is "a sign of consecration."[89]

In a letter to the editors of the *National Catholic Reporter*, John Ryan said that he had been educated by the IHMs and truly loved them. But he thought that "very much of today's whoop-de-do, celebratory joy-joy-joy, smile even-in-your-sleep, supercharged adolescent pop-art religion is eloquent bunk." He hoped that the Holy See would reverse "its ruling and allow the Sisters to complete their experimentation because if they are allowed to come regularly into contact with real life, real life will do for them what it does for honest lay people: it will grow them up."[90]

Joseph R. Thomas, managing editor of the Newark *Advocate* thought that Father Greeley had "overstated the case" when he said that the ruling is "one of the greatest tragedies in the history of American Catholicism." He didn't see anything "unreasonable of itself in the decision" and that the "Sisters could accommodate themselves to these directives without too much difficulty."[91] Joseph A. Brieg, while noting that "emotionally, like most people," he tended to side with the Sisters, he also felt that emotion cannot substitute for facts." He worried that many supporters of the IHM community had "left public opinion uninformed or poorly informed."[92]

When asked about the possibility of any alteration of its decision, a spokesman for the Sacred Congregation of Religious stood by the four point ruling but added, in response to a question from Desmond O'Grady, that "the case is not closed as long as there is agitation against it."[93]

It was at this juncture that the Sisters inaugurated "Project Petition," a drive to collect 5,000 signatures on a petition to Pope Paul VI in support of their renewal efforts. The drive didn't propose to make any value judgments on the content of their program, nor did it "intend to criticize church authorities locally." Rather, it regretted "the public barrage of criticism which has all but stifled the opportunity for the sisters to carry out and quietly evaluate the results of their renewal program."[94] Interestingly, there was never any great landswell of support for the Sisters among other communities, locally or nationally. According to the *National Catholic Reporter*, 3,000 U.S. nuns signed the petition, "the largest number of U.S. nuns who had ever put their names to a public petition." But that number represented a relatively small percentage of the 175,000 Sisters then serving in the United States.[95] Robert Strickland spearheaded the drive for signatures, pointing out that "there had been no opportunity for the Church at large to voice its opinion on the matter to the Vatican."[96] No final figures were given as to the total number of signers, but the drive proved to be a disappointment to the Sisters and their supporters. The editors of *Commonweal* joined the petition movement when, in their issue for April 5, 1968, they suggested that concerned readers "express their protest directly to the President of the U.S. Conference of Catholic Bishops."[97]

The chorus of supporters gradually expanded into the non-Catholic fold. In a separate petition, 194 prominent churchmen urged the Holy Father "to reconsider the decision made by the Congregation of Religious." Signatures included Dr. Harvey Cox,

Reinhold Niebuhr, Martin Marty, Robert McAfee Brown and the Right Reverend Arthur Lichtenberger, presiding Bishop of the Episcopal Church in the United States.[98]

Petitions to Rome are invariably answered, in one form or another. In this instance, the Holy Father asked the Sacred Congregation for Religious to re-open the case by appointing a four-man committee to examine the issues in dispute. Archbishop James V. Casey (Denver) was appointed to chair the committee which would be composed of Bishop Thomas A. Donnellan (Ogdensburg), Auxiliary Bishop Joseph Breitenbeck (Detroit) and Reverend Thomas R. Gallagher (Apostolic Delegation).[99] Appointment of the review committee was "considered as a small victory for the nuns" in some quarters.[100]

One newspaper suggested that "our American bishops might well discuss and seek a solution to this controversy at their spring meeting in Saint Louis."[101] When the prelates assembled, on April 22nd, Archbishop John Dearden, Chairman of the Conference, mentioned having sent a letter to the Holy Father expressing apprehension and some alarm over the reaction by members of different religious communities to Cardinal Antoniutti's decision. McIntyre objected strenuously, saying Dearden's letter was inaccurate and reflected his bias about the matter. The heated confrontation ended with Bishop Floyd Begin of Oakland saying that the bishops of California agreed completely with the stand that had been followed by the Archdiocese of Los Angeles. Archbishop Thomas Connolly protested that Dearden had no right to speak for the conference in this matter, to the Holy Father or to anyone else.[102]

The committee headed by Casey held its first meeting within a few weeks of its appointment. In addition to interviewing any and all members of the Immaculate Heart community, it met with bishops, pastors and other concerned persons. The atmosphere was exceedingly cordial on both sides. A spokesperson for the IHMs said that "we feel that, if any sort of decision is to be forthcoming from this group, it will be fair and just."[103]

From the outset of their deliberations, the question was not whether there would be renewal, but how much, in what direction and for how long. The committee recognized that any effective solution would have to go beyond interpreting this or that rule in the context of renewal. Viewpoints among the nuns had polarized into two clearly opposing camps, neither of which was any longer open to compromise with the other.

Archbishop Casey was quoted as being "very impressed" by certain aspects of the Immaculate Heart community, saying that they "are dedicated to their apostolate."[104]

The committee completed its work expeditiously and, on June 5, its decision was handed down in Los Angeles. It read as follows:

> In virtue of directives and authority received by the undersigned members of the Pontifical Commission, we hereby make the following dispositions in the matter of the difficulties that have arisen in regard to the California Institute of the Sisters of the Most Holy and Immaculate Heart of the Blessed Virgin Mary.
>
> 1. Notice has been taken with regret that an internal separation exists among the members of the Institute. For practical purposes, and while a final decision by the Holy See is pending, two groups are recognized. Each is authorized to act separately and is given the necessary faculties;
> 2. Those Sisters who intend to remain united to the original Institute are placed under the temporary direction of Sister Eileen McDonald, residing in the motherhouse of Los Angeles, who is given faculties for their government and work and may proceed to agreements regarding the schools with the diocesan authorities;
> 3. The Sisters, under the direction of Sister Anita, who intend to follow the Decrees of the recent General Chapter are given a reasonable time to reflect and come to a definitive decision to be submitted to the Holy See;
> 4. Financial questions will be settled in due time. Meanwhile, extraordinary acts of administration should be referred to the Pontifical Commission.[105]

In effect, the decree said that those involved in renewal could proceed "with their new program until the Pope makes his own decision."[106] According to John Dart, religion editor for the Los Angeles *Times*, the decision was "gratefully received by the sisters and the diocesan authorities in a spirit of mutual cooperation and understanding."[107] At the same time, it was reported that the IHM sisters were being individually polled to see which group they wished to join. As previously announced, the Immaculate Heart general chapter was scheduled to meet on June 24 to review their renewal program.

In most areas, the decision was accepted if not joyously, at least as inevitable. Msgr. Francis Maurovich wrote that all sides were "to be commended for the way" in which the case was resolved. He considered it "a tribute both to the Los Angeles Chancery and to the

Sisters that the decree was received in a spirit of mutual cooperation."[108]

There was some minor displeasure. The editor of the Louisville *Record*, for one, said that the decision was "a way out and not a solution" and hoped that it wouldn't become a pattern for other religious communities, because, as he said, "splitting up seems to be a very uncatholic solution for a Church that is committed to finding within itself room for all kinds of views."[109]

Meanwhile, the Los Angeles Chancery announced on June 18th that "all but one of the 32 parochial and secondary schools previously staffed by Immaculate Heart nuns are expected to reopen in the fall."[110] The gaps in staffing were filled by members of fifteen other religious orders and whatever Immaculate Heart Sisters elected to remain in the archdiocesan school system. Only one school was to be closed. Our Lady Queen of Angels, a girls' high school, which had already been earmarked to shut down because of dropping enrollment. Later in the summer, it was announced that the Sisters of the Immaculate Heart of Mary, those who split from the larger group, would help to staff nine of the schools. Their superior, Sister Eileen, said that "the group is relatively small, but its quality is distinguished. Every Sister assigned to administration and teaching has at least her Bachelor's degree and the appropriate California State teaching credential as well."[111] Eleven had master's degrees and three possessed doctorates.

There is, of course, much more to the Immaculate Heart story, but inasmuch as McIntyre's involvement was chiefly with the educational aspect of the renewal program, it effectively closed for him with the staffing of the schools from which the community had withdrawn. The cardinal's retirement, which occurred the following year, left him out of the final chapter completely. The biographer of his successor may want to pursue the story to its conclusion.

There were no winners in this long and complicated struggle, nor could there have been. From the very beginning, McIntyre's primary concern was about the staffing of archdiocesan schools. Though he held strong views about the ultimate effectiveness of the renewal process as adopted at Montecito, he was willing to leave that matter to other ecclesial authorities.

Without impugning any of the combatants, it has to be said that McIntyre's stance was rather consistently misrepresented and overplayed to the press and others. An example would be the question of the "habit." That he paid scant if any attention to the "habit issue" is obvious enough. In 1957, he welcomed and encouraged the Society Devoted to the Sacred Heart into the Archdiocese of Los Angeles and they wore no religious habit at all but went about their apostolic work "wearing simple street clothes, in order to be more accessible to everyone they met in their field of the apostolate."[112]

Neither the Sacred Congregation of Religious nor the Apostolic Commission ruled on what McIntyre considered the most important issue, the "ultimatum" presented to him after the initial chapter meeting. This writer can find no documentation anywhere that even suggests that the Sisters were "fired." Such a fallacious contention, which is the crux of statements and innuendoes about McIntyre's involvement, simply cannot be substantiated.

Even his foes concede "that under his leadership, a far sighted and efficient school expansion program made the archdiocese the envy of many others."[113] A goodly portion of that credit goes to the Immaculate Heart Community which, prior to 1968, staffed about a tenth of the archdiocesan schools.

However one interprets the activities of the Immaculate Heart Sisters between 1967 and 1970, it cannot be denied that their actions marked the beginning of "the demise of the greatest instrument of evangelization the universal Church had ever seen, i.e., the American parochial school system."[114]

Notes to the Text

1. Mother Humiliata subsequently resumed her baptismal name. She will be referred to herein as Sister Anita Caspary.
2. The legal title for the community was the longest of any listed in the *Official Catholic Directory* published by P. J. Kenedy and Sons.
3. Camden *Catholic Star Herald*, November 17, 1967.
4. Davenport *Catholic Messenger*, November 23, 1967.
5. *Memories & Hopes* (Dublin, 1992), p. 224.
6. The program was supervised by the Western Behavioral Science Institute at La Jolla.
7. This interview, conducted by Dr. William Marra, can be found in *The Latin Mass. Chronicle of a Catholic Reform* (Special Edition, 1994), Pp. 12-17. This essay was condensed from Coulson's "Tearing Down the Temple"- which appeared in *Fidelity* (December, 1983), 18-22. In an interview with George Neuman, Coulson made reference to the Franciscan scandal that was unearthed in 1994 at Saint Anthony's Seminary, Santa Barbara. He attributed that entire scenario to the influence of Rogerian theories on the friars, noting that of the eleven friars who abused seminarians, only two were assessed to be pedophiles. "The rest were victims of bad philosophy and that philosophy was Rogerian." *National Catholic Register*, March 19, 1995.
8. *The Buried Life. A Nun's Journey* (New York, 1971), p. 154.
9. See Cal Samra, "More Therapists than Priests," *The Catholic World Report IV* (August-September, 1994), 57.
10. Walter M. Abbott, S.J., *The Documents of Vatican II* (New York, 1971), p. 465.
11. Denver *Register*, November 26, 1967.
12. AALA, Sr. Francis Borgia, I.H.M. to James Francis Cardinal McIntyre, Los Angeles, October 10, 1967.
13. AALA, Office of the Community Education Board, Los Angeles, October 14, 1967.
14. December 25, 1967, 45.
15. AALA, Sr. Anita Caspary, I.H.M., Press Release, November 9, 1967.
16. AALA, James Francis Cardinal McIntyre Memorandum-l, October 16, 1967.
17. *Ibid.*, Memorandum-2, October 16, 1967.
18. *Lift Up Your Hearts*, October 16, 1967.

19. October 16, 1967.
20. October 18, 1967.
21. November 10, 1967, 160.
22. New York *Times*, November 14, 1967.
23. AALA, James Francis Cardinal McIntyre to Ildebrando Cardinal Antoniutti, Los Angeles, October 18, 1967.
24. AALA, Sr. Anita Caspary, I.H.M. to James Francis Cardinal McIntyre, Los Angeles, October 23, 1967.
25. AALA, Sr. Anita Caspary, I.H.M. to Sisters, Los Angeles, October 23, 1967.
26. AALA, James Francis Cardinal McIntyre to Sr. Anita Caspary, I.H.M., Los Angeles, October 24, 1967.
27. AALA, Sr. Francis Borgia, I.H.M. to James Francis Cardinal McIntyre, Los Angeles, October 24, 1967.
28. Los Angeles *Times*, November 9, 1967.
29. *Ibid.*
30. November 15, 1967.
31. *The Tidings*, November 17, 1967.
32. *Ibid.*
33. LXX (November 13, 1967), 26.
34. The *Catholic Messenger*, November 23, 1967.
35. *While the Winds Blew* (Wilkes Barre, 1968), p. 88.
36. The *Catholic Voice*, November 29, 1967.
37. November 30, 1967.
38. *The Wanderer*, November 23, 1967.
39. AALA, Sr. Anita Caspary, I.H.M. to James Francis Cardinal McIntyre, December 18, 1967.
40. LXXV (January, 1968), 10.
41. AALA, James Francis Cardinal McIntyre to Sr. Anita Caspary, I.H.M., Los Angeles, January 1, 1968.
42. AALA, Sr. Anita Caspary, I.H.M. to Pastors, Los Angeles, January 8, 1968.
43. AALA, Sr. Anita Caspary, I.H.M. to Parents, Los Angeles, January 8, 1968.
44. *The Tidings*, January 12, 1968.
45. January 26, 1968.
46. January 17, 1968.
47. *The Tidings*, January 26, 1968.
48. *National Catholic Reporter*, January 24, 1968.
49. Los Angeles *Times*, January 13, 1968.
50. January 25, 1968.
51. Long Beach Independent *Press Telegram*, January 21, 1968.
52. *National Catholic Reporter*, January 17, 1968.
53. *The Monitor*, February 8, 1968.
54. *National Catholic Reporter*, January 24, 1968.

55. *The Tidings*, January 26, 1968.
56. *National Catholic Reporter*, January 31, 1968.
57. Los Angeles *Times*, February 1, 1968.
58. *The Los Angeles Loyolan XLV* (February 5, 1968), n.p.
59. New York *Times*, February 10, 1968.
60. Los Angeles *Times*, February 5, 1968.
61. XCI (February 16, 1968), 73.
62. LXVIII (January 13, 1968).
63. *Catholic Star Herald*, January 19, 1968.
64. Brooklyn *Tablet*, February 8, 1968.
65. *National Catholic Reporter*, February 28, 1968.
66. Los Angeles *Times*, January 18, 1968.
67. Long Beach Independent *Press Telegram*, January 21, 1968.
68. *National Catholic Reporter*, February 2, 1968.
69. AALA, Joseph T. McGucken to James Francis Cardinal McIntyre. San Francisco, October 31, 1967.
70. AALA, Thomas Gallager, O.P. to James Francis Cardinal McIntyre. Washington, D.C., November 4, 1967.
71. AALA, James Francis Cardinal McIntyre Memorandum, Los Angeles, November 25, 1967.
72. AALA, Joseph T. McGucken to James Francis Cardinal McIntyre, San Francisco, February 9, 1968.
73. AALA, Ildebrando Cardinal Antoniutti to Thomas R. Gallagher, O.P., Rome, February 21, 1968. The contents of this letter were given to the *National Catholic Reporter* which published them on March 13.
74. AALA, Ildebrando Cardinal Antoniutti to James Francis Cardinal McIntyre, Rome, January 22, 1968.
75. March 10, 1968.
76. Los Angeles *Times*, March 12, 1968.
77. *Ibid*.
78. AALA, Sister Eileen MacDonald, I.H.M. to James Francis Cardinal McIntyre, Los Angeles. March 12, 1968.
79. March 13, 1968.
80. San Fernando *Valley Times*, March 16, 1968.
81. *The Catholic Voice*, March 27, 1968.
82. Quoted in Los Angeles *Times*, March 18, 1968.
83. *Ave Maria*, CVII (March 30, 1968), 2.
84. "Heroines and Humbug," *Commonweal* LXXXVIII (April 5, 1968), 64.
85. *National Catholic Register*, April 14, 1968.
86. Denver *Register*, March 22, 1968.
87. Arizona *Register*, March 28, 1968.
88. Quoted in *The Tidings*, March 22, 1968.
89. *The Pope Speaks* XII (1967), 31-32.

90. *National Catholic Reporter*, April 10, 1968.
91. April 4, 1968.
92. *Central California Register*, May 30, 1968.
93. *National Catholic Reporter*, March 20, 1968.
94. Los Angeles *Times*, March 26, 1968.
95. March 27, 1968.
96. *National Catholic Reporter*, April 3, 1968.
97. LXXXVIII, 64.
98. Los Angeles *Times*, April 13, 1968.
99. Los Angeles *Herald Examiner*, April 16, 1968.
100. Brooklyn *Tablet*, April 18, 1968.
101. Scranton *Catholic*, April 18, 1968.
102. AALA, James Francis Cardinal McIntyre Memorandum, Los Angeles, May 1, 1968.
103. *National Catholic Register*, May 26, 1968.
104. *Ibid.*
105. AALA, Decree, Los Angeles, June 5, 1968.
106. Los Angeles *Times*, June 7, 1968.
107. *Ibid.*, June 8, 1968.
108. *Catholic Voice*, June 19, 1968.
109. June 20, 1968.
110. Los Angeles *Times*, June 19, 1968.
111. *The Tidings*, July 19, 1968.
112. *America* (April 6, 1968), 437.
113. Les Rodney in the Long Beach *Press Telegram*, January 2, 1968.
114. George A. Kelly, *The Battle for the American Church Revisited* (San Francisco, 1995) p. 75.

21. *Father Dubay and the Batman Syndrome*[1]

During the spring and early summer months of 1964, James Francis Cardinal McIntyre came under criticism in certain circles for failing to take a public stand on the initiative to repeal certain provisions of the controversial Rumford Fair Housing Act.

On June 10, 1964, recorded in the Catholic annals of California as "D-Day," a sandy-haired twenty-nine year old cleric from the Archdiocese of Los Angeles became what one commentator called "the first priest since Luther to challenge his Cardinal in public."[2]

Father William DuBay chose an unseasonably hot day in early June for taking the unprecedented action of petitioning Pope Paul VI to remove James Francis Cardinal McIntyre for "gross malfeasance in office." In his fourteen page telegram, DuBay contended that the Archbishop of Los Angeles had "perpetuated inexcusable abuses" in two areas: refusing to educate Catholics about racial discrimination and conducting a "vicious program of intimidation and repression against priests, seminarians and laity who have tried to reach the consciousness of white Catholics in his archdiocese."[3]

At a subsequent press conference, DuBay indicated that he "was prepared to accept dismissal for his actions," but said that he had no plans on what to do "if it happens." He contended that "President Johnson is obviously giving more Christian leadership to Catholics than their own archbishop in Los Angeles."[4] He regretted that "I, as a priest, must accuse my bishop publicly, but all other means have failed. Letters, petitions, phone calls and even sit-ins and pickets at his office and residence have not moved the cardinal."[5]

Predictably, the priest was removed from his position as administrator of Saint Albert's Parish in Compton, but allowed to remain there performing his parochial duties.[6] While DuBay claimed there were other priests who shared his views, only one came forward and that was Father Terrence Halloran, a friend of many years. Halloran, however, did not endorse DuBay's tactics and stated flatly that he did "not feel the cardinal should be removed."[7] He had privately counseled DuBay against making public his letter to the Holy Father.[8]

On June 12, fifty-six pickets marched in front of the Chancery Office in support of Father DuBay. They were joined by members of Catholics United for Racial Equality (CURE), an organization not approved or endorsed by the archbishop.[9] The issue was broadened a few days later, when CURE asked the Apostolic Delegate to the Catholic Church in the United States, Archbishop Egidio Vagnozzi, to launch an "immediate investigation" into the civil rights violations in the Archdiocese of Los Angeles. "The sin of racism and related sins against justice and charity are being virtually ignored in the Los Angeles archdiocese, the moral health of all Catholics is in peril and the faith of many Catholics is being undermined." CURE leaders told the apostolic delegate that they were confident that the charges made by DuBay are true and "unless solutions are found, the image of the Catholic Church will suffer."[10]

Meanwhile, Bishop John J. Ward and others on the curial staff at Los Angeles were busily working behind the scenes to diffuse the incident. DuBay's lawyer had already advised him to avoid a collision course with the cardinal, pointing out that he had "already made his point in public and could honorably withdraw to protect his priesthood."[11] On June 18, DuBay was invited to the Chancery Office where he signed a statement saying that "in the light of recent happenings, and in fulfillment of my desire to express loyalty to Holy Mother Church and to the Archdiocese of Los Angeles," he renewed his ordination promises of reverence and obedience to the archbishop. The original statement, signed in the sanctuary of Immaculate Conception Church, was later renewed at Saint John's Seminary in the presence of Cardinal McIntyre and 231 priests who were on retreat at Camarillo.[12]

Further, DuBay was directed "to avoid all contacts with those persons who were part of this last week's demonstrations" at the chancery. Moreover, in the future, if "he believes that any injustice is done to him, he should use the normal remedies of recourse, and not the sensational method of appeal inaugurated at the time" of his recent press conference.[13]

In *The Tidings* for the following week, Msgr. Patrick Roche, the editor, said that "were it not for their serious overtones, the demonstrations of the past few days would require no answer. Without mentioning any names, he pointed out that those who are clamoring about justice are at the same time denying just consideration to the object of their attack. Violent charges have been made."[14] Roche noted that "the church has no apologies to make for the policy which she has followed in the long, arduous and painful pursuit of justice for all mankind... In this, the panorama of

Her churches, schools and social institutions, structured without discrimination of race, economic level or geographic locale, and constructed by the generous contributions of Her people from every walk of life, bears testimony to Her concern and love for all Her children."[15] The editor went on to say that "it is a pity that an ill-contrived and frenetic attempt is now being made to cloud and besmirch the record of accomplishment."

In the weekend issue of the Los Angeles *Times*, Dan L. Thrapp headlined his story: "End of Priest's Dispute With Cardinal Expected." He had heard that Father DuBay would "drop his campaign and be reassigned to another parish." He quoted Msgr. Benjamin G. Hawkes, the Chancellor, as saying that "so far as we are concerned, the case is resolved."[16]

Though Cardinal McIntyre never answered DuBay's specific allegations, he did make public a letter he had written on July 23, 1963, to Catholics United for Racial Equality (CURE).

We agree with you that this subject is one of present and pressing importance and that it is deserving of serious consideration.

The fact is that the Catholic Church has so regarded this subject for very many years. During these years, the Church has been amongst the foremost and the most persistent in supporting equality and equity for the Negro people of our country. Wherever the law and local custom permitted, the Church has practiced integration in its Churches, in its schools and in its social service departments.

It has been outspoken in declaring the fundamental and moral principles where abuses prevailed. These basic moral principles, therefore, have been applied in the service of religion, in the service of education and throughout our social agencies, as well as other institutions of a charitable character under the direction of religious.

It is our belief that such services as these, rendered quietly, consistently and as a normal aspect of parish life among our people, provide the most hopeful and effective means of promoting racial justice and charity.

On the other hand, the creation of special commissions and committees and the development of specialized programs, often formed in the heat of emotion and in the context of strong political overtones, can militate against the very ends they are designed to serve by arousing an acute sensitivity of racial differences rather than an absorption of them in the warmth of the brotherhood of Christ.

In this connection, we may note that our Catholic Negro people, by their constant loyalty to the Church and their support of all her programs, have manifested their satisfaction and agreement with the policies we have enunciated above.

No representative members of their community have indicated that they desire a change in these policies; in fact, some of them have expressed concern lest current agitation and demonstrations, even though well intentioned, may impede rather than augment progress towards racial justice.

Our policy has been one of acting and not of oratory. We shall abide by our practices of the past and continue our work and our constant service to the Negro people in the future, as we have in the past.[17]

Reaction to DuBay's allegations ran the gamut. In the *California Eagle*, a black weekly published by Loren Miller, the editor suggested that "the cardinal is clearly out of step with the Catholic Church in his racial attitudes and he has done his best to impose his out-of-date views on his own church and on the community."[18] Herb Brin, writing in *Heritage*, the Jewish weekly, contended that McIntyre "cannot avoid the issue. It will not go away."[19] In *Life* magazine, Shana Alexander said that "the mild little priest is no more a schoolboy than he is a hot-eyed zealot. He is a conscientious priest whose only error, if any, was to allow himself to be inspired by laymen who had less at stake than himself." She quoted DuBay as saying "I didn't want to be another Martin Luther. I didn't want to divide the Church. I just wanted to get the truth out."[20] A writer favorable to DuBay admitted that the "episode failed to polarize opposition to the Cardinal on the race issue." He quoted a priest close to DuBay as saying that "loyalty to a bishop is at the heart of what it means to be a priest. I would have been willing to say or do almost anything else, but asking that my bishop be dismissed is just too much."[21] Overall reaction in the press favored McIntyre over DuBay by substantial margins. An editorial in the Los Angeles *Outlook*, for example, said that "Father DuBay's protests against Cardinal McIntyre were premature." The priest "may have satisfied his own feelings but in doing so, he most definitely aroused the religiously weak as well as the ever-ready critics of the Catholic Church."[22] The editor of the Steubenville *Register* felt that "in the California incident, we think the Cardinal was very tolerant and forgiving."[23] In the Baltimore Catholic newspaper, the editor noted that "at a time when lawful authority is under so much attack around the world, Father DuBay's public challenge to his bishop presents a particularly distressful spectacle." While admitting that "nothing is more obvious than the ability of the race question to arouse strong emotions and to inspire dramatic action," the editor pointed out that even men with the same basic convictions on the subject sometimes sharply disagree about matters of timing and tactics.[24]

Among the many supporters of McIntyre's view that the issue was more political than moral was Lillian M. Murphy who wrote to the Reader's Forum of the Hollywood *Citizen News*: "I am going to take the liberty to speak for most of our Catholics who, as I, respect and appreciate our beloved James Francis Cardinal McIntyre as a true shepherd of his flock and as one who would lay down his life for his sheep regardless of their color."[25]

An earlier editorial in the same newspaper said that "no one doubts Father DuBay's good intentions. His methods, however, are something else again. He has put his superior, to whom he vowed absolute obedience, in a position where if the cardinal defrocks him (for which he has just cause under church law), he has created a martyr; if he condones the tirade in public news media, he is jeopardizing the church's position on the delicate church-state issue; if he transfers him to another archdiocese or publicly reprimands him, he leaves himself and the church open to criticism." The editorial concluded by saying that "unless Father DuBay can come up with something more credible, such as cases of discrimination within the church condoned by Cardinal McIntyre, then he is doing a disservice to both his superior and the church."[26]

Writing in the Texas *Catholic*, J.T. said that "one need not be in accord with every position taken by Cardinal McIntyre to say that it should take more than a young priest with more courage than common sense to send the press running gaily to their typewriters to fashion a scarlet whipping boy to the cause."[27] Joseph R. Thomas in the Newark *Advocate* said that "Father DuBay may have called attention to a problem, but the way he went about it certainly wasn't conducive to correcting it."[28]

Probably the most surprising observation was made in the pages of *America* where it was noted that these "angry young men" would "have a better chance of being taken seriously if they would avoid making themselves more obnoxious than they have to be." The essay went on to say that "the most annoying thing about them - we speak from a middle-aged point of view - is not so much what they say as the tone in which they say it. It is generally shrill, sometimes threatening. But most often it is accusatory. Those who disagree with them, one gathers, are not only mistaken but guilty."[29] Though it was hardly "one of the greatest crises in the

446

history of the archdiocese,"[30] as John Leo misquoted Bishop John Ward as saying, it was a most unfortunate occurrence which might have been avoided had there been better lines of communication between the parties involved.

As the summer months moved on, it was hoped that the unpleasant incident of "D-Day" would soon be relegated to the dusty files in the archdiocesan archives. In one of his less than prophetical statements, Daniel Callahan said that "by all odds, Father DuBay will probably not be heard from soon again; he will almost certainly drop from sight."[31] But there were ominous indications that the truce engineered by Bishop Ward and others was shaky. Leon Aubrey, director of CURE, proclaimed that "it is up to us to continue his work by further exposing the scandalous maladministration of this archdiocese."[32]

And there were rumblings from DuBay himself that he was gearing up for another assault. In a letter to *America*, he expressed pleasure "by the attention we are at last getting." He went on to state that "perhaps we can create new pressures within the Church"[33] to move its leaders to action. During this time, DuBay was busily writing an article on the "Democratic Structure in the Church" which was published in the fall issue of *Chicago Studies*, a publication loosely sponsored by the Archdiocese of Chicago. The lengthy essay asked whether "the Church's growing awareness of her divinely established nature allow for democratic institutions which guarantee the exercise of both authority and individual freedom."[34]

Displeased, to say the least, Cardinal McIntyre fired off a letter to his counterpart in Chicago, saying that he had read the article and found it "worthy of severe criticism." He reminded Albert Cardinal Meyer that the author had caused considerable turmoil by his charges that "the administration of this Diocese does not conform with his interpretation of independent freedom under democratic institutions."[35] The Apostolic Delegate was also made aware of the eighteen page essay and responded that he didn't feel that it was very profound. "It seems to me," said Archbishop Egidio Vagnozzi, "that it is little more than a collection of ideas with an attempt to join them together by a central theme." The delegate even suspected "that perhaps some one else wrote the article and Father signed it."[36]

Early the next month, a group of parishioners at Saint Boniface Church in Anaheim, where Father DuBay had been re-assigned, sent a petition to Cardinal McIntyre, asking that the cleric be transferred. They gave the following reasons:

1. His duties as an assistant are being seriously neglected in our large parish, understaffed for its size. Only the absolute minimum amount of time is spent on parish duties, which are quickly and summarily performed.
2. It is evident that he has no respect for ecclesiastical authority and disobeys deliberately.
3. It appears that a much greater emphasis is placed by him upon political problems rather than religious problems, as evidenced by his sermons and articles in various publications.
4. Because of the attitude and actions of Father DuBay, as set forth above, there is definite evidence of conflict and unrest within our parish, with some parishioners aligning themselves with Father DuBay and the others supporting your representative, our Pastor. This conflict, it is feared, will soon develop into a wide division in our parish.[37]

In summary, it is felt in the best interests of our parish, and the Church that Father DuBay be immediately removed from St. Boniface.

The Cardinal called DuBay into the Chancery and read him a letter in which he stated that the priest's status had been compromised "by articles you have written and had printed in newspaper and magazine publications, wherein you have taken occasion to disagree and to criticize well known policies of the Ordinary of the Diocese of which you are a member." He reminded DuBay that as a parish priest, he was functioning as a representative of the Church and its governing authority. And, in that capacity, "it is naturally expected in the minds of people at large and the parishioners in particular that your attitude and actions be in sympathy and conformity with the teachings and policies of which you are a spokesman."[38] For that and other reasons, he was being removed from Anaheim and re-assigned to Saint Monica's parish, where he would be full-time chaplain at Saint John's Hospital.

About a year after assuming the new duties, DuBay spoke before Robert Maynard Hutchins and the members of the Center for the Study of Democratic Institutions at Santa Barbara where he "proposed unionization of the nation's 58,000 Catholic priests." In particular, he called for an American Federation of Priests for "some means of collective bargaining to negotiate priestly wages, working conditions and to guarantee their professional freedom."[39] The priest said he intentionally used the word "union" rather than a

"The Sabbath was made for man and not man for the Sabbath."

AFP
THE UNION PRIEST
Official Publication of the American Federation of Priests

January, 1967   2   "Professional Integrity for Clergymen"   Vol. 2, No. 1

PRIEST UNION PROTESTS!
FATHER GARVIN SUSPENDED

In a recent letter to Archbishop John J. Krol of Philadelphia, the American Federation of Priests attacked the "arbitrary judgment and suspension" of Father Michael J. Garvin as a "flagrant, though common, violation of the rights of due process."

The letter went on to say: "The manner in which Father Garvin was summoned, convicted, suspended, and exiled to a retreat house is cause for concerted and effective action by all priests concerned with the mission of the Church and with their own pastoral effectiveness. The Star Chamber proceeding inflicted on him constitute a dangerous threat to the teaching of the Church on civil rights.

"How can the church promote the rights of man in society without protecting these very rights within its own institutions? How can the Church assume a posture of moral leadership if its bishops so disregard ethical norms of administration?

"The experience of democracy as well as the documents of the Second Vatican Council have taught us that guaranteed due process is a basic right of all individuals. This is especially true of those burdened with the grave responsibilities of the care of souls.

"There are many personal rights which even a bishop may not violate; and in any case the accused person deserves the protections of a fair hearing.

"In every proceeding involving a penalty, a priest should have the rights of elementary due process, including, at least: the right to a judgment by someone other than his accusers; the right to legal counsel at his discretion; the right to decline self-incrimination; the right to confrontation and cross examination of witnesses; the right to a public hearing at his discretion; the right to a record of proceedings and a written judgment; and the right of a prompt appeal.

"The suspension of Father Garvin is a crippling injustice against which we must loudly protest. But, even more, we are dedicated to removing the causes of such injustices by the establishment of the above guarantees."

FRATERNAL GROUP FOR DISCHARGED PRIESTS

CALIFORNIA TEACHERS UNION ENDORSES AFP

Santa Barbara, Calif. — Endorsement of a union for Catholic priests was voted recently by 250 delegates, representing 10,000 California teachers at the convention of the AFL-CIO California Federation of Teachers meeting in Santa Barbara.

The teachers declared that priests, like teachers, should be able to "participate in the decisions affecting their profession."

"This body endorses and supports the efforts of priests to obtain collective bargaining," the resolution stated. The convention "commended" the efforts of priests who are active in the American Federation of Priests.

The complete resolution reads: "Whereas it is necessary for priests as well as other workers to obtain professional working conditions and to participate in decisions affecting their profession,

"And whereas this can only be accomplished through collective and has used repressive measures to bring them back into active ministry. Adelphos will attempt to provide a basis of support for priests who have made their decision to start a new life in the secular world.

"Be it hereby resolved that this body endorses and supports the efforts of priests to obtain collective bargaining.

"Be it further resolved that this body commends the action of a handful of priests who are organizing the American Federation of Priests."

On January 3, a letter was sent to U.S. Catholic Bishops announcing the establishment of a Los Angeles-based fraternal association for discharged priests called Adelphos. The purpose of the group is to form a community of priests who are no longer in the active ministry and to aid them in securing jobs consistent with their background and professional standing. Adelphos is assisted in the task of job placement by a group of Catholic business men who have also cooperated in the formation of the group.

The membership of the group will remain confidential due to the current practice of reprisals taken against such priests. All business activities will be handled through the office of the American Federation of Priests in Santa Monica.

Adelphos will attempt to change public opinion on the status of discharged priests, who are often regarded as renegades. Until now, the Church has denied all responsibility for their welfare and has used repressive measures to bring them back into active ministry. Adelphos will attempt to provide a basis of support for priests who have made their decision to start a new life in the secular world.

All contributions and inquiries should be sent to Adelphos, 216 Pico Blvd. Room 11, Santa Monica, Calif. 90405.

Priest Draws Suspension For Clandestine Mass In Seminary Basement

Philadelphia — A parish priest has been suspended by Archbishop John J. Krol for conducting four unauthorized experimental Masses, among them a clandestine Mass in the basement of St. Charles Borromeo seminary.

The priest, Father Michael J. Garvin, 26, a curate at Holy Spirit Church in suburban Sharon Hill, reportedly was charged with more than a dozen violations of Church law including celebrating two Masses in one day without permission, concelebrating without permission, celebrating Mass without vestments and using a portable altar without permission.

Three of 11 seminarians who attended the Mass have resigned from the seminary at the request of seminary authorities.

One of the seminarians who resigned, James McMenamin, 26, said the Mass was arranged as a means of encouraging students who were "depressed and confused" by lack of action on the part of seminary officials in implementing suggestions contained in a "white paper" prepared last spring by major seminarians.

McMenamin said students were discouraged by lack of progress on the report when they returned from summer vacation and that some considered quitting the seminary.

"So to forestall what we felt were premature resignations and to strengthen the hope of everyone in the group, we arranged this Mass," he said.

McMenamin said most of the students felt the daily chapel Masses were "barren" and offered "little spiritual nourishment."

He said the clandestine Mass was scheduled for 11 p.m., a time when students were expected to be in their rooms.

McMenamin telephoned Father Garvin and asked him to celebrate the Mass. When he arrived he had been joined by another priest.

The Mass, McMenamin said, began with readings from "They Call us Dead Men," a book of essays by Father Daniel Berrigan, S.J., and from the Gospel of St. Matthew.

"Then we discussed our particular problem in the light of these readings," he said. "By exchanging insights, we tried to see our situation as a means of spiritual growth—a growth from hopelessness and crisis.

"We then sang hymns accom-
(Continued on Page 3)

Fichter Survey Reveals Need For Greater Priest Status

Rev. Joseph Fichter, S.J., author of a preliminary summary of data compiled in a survey of attitudes of diocesan clergy, pointed out in an interview with The Union Priest that the heart of the report is not the priests' concern with celibacy but, rather, "the overwhelming evidence that they are most seriously concerned with the status and roles of non-pastors in their relationship with the bishop."

The 58-year-old Stillman professor of Roman Catholic studies at Harvard University, said that the press had made the most of the report that 62 per cent of Catholic priests believe that priests should have the freedom to marry. "But what is more significant," he added, "was the fact that close to 95 per cent favored the establishment of tenure policy, grievance machinery and a diocesan personnel board. In short, the structural data in their response is far more important."

When asked whether any changes will take place as a result of this study, Fichter answered: "It is my very sincere anticipation, one which I expressed to every ordinary of the country as I sent them a copy of the report, that changes will occur as a result of this study. The priests have had the opportunity to express themselves. And I believe that the response has been a significant and sincere indication of the way in which priests want their bishops to go."

Speaking of the priests' union as a means to implement the above goals, Fichter stated: "There is a semantic problem with the union. People find the words 'union' and 'power' irritating. Not that priests do not need to use power to achieve their ends. The Chicago association of priests certainly made use of power as they confronted Archbishop Cody with the decisions of some 1,300 priests. And the publication of a survey, such as this, exercises a similar pressure on bishops. I don't believe that it is time any more to keep silent about such issues in the Church. By bringing them out into the open, I think we will be able to keep the bishops honest."

Fichter said that the preliminary report of his survey was sent to the ordinaries of the country before its appearance in the December 14 issue of the National Catholic Reporter. The survey was sponsored by committees of laymen and priests in various cities of the country and by the Reporter, which holds the copyright to the report. Fichter also stated that he was not sure how the results of the rest of the survey would eventually be published.

Among the results receiving the most public attention so far are these figures:

- 62 per cent of the 3,000 priests who replied believe that diocesan priests should have the freedom to marry.
- 31 per cent either probably or unquestionably would marry if given permission.
- 94 per cent favored a priest should have the chance to face his accusers before being penalized.
- 86 per cent favored a personnel office to work out the assignments of diocesan priests.
- 94 per cent favored a diocesan senate of priests.

THE AMERICAN FEDERATION OF PRIESTS
216 Pico Boulevard
Santa Monica, California 90405

Nonprofit Org.
U.S. Postage
PAID
Los Angeles, Calif.
Permit No. 26345

T VICTOR'S
8634 HOLLOWAY DR
W HOLLYWOOD 46 CALIF
90046

Ass. Assistant Pastors, Unassisted Pastors, Priest Teachers, Chaplains

William H. DuBay

A frank appraisal of the present state of the Catholic Church, emphasizing the necessity for the Church to employ her human re-

THE sources to solve human problems

HUMAN CHURCH

softer word like "association" because priests, like teachers, are employees.[40]

Calling collective bargaining the chief goal of the union, he described it as "an orderly process by which priests can arrive at a formal contract with their chancery on the issues of professional standards and rights, personnel practices and wages." He listed ten demands:

1. Due process through a grievance machinery which has binding arbitration as the final step.
2. Tenure policy which guarantees priests a fair hearing by peers prior to suspension.
3. Transfer policy which protects priests from arbitrary and oppressive transfers at the hands of chancery officials.
4. Freedom to preach.
5. Uniform leave policy which excludes chancery whim.
6. Open personnel file.
7. Freedom of residence.
8. Promotional policy which assigns pastorates without chancery favoritism.
9. Professional salary schedule which eliminates the buying and selling of religious services and which makes priests independent of the wealthy.
10. Definition of professional responsibilities which excludes mandatory fulfillment of such nonprofessional chores as money-counting, rectory-watching, bookkeeping, fund-raising and janitorial tasks.[41]

In 1891, Pope Leo XIII put it down as a "general and lasting law" that working people should form associations for the legitimate pursuit of benefiting "body, soul and property." Since that time, labor unions had become a force in modern society, rivaling in power the largest corporations and even government itself. And now, seventy-five years after Leo's *Rerum Novarum*, a youthful priest in Los Angeles, had proposed and, in fact, inaugurated, a program for unionizing the clergy to protect what he described as "their exploited interests." The editor of the Boston *Pilot* commented, tongue in cheek, that "it must be a great consolation to Pope Leo, looking down from the quiet regions, to find that his advice on unions has finally penetrated even the ranks of the clergy!"[42]

Press reaction to DuBay's proposal of a labor union for members of the clergy was almost unanimously unfavorable. The editor of the *National Catholic Reporter* told his readers that "Catholic newspaper editorial writers operated on Father William DuBay and his proposal for a priests' union with scalpel and needle. They cut both up pretty badly." The same writer went on to observe that "none of the newspapers sampled during a two-week period endorsed the labor union proposal."[43] Pat Scanlon, writing in the Brooklyn *Tablet* couldn't recall "any other subject matter upon which so many papers cast ridicule."[44]

Los Angeles' "labor priest," Father Joseph V. Kearney, called the proposal for a unionization of priests "a nutty idea - the wrong answer to the actual problem." In his role as spiritual advisor to the Catholic Labor Institute, Kearney did admit that "talk about a priests' union represents a very considerable movement in the Church to recognize the need to open a line of communication" for the clergy.[45] That sentiment was underscored by Msgr. Charles Owen Rice, one of the founders of the Association of Catholic Trade Unionists and probably the most respected contemporary authority on the subject, who said plainly that "priests have no legal rights; we are different," he said, "we are not employees and do not work for money." He went so far as to say that "if a union is organized, it will become just a refuge for cry babies. Priests have no more moral right to belong to a union than soldiers."[46]

The syndicated writer, Father John B. Sheerin, provided an historical perspective by pointing out that DuBay's call for a union of priests "is not a new idea. At least forty years ago, a European priest urged the formation of labor unions for priests, but his suggestion met with little support from the clergy of Europe."[47] The editors of *Commonweal* felt that "a union would also tend to legitimize the notion that priests are little more than 'employees' of the Church. But this is surely a wrong conception of the priesthood, even if the reality of the present situation seems to suggest nothing more exalted than that. A union would institutionalize a *de facto* evil."[48]

Though admitting that "some of the demands he wants his proposed union to make are not unreasonable," the editor of the Brooklyn *Tablet* said that "Father DuBay has hit upon the wrong means for attaining a worthy and worthwhile goal."[49] Msgr. John Sheridan, feeling that DuBay's initial bid for public attention was engineered by publicity professionals, said that "unfortunately, the press is so interested in exploiting the sensational, the rebellious and the absurd, and the public knows so very little about the spirit and philosophy of the Catholic priesthood, that some people do not appreciate how ludicrous the idea of a priests' union is."[50]

Interestingly, DuBay's call for a labor union for priests was opposed by a number of people who had earlier supported him. John Leo, for example, said that while the priest "has put his finger on a number of things that are badly askew both in the status of the priest and in the Church at large ... his plan of a union of priests is not what we're looking for. In fact, I think it's a crazy idea." DuBay's proposal struck him as "an act of despair on the part of a dedicated, well-educated priest who knows what the Church ought to be, but isn't."[51] *Ave Maria* magazine said editorially that "efforts to form an American Federation of Priests will be decisively rejected because it will prove offensive to priests throughout the nation."[52] Father Andrew Greeley weighed into the fracas by noting that "DuBay's tactics - the formation of a union - are clearly naive; but his strategy - definition of certain rights for priests - is also inadequate."[53] Finally, Mary Daly said that despite DuBay's relevance, he "lacks the discernment essential to sound theology."[54] There is no record of any member of the nation's hierarchy even commenting on the notion of a union for clergymen, with the exception of crusty Richard Cardinal Cushing of Boston who bluntly dismissed the idea as "absolute nonsense."[55]

Roman officials rarely respond directly to local problems, but prefer to speak in generalities that leave little room for doubting official thinking. Hence it came as no great surprise when Pope Paul VI, in an audience to parish priests, Lenten preachers and clergymen of Rome, chided those who "think it is incumbent upon them to start a total revision of ecclesiastical discipline, maintaining that Canon Law is outdated and an anachronism." Such priests, he said, "are an affliction to the Church, disintegrators of Her spiritual and social fabric. They are an affliction to themselves, depriving themselves of the merit of spontaneous filial and manly obedience and of the comforting effects of humility, good example and confidence."[56]

There wasn't even any support from the AFL-CIO, whose president, George Meany, "scoffed that trade unions are intended to help those who work for wages and not independent contractors." He went on to say that "I just don't see anything the American trade movement can do for priests."[57] Even Father Albert Blatz, vice president of the American Federation of State, County and Municipal Employees, a 275,000 member international union, disliked the idea saying that he was "firmly opposed to the idea of a union for clergy."[58]

About a week after his unionization "bombshell," the pastor at Saint Monica's Parish, Msgr. Raymond J. O'Flaherty, released a statement saying that because there was widespread "dissatisfaction on the part of the medical staff and patients" with Father DuBay's services at the hospital, partly due to his "excessive publicity . . . I have asked him to move back to the church from the hospital."[59] O'Flaherty denied that his action was taken at the behest of Cardinal McIntyre or anyone on his staff."[60]

Several days later, according to his own account, DuBay was summoned to the chancery where he was told to submit "all future public statements in writing to the cardinal for clearance or face immediate suspension from functioning as a Catholic priest." The next morning, he announced that "today, I returned to the chancery and informed the cardinal that I could not allow myself to be muzzled, because I believe submission to prior censorship and silencing to be fundamentally immoral and an abdication of a priest's responsibility to be honest even when threatened."[61] He was then told, again in DuBay's words, "that I was suspended from the priesthood."

The facts released by DuBay about his suspension were substantially those reported in *The Tidings* later that week. In its elaboration of the event, the archdiocesan paper said that "following his decision, a statement issued by the Chancery Office announced Father DuBay's suspension, citing as its cause his cumulative and contumacious irreverence and disobedience to the promises made at priestly ordination, his disregard of pledges made since that time to obey his superiors."[62]

Though the archdiocese had offered DuBay "hospitality in a religious house of its selection," the priest told interviewers that he planned to take up residence at the Synanon Foundation, a center for the rehabilitation of narcotic addicts in Santa Monica.[63] Officials there expressed a willingness to have him, but insisted that he disavow his membership in the Socialist party, a revelation that he made a few days earlier in an off-handed comment to reporters.[64]

One clerical wag suggested that DuBay's proposal for unionization of the clergy was an "ecclesial stillbirth." What few people knew was that this subject would be featured as a chapter of a book on which DuBay had been working for some time.[65]

Just as the union issue began fading from the pages of the nation's press, Doubleday announced the publication of Father DuBay's treatise on *The Human Church*, a 192 page volume which advance flyers advertised as "a frank appraisal of the present state of the Catholic Church." The author was portrayed as taking "a hard but constructive look at the attitudes of the Catholic Church" which, he concluded, was "not living up to its mission." DuBay proposed, "as an answer to the Gospel's demand to love thy neighbor, a non-religious church mobilized to support the human development of the world." It was surely a thunderous proposal and *Time* magazine weighed in early with the observation that DuBay "puts forward a program of reform that makes the ideas of Luther seem positively papalist by comparison."[66]

Though Dale Francis thought it was inconceivable that "any Catholic reviewer could possibly praise"[67] the book, some did. Father William Nerin, for example, writing in the St. Louis *Review*, said that "there is much in this book that needs to be thought through, discussed, contested and investigated before an honest critique can be made." He felt that DuBay had "something of a prophetic vision" for the Church and, in that vein, "he and his book serve the Church."[68] Geddess MacGregor, Dean of the Graduate School of Religion at the University of Southern California, said *The Human Church* was "a book for the reflective faithful to read and to ponder well in their minds and hearts." But then, he acknowledged that "were not the whole idea out of fashion ... this courageous book ... might have some claim"[69] for being on the *Index of Forbidden Books*.

A writer in San Francisco's Catholic newspaper said that "the book does contain suggestions worthy of consideration, although these tend to be lost sight of because of the bias and misguided zeal of the author." He went on to observe that "in commenting on the tone and style of the book, one cannot help thinking that it was written in the following setting; a Bible on the right, a Concordance on the left, a publisher's deadline notice in front and center, and opposite it, a typewriter activated by an angry young man."[70] John Cogley wrote in the New York *Times* that it was "a book of less than 200 pages but pushed tight as a walnut with ideas."[71]

Father William Cunningham said that "it is a good book, in fact, quite excellent," but he predicted that "heresy hunters will have a field day" with it. Examples abound, such as "what is taught (religion) or how it is taught is not so important as who teaches," and "Yahweh was the first atheist, the great iconoclast and demythologizer" and "Christ needed an anti-religious church and He founded the first unseminary."[72]

The overwhelming quantity of reviews were negative in tone. The nationally syndicated book reviewer, Msgr. John S. Kennedy, said that "the point is that the book adds up to a set of plans and specifications for a church other than the one which has existed and functioned for many, many centuries." Despite occasional flashes of insight, occasional proper criticisms, "it is a reckless performance."[73]

Never a McIntyre fan, Garry Wills said that the DuBay volume "makes one sympathetic with any superior who had to deal with him."[74] Father John Boyle described the book as "a mishmash of unassimilated and contradictory ideas ... a book that had been better left unwritten."[75] In another review, Father Joseph G. McGroarty referred to the book as product of little merit and dubious importance" in which most of the "standard objections of the Church's bitterest enemies are resurrected."[76]

In an unsigned editorial for the Steubenville *Register*, it was alleged that the book "abounds in half-truths, suspect theological formulizations, sloppy thinking and overstatements."[77] Father Philip Mueller described the book as "hastily conceived and not well thought out."[78] Finally, Father Joseph Meenan of Pittsburgh felt that the volume "is a release of pent-up thoughts and emotions of an angry young cleric."[79]

The DuBay volume didn't fare much better in the magazines and journals. In *Act*, Elliott Egan, a Carmelite, said that "you will search the book long and hard for even occasional, let alone frequent references to the Fathers in order to justify the accolade that the work rests on a study of Patrology."[80] In the prestigious clerical journal, *Homiletic and Pastoral* Review, Father Regis Appel called it "an unfortunate book" which ignores totally Vatican II's constitution on the Church.[81]

A reviewer for *Pastoral Life* said that "it's too bad that the text reflects more of a spirit of opposition than fusion."[82] Father Theodore Vittoria said that "this book seems to represent more the product of hurt feelings on the part of the author, than a bold, direct and creative contribution." Even Andrew Greeley was unimpressed. Writing in *Sign* he observed that "the trouble with *The Human Church* is not that it is revolutionary but that it is dull - maddeningly, insufferably dull." DuBay's "style does not get beyond the simple declarative sentence, with a rare adverb and a very rare qualifying or dependent clause."[83]

James A. Cunniffe, writing in the *Reign of the Sacred Heart*, noted that "with its endless, repetitious theorizing and its unrelieved social science jargon," the book "is not an easy thing to get through - not even if you go for the party line."[84] In a magazine that perhaps reached more readers than any other, James F. Andrews said that "this book is the theological meditation of a man in particular circumstances." He further noted that "if Father DuBay's vision is correct, the renewal of the Church in Los Angeles is going to be an unchristian affair. We hope his vision is faulty."[85] Finally, writing in the *St. Joseph Magazine*, a reviewer said that while sympathizing with DuBay's good intentions, it must be said that he has written a bad book. His charges lack substance; he flails with his literary lance when he should have directed it to the heart of the problems he has encountered.[86] Though at least one writer predicted that "the book, no doubt, will enjoy a big sale" and be a "commercial success,"[87] only 11,000 copies were actually sold and the writer received no royalties.[88]

Seemingly undaunted by the largely negative reaction to his book by the Catholic press, which he characterized as "a sycophant press,"[89] DuBay took to the lecture circuit. On April 20, 1966, he told students and faculty at Claremont College that "the world needs one church and it must develop a tolerance for heresy." Described enthusiastically by the local paper as "one of the most controversial figures in recent church history," DuBay presented "his violently unorthodox views in a calm, serious manner."[90]

A week or so later, he gave a lecture at Long Beach State College where he "accused the Church of having tacitly or actively promoted segregation in many instances." He called for a "working alliance of denominations to eliminate prejudice and segregation in the nation."[91] Then he went on to Los Angeles State College where he spoke on "Church Relationship to Civil Rights and Civil Liberties." In that presentation, he said that "anything that will check the divergence of the Church will help promote the cause of civil rights."[92]

DuBay kept writing too, although his style changed markedly, giving some credence to the widely-held opinion that there had been a ghost writer for *The Human Church*. He submitted articles to a number of journals, including *Jubilee* magazine. In an essay for the *Saturday Evening Post*, he called again for reforming the Church and advocated doing away with laws giving tax exemption to churches, noting that "there was a crying need for the Church's internal reform."[93] He received some justifiable flack from Val King who pointed out that DuBay's portrayal of property exemption for the Church in California was inaccurate and erroneous. King lamented that "it's obvious that Father DuBay didn't bother checking out the facts before firing his broadside at the Church."[94]

During a press conference DuBay gave in San Diego on June 29th, the priest warned that "if his appeal to the Vatican for reinstatement were denied, he would sue the Church in civil courts."[95] Just a month or so later, on August 9th, Archbishop Egidio Vagnozzi disclosed that DuBay's suspension from his priestly duties had been upheld by the Roman Curia. The Apostolic Delegate also noted that Vatican officials had directed DuBay to withdraw from circulation his recent book, *The Human Church*.

Predictably, DuBay promised to appeal the decision, saying flatly that he absolutely would "not withdraw the book from circulation" and that he was "deeply scandalized" by the attempt to keep the book from the American public.[96] He later assured a telephone interviewer that "neither he nor his publisher ... intended to honor the Vatican decision about the book."[97]

That the whole affair had slipped to the back burner of public interest is evident by the almost total lack of criticism of the Holy See's action. Only in the pages of *America* could one find an editorial bemoaning the fact that "no witnesses were called, no opportunity to cross-examine was afforded either party and there was no oral argument."[98]

On October 18, 1966, financed "by contributions from 100 Catholic priests in various parts of the United States," DuBay opened headquarters of his labor union in a new building across the street from the Civic Auditorium in Santa Monica, California. At a press conference on that day, the priest promised that "membership will be kept confidential to protect members from reprisals at the hands of diocesan administrators."[99] "This union," DuBay said, "is being formed for the Church, not against the Church. It is in fact to guarantee the integrity of the Church that we have taken this action." He further explained that "processing of grievances and other forms of union activity leading to formal collective bargaining with chanceries will be initiated in direct proportion to the number of priests who join and form strong locals."[100]

Beyond recording the fact, the local press gave only scant attention to the opening of the union office. Dale Francis, a prominent observer of Catholic events in the United States, said that DuBay was "intent on changing the image of priests" and he predicted that if that event actually came to pass, it "would bring forth a burst of anti-clericalism."[101] Father Joseph Hilbert told his readers that "the American Federation of Priests will probably die in infancy and will not even merit a footnote in future Church history texts."[102]

Father Francis F. Brown, writing in the Steubenville *Register*, said the union had two evident strikes against it: "Both priests involved in its earliest organization stages are suspended" and "the invitation to join the union for $25 would appeal almost without exception to only the disenchanted among the nation's 50,000 priests." He went on to observe that "the guarantee that members' names will be kept confidential should be sufficient sign that the union is not really making its appeal to the typical American priest."[103]

Early in August of 1966, DuBay revealed in an interview appearing in *The Wanderer*, that he was contemplating issuance of a national newspaper. He said the purpose of *The Union Priest* would be "to circulate amongst all the clergy throughout the United States and to help them organize their own locals ... and to provide leadership in this movement."[104] The newspaper appeared on the newsstands in November. In its premier issue, the editor said that "if priests are to share in the great reforms going on in the Catholic Church, they must till their own plot of ground first, and bring to the priesthood the highest levels of professional competence and integrity." While calling on lay people "and others who are interested in the priest-union development for assistance, DuBay

Rev. William H. DuBay

Father DuBay at a press conference.

THE

Commonweal

Catholicism
In
Los Angeles

A Church of Silence
A. V. Krebs, Jr.

The DuBay Case
John Leo

VOLUME LXXX, NO. 16   JULY 10, 1964   TWENTY-FIVE CENTS

declared that not every priest would be eligible to join the American Federation of Priests."[105] Those in management or supervisorial positions would necessarily be eliminated.

The proto issue of *The Union Priest* contained what the Federation called "endorsements" of the union by Father Richard McSorley of Georgetown University and Theodore Bikel, vice president of Actors Equity Association, AFL-CIO. McSorley wrote that "it is not true to say that the social teachings of the Church do not apply to our own structure," while Bikel wrote that he saw nothing incompatible about priests wishing to be adequately recompensed.[106]

The newspaper listed the union's goals as grievance machinery, policies on transfers, tenure and leave, and professional standards and salaries. "Only after priests have brought their bishop to the bargaining table and worked out a contract - the essence of unionism will they be free to do the job for which they were ordained."[107]

According to the *National Catholic Reporter*, copies of the newspaper were sent gratis to 40,000 priests in the United States. There was no advertising, even though an appeal for ads was carried in every issue of the paper.[108] The last issue, which appeared in May of 1967, told about a trip DuBay took to Washington, Philadelphia, New York, Cleveland and Saint Louis to "sell the union idea and ascertain feelings and attitudes of priests towards their situation." An estimated 300 heard him at those five places. When asked if he had any luck in selling the union, DuBay answered: "Well, we don't have any independent locals going yet. But I was able to interest several priests in organizing some locals in their respective areas."[109] In fact, no locals were ever established, not even in Los Angeles.

Despite the widespread unpopularity of the whole union notion, especially among priests, there were pockets of support for DuBay. Eric Cohen, for example, toured the union offices in late 1966 and later wrote a most favorable essay in USC's *Daily Trojan* about "the maverick Roman Catholic priest." He concluded by saying that "while DuBay's reforms seem harsh, rather than recoiling in dogmatic disapproval, serious consideration should be given to the basically sound intent of these reforms" in the Church.[110]

For about a year after abandoning his campaign for unionizing the Catholic clergy, little was heard from William H. DuBay. He went into semi-seclusion at his parents' weekend home in the San Jacinto mountains and sought employment as a park ranger in order "to help others develop an appreciation for the woods and nature."[111] He told the Los Angeles *Times* in an interview that, by then, he was "pretty alienated from organized religion."[112]

Then, the August 9, 1968 issue of the Idyllwild *Town Crier* announced in bold headlines that "Priest-Ranger to Marry in Campus Ceremony." The next day, he exchanged marital vows with twenty-nine year old Mary Ellen Wall, in the presence of the Reverend Mason C. Harvey, a Presbyterian minister and a hundred well-wishers. A writer described the event in these words: "Garbed in a Nehru jacket with a chain around his neck, DuBay joined the procession out of the Catholic Church with his marriage at the Idyllwild School of Music and Arts."[113]

A few weeks later, Dan L. Thrapp reported that DuBay and others had acquired the old Tyrol restaurant at Idyllwild "as a center for the development of ecological consciousness." The purpose of their new "Mountain Forum" would be "to provide new opportunities for interdisciplinary and intercultural study, research, discussion and presentation of topics relating environmentally to social planning."[114]

With his entry into the environmental field, DuBay's popularity among his earlier followers, already greatly diminished, plummeted even further. When the "hippie priest" came to speak at Rio Hondo Junior College in Whittier, he was described as being as "anxious to get answers to his own questions as to give answers to students' questions." His "appearance was disturbing in his restlessness" as the audience questioned his motives for leaving the Church. He was quoted as saying "I only wish I knew what I am going to do after this lecture tour."[115]

Things didn't improve appreciably as DuBay continued the tour. Jim Bardwill reported that the "Ex-Catholic Priest DuBay Badly Received at Forum; Philosophy Laughed At." He said "from priest to atheist, from cassock to bell-bottoms and from crewcut to beard is the changing story of the ex-Catholic priest William DuBay who recently rambled on his philosophy during a lecture in the Campus Center."[116]

As late as July of 1969, when asked whether he had been right in the "startling action" he had taken several years earlier, DuBay responded "yes," and said "he would to it again."[117] But he seems to have had subsequent doubts. Writing on "The Fragile Marriage of an Ex-Priest," he admitted a year later that after his book on *The Human Church* appeared, he began to believe his own publicity. "All image and very little real substance. I was a good setup for personal disaster."[118] The essay provided deep personal insight which DuBay had discovered with the help of Dr. James Ferguson, a psychiatrist.

Father James B. Nugent, in a response to the article in the popular *Women's Magazine*, said that the essay "is interestingly written and has the ring of sincerity and frankness. There is not much in it of the polemical bitterness against the Church that one might expect." As far as what DuBay said about deficiencies in his training, Father Nugent said these become apparent "only if he chooses to abandon his vows as DuBay did."[119]

In September of 1972, DuBay separated from his wife, Ellen. He later took a position with Stonewall, a residential treatment center for homosexuals who are parolees, probationers or alcoholics. It was while there, in December, that DuBay wrote an essay for *The Advocate* in which he acknowledged that he was a homosexual. "The temporary difficulty of coming out as a homosexual is nothing in comparison with the years of trying to be someone I wasn't," he said.[120] The following April, DuBay's wife asked the court to dissolve her marriage "because of irreconcilable differences."[121]

The passing of thirty years has done little to enhance the image or the causes of William H. DuBay. With the possible exception of Chicago's still-active Association of Catholic Priests, which DuBay dismissed as a "company union,"[122] there is no evidence that his proposals and ideas have had any lasting effect on the structure of the Catholic Church in the United States or elsewhere.

In a subsequent interview, DuBay even exonerated the man whom he targeted as the cause of his original complaint, conceding that "Cardinal McIntyre is totally without prejudice ... he is one of the most conscientious churchmen of our time."[123] Writing in the *National Catholic Reporter*, DuBay further noted that McIntyre "has been tapping the surplus funds of wealthy suburban parishes for 20 years and putting millions of dollars into development of excellence in ghetto schools." He went on to observe that "the best schools in McIntyre's system are in the ghetto."[124]

Notes to the Text

1. This title was suggested by the headliner for an article appearing in *Our Sunday Visitor* for March 20, 1966, in which Dale Francis contended that Father DuBay "is a victim of the Batman Syndrome, a combination of symptoms that have affected a wide range of young priests, seminarians and angry laymen."
2. Robert Blaire Kaiser, Oklahoma *Courier*, August 7, 1964.
3. Letter reproduced by the NCWC News Service, June 19, 1964.
4. Los Angeles *Times*, June 12, 1964.
5. Los Angeles *Herald-Examiner*, June 12, 1964.
6. *Ibid.*
7. San Fernando Valley *Times*, June 13, 1964.
8. The only other priest to totally identify with DuBay was Father Brendan Nagle who came aboard at the time the union was inaugurated.
9. Los Angeles *Times*, June 16, 1964.
10. *Ibid.*, June 17, 1964.
11. John Leo, "The DuBay Case," *Commonweal* LXXX (July 10, 1964), 480.
12. AALA, John J. Ward Memorandum, Los Angeles, June 18, 1964.
13. *Ibid.*
14. June 19, 1964.
15. Quoted in the Los Angeles *Herald-Examiner*, June 19, 1964.
16. June 19, 1964.
17. *The Tidings*, July 3, 1964.
18. June 16, 1964.
19. June 18, 1964.
20. LVI (June 26, 1964), 41.
21. John Leo, *op. cit.*, 481.
22. June 18, 1964.
23. June 25, 1964.
24. Baltimore *Review*, June 19, 1964.
25. June 22, 1964.
26. June 17, 1964.
27. June 27, 1964.
28. July 9, 1964.
29. CXI (August 15, 1964), 150-151.
30. John Leo. *op. cit.*, 479.

31. "In Praise of DuBay," *Commonweal* LXXXX (June 22, 1964), 408-409.
32. Quoted in the Los Angeles *Times*, June 19, 1964.
33. September 19, 1964, 274-275.
34. III (Fall, 1964), 133-151.
35. AALA, James Francis Cardinal McIntyre to Albert Cardinal Meyer, Los Angeles, December 3, 1964.
36. AALA, Egidio Vagnozzi to James Francis Cardinal McIntyre, Washington, D.C., December 22, 1964.
37. AALA, John Quatannens to James Francis Cardinal McIntyre, Anaheim, January 29, 1965.
38. AALA, James Francis Cardinal McIntyre to William H DuBay, Los Angeles, February, 1965.
39. San Fernando Valley *Times*, February 23, 1966.
40. *National Catholic Reporter*, February 23, 1966.
41. Whittier *Daily News*, February 22, 1966.
42. Boston *Pilot*, February 26, 1966. Reprinted in *The Tidings*, April 4, 1966.
43. March 23, 1966.
44. March 17, 1966.
45. Los Angeles *Herald-Examiner*, February 24, 1966.
46. Steubenville *Register*, March 3, 1966.
47. Miami *Voice*, March 11, 1966.
48. LXXXIII (March 11, 1966).
49. March 3, 1966.
50. Santa Monica *Evening Outlook*, March 2, 1966.
51. *National Catholic Reporter*, March 2, 1966.
52. Quoted in the Los Angeles *Herald-Examiner* March 3, 1966.
53. Scranton *Catholic Light*, March 24, 1966.
54. "Hans Küng" in Wm. Jerry Boney and Lawrence E. Molumby, *The New Day* (Richmond, 1968), p. 139.
55. Los Angeles *Times*, May 18, 1966.
56. *Delmarva Dialog*, February 25, 1966.
57. *Time* LXXXVII (March 4, 1966), 86.
58. National *Catholic Reporter*, May 11, 1966.
59. Los Angeles *Herald-Examiner*, February 24, 1966.
60. Los Angeles *Times*, February 24, 1966.
61. Los Angeles *Herald-Examiner*, February 26, 1966.
62. March 4, 1966.
63. Los Angeles *Herald-Examiner*, February 26, 1966.
64. Los Angeles *Times*, February 26, 1966.
65. AALA, Press Release, New York, March 4, 1966.
66. LXXXVII (March 4, 1966), 86.
67. May 18, 1966.
68. March 18, 1966.

69. Los Angeles *Times*, March 27, 1966.
70. *The Monitor*, March 11, 1966.
71. March 4, 1966.
72. Michigan *Catholic*, March 3, 1966.
73. April 1, 1966.
74. *National Catholic Reporter*. May 4. 1966.
75. Davenport *Catholic Messenger*, August 18, 1966.
76. Brooklyn *Tablet*, March 17, 1966.
77. April 14, 1966.
78. Edmonton *Western Catholic Reporter*, April 21, 1966.
79. Pittsburgh *Catholic*, September 15, 1966.
80. LXVI May, 1966, 12.
81. LXVI (June, 1966), 789.
82. XIV (June, 1966), 376.
83. XXXXV (May, 1966), 57.
84. May, 1966.
85. *Ave Maria*, CIII (April 9, 1966), 19.
86. April, 1966, p. 140.
87. Joseph G. Moriarty in *The Brooklyn Tablet*, March 17, 1966.
88. *Time*, August 19, 1966, 74.
89. Claremont *Courier*, April 23, 1966.
90. Pomona *Progress Bulletin*, April 21, 1966.
91. Long Beach *Press Telegram*, May 7, 1966.
92. Los Angeles *Collegian*, May 10, 1966.
93. CCXXXIX (June 4, 1966), 10-11.
94. San Francisco *Chronicle*, June 2, 1966.
95. Los Angeles *Herald-Examiner*, June 30, 1966.
96. Los Angeles *Times*, August 10, 1966.
97. New York *Times*, August 10, 1966.
98. Quoted in *Church World*, October 7, 1966.
99. Los Angeles *Herald-Examiner*, October 19, 1966.
100. *Ibid.*
101. *Our Sunday Visitor*, November 11, 1966.
102. Harrisburg *Catholic Witness*, December, 1966.
103. November 3, 1966.
104. August 11, 1966.
105. *The Union Priest* (November, 1966).
106. Quoted in the *National Catholic Reporter*, November 11, 1966.
107. *The Union Priest, Op. cit.*
108. November 23, 1966.
109. *The Union Priest* (May, 1967).
110. November 30, 1966.
111. Idyllwild *Town Crier*, August 9, 1968.
112. August 9, 1968.

113. *The Herald of Freedom* V (September 6, 1968), 3.
114. Los Angeles *Times*, October 19, 1968.
115. Bob Copperstone in the San Gabriel *Valley Tribune*, March 6, 1969.
116. Pierce College *Roundup*, March 17, 1969.
117. Los Angeles *Herald-Examiner*, July 13, 1969.
118. *McCall's* XCVII (September, 1970), 133.
119. Steubenville *Register*, September 3, 1970.
120. *National Catholic Reporter*, March 17, 1972.
121. Los Angeles *Times*, April 25, 1972.
122. Steubenville *Register*, November 3, 1966.
123. *The Wanderer*, August 11, 1966.
124. *National Catholic Reporter*, June 5, 1968.

22. Racial Issues

P robably the most glaring deficiency in the McIntyre regime was its almost total lack of appreciation for public relations and its role in the Catholic apostolate. That shortcoming became increasingly more prominent in the years after Vatican Council II and the gradual shift of McIntyre from an offensive to a defensive episcopate. Nowhere is this deficiency more obvious than in the subject of racial relations, especially with regard to the enormous influx of Afro-Americans into Los Angeles and the ever-more sophisticated demands of advocacy groups.

A close scrutiny of McIntyre's views about minorities reveals a man intensely concerned about the equity of their stature in both Church and state. His failure to communicate his position publicly can only be explained by the utter amateurishness of the communications network then used by the archdiocese.

PROPOSITION 14

Involvement of the hierarchy in political matters has a number of precedents in United States Catholic annals. Rarely, however, has such activity created as much attention as that aroused in California during 1964, when efforts were initiated to repeal by constitutional amendment certain provisions of the controversial Rumford Fair Housing Act. Even more outstanding than the campaign itself, was the *apparent* disagreement among the local bishops on the issue, a factor which, for practical purposes, dissipated their influence on the thorny subject.

Any discussion of the hotly-contested Proposition 14 must advert, at least in passing, to the question of whether the proposed amendment itself involved a moral judgment, for it was precisely that point which divided California's hierarchy. In a joint statement, issued during August of 1964, the eight residential bishops reasserted traditional Catholic teaching that "discrimination based solely on race, color, nationality, or religion cannot be reconciled with the truth that God has created all men with equal rights and equal dignity."[1] Three of the ordinaries, though not personally responsible for introducing the "moral" theme into the campaign, went a step further and put themselves on record as seeing such an issue at stake in the proposition in question.

Injection of the "moral" note into the controversy ultimately worked against the opponents of the constitutional amendment. Efforts to apply Pope John XXIII's statement that "every human being has the right to freedom of movement and residence"[2] were resented by certain Catholics familiar with *Pacem in terris* for, in its proper context, the phrase obviously had in mind the involuntary displacement of captive peoples in Iron Curtain areas, a situation hardly comparable even in that locale *Newsweek* labeled "The Mississippi of the U.S. Roman Catholic Church."[3] Proponents of Proposition 14 also had recourse to papal pronouncements and in defense of their position appealed to *Rerum novarum* and Leo XIII's remark that "it is precisely in [the] power of disposal that ownership consists, whether the property be land or movable goods."[4] In neither case could any positive note be attached to the actual selling or purchasing process since there is no absolute equation between the right to *acquire* property and the prior right to *hold* it.

While no conscientious Catholics openly disagreed with the national bishops' statement of 1958 that "the heart of the race question is moral and religious," many saw the Rumford Fair Housing Act, part of which Proposition 14 sought to repeal, not so much as a case of moral discrimination as one of law making about such practices. In most instances, the votes cast for the amendment by Catholics were not directed against any particular race or group but favored individual liberty for everyone equally.

The refusal of the Archbishop of Los Angeles publicly to commit himself on the question, though it was interpreted differently in various circles, apparently grew out of his belief that Catholic principles of jurisprudence lie somewhere between rigidity in law and recklessness in liberty. This conviction, hardly a novel one, was held by a number of progressive writers who felt that "society cannot and does not admit that every claim to freedom of action based on an individual's or a group's conscientious beliefs is a natural right that must be satisfied."[5]

As the San Francisco *Monitor* noted after the campaign, the crux of the whole question was "whether this right over one's private property occasionally needs limitations, and, if so, have we reached a point in California where it is necessary to limit this right by government regulation to avoid discrimination.[6] The electorate of California, 21% of it professedly Catholic, answered this question in the negative. While the democratic process itself is hardly the determinant of morality, the election outcome did indicate a grass-roots reflection by Catholics of episcopal involvement in questions, the moral quality of which is doubtful.

After almost a year's activity to induce an endorsement of the Rumford Fair Housing Act from the Archbishop of Los Angeles, Father William DuBay attempted to force the cardinal's hand by a widely publicized plea to Pope Paul VI. In retrospect, it seems that this particular incident backfired for, as one journalist pointed out, "it is still true that the risks one takes must be measured against the chances of success. Father DuBay ignored that axiom to the detriment not only of himself but of the Church and the Negro in Los Angeles as well."[7] Without any question, the refusal of James Francis Cardinal McIntyre to formally answer the charges of his recalcitrant cleric and the subsequent curtain of silence which descended over the affair was interpreted by many people as an endorsement of the amendment.

What the cardinal's actions might have been had the DuBay affair never occurred, is another question. Except in the matter of taxation of Catholic schools, where principles of strict justice were at stake, McIntyre had consistently avoided commenting on political matters, believing that "when an issue is submitted to the people for vote, it does not behoove the Archbishop of Los Angeles to encourage the clergy to presume to direct the faithful in the expression of their individual judgment and consequent vote."[8]

John Leo, whose earlier article in *Commonweal* left little doubt about his opinion of Southern California's archbishop,[9] noted later that the cardinal's position "cannot be condemned out of hand. Regardless of what we think of Proposition 14, we must admit he is on to a great truth when he says that Catholics do not want their bishops intervening in politics." He further observed that "ironically, the very Catholics who brought pressure to bear on the Cardinal to speak out are the ones who normally could be expected to resist any attempt by a bishop to tell them how to vote." Leo saw McIntyre as agreeing "that the political order belongs essentially to the layman, and that in ordinary circumstances, bishops should confine themselves to the teaching of principles for the layman to apply in the natural order."[10]

Others, while failing to go along with the cardinal's alleged position on the proposed amendment, expressed accord with his noninterference policy. H.F. Schilling of Pasadena wrote to the Los Angeles *Times* to repeat an old German proverb: "speech is silver, silence is gold. Many of your readers join me in commending Cardinal McIntyre for being on the gold standard."[11] A Catholic laywoman, actively opposing the amendment, decried "the whole effort to smear an aging man who was responsible for the advent of the first Negro nuns to his archdiocese" and pointed out that such energy and time could be better employed in other areas.[12]

Few voters were won to the "No" camp by the intemperate attacks of certain extraterritorial journals which attempted to portray Southern California under the merciless "tight control" of an archbishop who taps phone lines, passes out bumper stickers and personally censors all sermons on racial matters.[13] The most spectacular of the diatribes, launched by Edward Keating in *Ramparts*, can be best epitomized by the words *sic semper tyrannis*[14] which he placed over the cardinal's picture. Although slow to do so, the nation's Catholic press eventually reacted to this unwholesome procedure. The Georgia *Bulletin*, which saw "justification for disagreeing with some of the views and positions of Catholic leaders in the Los Angeles area, termed the Keating attack on McIntyre as "an unforgivable piece of writing... more reminiscent of yellow journalism than Catholic culture."[15]

There were other departures. Commenting on an article by Dorothy Day in the *Catholic Worker*, the editor of *Ave Maria* noted that "too many people like some of the laity in Los Angeles, wait for a bishop or Cardinal to make everything safe and official before they will move." Observing Miss Day's personal attitude toward Church authority over the years, the writer confessed after reading her article that "we feel a little cleaner now, and a little surer, and somewhat ashamed."[16]

Probably a good number of undecided voters were influenced by the spectacle of a young priest attacking one of the nation's most dynamic prelates with the shaky charge of failing "to exercise moral leadership." This mood was expressed editorially by Hollywood's *Citizen News* which saw it as "an unfortunate circumstance when a man of God whose life has been replete with good works for the benefit of man and his church gets caught in a maelstrom of circumstance wherein he can't emerge without losing."[17]

But did McIntyre lose? If he favored the amendment, as many have conjectured, he did not. Beyond the small group of people immediately surrounding the "angry priest," many of California's Catholics saw Father DuBay as one of those young clerics whom Pope Paul spoke of as "moved by the good intention of penetrating the masses or particular groups, somehow getting mixed up with them instead of remaining apart, thus sacrificing the true efficacy of their apostolate to some sort of useless imitation."[18]

Nine of California's fourteen bishops made no commitment on the issue, while five of the prelates openly endorsed a "No" vote on Proposition 14. Strongest of the statements was that of the Most Reverend Floyd Begin, Bishop of Oakland, who viewed the amendment as "of such a nature as to contradict what is clear and universal Catholic teaching on the rights and duties of those who own property.[19] The Archbishop of San Francisco originally opposed the measure on constitutional grounds alone, for which there was a strong case. Though he recognized "room for legitimate differences of opinion among Catholics regarding the legislation," Joseph T. McGucken issued a pastoral letter from Rome in late October defending the right of the Church "to speak out on the moral issues involved" and clearly, though not specifically, urging defeat of the amendment.

While Bishop Begin said unequivocally that Proposition 14 was "a moral issue insofar as it concedes absolute rights to property owners with no reference to the rights of others," most of the prelates carefully skirted the "moral" aspect of the question, at least in their official statements. The bishops of Sacramento and Santa Rosa joined other members of their province in opposing the amendment and Stockton's bishop, Hugh Donohue, was among the three signatories of the opposition argument mailed to voters by the Secretary of State's office. Reaction to the stand taken by the northern bishops was mixed. One commentator felt that "generally, the Catholic opposition was strong enough to make one realize that many Catholics simply did not accept the authority or the ability of bishops and clergy to speak on the moral implications of this political issue."[20] This view was heard in other quarters. *The National Catholic Reporter* agreed that "at the prudential level, ...a priest or bishop is no more competent than the next man; and if he exceeds his competence by imposing his political judgments on the laity he may well be abusing his spiritual authority and keeping the laity in diapers."[21]

A committee of prominent Catholic laymen at Los Altos reacted to Archbishop McGucken's position in a manner almost as unparalleled in America's ecclesiastical history as the DuBay incident in Los Angeles. Their formation of a "Catholic Yes on Proposition 14" organization grew out of "mass indignation to the church becoming politically active in the anti Proposition 14 battle."[22] Their full-page advertisement, appearing in the Bay City's newspapers on October 28, 1964, was a copy of a letter sent to McGucken:

> Many of your devoted subjects who have tried to live and think as good Catholics all their lives have suddenly found themselves at odds with some of their clergy. The bone of contention is Proposition 14.
>
> Many of our clergy believe and teach that our legislators will be precluded from passing housing legislation if

Proposition 14 is adopted. This is untrue. Our legislators can pass any law they choose subject to approval by the people of the State by vote.

The Catholics of whom we speak are told that there is only one side to Proposition 14. Yet our reasoning, based on Catholic training, tells us that this is not true.[23]

The highly respected Thomas P. White, former State Supreme Court justice, spoke for countless other Catholics when he said, in defense of the silent Archbishop of Los Angeles, "we would resent and criticize our clergy if they undertook to advise us on our conduct at the ballot box."[24] That White's opinion was substantially correct was at least indicated at the polls on November 4th when the measure won a tremendous endorsement of almost 2 to 1. As one eastern paper reported: "Observers throughout the state said that the result of the balloting on Proposition 14 could not be described other than as a defeat for a great proportion of the state's clergyman."[25] In a multiple interview carried by *The Commonweal* for its jubilee, one journalist chided those clamoring for more prelatial leadership in political matters and wondered "if liberals haven't consistently been playing the game both ways. If it is a measure they like, they ask the bishops to intervene. Otherwise they are quick to point out that political order belongs to laymen."[26]

It is hard to say whether McIntyre's silence or the northern bishops' open endorsement won more votes for proponents of the amendment. Only one of the state's fifty-eight counties disapproved of Proposition 14 and that by a narrow margin of nineteen votes.[27] Generally, Southern California recorded a higher percentage of affirmative ballots but much of that can be attributed to a traditionally conservative block of votes in that area. A definitive estimate of the hierarchy's influence and effectiveness (or lack thereof) must await further study for there were other powerful interests at work on both sides during the long struggle, such as the circular letter mailed to the state's Catholic clergy by the theology department of the University of San Francisco, wherein it was stated categorically that "any Catholic who feels that he may vote for this measure has an erroneous conscience and is morally obliged to correct it in the light of Christian principles."[28] That these tactics were unappreciated seems obvious enough, but their real effect cannot yet be weighed.

This much can be said, that such comments as John O'Connor's that "incipient racism - a shameful heritage of by-gone, ghettoed years, was behind the victory of Proposition 14"[29] are totally unfounded and indefensible. In the total analysis, it must be remembered, as a black minister in Los Angeles pointed out, that "in the west especially in the southern California area, we have most of the provisions of civil rights justice on the books and in the attitudes of the people,"[30] a statement recalling Yves M.J. Congar's study for UNESCO in 1953 wherein the distinguished Dominican theologian concluded that Negroes in California "suffer no discrimination."[31] The UNESCO survey was confirmed as late as November, 1964, by a report of the National Urban League which stated: "Living standards of Negro families in the Los Angeles area are the highest in the nation."[32]

While Los Angeles leads the nation in percentage of acceptable housing, both rental and owner-occupied, no one denies that there have been and are "pocketed inequalities" and efforts are being made to meet these problems. As the Archbishop of Los Angeles said after the campaign, "the approval of Proposition 14 does not repeal the serious moral obligation of all persons to avoid racial discrimination and segregation."[33]

The question remains, however, concerning the manner of remedying these serious ills in modern society.[34] It would seem, from the incidents related above, that California's Catholics preferred to have their bishops remain aloof from politics, except in those rare cases where a specifically, *well-defined* issue of justice or morality is at stake. The Golden State's Catholics apparently wanted more emphasis placed on taking the slums out of the people than the people out of the slums, for then and only then, did they see the Church and its collegially endowed episcopate empowered to speak. Catholics respected the opinions of their bishops - but apparently only in areas of faith and morals. There alone did they see legitimate magisterial competency.

CURE

The Catholic Interracial Council, which predated McIntyre's arrival in Los Angeles, had been organized by Dan Marshall shortly after World War II as an "advisory" agency for the Archdiocese of Los Angeles. It had acquired some displeasure with the Cantwell regime for its attack on "the Jim Crow policy" of the local Knights of Columbus, the archdiocesan girls high school, Catholic hospitals and residential restrictive pacts.[35]

The council had achieved a major civil rights victory in 1948, when it provided legal sponsorship for a priest who wanted California's seventy-six year old miscegenation marriage law overthrown. On October 2 of that year, the State Supreme Court, in a 4-3 decision, ruled the law unconstitutional.

Father George Dunne, in his memoirs, charged that "one of the first things he (McIntyre) had done after his arrival in Los Angeles was to order the dissolution of the Catholic Interracial Council.[36] Dunne's accusation needs to be examined in the context of the times. McIntyre had been advised by his lawyers to have all agencies bearing the name "Catholic" placed under the archdiocesan umbrella for liability reasons. It was the council's refusal to adhere to that directive that brought about its disbandment and not McIntyre's displeasure with its policies.

Catholics United for Racial Equality (CURE) was organized early in June of 1963 by a group of Catholics concerned about interracial justice in the United States and California. It was a group "interested in lay Catholic action . . .in the field of race relations and social justice."[37] Early on, the leaders of CURE decided to confront McIntyre by staging "sit-ins" at the Chancery Office and outside his home in Fremont Place. During the first of those incidents, Sue Welch and Alan White left behind a handwritten note outlining the objectives of their group.

Among the initiatives proposed by the CURE group were the formation of an officially approved Catholic Interracial Council, an episcopal letter on specific moral aspects of discrimination, the encouragement of more frequent sermons on social justice, better coverage of race-related news in *The Tidings* and, wherever possible, the recruitment of black teachers to fill openings in white secondary and elementary schools.[38]

The cardinal responded with a letter which said that the Catholic Church had "been amongst the foremost and the most persistent in supporting equality and equity for the Negro people of our country. " He said it had "been outspoken in declaring the fundamental and moral principles where abuses prevailed. These basic moral principles, therefore, have been applied in the service of religion, in the service of education and throughout our social agencies, as well as other institutions of a charitable character under the direction of religion."

McIntyre went on to observe that "it is our belief that such services as these, rendered quietly, consistently and as a normal aspect of parish life among our people, provide the most hopeful and effective means of promoting racial justice and charity." He believed, on the other hand, that "the creation of special commissions and committees and the development of specialized programs, often formed in the heat of emotion and in the context of strong political overtones, can militate against the very ends they are designed to serve by arousing an acute sensitivity of racial differences rather than an absorption of them in the warmth of the brotherhood of Christ."[39]

In a letter addressed to Anne Reher, he wrote that he "had worked with this problem for forty years." He was well familiar with the great efforts made by the Church, its representatives and by missionaries on behalf of the colored people here in the United States as well as in foreign lands. "The policy of the Church has been sustained as one of action and not one of oratory or conference alone. Our policy has been one of accomplishment for the benefit of the Negroes."[40]

McIntyre's response was released to the press which reported that "demands for black nuns in white schools and white nuns in black schools" was insulting to church authorities and the Negro community" which is not what McIntyre had said.[41] Sue Welch was quoted in another paper as saying that "faint hearted episcopal leadership in the quest for racial justice in this diocese is not less than the abrogation of pastoral duty and the denial of a Christian charity and human justice."[42]

In an attempt to embarrass McIntyre nationally, the leaders of CURE addressed a letter to all the bishops of the United States which they mailed on September 9, 1965. As a rationale for their actions, the signatories cited the *Constitution on the Church* which said that the "laity should openly reveal their needs and desires with that freedom and confidence which is fitting for children of God and brothers in Christ."

Their concern was "the state of the Church in Los Angeles." They charged that the teachings of the Church on matters of social justice (especially the race problem) and the liturgy are carried out only with greatest difficulty in Los Angeles. In particular, they said that Mass facing the people, offertory processions, and the use of "postures" were discouraged or not allowed. But what distressed them more than that was the prevalent attitude of indifference and coolness toward the renewal of the life of the Church." They repeated the unfounded charge that "it is widely known that the priests of the archdiocese are under implicit, if not explicit, directions not to preach or write directly on the racial tension and injustices underlying the tragic riots in Los Angeles."[43] They felt that "the result of this official attitude on the part of the Hierarchy of Los Angeles" was in direct contradiction to the spirit of the teachings of the Magisterium of the Church and was "causing great and deep suffering and deprivation for many people."[44]

The letter was signed by 270 lay people from twenty-six states, excluding California for "fear of reprisals and threats of intimidation. " Among the signatories were Daniel Callahan and Joseph Cuneen of New York and John O'Connor who had recently left the employ of *The Monitor* in San Francisco.[45] Though relatively few Catholic newspapers printed the letter, which was sent to all of them, *The Monitor* of San Francisco ran the story under the masthead "Laymen Concerned over Church in L.A." It asserted that "the letter represents the first time that laymen from all over the United States have addressed themselves to all the U.S. bishops at one time on a particular subject."[46]

McIntyre lost no time in sending a telefax to Msgr. Francis Quinn, the editor, complaining that "neither the letter nor the article attributes the statements and insinuations therein to any qualified or recognized source. It quotes the number of supposed signers, but does not identify them." McIntyre thought that "this type of newspaper writing is in violation of the ethics, norms and practice of the newspaper profession." He also felt that "the attack and insinuations in the article are slanderous and scandalous because they are contrary to the truth." The cardinal said that the whole presentation was "unfair for evidently no attempt was made to confirm with official sources any of the charges made in the letter. " McIntyre demanded that his telefax be printed in the next issue of the paper, and it was on September 23rd.[47]

The cardinal also sent a letter to Archbishop Joseph T. McGucken saying that appearance of the letter in *The Monitor* came as "a complete shock to us.... We cannot find that any other papers in the West carried the story except *The Monitor* and the *Catholic Voice*" of Oakland.[48] Msgr. Quinn replied, expressing his "apology for the article" saying only that he was "very sorry for the pain that the article may have caused." He had heard from Archbishop McGucken, who was in Rome, and the archbishop had also objected "to the erroneous statements and implications of the letter." Quinn offered no explanation as to why the article appeared.[49]

In addition to printing McIntyre's telefax the following week, the paper ran a long interview with Bishop John J. Ward in which the southland's auxiliary said that "implementation of the new liturgical norms is being carried out in Los Angeles in letter and spirit." After enumerating the directives already issued to pastors in Los Angeles, Ward added that "His Eminence has never prohibited celebration of Mass facing the people, if the altar so permits." And he pointed out that new churches were being provided for such Masses. Already fourteen had been completed and twenty-two more were on the drawing board.

Alphonse Antczak speaking for *The Tidings*, was quoted as saying that "the archdiocese had adhered to the teaching of the Church as enunciated by the hierarchy of the nation and by the bishops of the state. Through its parishes, schools, social and welfare agencies, the archdiocese has supported a consistent and positive policy of racial equality." Referring to President Lyndon Johnson's recently expressed concern about the "erosion of family life," Antczak said that "the persistent work of the archdiocese has been to bedrock and structure family life by imparting the education needed for living a morally and materially fruitful life."[50]

When Archbishop Egidio Vagnozzi, the Apostolic Delegate, received a copy of the letter addressed to the bishops, he expressed to McIntyre his view that it represented "the action of a well-organized conspiracy. Persons outside of Los Angeles would not have any information other than what they read in the newspapers or was told to them."[51]

McGucken was furious when copies of *The Monitor* reached him in Rome. He wrote a four page letter to Quinn saying that he didn't think the follow-up article in the paper was adequate. He then said that "a Catholic paper, which must be governed by moral principals, can never stoop to defamation and calumny, as that article did, with cowardly anonymity. He couldn't help feeling deeply indignant and ashamed that "a paper published in my name should have lent itself to a campaign of vilification already well known and despised by the Bishops of the country and many others, some of whom have sent me cablegrams of protest." The Archbishop of San Francisco bemoaned the fact that the writers of the letter had never bothered to check their facts. He referred to the new churches in Los Angeles "which have altars built for Mass facing the people, and all those now being designed." He pointed out that "pastors have been given full permission to implement the new liturgy, and are doing it gradually, as the Holy See has suggested." And he opined that "if they made changes more slowly than we have done, perhaps they will have less abuses to correct and better results in the long run."

McGucken was clearly resentful of the attacks made on the jurisdiction where he had worked for most of his life. He recalled that "the Archdiocese of Los Angeles, in the field of Social Service, Charity, Education, Vocational and Technical Training has done far more for minority groups. than any diocese in the West." He concluded by saying that "it is one thing to talk to each other about racial justice and quite a different thing to get out into the field and work with creative and on-going programs which really serve to elevate and benefit in a permanent way those who suffer discrimination and disadvantage. No matter how much we may differ with regard to policy on legislation, we have no right to carry on a program of vindictiveness, and much less to defame others by broadcasting exaggerations, half truths and outright falsehoods."[52]

Bishop Floyd Begin of Oakland also apologized that the article had appeared in the *Catholic Voice*. He was "embarrassed and angry" when he saw the letter in his diocesan newspaper, saying that "neither I nor my Editor, Father Maurovich, knew anything

478

about it." He signed off by saying that "Your Eminence knows that I have nothing but praise and envy over what you have accomplished in Los Angeles. I am sure that is the feeling of all the Bishops of California or any other Bishop who is well informed."[53]

Quinn never disclosed why the article appeared or who was responsible. He wrote to McIntyre, expressing sorrow over the matter, but saying only that he hadn't seen the article until after it had appeared in print. He could attribute "no source to the article locally."[54] Msgr. Thomas Bowe, acting Vicar General for the Archdiocese of San Francisco, wrote to McIntyre that "the selection was made by one of the lay staff of *The Monitor*." It had been received from a Miss Ethel Soussa, one of the signers, who operated the Junipero Serra Shop on Maiden Lane in San Francisco. He supported the editor, saying that "neither Monsignor Quinn nor myself were aware of the decision to print the letter until it appeared in the published edition."[55]

What seems to have happened was this. Quinn was away on vacation and was unaware of the matter until informed by phone from Bowe. Though he discovered after the fact that John O'Connor, former editor of *The Monitor*, was the culprit, Quinn assumed full responsibility since it happened on his "watch." No one who knew Quinn, later Bishop of Sacramento, would ever have held him personally responsible, including McGucken.

In a letter to John K. Ford, Quinn repeated his "respect and reverence for His Eminence, Cardinal McIntyre," noting that he had occasion to work under his direction in several statewide and diocesan matters through the years. He assured Ford that "*The Monitor* does not subscribe, and I do not subscribe, to the attacks made on the Cardinal from time-to-time in the press." He regretted "very deeply the unjournalistic characteristics of the article which appeared in the September 16 issue of *The Monitor*." When Ford sent a copy of the letter to McIntyre, the cardinal wrote atop the letter: "Matter closed."[56]

There were many members of CURE who felt that the organization's confrontational attitude had served neither them nor the Church well. Out of their displeasure was born the Catholic Human Relations Council of Los Angeles whose avowed purpose was "to establish, maintain and promote better relations among the peoples of this community through the practical application of the Christian principles of charity and justice to be achieved through example, education and social action as expressed by the Catholic Bishops of the United States in their joint statements of 1943, 1958 and 1963 and relevant papal encyclicals."[57]

McIntyre found this latter group considerably more conciliatory, describing the Catholic Human Relations Council as aspiring "to represent Catholic thought and policy in conjunction with fringe commissions, but refusing to accept a chaplain or clerical director." He pointed out that only their unwillingness to have a chaplain kept them from having "approval from the Archdiocese of Los Angeles."[58]

KNIGHTS OF PETER CLAVER

One of the largest and oldest of the Catholic fraternal orders, the Knights of Peter Claver are mostly black, though membership is open to Catholics of all races and colors. Cardinal McIntyre once remarked that the "Knights were always a source of comfort, consolation and edification."[59] He had worked closely with them in New York and after his transfer to Los Angeles, McIntyre became even more outspoken in his regard for the Knights.

The first council was established in California in 1941. Chartered under the name Queen of Angels, this council was headquartered at Los Angeles. Acting at McIntyre's invitation, the Knights met in Los Angeles for their 11th Annual Western District Conference in June, 1964. McIntyre went to Verbum Dei High School, the nation's first Catholic secondary school to have an Afro-American principal,[60] where he offered Holy Mass for the assemblage.

THE CIVIL RIGHTS BILL

When President Johnson signed the landmark Civil Rights legislation in July of 1964, McIntyre was among the first to issue a statement. He said he was "happy that the elected representatives of the people have kept faith with the Constitution of the United States and the benign spirit of Abraham Lincoln." He said that "we are confident that the provisions of this new law will be accepted and obeyed with docility, understanding and Christian love."

He called the rights act "a concrete expression of the conscience of all men of good will" and added: "The formation of that conscience has been the concern and the work of the Church for many long years. To this end, she has labored by precept and example to instill in men's hearts those lessons of human dignity and human equality which flow from Christ's teachings."[61] The cardinal said it was an "additional reason to rejoice" at the bill's enactment that "its provisions reflect the healthy climate of racial justice which prevails here in our state and in our archdiocese." "The people of Los Angeles have supplied a living example of those moral principles which are now enshrined in the law of our land,"[62] Cardinal McIntyre declared.

A spokesman for the Catholic Human Relations Council "approved McIntyre's statement endorsing the Civil Rights bill" but asserted that "the cardinal's comment did not go far enough."[63] Governor Edmund G. Brown also applauded the cardinal's action as "a welcome expression of the moral leadership which will be so important in making possible implementation of this historic law."[64]

Even John O'Connor jumped momentarily on McIntyre's bandwagon, noting that McIntyre "expressed happiness at the President's signing of the bill, calling it a concrete expression of the conscience of all men of good will."[65] On August 24, the day the Democrats opened their Atlantic City convention, the California bishops put their signatures to a letter addressed to all their people. The letter urged the formation of a right conscience in public affairs and a healing of the wounds of discrimination. Cardinal McIntyre's name - like that of Abou Ben Adhem - headed all the rest.

When Martin Luther King, the Baptist minister who brought the spirit of Christ to the movement for racial justice, was assassinated, the ecclesial leaders of Los Angeles scheduled a memorial service at the Los Angeles Memorial Coliseum, followed by an unprecedented ecumenical gathering at the First Methodist Church. In one of his few appearances at a Protestant Church, James Francis Cardinal McIntyre delivered a brief eulogy in which he said the "we join the nation in sympathy for the cause espoused by Dr. King. We pray that this sacrifice may hasten the realization of the peace and happiness in an united people of our beloved country." He said that the Catholic community would "pray for the happy repose of Dr. King, a champion for a just cause, and for his bereaved family. " His Eminence also suggested that individual parish communities might want to join him in memorializing Dr. King at their weekly services.[66]

WATTS RIOTS

McIntyre was a hands-on administrator, not only in the curial offices but in the parishes, schools and agencies under his mantle. It was a rare day when he didn't administer Confirmation, inspect a building site or visit a convent, hospital. or school somewhere in the four county archdiocese. Few churchmen in the United States knew their people better or moved among them more frequently than the cardinal.

Though his claim that there was no racial "problem" in Los Angeles was discounted and criticized widely in the press, the cardinal based that view on personal experience not on surveys or exit polls. Interestingly, from the perspective of thirty years, he appears to have been considerably more right than wrong. An example would be the Watts Riots where, clearly, there were reasons other than racial for what Theodore White called a "Festival of Hate."

The riots broke out on August 11, 1965 in a district populated mostly by Afro-Americans and Mexican-Americans southwest of downtown Los Angeles in an area known as Watts. The actual catalyst was the arrest of a black man for drunken driving by a member of the California Highway Patrol. An angry crowd gathered and soon turned into a mob whose fury grew more intense when additional police arrived. Roving bands set cars ablaze, shot at fire trucks and looted and burned shops belonging to whites, destroying buildings in a 534 block radius. Local officials could not control the violence until Governor Edmund G. Brown called in the National Guard. Thirty-four people were killed and over a thousand were injured during the ensuing five days.

Cardinal McIntyre lost no time in responding to the riots. He issued a statement on August 13 asking Catholics to use their influence to counter the rioting in Watts:

> I am grieved that the splendid spirit and high moral integrity of Negro people in our beloved city of Los Angeles is being besmirched by the happenings of recent days.
>
> The uprising has seemingly been without presentation of grievances for adjudication and settlement. Hence, the uprising seems an instigated revolt against the rights of neighbor and the preservation of law and order.
>
> The responsibility for the depredations has not been declared. Hence, there is no recognized authority for negotiation and settlement. I urge our devoted Catholic people to protest and to discredit the prevalent depredations and to use their influence so that seemingly unjustified demonstrations and violence may cease. Progress is obtained only through the medium of law and order and respectful recognition of the rights of others.[67]

Not content with rhetoric, the cardinal set in motion a gigantic relief operation whereby seven tons of food was sent to the Watts district by the Archbishop's Fund for Charity. Personnel from Catholic Charities visited Watts daily to determine the needs of the people. A survey of the ninety-five Catholic facilities in the area disclosed that no harm had come to any one of the seventy-five priests, 300 sisters, seven brothers and numerous lay persons attached to Catholic institutions or agencies. It was a large area in which the church maintained twenty-eight parishes, twenty-seven convents, twenty-three elementary schools, five high schools, a college, a hospital and numerous other Catholic activities.

It is interesting to recall the comments of arm-chair observers, many of whom had never been to California, on the question of causality. William X. Kienzle, writing in the *Michigan Catholic*, for example, charged that "one could dispute whether the Archdiocese of Los Angeles is in any way committed to the racial question. But no one could argue its popular image. And that image is one of silent detachment." The writer credited "the Archdiocese of Los Angeles with having a policy that divorces it from any meaningful involvement with today's racial crises."[68]

An editorial in the Dubuque *Witness* proclaimed that "the program to get social justice for a large segment of the Los Angeles area has received no impetus from the Church"[69] and the *Catholic Universe Bulletin* quoted Dr. Martin Luther King as hoping that Cardinal McIntyre would be as vigorous in condemning conditions causing the riots as he was in condemning the violence.[70]

Leon Aubrey, director of Catholic United for Racial Quality (CURE), dispatched a letter to Pope Paul VI asking that the Cardinal McIntyre be removed for his "refusal to mobilize Catholics and to work for fair employment, housing and education" which, he claimed, "contributed to the current racial outbursts."[71]

Those living in the area had a totally different appraisal than did their eastern confreres. Father Louis F. Knight, administrator of Ascension parish in Watts, told reporters that the cardinal "did all he could," pointing out that McIntyre "had done more for the good of race relations than anyone else." He called CURE's writing to the Holy Father a "vicious, impertinent" attack and said that CURE's "public statement contributed to the unrest."

Father Knight, whose parish was in the eye of the racial hurricane but did not sustain any damage, said that even the black leaders were terrified by the riots. He said "the good Negro is perturbed about it and wants no part of it." He added the rioting had nothing to do with race troubles when it began and that it had "absolutely nothing to do" with the cardinal's earlier stand on civil rights. He said the Catholic Negro community in Watts has been "very respectful to the Church and Cardinal here," as evidenced by the fact that none of the Catholic churches, schools or hospitals in the area had been damaged. Park Hospital, a public institution, was attacked by a mob and National Guardsmen had to be called to aid police quell the rioting, arson and looting. Knight said the rioting began with a gang of hoodlums and then mushroomed and leaped to other areas.[72]

Another priest told reporters that "repeating the argument that the Negroes are underprivileged continued until finally they believed it and took unnecessary and drastic action." Father Anthony Harris of St. Lawrence Brindisi said that "civil rights might have figured into the beginning of it all" but "after it got started, it wasn't a race riot at all." He said it became just a mob excitement, largely among young people.[73]

Father Knight wrote a letter to the editor of the *National Catholic Reporter* complaining that the paper had "quoted and misquoted" him and asking that his views on the whole issue of the Watts Riot be published for the record. Therein, he pointed out that when the irresponsible element among the colored population take the law into their own hands, it is manifestly unfair to blame the colored population as a whole." He observed that "the consciousness of Our God given dignity as human beings is a far stronger bond of unity than any distinction of color, race or social position." He believed it was "the function of the whole Church, ministering through its parishes and schools, to teach these bonds of unity and to condemn criminality among ALL people. To this end, the Archbishop of Los Angeles has exercised his genius and his love for God to provide parishes and school and the priests and sisters to staff them. Through these dedicated people teaching in ALL parts of the Archdiocese, Cardinal McIntyre has done more for the good of race relations than any one else. Part of the cardinal's campaign to assist in good relations between all peoples has been to build churches and schools in areas where people could not afford them. This is made possible by those who can better afford it giving to those who are less fortunate financially but equally fortunate in their human and Christian dignity. The cardinal, in his foresight, has been doing this for the past 20 years. There are those who have recently jumped on the racial band wagon and attacked the cardinal's policy, seemingly unaware that the one thing agreed upon by all in this complicated problem, is the necessity for the education of ALL people in the human dignity of ALL Men." Father Knight concluded his lengthy letter by suggesting that the newspaper should do some soul searching: "Is it possible that through giving undue publicity which is indicative of disrespect for legitimate authority, they have in some way contributed to the lawlessness that has been prevalent in Los Angeles? Is it possible that through NOT publicizing that which is constructive, they have contributed to that which is destructive? Is it possible that a desire for the novel and sensational has prevailed a desire for the truth?" To Knight's question, the editor replied that "it's possible."[74]

The cardinal regarded the rioting in Watts as a genuine tragedy for the whole community, a tragedy that affected citizens of every race and creed. He was distressed that a wrongful and distorted image of the city had been projected across the nation and around the world. That such a situation could happen was a startling reminder of the narrow line dividing an ordered society and anarchy. Acknowledging that there were wrongs and injustices in Los Angeles as indeed there were in most large cities of the nation, McIntyre had worked hard over the years to insure that every single Catholic in his jurisdiction worked within the proper framework and established legal process in solving problems.

In an editorial for *The Tidings*, Msgr. Patrick Roche noted that "the theory of non-violent demonstration, accompanied by the proclamation that one's conscience supersedes the law, has proved a dangerous antidote to prescribe for a social malady whose roots are long and deep." He felt that the rioting was "a hard-core enterprise, skillfully directed and catching up in its grip a number of criminal elements, arsonists and loot-seekers." Roche saw no evidence to support the contention that the incident was caused "by the economic and social oppression" of the black people. "Too often has the charge been made, by eager zealots more addicted to publicity than to facts, that this is a segregated city. Statistics speak otherwise." Roche quoted a survey of sixty-eight major U.S. cities made by the National Urban League in November of 1964 which found that "living standards of Negro families in the Los Angeles area are the highest in the nation. The study disclosed that in major population centers Los Angeles Negroes led the country in: a) percentage of acceptable housing, both rental and owner-occupied; b) percentage of skilled, professional or other white collar employment; c) median family income."

The survey went on to reveal that black ownership was at its best in Los Angeles. Of the 70,942 owner-occupied housing units here, 92 percent were declared sound by the government, upon whose investigations the Urban League relied in its survey. The survey found 19,447 substandard Negro renter-occupied housing in Los Angeles. Those 19,447 units constitute but 19 percent of the total Negro renter-occupied housing in Los Angeles - the smallest percent in the 68 cities surveyed. Moreover, Los Angeles, along with Gary-Hammond, Indiana, ranked at the lowest point in the scale of the survey for the number of Negro families living on "poverty" incomes. The Urban League based its "poverty" designation on an income of $3,000 or less per year, and placed middle-class status at an income level of $6,000 per year.

Given such statistics, Roche felt that "rebellion born of poverty" could not be alleged as the root cause of the riots. He concluded by saying that "essentially, painful though it may be to admit, it was a spirit of incredible lawlessness which brought about the disaster of riot in Los Angeles. According to the annual FBI national crime reports, this is a spirit growing apace throughout the whole land. And it was focused with terrible intensity here in our city."[75]

An editorial in the Miami *Voice* pretty much agreed with Roche's views, saying that "the nation makes a mistake if it regards what is happening in California as a racial demonstration. It isn't. It is a piece of violence which is savagely lawless, and which amounts to an open insurrection against all law and order. People who kill, who burn homes and stores and cars, who loot, and steal and terrorize a city, are not racial leaders in any sense of the word. They are simply criminals and should be dealt with as criminals."[76]

Theodore H. White, the prominent historian and commentator on the American scene, wrote an essay for the Los Angeles *Times* in which he came to much the same conclusions. He pointed out that per capita income for Negroes in Los Angeles was higher than for any other Negro community in the country. Crime was lower, as was welfare. Illegitimacy rates, though high, trailed the terrifying rates of the East. He went on to note that the mayor had been elected with substantial Negro votes, and the governor was a recognized champion for Negro rights. The police commission had a Negro member and the city council had three members which meant it was over represented statistically. He faulted, as did others, the role and control of radio and television, noting that coverage, "masterpiece of visual instant reportage," tended to exaggerate reports of sniping and killing, both of which added to white panic. Saying that "in Los Angeles there exists the most politically successful Negro community in the land." White wondered if "we must start all over again in our thinking."[77]

The conclusions of the governor's commission on the Los Angeles Riots, commonly referred to as the *McCone Report*, was issued December 7, 1965. It was a succinct, compact and to-the-point report containing no evidence of partiality. The report emphasized that human life must involve an acceptance of obligations as well as a demand for rights. It pointed out the peril of a developing pattern of unpunished violence and disobedience to law throughout the nation, and the explosive character "of exhortations, here and elsewhere, to take the most extreme and even illegal remedies to right a wide variety of wrongs, real and supposed."

It evaluated the philosophy underlying many current welfare and social service programs and found it defective because "a truly successful welfare program must whenever feasible, create an initiative and an incentive on the part of the recipients to become independent of state assistance. Otherwise, the welfare program promotes an attitude of hopelessness and permanent dependence." Besides the solid philosophy which the commission report provides, it also furnishes statistical evidence of the social health of Los Angeles. Despite allegations of superficial academic critics, often far removed from the local scene, Los Angeles has been a generous and receptive haven for so-called minority groups, both Afro-American and Mexican-American.

The report noted that within the period of 1940 to 1965, while the county's population was trebled, the Negro population had increased almost tenfold, from 75,000 to 650,000. That this assimilation had taken place over that period along normal and peaceful patterns is an accolade to the community itself and to all the varied racial and ethnic groups which comprise it. "The opportunity to succeed," the report stated "is probably unequaled in any other American city." Moreover, only about two percent of the entire Negro population were involved in the August disorders. That itself, is a testimony to the healthy pattern of assimilation, as well as a tribute to the character of our fellow citizens of the Negro race.[78]

McIntyre never denied that there were racial overtones in Watts riots. That would have been like denying that slavery was an issue in the Civil War. The riots erupted in a depressed, heavily black area. Yet the racial aspect was only a secondary, albeit important issue.

In the fall of 1965, the Los Angeles Urban League and the Archdiocese of Los Angeles entered into an arrangement to establish an employment program for people living in the riot area. Parishes throughout the four county archdiocese were asked to participate in providing "leads" for the Job Finding Bureau which operated out of the Catholic Charities building in downtown Los Angeles. The cardinal sent a letter describing the operation to all pastors and administrators, explaining the need for relieving unemployment. In announcing this innovative program, Wesley R. Brazier, executive director for the Urban League, commended McIntyre "for a very practical plan to assist people in the riot area."[79]

In mid 1966, a specially formed committee of priests working in the Watts area met for discussion and consultation. They were men of experience, sensitivity and proven zeal who knew first hand the cultural climate and social circumstances of the area. Following their meeting, the committee issued a statement expressing their common concern and embodying certain recommendations flowing from their gathering. So impressed was Cardinal McIntyre that he directed that their statement be printed in *The Tidings*.

The recurring acts of violence in the south Central and south Eastern section of the Los Angeles area are a source of deep concern to us who are committed to the spiritual welfare and guidance of the people of this area. Therefore, we, the Pastors of the Catholic churches located here, feel it appropriate that we express our reactions to the problems involved in this situation, in the hope that our collective experience may direct some light as to their solution.

It is our conviction that an extremely small percentage of the residents are guilty of any participation in these acts. The members of our congregation and many others with whom we have discussed the matter deplore the attacks on persons and property by a small number of people who do not represent the large body of responsible and conscientious members of our community.

We do not minimize or overlook the unfortunate social and economic conditions which are a contributing factor to the incidents in question, and we support all constructive efforts to alleviate these conditions.

We are aware of the feeling of distrust which exists between many of the residents and law enforcement personnel. We support and encourage all activities aimed toward better understanding, confidence and cooperation, and which will help eliminate tension-producing fear on both sides because fear can so easily spark regrettable incidents.

We feel that it is urgent that everyone in a position of responsibility, all leaders, and those aspiring to leadership, use the utmost restraint and prudence in public statements in order to avoid provoking tempers that are already too much on edge. The same caution should be observed with regard to statements which seem to attribute to a whole community or ethnic group responsibility for actions of a few.

It is well known that in times of unrest and tension exaggerated and sensational publicity given to violent acts excites some others to follow a pattern of lawlessness. Another result can be an erroneous estimate by the public of the gravity of the situation, leading to unfortunate and unwarranted reactions.

It seems to us most necessary, therefore, that all communications media exercise the highest degree of editorial responsibility in this matter, lest they should unintentionally fan the flames of human emotions and increase tension and violence.

Finally it is our fervent hope and prayer that all people will increasingly come to look on their fellow men as brothers, without regard to race, color or religion. This bond of brotherly love, uniting men as children of God, will eliminate fear and distrust, and bring all of us to work in harmony for the solution the problems that are troubling our city and county.[80]

It was indeed ironical that James Francis Cardinal McIntyre was criticized in certain quarters for his policies and views towards black people, for whom he always exhibited concern and love. He had known discrimination first hand, even before his native Harlem turned black. He had been all the things excoriated by the Ku Klux Klan: he was Irish, he was Catholic and he was poor. Yet, in his long life in the ministry, McIntyre probably did more to alleviate the causes of poverty than any other single American churchman by developing the largest parochial system in the nation, where all youngsters were welcomed, irrespective of race, color or social status.

The cardinal subscribed to the theological teachings of Father Raymond A. Tartre, National Director of the Priests Eucharistic League, who said that "the average Catholic layman wants and begs from the Church that it should enunciate and elucidate the principles of Christ, and point out with vigor their application to existing conditions, without its representatives becoming personally involved on the pragmatic level." Tartre felt that "the layman knows instinctively that the priest's place is not at political caucuses or on social band wagons. The Catholic layman wants the priest to form him for Christian leadership that he may be equipped with true knowledge of Christ's teaching. Then he, the layman, will go and mix up with godless socialists, the purveyors of immortality, the proponents of gross injustice and others of that ilk."[81]

McIntyre believed that the problem was not whether or not the church should be committed to the building of the social structure, but to what extent, to what degree and in which areas the Church must be involved in order to exercise its beneficent influence. McIntyre saw his role and that of his brother priests as leading the laity to a fuller understanding of their specific role as Christian witnesses to the world; an objective he felt was most fully realized through a religious-oriented school system available to all Catholics everywhere.

Notes to the Text

1. Los Angeles *Herald-Examiner*, August 24, 1964. This statement alone gives life to unfounded charges by such people as John Donovan that "McIntyre seems to have some racist attitudes." See "Cardinal McIntyre and Race Relations in Los Angeles in the 1960s," *Perspectives* XVIII (1991), 43.
2. *Pacem in Terris* (New York, 1963), 25.
3. *Newsweek*, LXV (January 11, 1965), 57.
4. *Rerum Novarum* (New York, 1939), 6.
5. Francis Canavan, "Conscience and Pluralism," *America* CX (April 18, 1964), 539.
6. San Francisco *Monitor*, November 12, 1964.
7. Joseph R. Thomas in the Newark *Advocate*, July 9. 1964.
8. *The Tidings*, July 31, 1964.
9. Cf. The *Commonweal* LXXX (July 10, 1964), 477-482.
10. *National Catholic Reporter*, November 18, 1964.
11. Los Angeles *Times*, June 28, 1964.
12. Alice Ogle in *National Catholic Reporter*, November 25, 1964.
13. Such accusations were actually made by A.V. Krebs, Jr., in "A Church of Silence," *Commonweal* LXXX (July 10, 1964), 467-476.
14. In an advertisement in *The Reporter* XXX (October 22, 1964), 55; the words are, of course, the slogan of John Wilkes Booth and the motto of the State of Virginia.
15. Georgia *Bulletin*, October 29, 1964.
16. *Ave Maria* C (September 19, 1964), 16.
17. Hollywood *Citizen News*, June 17, 1964.
18. *Ecclesiam Suam*.
19. San Francisco *Monitor*, June 26, 1964.
20. Neils J. Anderson, "Proposition 14 and the Liturgy," *America* CXI (November 21, 1964), 658.
21. *National Catholic Reporter*, November 4, 1964.
22. San Jose *Mercury*, September 10, 1964.
23. San Jose *News*, October 1964.
24. Los Angeles *Herald-Examiner*, July 28, 1964.
25. Camden *Star Herald*, November 13, 1964.
26. *The Commonweal* XC (November 20, 1964), 266-267.
27. The verified count by the Secretary of State gave 4,526,460 votes in favor of the amendment and 2,395,747 against.

28. Statement of September 28, 1964, mailed out under the letterhead of the University of San Francisco Theological Faculty.
29. *The Monitor*, November 12, 1964.
30. Statement of the Reverend Nathaniel Lacy, quoted in *The Monitor*, July 17, 1964.
31. *The Catholic Church and the Race Question* (Paris, 1953), p. 49.
32. According to the report, printed in the Los Angeles *Herald-Examiner*, November 29, 1964, Los Angeles ranked with Gary-Hammond (Ind.) at the bottom of the scale in a survey concerned with Negro families living on poverty incomes.
33. Los Angeles *Times*, November 7, 1964.
34. On May 16, 1966, the California State Supreme Court declared Proposition 14 unconstitutional by a vote of 5-2.
35. *Commonweal* XC (July 10, 1964), 474.
36. *King's Pawn* (Chicago, 1990), p. 211.
37. AALA, Statement by Sue Welsh, Los Angeles, July 19, 1963.
38. AALA, "What does C.U.R.E. Want?", no date.
39. AALA, James Francis Cardinal McIntyre to Sue Welsh *et al.*, Los Angeles, July 21, 1963.
40. AALA, James Francis Cardinal McIntyre to Anne Reher, Los Angeles, July 23, 1963.
41. Los Angeles *Herald-Examiner*, July 28, 1963.
42. Los Angeles *Times*, July 28, 1963.
43. This is nonsense. This writer wrote an article on "The California Bishops and Proposition 14" which appeared in *Front Line* III (Spring, 1965), 176-184.
44. AALA, Open Letter to the Bishops of the United States, n.p., September 9, 1965.
45. *National Catholic Reporter*, September 22, 1965.
46. September 16, 1965.
47. AALA, Western Union Telefax, James Francis Cardinal McIntyre to Francis Quinn, Los Angeles, September 26, 1965.
48. AALA, James Francis Cardinal McIntyre to Joseph T. McGucken, Los Angeles, September 21 1965.
49. AALA, Francis Quinn to James Francis Cardinal McIntyre, San Francisco, September 22, 1965.
50. *The Monitor*, September 23, 1965.
51. AALA, Egidio Vagnozzi to James Francis Cardinal McIntyre, Washington, D.C., September 23, 1965
52. AALA, Joseph T. McGucken, to Francis Quinn, Rome, September 28, 1965.
53. AALA, Bishop Floyd Begin to James Francis Cardinal McIntyre, Oakland, September 22, 1965.

54. AALA, Memorandum by James Francis Cardinal McIntyre, Los Angeles, September 22, 1965.
55. AALA, Thomas Blew to James Francis Cardinal McIntyre, San Francisco, n.d.
56. AALA, Francis Quinn to John K. Ford, San Francisco, September 30, 1965.
57. AALA, Undated brochure.
58. AALA, James Francis Cardinal McIntyre to Egidio Vagnozzi, Los Angeles, September 10, 1965.
59. Francis J. Weber, *Vignettes of California Catholicism* (Los Angeles, 1988), p.295.
60. *Viz.*, Father Joseph Francis, S.V.D., later Auxiliary Bishop of Newark, *The Tablet*, June 11, 1964.
61. *Southern Cross*, July 9, 1964.
62. Los Angeles *Times*, July 3, 1964.
63. *Ibid.*, July 4, 1964.
64. AALA, Edmund G. Brown, to James Francis Cardinal McIntyre, Sacramento, July 3, 1964.
65. "The Honey and Vinegar in Tomorrowland," *The Sign* XXXIV (December, 1964), 79.
66. Los Angeles *Times*, April 6, 1968.
67. *Ibid.*, August 14, 1965. The statement was repeated in its entirety in *The Tidings* for August 20, 1965.
68. August 19, 1965.
69. *Ibid.*,
70. August 20, 1965.
71. *The Catholic Messenger*, August 26, 1965.
72. Cleveland *Catholic Universe Bulletin*, August 20, 1965.
73. *The Tidings*, August 20, 1965.
74. *National Catholic Reporter*, September 8, 1965.
75. January 7, 1966.
76. August 20, 1965.
77. August 22, 1965.
78. For the full text, see *The Tidings*, January 7, 1966.
79. *Ibid.*, October 22, 1966.
80. June 10, 1966.
81. "The Church and Social Movements," *Emmanuel* LXXI (July-August, 1965), p. 293.

23. Advice, Advisors and Friends

C ontrary to popular myth, McIntyre rarely acted unilaterally on any issue. He had a wide and assorted group of collaborators whose advice he sought on all the major decisions of his tenure. Chief among his advisors was the Board of Consultors for the Archdiocese of Los Angeles, composed of as many as eighteen members. They met at least monthly for all day sessions and the minutes of those gatherings, filling no fewer than thirty-one bound volumes, are available to researchers at the archdiocesan Archival Center in Mission Hills.

Customarily, Cardinal McIntyre would appoint committees for all the major issues and challenges of the time and he would insist that formal reports be submitted in writing to the Board of Consultors. There were no secrets or clandestine meetings and even the most sensitive topics were submitted to those knowledgeable in the field.

The corporate process used by the cardinal allowed and encouraged input from every level of the curial offices. He insisted on being informed on all issues, but rarely reversed or even questioned recommendations made at a lower level. It is historically ironical that the churchman who pioneered so many contemporary chancery procedures has never been recognized for his managerial and collegial skills. Even his antagonist, John Cardinal Dearden, admitted at his funeral that "McIntyre wrote the book on modern curial activity."

Unlike less secure leaders, McIntyre was never intimidated when subordinates were singled out for recognition. He not only tolerated but encouraged his confreres to excel in their work for the Lord and he rejoiced at their success. An example would be his relationship with his auxiliary, Bishop Timothy Manning, who was acknowledged to be among the finest speakers in the American hierarchy. The cardinal never felt any celebration was complete unless Manning spoke. His usual suggestion was: "I'll preside, you speak." And he was always solicitous to see that the archdiocesan newspaper got the texts of Manning's talks.

In addition to the Board of Consultors and the several other bodies of official advisors, there were people that McIntyre relied on for their special expertise. Mentioned here alphabetically are some of those who wandered in and out of the cardinal's life between 1948 and 1970.

MSGR. ANTHONY J. BROUWERS

The memory of Msgr. Anthony J. Brouwers (1912-1964) remains very much alive, especially among the Lay Mission Helpers. Born in Los Angeles, young "Tony" Brouwers attended Sacred Heart Parochial School, Cathedral High and Los Angeles College. He was ordained a priest in Rome on December 8, 1938. A few years later, he was appointed to the archdiocesan matrimonial curia. In 1947, he became secretary to the then Bishop Timothy Manning and the following year, he was named director for the Propagation of the Faith.

Always a popular speaker, the energetic young priest was a favorite of young and old alike. In 1950, he established the Saint Vibiana's Guild to encourage and train aspiring artists. Five years later, the far-sighted priest "began one of the most advanced and visionary developments in the Church"[1] with his establishment of the Lay Mission Helpers, a group of people who volunteered to serve a minimum of three years in the missionary outreach of the Church. The next year, he founded the Mission Doctors for the same purpose. Since the first departure ceremony on July 4, 1956, several thousand people have been sent to the missions, all because a dynamic priest had the courage to pursue a dream.

Honored by two pontiffs, Brouwers was made a papal chamberlain by Pope Pius XII in 1950 and a domestic prelate by Pope John XXIII in 1959. The Papal Volunteer program inaugurated by the Holy See was modeled in great part on the program developed in Los Angeles. The monsignor was active in a host of other projects too. And somehow he found time to administer the busy, inner city parish of Saint Paul between 1959 and 1964. Monsignor Brouwers made four extended tours of the African continent to determine the needs of the missions there and to visit the Lay Mission Helpers already at work in that huge area. He authored a weekly column, "Mission Chats," for *The Tidings* where he kept alive the spiritual and physical challenges of the missions.

His final missionary labor was on the frontier of suffering. Though stricken with spinal cancer in his last years, he never slackened his pace or lessened his enthusiasm. As mentioned in an editorial by

Alphonse Antczak in *The Tidings*, "it should not be forgotten that there was a holy man here named Anthony Brouwers. *Que en paz desance.*"

ASA VICKERY CALL

Probably McIntyre's closest friend and advisor was Asa Vickery Call (1892-1974), honorary chairman of the board for Pacific Mutual Life Insurance Company. Born in his parents' home on the corner of Pico Boulevard and Hill Street, Asa attended Polytechnic High School and the University of Southern California Law School.[2]

Starting as a lawyer in private practice, he went to work for Pacific Mutual Life in 1933, where he became president a decade later. He led that company into becoming one of the country's biggest and healthiest underwriters. He also served on the boards of Standard Oil of California, North American Aviation, Southern California Edison and the Stanford Research Institute. He also served a term as president and director of the Automobile Club of Southern California.

Politicians and corporate executives trusted Call for his directness, energy and lack of pretense. He became a leader, spokesman and powerful broker in the city's highest echelons. He helped to organize such important projects as the Los Angeles Civic Center complex, the Music Center, the California Water Project and the McCone Commission. Even "those who opposed him on specific issues came to like him, to trust his integrity and respect his effectiveness in politics."[3]

Call was exceedingly gracious with his time and talent for the Archdiocese of Los Angeles and Cardinal McIntyre made few major decisions without running them past Mr. Call. In 1967, he was one of the first non-Catholics named a Knight of Saint Gregory by Pope Paul VI.

MSGR. JOHN J. CAWLEY

Msgr. John J. Cawley (1882-1953) served as Vicar General for the Archdiocese of Los Angeles and its predecessor jurisdictions longer than any other person, a total of twenty-nine years. Born in Ireland's County Sligo, Cawley was educated at Maynooth College and ordained to the priesthood in 1906. During his earliest years in the ministry, he taught at Saint Nathy's College and, later, at Maynooth. He came to the Diocese of Monterey-Los Angeles in 1909 and served in positions in Los Angeles and Watsonville until 1917 when he was appointed chancellor and secretary to Bishop John J. Cantwell. He was made a monsignor in 1920.[4]

During his many years as Rector of Saint Vibiana's Cathedral and Vicar General, Cawley's name was often mentioned as a candidate for the bishopric. But, as was the common talk among clergy of earlier times, he preferred remaining in his role as assistant to Cantwell. When McIntyre came to Los Angeles, one of his first actions was that of confirming Cawley in his dual leadership role. Early on, McIntyre recognized Cawley for what he always was, a churchman, one who lived and breathed only for the service of God's people. Fittingly, he died enroute from the Eternal City after witnessing the Archbishop of Los Angeles being enrolled in the Sacred College of Cardinals. Speaking at his funeral, the cardinal said that "our hearts are melted with grief that the Lord has seen fit to take to his reward the pastor of our cathedral."[5] Interestingly, Cawley had been scheduled to speak from that very pulpit, welcoming McIntyre back to his Southern California.

CARRIE ESTELLE DOHENY

One of the most interesting and generous persons in McIntyre's coterie of friends was Carrie Estelle Doheny (1875-1958) who lived in a magnificent home at #8 Chester Place in Los Angeles. Known as a woman of vivid personality and irresistible charm, Mrs. Edward L. Doheny was endowed with that buoyant vitality, quick mind and grasp of practical affairs discernible only in personalities deeply etched in the chronicles of history.

Born in Philadelphia on the Feast of Our Lady of the Angels, August 2, 1875, Carrie spent her earliest years in Marshalltown, Iowa, coming to Los Angeles in 1897. With her marriage at Albuquerque to Edward L. Doheny, on August 22, 1900, she rose, as only a rarely gifted woman could have done, to the opportunities open to her as the wife of a man of wealth. During the years of her wedded life, Carrie Doheny traveled widely with her husband. She reached the high noon of her long life on October 25, 1918, when Bishop Joseph S. Glass of Salt Lake received her into the Catholic Church in New York's Saint Patrick's Cathedral.

In 1930, when Mr. Doheny's health began to fail, the couple settled down to a quieter life at their home in Chester Place, a park-like estate near the corner of Adams Boulevard and Figueroa Street in Los Angeles. Mrs. Doheny carried on her husband's philanthropic activities after his death. Among other institutions benefiting from her generosity were the Los Angeles Orphanage, the Orthopedic and Children's Hospital, Saint Vincent's Seminary and the Vincentian House of Studies in Washington, D.C. In 1956, she erected a five-story building to house the constantly expanding Estelle Doheny Eye Foundation of Saint Vincent's Hospital. In 1940, in memory of her late husband, Mrs. Doheny erected a magnificent library at Camarillo, adjacent to Saint John's Seminary. The top floor of the edifice was set aside for the rare books, manuscripts and works of art known throughout the world as the "Estelle Doheny Collection. "

Besides the Carrie Estelle Doheny Foundation, established in 1949 for the advancement of education, medicine, religion and science, Mrs. Doheny engaged in countless personal charities, unknown, unheralded, and sometimes unappreciated. Recognition of her many charitable activities came on June 29, 1939, when Pope Pius XII conferred upon her the title of papal countess, the first such bestowal of pontifical nobility ever granted in Southern California. Some years later she was named "Woman of the Year" by the Los Angeles *Times*. She discussed all her benefactions with McIntyre and never made a decision without his approval and benediction.

Though she was forced to spend the last seventeen years of her life in a world dimmed by glaucoma, Carrie Doheny remained a vital, magnetic woman whose sparkling brown eyes and radiant smile were the outward expression of a warm and generous heart. With the death of Mrs. Doheny, it could truly be said, "Her true riches were not the material wealth which was forced upon her, but the eternal, unchanging treasures of fortitude, wisdom, unselfish devotion to those she loved, and a radiant joy in serving God with her whole heart."[6]

MSGR. BERNARD J. DOLAN

The "institutional memory" for the Archdiocese of Los Angeles, Bernard J. Dolan (1890-1968), knew the terrain, clergy, religious and laity of the area like few others. He was a valued and treasured member of McIntyre's inner circle.

A native of Ireland, he was raised in Worcester, Massachusetts. After studies at Holy Cross College, he became a clerical candidate for the Diocese of Monterey-Los Angeles. He was ordained by the legendary James Cardinal Gibbons at Baltimore's cathedral in 1919.

Father Dolan served as pastor of Saint Joseph's, La Puente, until 1923 when he was appointed secretary to Bishop John J. Cantwell. A year later, he became chancellor, a post he occupied until 1938 when he was entrusted with the pastorate of Saint Anthony's in

Long Beach. He was named papal chamberlain in 1932 and advanced to the domestic prelacy in 1937. He was made a Protonotary Apostolic in 1954.

Dolan was noted for his speaking skills, preaching at the episcopal consecrations of Stephen Alencastre (1924), Thomas K. Gorman (1931), Joseph T. McGucken (1941) and Alden J. Bell (1956). He served in a multitude of positions in the archdiocese and was a consultor for many years. Bishop Timothy Manning eulogized him as "above all, a parish priest."[7]

DANIEL J. DONOHUE

Because his father had known and studied at Fordham University with Francis J. Spellman, who later became Archbishop of New York, Daniel J. Donohue (b. 1919) was personally acquainted with many members of the American hierarchy, including Archbishop J. Francis A. McIntyre before he came to Los Angeles.

Born at Jersey City, Daniel studied philosophy at the Catholic University of America. He later became affiliated with the Hospitaller Brothers of Saint John of God at their foundation in Los Angeles. Subsequently he left the Brothers and entered the diocesan seminary in San Diego. After serving on the staff of Bishop Charles F. Buddy, Daniel decided that his vocation would find its maximum fulfillment outside the ministry.

Daniel had known Bernardine Murphy since 1940, when she came regularly to visit the Brothers at their residence in Los Angeles. On several occasions, he had advised her about benefactions to charitable organizations. Their relationship grew closer in the months after he left San Diego and, on January 16, 1954, they were married at a ceremony witnessed by James Francis Cardinal McIntyre in the archiepiscopal chapel in Fremont Place.

In 1957, the Donohues established the Dan Murphy Foundation, a charitable trust funded by the Murphy fortune which had been accumulated from various sources, including California Portland Cement. With first Bernardine and later Daniel Donohue as Chairman of the Board, the Dan Murphy Foundation has been active in supporting charities, mostly those associated with the universal apostolate of the Roman Catholic Church.

After Bernardine's sudden and unexpected death on March 5, 1968, Daniel continued the traditions of charity inaugurated by his wife. Personally and through his position as chair of the Dan

Murphy Foundation, he was the most generous benefactor to the Archdiocese of Los Angeles during McIntyre's time.

WILL DURANT

One of the cardinal's oldest friends was a man who had been excommunicated by the Catholic Church, something that was never mentioned in their relationship. *Time* magazine conferred the ultimate honor upon Will Durant (1885-1981) when it described him as the "Biographer of Mankind." Indeed he was that and more - he signed one of his last letters as "another lover of Christ."

A graduate of Saint Peter's College, Massachusetts-born Durant studied at Seton Hall Divinity School. Shortly after leaving the seminary, the young philosopher drifted away from the Church. In later years, Durant claimed that his estrangement from the Church was all Spinoza's fault. Having read *Ethics*, he had allowed himself to be overly influenced by the 17th century pantheist. In January of 1912, Will was formally excommunicated by Bishop John J. O'Connor of Newark. *The Evening News* reported on that occasion that "no Catholic should henceforth associate with him in any avoidable way." The following year, Will met Ida Kaufman, whom he referred to as "Ariel" after the imp in Shakespeare's "The Tempest. " The two were married soon thereafter, a union that lasted for sixty-eight years.

Though trained as a philosopher, Durant spent most of his life writing *The Story of Civilization*, an eleven volume series that propelled the author into almost all the world's major libraries and research centers. The masterful series, written in collaboration with Ariel, chronicled 10,000 years and sold more than two million copies. Volume Ten on "Rousseau and Revolution" won the coveted Pulitzer Prize.

Though Will remained outside the Catholic fold, he had a love and affection for the Church which surfaced in his later writings. He admitted, for example, in *The Lessons of History*, published in 1968, that "even the skeptical historian develops a humble respect for religion, since he sees it functioning and seemingly indispensable, in every land and age."[8] In another place, he noted that "Catholicism survives because it appeals to imagination, hope and the senses; because its mythology consoles and brightens the lives of the poor; and because the commanded fertility of the faithful slowly regains the lands lost to the Reformation."

McIntyre had gotten to know Will and his wife through the intervention of Dr. James W. Fifield. On one occasion, at a private luncheon given for the Durants at the Townhouse on Wilshire

Boulevard, McIntyre publicly referred to Durant as his "favorite historian. " Over the years, Durant also remained in contact with a number of Jesuits, including Father Herbert Ryan, the stepson of his sister, Ethel. It was Father Ryan who reconciled the famed historian to the Church prior to his death on November 7, 1981. "Civilization," Durant once observed, "is a stream with banks." Most historians, he thought, concentrate on the stream, "which is sometimes filled with blood from people killing, stealing, shouting." Durant was devoted to what happened on the banks. There, "unnoticed, people build homes, make love, raise children, sing songs, write poetry, whittle statues" or write about it all.

DR. JAMES W. FIFIELD, JR.

During his thirty-two years as Pastor of the First Congregational Church of Los Angeles, Dr. James W. Fifield, Jr. (1899-1977) became one of the truly significant figures in American Protestantism. Born in Chicago, he studied at Oberlin College, the University of Chicago and the Chicago Theological Seminary. Ordained a Congregationalist minister in 1924, Dr. Fifield served at various pastorates before coming to Los Angeles in 1934.

Bishop John J. Cantwell encouraged Fifield to accept the pastorate of the First Congregational Church and the two religious leaders forged a friendship that lasted for many years. By 1942, the impressive Gothic church on Commonwealth Avenue had become the largest Congregational fellowship in the world, with 4,317 registered members and over 20,000 parishioners.

In 1959, Fifield established The Freedom Club movement which rapidly spread nationwide. His radio program was aired over 600 stations and his television appearances were featured on forty channels around the country. In addition to numerous books, Dr. Fifield wrote a weekly column for the Los Angeles *Times* which, in syndication format, reached over eight and a half million readers. By the 1950s, Fifield was easily the most outstanding Protestant leader in Southern California.

Back-to-back neighbors in Fremont Place, Fifield and McIntyre often took evening strolls together during which they discussed the major challenges facing religion and religious leaders during those years. At that time, Fifield was the most prominent and outspoken Protestant leader in Los Angeles and it is historically significant that they were such close friends and confidants, a relationship that spilled over many times into the public arena.

500

MSGR. BENJAMIN G. HAWKES

McIntyre's closest priestly collaborator and confidant was Msgr. Benjamin G. Hawkes (1919-1985) who served the cardinal successively as secretary, chancellor and vicar general. Born in Lakeport, New York, Benjamin George Hawkes acquired his earliest religious training at Saint Vincent's School in Buffalo. Later, his parents and older brother, William, moved to Los Angeles, and Benjamin completed his primary education at Immaculate Heart of Mary in Hollywood

In 1932, he enrolled at Los Angeles College, the preparatory seminary for the Diocese of Los Angeles-San Diego. Upon graduating, he entered Loyola University, where he majored in economics. In 1940, he joined the staff of Lockheed Aircraft Company and there he rapidly advanced in the accounting department to the position of steward. At the end of World War II, Benjamin sought out the advice of Fathers Vincent Lloyd-Russell and Charles Casassa and then decided to complete his theological studies at Saint John's Seminary as a clerical candidate for the Archdiocese of Los Angeles. He was ordained priest on April 26, 1950.

After two years as a curate at Saint Michael's Parish in central Los Angeles, Father Hawkes was named secretary to Archbishop J. Francis A. McIntyre. Early the following year, he accompanied the archbishop to Rome for his formal investiture as the first American cardinal of the far west. During the following thirty-three years, Msgr. Hawkes served in the curial offices of the archdiocese as secretary (1952-1962), Chancellor (1962-1967), and Vicar General (1967-1985). He was also active in other areas as a Board Member for the Dan Murphy Foundation, a trustee for The Catholic University of America and Vicar Delegate for the Military Ordinariate.

In 1965, Msgr. Hawkes began his long association with Saint Basil's parish, first as consultant for the new church and, from 1969 onwards, as canonical pastor. The completed Saint Basil's was aptly described by the Mayor of Los Angeles as "one of the most significant examples of contemporary church architecture in the world."

In his penetrating study "Inside the Power Structure of the American Catholic Church," Jesuit Thomas J. Reese explains how the McIntyre influence stretched beyond his own tenure into that of his successor, Timothy Manning. By carefully considered design, Manning, who cared little for administrative duties, designated Hawkes to act as his Vicar General for Finance or chief operating officer, a role in which Hawkes supervised and coordinated all archdiocesan agencies. While technically only in charge of finance, Reese pointed out that "since most things cost money, Hawkes exercised sweeping power in Los Angeles."[9] Though they held little affection for one another, Manning and Hawkes devised a working relationship that was unique and effective in American ecclesial annals. While everything related to finance and administration was completely entrusted to him, Hawkes did nothing of any magnitude without advising the archbishop before he did it.

In many ways, Hawkes was a clone of McIntyre. He believed, for example, that the haves should help the have-nots. He didn't feel that a suburban parish should have sixteen classrooms when an inner city parish couldn't afford eight. In his view, the archdiocese should come to the assistance of a new parish. He explained it this way: "When we start a new parish - we do one or two a year - the cardinal gives the parish the property. Then we build what we think the place and the location needs. That would be a rectory and a multipurpose building for a church. Half of the multipurpose building might provide four classrooms, but it could also be used for Sunday Masses. What it usually costs is $2 million and the archdiocese gives the parish up to $1 million. That is the only way the people can handle it. Five percent on $2 million is a large portion of your collection for interest."[10]

Always a realist, Hawkes frequently reminded pastors that no archdiocese has unlimited resources and many have very limited funds. He said that "a diocese can give to the People of God only what the People of God can pay for." Operating in the b.c. era (before computers), Hawkes knew more about the parishes of Los Angeles than could ever be put on a computer. He was a one man operation. After his retirement and death, he was replaced by a host of professionals who had to build a system from scratch. In an interview, Cardinal McIntyre casually referred to Msgr. Benjamin G. Hawkes as the archdiocesan "concert-master."

> The concert-master selects the programs, rehearses the orchestra and then steps aside for the conductor. The musicians often bristle at the concert-master's methods, but they all respect his ability to blend their individual efforts into soothing music.[11]

Although Monsignor Hawkes did not succeed McIntyre in title, he surely did in fact. With the blessings and encouragement of McIntyre's successor, Hawkes became the most powerful and influential ecclesial figure in Southern California throughout the Timothy Manning regime. By virtue of his shrewd managerial skills, he paid off the remaining indebtedness of McIntyre, financed the fifteen year tenure of Manning and stockpiled a treasury of well over $100 million dollars which made possible and still sustains many of the innovations inaugurated by Cardinal Roger Mahony.

FATHER WILLIAM J. KENNEALLY

Father William J. Kenneally, C.M. (1911-1977), rector of Saint John's Seminary during the tumultuous years of Vatican Council II, was a scripture scholar whose influence on McIntyre was obvious in many quarters. A native of Los Angeles and an alumnus of old Saint Vincent's College, Father Kenneally celebrated his first Mass in Saint Vincent's Church in 1933. He did graduate work at the Angelicum and Pontifical Biblical Institute in Rome, where he was a classmate and close friend of Karol Wojtyla who later became Pope John Paul II.

Having served as rector of Saint Thomas Seminary in Denver (1948-1957), Kenneally came to Camarillo as rector in 1958, a position to which he clung for nine years.[12] A captivating speaker and a convincing reactionary, Kenneally served as McIntyre's *peritus* at several sessions on the Vatican Council. Because the cardinal had little expertise in either scripture or theology, he usually accepted Kenneally's recommendations with little or no question. As one cleric suggested, "Kenneally's theology was only slightly less antiquated than his sources." He once conned the cardinal into preparing and delivering a talk on the priesthood from a copy of *Sancta Sophia, Or Holy Wisdom* published in 1906![13] He did not serve the cardinal well.

MSGR. THOMAS McCARTHY

A promising young priest who never really reached his ultimate potentially was Thomas McCarthy (1911-1978). In 1942, shortly after receiving a doctorate in psychology at the Catholic University of America, Father Thomas McCarthy was named editor of *The Tidings* by Archbishop John Cantwell. His facile mind quickly mastered the intricacies of journalism and, before long, the paper was achieving added local distinction and merited national acclaim.

McCarthy opened the pages of *The Tidings* to new columnists and fresh features that appealed to all levels of Catholic readership. He was once quoted as saying that "the essence of journalism is sensation on the wing." A scholar himself, McCarthy enlarged the paper's library and outlined procedures whereby staff members could study as they prepared their stories for publication. Each employee was encouraged to read a book every month. McCarthy's system worked too and, in 1945, a writer in the Los Angeles *Herald Express* said that "in its own specialized field, *The Tidings* has become one of the leading Catholic papers in the nation." Editorially, the paper kept abreast of the times. McIntyre was enamored of McCarthy and often noted that he was "the finest jewel I inherited when my predecessor went home to God." A man with a high sense of morality, McCarthy was easily outraged. He fearlessly waged personal feuds with such luminaries as Drew Pearson ("vicious slander and irresponsible smearing") and Louella Parsons ("cheap, meretricious twaddle") and with any other careless columnist who trod on the truth.

McCarthy's successor at *The Tidings* said that it was always his aim to give the paper proper proportion lest it merit Meneken's sophomoric jibe of a "dismal diocesan rag." And so, *The Tidings* became everybody's newspaper, with features for every member of every household, not alone an archdiocesan chronicle, but concerned as well with the momentous issues at home and abroad, in the turbulent years that have now passed. Msgr. William North went on to observe that McCarthy's pen "surveyed the contemporary scene with courage and conviction. It was slow to wrath except when Christian principles were openly affronted. Hedging was foreign to his resolute and independent mind. And integrity belonged to the essence of his character."

McCarthy early on entrusted the business affairs of the newspaper to Robert S. Labonge, a seasoned journalist who looked after the editorial department and Robert F. Nichols who became business manager. By the time of his retirement from the editorship, one writer said McCarthy had been "our most forceful spokesman" in every arena of public affairs. "And he has been to all a zealous, kindly priest; and to many, a fast and faithful friend."[14]

McCarthy remained at the helm until 1949, when, in the words of *Time* magazine, "the editor of the hard-hitting Los Angeles Catholic weekly, *The Tidings*, and .a leader among the younger, liberal element in the Church," was appointed director for the Bureau of Information attached to the National Catholic Welfare Conference in Washington. That McCarthy's tenure at *The Tidings* was successful is attested to by circulation figures which show that by mid-1949, there were no fewer than 42,495 subscribers to the paper.

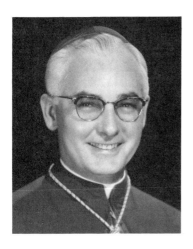

Auxiliary Bishop Alden J. Bell   *Msgr. John J. Cawley*

Msgr. John Clarke   *Msgr. John Devlin*

Msgr. Benjamin G. Hawkes

Msgr. Thomas McCarthy

Msgr. William R. North

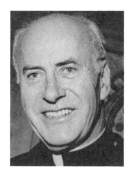

Msgr. Patrick Roche

Msgr. Thomas F. Fogarty

Auxiliary Bishop John J. Ward

MSGR. MARTIN McNICHOLAS

Martin McNicholas (1903-1967), born in Baltimore, Maryland, was raised in Ireland and received his early education at Saint Nathy's College (Ballaghadeneen) and Saint Patrick's College (Carlow). Completing his priestly studies at Saint Patrick's Seminary, Menlo Park, he was ordained in 1925 at Saint Vibiana's Cathedral by Archbishop Edward J. Hanna.

Father McNicholas did post graduate work at the Catholic University (Washington, D.C.) and Saint Apollinare (Rome), where he received a doctorate in Canon Law. Between 1931 and 1937, McNicholas served as archdiocesan superintendent of schools. He became pastor of Saint Anselm's parish in 1933 and, a dozen years later, crowned his pastoral accomplishments by building a church for Saint John the Evangelist parish that was considered one of the most modern in the nation. He was made a domestic prelate in 1943.[15]

That Msgr. McNicholas was an organizational genius was early recognized by McIntyre. He had conducted the first archdiocesan campaign for funds to build the major seminary in 1937 and in the years after 1949, he directed educational campaigns that financed the erection of over a hundred schools. His basic techniques for fund raising are still used and many consider him to be a pioneer in that important work.[16]

McNicholas was appointed Vicar for Religious in 1953, Vicar Delegate for the Military Ordinariate in 1955 and an archdiocesan consultor in 1956. He also worked in the matrimonial tribunal and was moderator of the annual clergy conferences.

MARY YOUNG MOORE

McIntyre had known Mary Young Moore in New York and, after arriving in Los Angeles, he visited her several times a year. Born in Immaculate Conception parish in Los Angeles on November 7, 1882, the daughter of Robert B. and Mary C. (Wilson) Young, she was raised in the south central area of the city. Miss Young studied at the old Immaculate Heart College and was later active in the National Conference of Catholic Charities where she befriended Father William Corr. She was a member of the Academy of Political Sciences and the Catholic Women's Club in the 1930s.[17]

In October of 1940, on the recommendation of Archbishop John J. Cantwell, Mrs. Moore was awarded the *Pro Ecclesia et Pontifice* medal by the Holy Father. In 1946, she was made a Dame of the Holy Sepulchre and, four years later, a papal countess upon the request of Archbishop Francis J. Spellman of New York.

Mrs. Moore lived in a home at Hoover and Olympic in Los Angeles. Later, she purchased property at Figueroa and 7th Street which subsequently became the headquarters of Barker Brothers Department Store. There is no archival evidence of when she married her husband. A heavy-set woman of regal bearing, she later moved to Altadena, where she became a parishioner of Msgr. Corr. Mrs. Moore was the principal benefactor for the magnificent parochial Marian Shrine modeled after that of Our Lady of Lourdes in France.

In a history of Saint Elizabeth parish in Altadena, the late Msgr. Robert Brennan felt that it was "not out of place to pay special tribute to Countess Mary Young Moore for her unassuming yet constant and munificent offerings to the parish over many years." Brennan went on to say that "the convent itself was erected as a personal memorial to her mother and grandmother." He concluded by saying that "now that she has passed from the local scene Countess Mary Young Moore is still very much alive, and it is well to be mindful of her and to pray that her goodness to us will receive its blessed reward."[18]

Mrs. Moore's charities were not restricted to Altadena. She also assisted Msgr. Bernard Dolan of Long Beach by donating the property (or the cost of it) for Saint Anthony's School. Mrs. Moore's wealth probably came from oil. She owned a gasoline station across the street from Saint Elizabeth's Church in Altadena and, when she died, the station was willed to the parish. At some unrecorded date, Mrs. Moore, by then a widow, moved to New York where she became a confidant of Francis Cardinal Spellman and his coadjutor archbishop. She appears to have been a shrewd business woman and reportedly owned a considerable amount of real estate in the Empire State.

Mrs. Moore died at the advanced age of eighty-eight on October 23, 1971. Terence Cardinal Cooke of New York was the principal celebrant of her Requiem Mass which was offered at Saint Philip's Church in Pasadena. Always a shy woman, Countess Moore's charities were as unheralded as they were manifold. She is remembered chiefly today by students at Moore Catholic High School in Staten Island, New York.

MSGR. WILLIAM E. NORTH

William E. North (1904-1989) was one of Southern California's unique and colorful clergymen. Born in Chicago, young North attended Resurrection parochial school there and old Saint Patrick's conducted by the Christian Brothers. He began his studies for the ministry at Quigley Seminary. Upon completion of his theological courses at Saint Patrick's Seminary in Menlo Park, North was ordained priest by Bishop John J. Cantwell in Saint Vibiana's Cathedral on May 31, 1931. Five years later, Father North completed his doctoral studies at the Catholic University of America with publication of his monumental study on *Catholic Education in Southern California*, a 227 page dissertation that won wide acclaim in scholarly circles.

North was appointed superintendent of Catholic Schools for the Archdiocese of Los Angeles in 1937 and, a dozen years later, was named editor of *The Tidings*, a position he occupied until 1957. He was honored by the Holy Father in 1950 and 1953. During his years at *The Tidings*, North built the edifice housing the editorial offices on Ninth Street, tripled the circulation through a cooperative plan with Catholic schools and won national attention and honors for his writings. Under North's gentle but persuasive leadership, new emphasis was placed on local features. Each member of the paper's staff was expected to write one feature story a week and writers learned to use a press camera to illustrate their stories.

There was no dearth of feature material. The archdiocese was in the midst of its greatest era of expansion, with the Catholic population doubling in the post war years. The face of the area was changing. Whole new residential communities replaced the fields and groves that earlier covered the valleys and hillsides of the city and its environs.

North was the co-architect with McIntyre of two successful campaigns to remove taxation from non-profit, private schools via the electoral process. The positive results were all the more remarkable in view of the minimal and reluctant support from the Archdiocese of San Francisco. North's tenure at *The Tidings* could be best classified as the "golden years." The paper reached its greatest growth, expanding its size and its staff considerably.

The accomplishments at 1530 West Ninth Street were noticed at higher levels of the American Church. In 1951, for example, *The Tidings* won the Gold Medal from the Catholic Press Association for editorials appearing in *El Rodeo*. And, in 1956, *The Tidings* was honored for being the "best Catholic newspaper in the United States." In an address to the Archdiocesan Council of Catholic Women, North said that "an editor is one of God's abandoned creatures who is doomed if he does and doomed if he doesn't. The word is doomed! The only thing he can safely write about is the weather and the Natural Law, because there is nothing anyone can do about the weather and little anyone knows about the Natural Law."[19]

Throughout his long life, North was plagued by illness. Twice he was hospitalized for some months with tuberculosis and never did he enjoy more than marginal health, a factor which figured prominently in his refusal to be considered for the bishopric in 1955.

MSGR. PATRICK ROCHE

Among the most influential men in McIntyre's life was Patrick Roche (1912-1982) who served as editor of *The Tidings* from 1957 to 1973. Born in Lynn, Massachusetts, Patrick graduated from Holy Cross College before entering Saint Mary's Seminary in Baltimore as a clerical candidate for the old Diocese of Los Angeles-San Diego. He was ordained in 1938.

During the earliest years of his ministry, Father Roche worked mostly in educational assignments, both as assistant principal and associate superintendent for Catholic Schools. Like his two sacerdotal predecessors, Roche held a doctorate from the Catholic University of America and that training served him well for the sixteen years he shepherded the grand old lady of the Catholic press. Succeeding North as editor of *The Tidings* was a tremendous challenge. Yet, there was still a steady flow of local news stories about the continued growth of parishes and schools, development of the seminary system, expansion of the Confraternity of Christian Doctrine and the activities of such organizations as the Lay Mission Helpers who were sending people from Los Angeles to missionary areas around the world.

It was Msgr. Roche who encouraged this writer to begin "California's Catholic Heritage" in 1962 so that "contemporary peoples could learn about and profit from the accomplishments of their forebears along California's El Camino Real." Just a few days before his passing, Msgr. Roche gave one last "push" to the apostolate of the Catholic historian: "Keep writing, Frank. People don't remember much about what they hear or see, but they rarely forget what they read. There's something about the written word that touches the soul."[20] He went on to observe that "Catholics walk taller when they learn about their roots. The honest writing of history is an apostolate that influences the mainspring of the commonwealth." Roche frequently quoted and endorsed John Steven McGroarty's definition of a friend which states that "a friend is one who writes the faults of his brothers and sisters in the sand for the winds to obscure and obliterate and who engraves their virtues on the tablets of love and memory."

Those who read Roche's weekly *El Rodeo* columns were as impressed by his style as they were by their content. To the very last, the monsignor was a master of phraseology. The record needs to show that Roche departed significantly from his predecessors insofar as he was exceedingly conservative, almost reactionary in many of his views. During his editorship, *The Tidings* lost much of its credibility among those imbued with the so-called "spirit" of Vatican Council II. Yet, when he retired, he was praised for his "sensitive and capable management of the paper. *The Tidings* has reflected a true image of the Church and the Archdiocese under your loyal priestly mind and heart."

JOSEPH SCOTT

Though he never ran for nor occupied any political position during his life, Joseph Scott (1866-1958) was "the great elder statesman of the west and one of its most beloved citizens." It would be difficult to say whether the growth of the city paralleled the life of Joseph Scott or vice verse. Born in Penrith, England, Joseph Scott was educated at Ushaw College, Durham, where he had the privilege of studying under Raphael Merry del Val, later papal Secretary of State under Pius X. After his graduation from London University, Scott came to the United States in 1889, and was admitted to the bar five years later.

The Los Angeles of those years had seemingly little to offer but in the City of Our Lady of Angels Joseph Scott found his wife, his career and his fame. Of the eleven children born to Joe and Bertha Roth, two became priests, one a judge, and all became respected members of a society that owed a large debt of gratitude to their loving father. Scott never held public office except for a short tenure as President of the Los Angeles Chamber of Commerce and the City Board of Education some years after the turn of the century. Rather, he devoted his energies to social and cultural betterment which he felt was easier and less conflicting for a private citizen. A patriot, nationally famous for his sterling leadership in public affairs, Joseph Scott preferred to sit on the sidelines; nevertheless, he was a powerful force in the Republican Party as is evidenced by the privilege accorded him in 1928 of nominating Herbert Hoover for the presidency.

Though Scott was already a legendary figure by the time McIntyre came to Los Angeles, the new archbishop immediately brought the jurist into his inner circle of advisors. He was the first one invited by McIntyre to accompany him to Rome for the conferral of the cardinalate in 1953. A tribute printed in the *Congressional Record* to commemorate Scott's ninetieth birthday spoke of Scott's "driving ambition and his boundless energy that wrote an American success story for him." One member of Congress noted that "if any man has lived a more full and vigorous and useful ninety years than Joseph Scott, I have yet to hear of him." The fame which Scott acquired for his achievements as a patriot and civic leader never clouded his brilliance as an outstanding and respected member of the legal profession. The list of his favorable court decisions over more than fifty years is exceedingly impressive. Eulogized by the press as "Mr. Los Angeles," Joseph Scott was, in the words of James Francis Cardinal McIntyre, "a gentleman of God, a noble citizen, a soldier of truth and justice."[21] Los Angeles has its long list of benefactors, but as Herbert Hoover once observed, "I will suggest to you that one of the men, perhaps the greatest of the men of this city have kept the democracy functioning with its tolerance, with its willingness to action taken with its constant devotion to public service is Joe Scott."

He was not just a statesman who was a Catholic, he was a "Catholic statesman." His name was at the head of every group of laymen and no one has yet had the time to tabulate the number of organizations to which he belonged or the ones which he helped to finance. Perhaps no other Catholic layman was a more articulate and zealous proponent of the Church. Certainly no one maintained that position so long or so consistently. He used his stature as a statesman to further Catholic ideals, not a common virtue in America's Catholic annals.

BISHOP FULTON J. SHEEN

McIntyre's relationship with Fulton J. Sheen (1895-1979) stretched back to the mid-1920s. Known as the "microphone of God,"[22] Sheen's life began over his father's hardware store in El Paso, Illinois, near Peoria. He earned a doctorate at Louvain University and later taught at the Catholic University of America.

A pioneer radio preacher whose programs drew 6,000 letters a day, he wrote more than fifty books. In 1950, he became national director for the Propagation of the Faith and a year later, was appointed Auxiliary Bishop of New York. He first appeared on television in 1952, and his program, "Life is Worth Living" eventually pulled twenty million viewers in the weekly ratings war. A 1953 poll of journalists proclaimed Sheen TV's Man of the Year.

Although they often disagreed on matters, neither McIntyre nor Sheen ever allowed their differences to show. In a letter to McIntyre, when both were preparing for the end, Sheen said "You will probably not recall that I once asked you to hear Mrs. Luce's confession when she came into the Church. I asked Clare

512

beforehand what kind of man she wanted to hear her confession. She answered: One who has seen the rise and fall of kingdoms."

FRANCIS CARDINAL SPELLMAN

No two churchmen in the history of American Catholicism were more unalike or closer friends than the cardinal archbishops of New York and Los Angeles. Almost daily they spoke by telephone, a habit that deprived historians of any record of their fascinating conversations.

Born in 1889, Spellman was ordained at Rome in 1916. His earliest priestly years were spent in Boston. In 1925, he was named to the Vatican Secretariat of State, the first American ever to hold a position there. Named Auxiliary Bishop of Boston seven years later, Spellman was consecrated by Eugenio Cardinal Pacelli in Saint Peter's Basilica. With the death of Patrick Cardinal Hayes, Spellman became Archbishop of New York. He was raised to the Sacred College of Cardinals on February 18, 1946.

Though he personally despised Spellman, Msgr. John Tracy Ellis, historian of the American Catholic Church, admitted that Spellman was the most widely known, highly respected and fully informed churchman in North America. Through his close relationship with "Spellie, " McIntyre was privy to the innermost workings of the Catholic Church in the United States and throughout the world.

THOMAS P. WHITE

Another jurist frequently consulted by Cardinal McIntyre was Thomas P. White (1888-1968), a man for whom justice was the keystone of a long service to the commonweal.

Thomas Patrick, the son of Peter White and Catherine Clark, was born in Los Angeles. His early education was acquired at Sacred Heart and old Saint Vincent's College. After leaving school in 1905, White took a business-college course in shorthand and typing, at the conclusion of which he entered the employ of Santa Fe. When he left the railroad in 1908 to begin the study of law, he was assistant to the trainmaster at Needles. Following a distinguished three-year stint at the University of Southern California, during which time he represented the institution on its intercollegiate debating team and acted as student body president, White graduated in 1911 with a legal degree.

For several years, the young attorney practiced his profession with the firms of Randall, Bartlett and White and, later, with

Irwin, White and Rosecrans. In 1913, when Henry H. Rose became Mayor of Los Angeles, the Board of Supervisors named Thomas P. White to the former's unexpired term on the Police Court as Justice of the Peace. The following year, he was elected to a full term. Though, at the age of twenty-five, White was the youngest jurist in the United States, his years on the Police Court brought about the innovation of the famed woman's court, first of its kind in the nation. Judge White also inaugurated a probation department for the inferior courts in 1915, and two years later the first work-farm for rehabilitation of inebriates.

Between 1919 and 1931, White engaged in private practice and soon gained a reputation as one of the city's most outstanding trial attorneys. He returned to the bench in 1931, when Governor James Rolph named him to the Superior Court. While serving in the latter position, Justice White was assigned by the Judicial Council as a *pro-tempore* member of the District Court of Appeals. In 1937, Governor Frank Merriam named the well-known jurist Associate Justice of the District Court, to which position he was elected and re-elected by the people. He was advanced to the presiding judgeship by Governor Earl Warren in 1949.

White's appointment to the California Supreme Court in 1959 "capped one of the grandest judicial careers on record" and gave the judge the unique record of having served on the bench at every level of the state's judicial system. Upon naming the life-long Republican to the Supreme Court, Governor Edmund G. Brown noted that "Justice White has been a great jurist in California for more than thirty years. This appointment comes late in his career, but it carries with it a recognition of the gratitude and confidence of the people of California."[23]

Throughout his long and useful years, Justice White was an outspoken and respected member of California's Catholic community. He had served as State Deputy and Supreme Director of the Knights of Columbus, Grand President of the Young Men's Institute and the Los Angeles Archdiocesan branch of the Holy Name Union and, for sixteen years, as president of the southland's Saint Vincent de Paul Society. He was also a founding member of the Perpetual Adoration Society at the old Plaza Church. Equally active in civic affairs, the justice served on the Executive Board of the Boy Scouts of America, the Board of Directors of the Community Chest (now United Crusade) and faculty of Loyola College of Law.

White's car could often be seen in the parking lot of the Chancery Office during McIntyre's time. He would slip quietly into the building, unannounced but always welcomed by the cardinal for his solid and useful advice on the many legal problems confronting the archdiocese.

Notes to the Text

1. Francis J. Weber, *California Catholic* (Mission Hills, 1992), p. 145.
2. Los Angeles *Herald-Examiner*, May 30, 1971.
3. Los Angeles *Times*, June 20, 1978.
4. Francis J. Weber, *The Pilgrim Church in California* (Los Angeles, 1973), Pp. 198-199.
5. *The Tidings*, January 23, 1953.
6. Francis J. Weber, *Catholic Footprints in California* (Newhall, 1970), p. 95.
7. *The Tidings*, August 30, 1968.
8. Quoted in Francis J. Weber, *Vignettes of California Catholicism* (Mission Hills, 1988), p. 461.
9. Thomas J. Reese, S.J., *Archbishop* (San Francisco, 1989), p. 109.
10. *Ibid.*, p. 168.
11. Francis J. Weber, *Vignettes of California Catholicism* (Mission Hills, 1988), p. 101.
12. *The Tidings*, February 18, 1977.
13. *National Catholic Reporter*, May 17, 1967.
14. Francis J. Weber, *A Centennial History of The Tidings* (Mission Hills, 1995), p. 70.
15. Los Angeles *Herald-Examiner*, July 26, 1967.
16. *The Tidings*, July 28, 1967.
17. See Francis J. Weber, *Catholic California Essays* (Mission Hills, 1994), Pp. 32-33.
18. Robert E. Brennan, *St. Elizabeth Parish. A History of Early Rancho Days and of Fifty Parish Years* 1918-1968 (Altadena, 1968), p. 62.
19. Francis J. Weber, *A Centennial History of The Tidings* (Mission Hills, 1995), p. 80.
20. *Ibid.*, p. 92.
21. Francis J. Weber, *Readings in California Catholic History* (Los Angeles, 1967), Pp. 194-196.
22. *Time* CXIV (December 24, 1979), p. 84.
23. Francis J. Weber, *Catholic Footprints in California* (Newhall, 1970), p. 100.

24. Vocation Program

A vital part of any seminary program is recruitment. Prior to McIntyre's time, there was no formalized procedure in Los Angeles for identifying and encouraging young people prior to their entry into the seminary or convent. Within a few months after his installation, the archbishop wrote to the clergy pointing out "a vocation to the priesthood or sisterhood is a gift from God, given only" to a few. He said it was "a call that should be encouraged and likely youth should be advised to confer with their confessors for counsel and direction."[1]

In 1952, McIntyre established a Commission for Vocations and appointed Father Joseph E. Weyer to be its director. Two years later, he enlarged the commission to include a number of pastors and young priests to act as advisors. It was also in 1954 that the cardinal inaugurated the yearly practice of designating a vocation week in April. Sermons were to be preached in every parish on the subject of vocations and outlines were sent to those who wanted to use them. The cardinal also encouraged the Sisters to talk to youngsters in the schools on the priesthood and sisterhood. A special liturgy was to be held on April 11th "for the intention that God will grant us many vocations to the priesthood and religious life."[2]

The following year, McIntyre wrote to the pastors of parishes staffed by religious orders, noting that "as we survey the parishes from where the students of our Junior Seminary come, we note with some concern that most of the parishes conducted by Religious Communities are supplying no candidates for the secular clergy." While he understood that their first efforts would be to obtain vocations for their own communities, he suggested that there were also potential vocations for the secular clergy in their parishes. He said that he was "hopeful that as occasions may arise, prospective candidates for the secular clergy will be encouraged and directed to the Junior Seminary."[3]

Archdiocese of Los Angeles
Clergy, Religious and Seminarian Census

Year	Diocesan Priests	Religious Priests	Total Priests	Sisters	Brothers	Seminarians
1948	392	297	689	1965	92	319
1949	412	285	698	1980	90	356
1950	412	300	721	2175	100	342
1951	427	300	727	3000	114	315
1952	427	300	727	3005	114	429
1953	420	345	765	3023	115	343
1954	431	344	775	3057	142	429
1955	423	387	810	3066	157	445
1956	481	319	850	3077	175	440
1957	492	430	922	3245	186	466
1958	509	472	981	3245	202	483
1959	550	540	1090	3321	234	498
1960	571	590	1161	3370	262	510
1961	586	600	1186	3520	287	552
1962	614	620	1234	3735	295	587
1963	627	651	1278	3839	285	689
1964	662	687	1351	4281	345	728
1965	689	704	1393	4495	349	694
1966	714	733	1447	4590	335	668
1967	718	720	1438	4340	355	630
1968	701	720	1421	3934	312	592
1969	680	734	1414	3517	309	572
1970	679	755	1424	3226	292	465

Archdiocesan Statistics

Year	Parishes	Missions	Stations	Chapels
1948	221	44	20	91
1949	230	53	15	92
1950	234	43	16	143
1951	241	43	16	143
1952	245	53	13	167
1953	248	52	7	133
1954	252	50	14	130
1955	258	53	10	139
1956	269	51	15	145
1957	276	52	14	150
1958	281	55	11	170
1959	286	58	20	196
1960	287	50	14	195
1961	291	51	10	218
1962	297	44	8	232
1963	299	40	19	238
1964	307	44	13	257
1965	310	41	17	285
1966	313	40	18	314
1967	313	37	8	344
1968	312	33	10	340
1969	318	38	11	366
1970	321	38	11	366

Though the vocation director only devoted part of his time to the recruitment program, he was able to report, early in 1956, some notable accomplishments. Pastors had received sermon outlines, elementary schools had been provided with vocational materials, high schools had been visited by a team of priests, posters and literature had been dispatched to all schools, brochures had been provided to parents and guardians, a vocation rally was conducted, a speakers bureau established and the Serra Club had been approached for support.[4]

In 1961, when Weyer was forced to step aside because of ill health, the cardinal asked Father Lawrence Gibson to assume the duties of vocation director on a full time basis. Gibson dramatically expanded the program and, over the ensuing years, initiated policies that became the envy of the nation. Among the many new measures adopted were annual visitations of the primary and secondary Catholic schools in the archdiocese, enlistment of a team of priests to give vocational talks, utilization of the Serra Club in encouraging vocations, transporting potential candidates to the seminaries, holding of weekend retreats at the seminary for 7th and 8th graders and the formation of an extensive file of youngsters interested in some aspect of the program.

Sermon outlines were provided for use in parishes and priests were asked to identify, speak with and encourage young people expressing an interest in the priesthood or sisterhood. Recruitment kits were made available, spelling out the purpose and need for priests, spiritual opportunities, intellectual challenges, physical and social facilities, cost analysis, qualifications of candidates, who is called, function of Latin, how to deal with uncertainty and where to obtain further information. Several vocation movies were produced and made available to interested organizations, spelling out in great detail the mechanics of identifying and pursuing a call to God's service.

In April of 1968, Cardinal McIntyre issued another of his many letters on the subject of vocations, this time calling the clergy's attention to the fact that Pope Paul VI had designated Good Shepherd Sunday as a World Day of Prayer for Vocations. Sixty churches throughout the archdiocese were selected "to have a special Holy Hour for vocations." The cardinal felt that renewed emphasis should be placed on the need for prayer in the overall process of identifying and encouraging vocations.[5]

Beyond encouraging young men to enter the archdiocesan seminary, the cardinal also approved formation of a parallel recruitment program for religious orders of men and women. In 1964, he established a Council for Sisters Vocations, with six different nuns representing the eighty three religious communities then active in the archdiocese. A full time Sister was added to the staff of the Vocation Office. The first issue of the *Bulletin for the Council of Sisters Vocations* was released in February of 1965.

RELIGIOUS LIFE

Like most of his contemporaries, James Francis Cardinal McIntyre had profound respect and admiration for the religious men and women who brought the Catholic school system and health care facilities in the United States to a pinnacle of service and excellence unparalleled in the religious annals of any country. The cardinal verbalized his feelings and those of most American Catholics in an address commemorating the centennial of the Sisters of Charity of the Incarnate Word at Houston, Texas, on October 1, 1966.

He observed that among the various vocations and ways-of-life accepted by womanhood in history, "none has acquired a distinction, an acknowledged holiness, a reverence and a respect as have the sisterhoods of the Roman Catholic Church throughout the world. They have acquired a status that is unique, exalted and universally respected." McIntyre regarded the development of religious communities as providing a record that "is pre-eminent for virtue, devotion, sacrifice and all for the love of God and the love of neighbor." He went on to say that the unifying element of these women was "to live in protected communities, dedicated to prayer, to education and good works on behalf of the poor and afflicted." Down through history, "these groups took upon themselves diverse forms of work in assisting the needy, educating the youth and providing for the sick and poor and the neglected. Nothing was too menial, nothing too magnanimous, nothing too sacrificing as long as it was done from the motive of the love of God and the charity of Christ." As their numbers increased, norms of religious life were established which "attracted the nobility and the most humble. They drew from all branches of life, society and influence. Their primary purpose and objective was to love and serve Almighty God and thus promote the salvation of souls."

McIntyre noted that in these pursuits, "they attained the highest of earthly and social accomplishments in education and culture. At the same time, they developed the most scientific and efficient standards in their care of the maimed and afflicted, the chronically and permanently ill and suffering. With all these human qualities expressing true charity, their primary purpose was the sanctification of their own souls by lives of prayer and mortification." This work, over the years, allowed for the highest kind of excellence in administrative and educational endeavors.

The cardinal said that "the holiness, the sanctity, the prayerfulness, the sacrifices of religious women throughout the centuries have been phenomenal. It truly reveals the presence of God in and amongst these chosen servants. To the world at large, this type of life has been a great edification and a tremendous stimulant to virtue and a love of God that is inestimable." Though he was not wedded to the concept of the traditional "habits" worn by many religious communities, he did observe that much of the reverence and respect accorded to Sisters was due to "the type of costume and the uniformity of fashion that tells the world that wearers are worthy of special treatment. The religious habit, whatever form it takes, "denotes internal qualities that surpass ordinary consideration." McIntyre concludes by admitting that he looked "with apprehension and some alarm as the fashions of our time seem to be making an attempt to intrude beyond the barriers of custom and principle that have been the guideposts, the protectors and the sanctifiers of holy women for centuries."[6]

Several years later, addressing a group of religious superiors, McIntyre said that "we hear much today of nuns embracing new activities - new professions." The phase today is to "become closer to the people. May we ask, who in all history and in all times and under all circumstances have been closer and more effective in all known fields of charitable endeavor than has been the nun. From battlefields to hospitals, to schools, to homes for the poor, to homes for the aged, to assistance in the very homes of the poverty stricken, the apostolate as nuns knows no limits and appears in all circumstances. They have survived and suppressed all contrary circumstances and, through it all, maintained and conveyed a holiness inspired by the realization of God's presence with them and with those they served. They have been a bulwark of faith."

He went on to say that "the character of the nun has inspired not only the children in the classroom but, through them their parents, and supply an ideal of holiness. This has affected the philosophy and the theology of the home and has been indirectly a factor of importance. The Sister in the school has been a most extraordinary person, living a life of prayer and sacrifice, a life of wisdom and penance, and all in the appreciation of the presence of God's graces about her in the manifestation of her love of neighbor for the love of God."[7]

On an earlier occasion, speaking to the Sisters of Saint Joseph at Orange about the Sister Formation movement, McIntyre expressed his personal view that many of the suggestions about "updating" religious life struck him as evidencing "a remarkable absence of common sense, good judgment and of sound reasoning."[8] McIntyre was referring to the notion of "experimentation" which had been introduced after the Vatican Council as a means for allowing religious to exercise a more relevant status in the modern Church. The cardinal agreed that religious attire and practices would profit by reasonable modernization, but he pointed out that past performance was a convincing argument favoring the existing system. Dismissing a program that was decades ahead of most other places of Catholic influence didn't make a lot of sense to him. He exhorted Sisters to be leaders, not followers, noting that exhortations to change from people like Cardinal Suenens were directed primarily at Europeans.

In urging American Sisterhoods to avoid becoming overly involved in changing a system that had proven immensely effective, McIntyre pointed out some of the pitfalls inherent in experimentation. First of all, the time element provided for experimentation was too long and, in some cases, open-ended; secondly, existing rules would be suspended, often totally, while nothing was put in place for the interim period; thirdly, there were virtually no provisions made for accountability either during or after the period of experimentation and, finally, American religious had everything to lose and little to gain by changing directions on the superhighway of service to God and neighbor.

For their part, many Sisters complained that they were not adequately compensated for their work, that they lacked the "equality" and recognition accorded to contemporary women and they were overly burdened with work all of which was true. What they had forgotten or overlooked was the fact that they had *freely* embraced a lifestyle based on the deprivation that flows from practicing the virtues of poverty, chastity and obedience. Catholic schools and hospitals had been successful, in large measure, because their religious staff voluntarily worked for only board and room in order to benefit children and patients who otherwise would not have had the opportunity of using those facilities. This they did for God who promises compensation in another life.

In any event, the cardinal predicted that convents would be depleted within a generation if there were a wholesale embracing of dramatic change in any direction. His suggestion that religious life in the United States should be fine-tuned rather than revamped got little support from other members of the American hierarchy, most of whom either doubted his dire predictions or were afraid of confronting what was fast becoming an explosive issue. With the passage of a generation, the McIntyre scenario has proven remarkably accurate. Those Sisters who remained found more "relevant" tasks than teaching in schools and nursing in hospitals, many of them taking positions that could be held equally well by people not committed by special vows to the service of the Lord.

McIntyre was no prophet, but he never wandered far from the simple way-of-life he knew in Harlem. While becoming a prince of the Church, he always remained a commoner in his personal lifestyle. He knew people - what they wanted in life, how they felt about issues, where they looked for encouragement and what motivated them. He instinctively knew that religious women were embarking on a disaster course and, understandably, he urged them to reconsider. He was one of the few American bishops who cared enough to express an opinion. For his trouble, he was ignored, belittled and profaned. Whether he was more right than wrong will be determined by a future historian.

PRIESTS' SENATE

Secular priests in the Archdiocese of Los Angeles were well provided for during the McIntyre years. They were compensated more generously than in any other ecclesial jurisdiction in the country and Los Angeles was one of the few areas where every priest was provided with a car and insurance. Even their social security fees were paid by the chancery. Yet, many complained that they needed a larger voice in the day-to-day management of the Church.

The movement towards establishment of the Priests' Senate in the various archdioceses and dioceses of the United States can be traced to the Decree on the Bishop's Pastoral Office, issued by the Vatican Council II on October 28, 1965. Therein it was stated that "included among the collaborators of the bishop in the government of the diocese are those priests who constitute his senate or council, such as the cathedral chapter, the board of consultors, or other committees established according to the circumstances or nature of various localities."[9]

McIntyre resolutely opposed formation of a Priests' Senate in the Archdiocese of Los Angeles because he felt that such a group was redundant in his jurisdiction because of the existing, highly effective, structural organizations already in place. In his opinion, the conciliar directive "was taken from the example of such dioceses as Los Angeles" where there had long been an extensive "collaboration" by the board of consultors which clearly was a representative body "established according to the circumstances or nature of various localities."[10] McIntyre's opposition to formation of a Priests' Senate was not then just a whimsical reaction but an opinion based on a valid premise of judicial interpretation.

In another memorandum, the cardinal spelled out in great detail the organization in the Archdiocese of Los Angeles which for many years had anticipated the circumstances expounded in the decree of the Vatican Council. Because this memo is so integral to McIntyre's rationale about the notion of a Priests' Senate, it needs to be reproduced here in its entirety.

According to the provisions of Canon Law, our Diocesan Consultors meet monthly and review in detail all of the operations of the archdiocese. Our sessions consume from three to five hours. Precise minutes of these meetings are kept. These constitute a detailed history of the archdiocese for the reason that at these meetings all the business of the archdiocese has been presented and discussed. All appointments of pastors are approved by the Council and all transfers of assistants are presented for their information. All permissions for the establishment of parishes; all permissions for the erection of churches, schools and buildings, all expenditures of money beyond a nominal amount are submitted to the Consultors for their action. To the Consultors are also presented programs of expansion and diocesan policy.

In addition to the Consultors, we have a Building Committee. This Committee meets weekly and reports on petitions made to the Council with regard to building and building contracts. They are largely a different group from the Consultors.

In addition, we have an Advisory Board of Education. This Board is a group numbering fifteen, and considers the operation and expansion of our elementary and high schools. The members are different from the above described committees. Our Department of Education consists of a Superintendent, two Brothers and two Sisters for our high schools and colleges, and a Superintendent, an assistant and six Sister Supervisors for our elementary schools.

We have a Board for the operations of the Confraternity of Christian Doctrine. This has a full time staff of four priests and an auxiliary staff of forty-five priests who teach adult education one day a week. A staff of Sisters also assist in this work.

We have a Welfare Bureau that works in conjunction with the United Way and from which it receives a substantial subsidy. On the staff of the Welfare Bureau, there are seven priests full time and a large lay staff. The Welfare Bureau is separately incorporated with a Board of thirty-one priests and lay people. This Board meets monthly.

The St. Vincent de Paul Society is established in each parish with lay members. Its supreme Board is composed of two priests and several lay members. This, too, is a very active and functioning group. Another group of twenty priests, brothers, sisters, and lay people function in the apostolate of vocations.

Our seminaries, major and minor, are separately incorporated with Boards of Directors composed of priests and lay people. These Boards meet at least annually and more often as occasion may require. The Chancery Office is open daily, morning and afternoon. The Auxiliary Bishops and Chancellor are available at all times for consultation and direction. Our Society for the Propagation of the Faith is supervised by two priests and has a substantial staff of helpers.[11]

The cardinal felt that, in many instances, ambitious and often ill-advised efforts to implement certain proposals of the council had involved "an unwarranted and exaggerated interpretation." He believed that in Los Angeles "there is functioning all the elements of a senate" in the "various collateral branches of the works of religion and social service."[12] Given those circumstances, he saw no need or function for an additional group known as a Priests' Senate.

McIntyre said that "while in some places of the world, the consultors were more in the class of Chapter Members, in the United States they have not had a liturgical standing nor have they functioned with regard to the recitation of the Divine Office. In the United States, they have functioned as administrative advisors. Therefore, the consultors are in all elements and qualification the Senate of the Ordinary."[13] Further, he argued, that the Cathedral Chapter, which in the United States was replaced by the Board of Consultors, was defined as the "senate and assembly" of the bishop in the Code of Canon Law.[14]

It is clear that McIntyre's opposition to establishing a Priests' Senate in the Archdiocese of Los Angeles had a solid rationale. In his view, there already was, at least in his jurisdiction, a body that performed all the functions predicated of a Priests' Senate. As a matter of fact, in many areas of the United States, bishops eventually came to a similar decision, combining the duties and even titles of Priests' Senators and Boards of Consultors into a single body of sacerdotal advisors. There is no record that McIntyre ever explained his position either to the priests themselves or to the press and that was a serious tactical mistake. Once again, his lack of communicational skills worked against him because many interpreted his failure to even discuss the issue as an unwillingness to implement a conciliar directive.

There were several unilateral attempts made by individual priests to establish groups that would evolve into a Priests' Senate. In 1966, the initial issue of *The Priestly Community* appeared, calling itself "a pastoral-personal newsletter for Catholic Priests in Los Angeles." It told how "a plan to confer with His Eminence over the possibility of a senate was transformed into a luncheon conference with Monsignor Hawkes, and showed us that dialogue in depth is possible even in short range meetings. Monsignor expressed his appreciation and showed an openness to further meetings." The editor of the newsletter admitted that "much remains to be done. The burden still rests with priests at the grass roots . . . there is need for dialogue on a deeper pastoral and theological level." As part of the envisioned program for elevating the morale of priests, "the first concern of all the Church," it was stated that "a number of Los Angeles priests have thought to make a serious effort to strengthen the priestly community. The program envisioned is totally constructive: irenic, open, and personal, not political; it has little structure; its intent is to improve communication by emphasizing the things which pull us together and inspire us, not issues which divide and weaken. This newsletter is part of the attempt."[15]

In January of 1967, a letter was sent to about forty priests in the archdiocese saying that "the second Vatican Council has stated that there should be in each diocese a senate of priests, representing all priests, which by its advice will be able to give the bishop effective assistance in the administration of the diocese." It stated that "many priests are hopeful that a senate of priests may soon be established in the Archdiocese of Los Angeles." Such a group would "endeavor in its structure and procedure to be representative of all priests and provide a forum for open communications among priests with the bishop." Auxiliary Bishop Timothy Manning was proposed as "chairman" of this group in which all members would be elected.[16] According to one report, the authors were called into "the chancery for a forty-five minute lecture by the cardinal,"[17] a fact that cannot be substantiated in McIntyre's desk calendar for that year.

At some time during those years, there appears to have been established an Association of Priests in the archdiocese. Its underlying purpose was to begin "a voluntary association to provide all of our priests with a better opportunity to exchange ideas, evaluate their own needs and those of their people, continue their own education, and keep up on developments in the Church affecting the pastoral ministry." While admitting that "any proposal of this nature is bound to run into immediate objections on the part of some priests," the "Steering Committee" said that such "objections could be met with the honest and guaranteed assurance that no special groups were being served, that no whining criticisms were afoot, that no rebellious, disobedient or cynical motives were in control." The letter said that "nothing about this proposal must be secret or anonymous," yet, no one signed the letter or provided any information except a mailing address on Wilshire Boulevard.[18]

During a meeting of the Junior Clergy for the Archdiocese of Los Angeles, early in May of 1967, Father Robert Delaney stood up after the formal program was concluded and "called for a standing vote on formation of a Priests' Senate." His suggestion took everyone by surprise, including the cardinal who immediately ruled him out of order and concluded the meeting with a prayer.[19] There were other incipient "associations" begun during those years and, in April of 1968, John Dart reported in the pages of the Los Angeles *Times* that "it is known that an association of priests sworn to secrecy exists in James Francis Cardinal McIntyre's Los Angeles Archdiocese." But he was told that "priests believe their numbers are not sufficient to announce their activities publicly."[20]

Later that year, the executive board of the National Federation of Priests' Council met in Hollywood for a three day session. At that time, Father Patrick O'Malley announced that 124 priests' groups throughout the country had affiliated with the National Federation. Every priest in the archdiocese was invited to attend a meeting at the Continental Hyatt House in Hollywood on December 11th. About a dozen appeared.[21]

The actual formation of a Priests' Senate had to wait for McIntyre's successor, much to the irritation of many priests in the Archdiocese of Los Angeles.

DEPARTURE OF PRIESTS

The exodus of priests from the active ministry, which became a hemorrhage in the years after Vatican Council II, brought about challenges without precedent in Catholic annals. While he deplored the whole notion of clerical departures and used every opportunity to propose alternative solutions to problem-plagued priests, McIntyre readily set up the necessary canonical procedures for dealing with the phenomenon. A priest in the tribunal was delegated to handle cases leading to laicization, along with other measures useful for the spiritual healing of petitioners. Not infrequently, McIntyre took a personal hand in dealing with alienated priests and often enough he was able to find a position for a troubled priest in another jurisdiction. He made it clear that he was "available" at any hour to discuss problems that surfaced from his priests.

There are no figures available about the number of priests leaving the active ministry in Los Angeles during the cardinal's tenure. If anything, the percentages were probably lower than the national average. One reason for that might have been that McIntyre kept the lid on longer than most of his episcopal colleagues. There was little equivocation about priestly behavior and demeanor in Los Angeles and that factor may have been the deciding factor in many cases.

FATHER JOHN B. THOM

Of all the heartbreaks endured by McIntyre during his twenty-two year archiepiscopate, none was greater than the tragic loss of a priest on his staff to an assassin.[22] A few minutes before two o'clock on the afternoon of July 23, 1965,[23] a neatly-groomed lady, wearing a green and white frock, presented herself to the receptionist of the Los Angeles Chancery Office, Miss Mary Sinclair, for an appointment with Father John B. Thom, who was serving as interim secretary to the cardinal.

Shortly after arriving back at the office from luncheon at the archiepiscopal residence, Father Thom greeted the auburn-haired visitor, who identified herself as Mrs. Dorothy M. Brassie. When she asked to speak privately, the priest ushered her into the adjoining conference room. At approximately 2:10 p.m., two muffled shots were heard from the chamber, after which Father Thom opened the door into the lobby, fell across the threshold, gasping: "My God, I have been shot . . . I have been shot!" The fatally-wounded priest, struck by twin bullets from a 32 caliber derringer,[24] sustained two wounds; one in the head which perforated the carotid artery, the other in the chest which pierced the right lung and heart, causing massive internal hemorrhaging.

When those standing outside the lateral entrance way to the conference room dashed into the chamber, Mrs. Brassie placed the short-barreled pistol on the table, and then calmly and unobtrusively seated herself in a corner of the room. By the time a priest had administered the last rites, an interval of about four or five minutes, Father Thom was in the throes of his death agony. Though muscular action continued for some additional moments, he apparently succumbed within ten minutes after being struck down. The ambulance attendants arrived soon and, though there was evidence of vital signs, they made no attempt to administer oxygen or in any other way to sustain life. Msgr. Edward Wade accompanied the ambulance to nearby Central Receiving Hospital, where Father Thom was pronounced dead-on-arrival. At 2:34, the cardinal was informed that the stricken priest had expired.

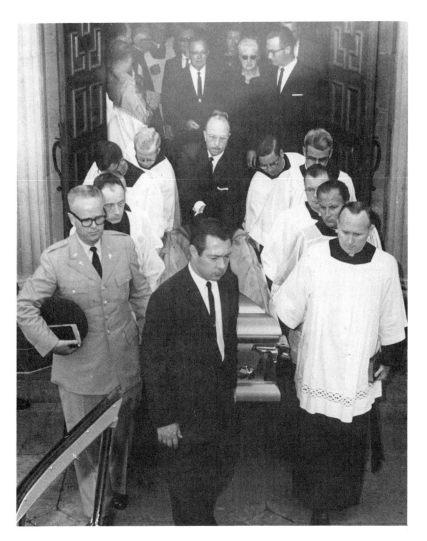

Funeral of the Reverend John B. Thom, 1965.

In Memory of

The Reverend

John B. Thom, S.T.D.

Born February 14, 1933
Ordained April 30, 1959
Died July 23, 1965

Meanwhile, the fifty-five year old assailant, a resident of the Atwater District of Los Angeles,[25] had been taken into custody and booked at Sybil Brand Institute on suspicion of murder. Subsequent investigation disclosed that Mrs. Brassie, who had disappeared from her Saint Louis home three years earlier, had previously contacted a prominent local detective, William R. Colligan, for "help against the Catholic conspiracy." The detective later recalled suggesting that the distraught woman "see a psychiatrist, to get herself certified insane."[26]

In her subsequent trial, Mrs. Brassie admitted having called the Chancery Office three times, on July 19th, in an unsuccessful attempt to secure a personal interview with the cardinal. On the following day, however, she did make an appointment, under an assumed name, to see Father Thom on July 23rd. During the course of her short interview with the priest, Mrs. Brassie, overcome with frustration at her "inability to obtain a personal interview with James Francis Cardinal McIntyre," pulled from her purse the gun she had purchased six weeks before at a Hollywood artillery store.[27]

Several "rambling, almost incoherent typed letters" were discovered in which Mrs. Brassie, a nurse who had been dismissed from her previous position "because of emotional instability," expressed "acute anguish" at being "tormented by Catholics and their collaborators" in her "home, on the street, at work, in business shops, etc., twenty-four hours a day, every day of the year, for four years."[28] In a letter unearthed in the Chancery Archives, she asserted that her persecutors had "concealed microphones and remote controlled relay switches that set off loud noises . . . monitored by persons in the immediate neighborhood."[29]

On August 4, Mrs. Brassie was bound over for Superior Court trial on charges of murder. She was subsequently convicted of second degree murder by Judge Herbert V. Walker, in a nonjury trial. Found innocent by reason of insanity, she was sentenced to Patton State Hospital on December 15, 1965.[30] Aside from a twenty-six hour period in April, 1967, when she absented herself from the hospital without authorization, Mrs. Brassie was a model inmate at the institution until, apparently cured, she was released in 1968.[31]

In his eulogy for the slain priest, Auxiliary Bishop Timothy Manning noted that when "this priest fell, there was something in his falling that was purposeful and willed by our providential God. It was not solely the consummation of a personal life consecrated to His service, but it had also a social and a priestly implication, a lesson needful for the healing of our present ills."[32]

Notes to the Text

1. AALA, J. Francis A. McIntyre to Priests, Los Angeles, June 1, 1948.
2. AALA, Joseph E. Weyer to Priests, Los Angeles, March 1, 1954.
3. AALA, James Francis Cardinal McIntyre to Priests, Los Angeles, October 12, 1955.
4. AALA, Joseph E. Weyer to Timothy Manning, Los Angeles, March 28, 1956.
5. AALA, James Francis Cardinal McIntyre to Priests, Los Angeles, April 17, 1968.
6. AALA, McIntyre Address "Centennial of the Sisters of Charity of the Incarnate Word," n.p., October 1, 1966. Reported by NC News Service, October 7, 1966.
7. AALA, James Francis Cardinal McIntyre. Talk to Religious Superiors, n.p., February 24, 1969.
8. AALA, McIntyre "Talk on Sister Formation," Orange, February 8, 1963.
9. Walter M. Abbott, S.J., *The Documents of Vatican II* (New York, 1966), p. 416.
10. AALA, "Archdiocesan Organization," Los Angeles, January 23, 1967.
11. AALA, Undated Memorandum appended to a letter mailed to James F. Johnson, Los Angeles, November 28, 1966.
12. AALA, "Archdiocesan Organization," Los Angeles, January 23, 1967.
13. *Ibid.*
14. *Codex Juris Canonicis* (New York, 1952), Canon 39.
15. AALA, *The Priestly Community* I, undated, #1.
16. AALA, Mimeographed letter, undated (January, 1967).
17. *National Catholic Reporter*, May 17, 1967.
18. AALA, Steering Committee to Priests, Los Angeles, n.d.
19. *National Catholic Reporter*, May 17, 1967.
20. Los Angeles *Times*, April 24, 1968.
21. AALA, Patrick O'Malley to Priests, n.p., December 8, 1968.
22. For a more lengthy and detailed account, see Francis J. Weber, "Father John B. Thom - A Memoir," *Emmanuel* LXXVIII (June, 1972), 256-259.
23. New York *Times*, July 24, 1965.
24. San Francisco *Chronicle*, July 24, 1965.
25. Los Angeles *Times*, July 24, 1965.

26. Thomas Fuchs, "True Detectives," *West* magazine in the Los Angeles *Times*, June 21, 1970.
27. Los Angeles *Times*, August 5, 1965.
28. Los Angeles *Herald Examiner*, August 4, 1965.
29. AALA, Dorothy M. Brassie to James Francis Cardinal McIntyre, Los Angeles, December 4, 1964.
30. Hollywood *Citizen News*, December 11, 1965.
31. Los Angeles *Times*, November 14, 1968.
32. *Ibid.*, July 29, 1965.

25. Inter Archdiocesan Matters

Among McIntyre's first innovations at Los Angeles was the inauguration of the Archbishop's Christmas Party for Children which was modeled on the one held annually for the youngsters of the New York Foundling Home at the Waldorf-Astoria Hotel.

McIntyre enlisted a group of civic-minded ladies who set up a committee to host youngsters from the Los Angeles Orphanage, Castelar Creche and other boarding homes under the supervision of the Catholic Welfare Bureau. It was agreed that the purpose of the event, which was held annually since 1949, would be "to provide a better Christmas for Catholic families on the dole." At the time, there were 467 families that fell under that label with roughly 1,020 children.

The party, held on December 17th at the Beverly Hills Hotel, was hosted by Jerry Colonna and featured sixty children ranging in age from two to five. Over 1,200 grown-ups were on hand to see "the wide-eyed wonder in the faces of children as they met Santa Claus, opened their gifts, watched Mount Saint Mary's girls dressed as nursery rhyme characters and listened to Christmas carols by the Cathedral Chapel boys choir."[1] After meeting each of the youngsters, the archbishop thanked the patrons and explained how the party would benefit the Catholic Welfare Bureau in its programs for the needy of Los Angeles.

In the following year's invitation, McIntyre reported that "the party was a grand success and we were able to distribute a substantial sum in gifts and good cheer to many families at Christmas time. "Besides," he noted, "the party itself was unique and brought to all present a distinct joy and a realization of the Christmas season."[2] Addressing himself to "children young and old," the archbishop said that "we are all children at Christmas time and we are happy to join with Santa Claus in this preview of Christmas."[3]

Those invited to the 1951 party were told that "more than a thousand families on public relief" would benefit. Through the Catholic Welfare Bureau, "Christmas baskets and gifts will be distributed from the proceeds. The event was enhanced that year by tumblers, jugglers and trained animals, as well as clowns, troubadours and choristers. Toys, noisemakers, candy, ice cream and cake were provided for the youngsters at their tiny tables."[4]

In 1952, the party was moved to the Ambassador Hotel on Wilshire Boulevard and, by that time, the party had "become recognized as most enjoyable. Parents and grandparents, as well as the young children enjoyed witnessing the little ones from our institutions and boarding homes rejoice in an old-fashioned Christmas Party amongst their elders."[5] Writing under her byline, "Society Women's Activities," Princess Conchita Sepulveda Pignatelli said that there was "no more inspiring and heartwarming sight than the awe and wonder in the eyes of needy tots when they gaze on a real Santa Claus and a gaily adorned Christmas tree laden with gifts, assuring them that they, too, have been remembered in this holy season."[6]

Each year the revenues grew and, by 1955, the event raised $18,364.31 which was a considerable amount in those days. And every single cent went to the Catholic Welfare Bureau for distribution to poor and indigent families. McIntyre kept a very tight string on the finances.[7] It was one of his favorite charities and he got personally involved every year, even to the extent of signing all the requests for funds. He only missed attending the event one year and that was 1955. He later offered his "humble apology," noting that he was grieved but "powerless" in a hospital bed.[8] The event became a holiday fixture among the southland's social events and generally it received attention in the local papers. One journalist reported in 1961, the thirteenth year of the event, that the party was held at the Beverly Hilton Hotel and was attended by 1,500 adults and children. Included among the attendees were youngsters from Little Flower Missionary Home, Los Angeles Orphanage, Mother Cabrini Day Nursery, Divine Providence Day Nursery, Saint Elizabeth Day Nursery and other Catholic institutions. Lawrence Welk was among the entertainers, as was Billy the clown and his cohorts, Al Killeen and Phil Reilly.[9]

In 1964, McIntyre came up with the idea of a "drop-a-coin" box for those who wished to support the Christmas Party. It was a novel idea that eventually proved popular, especially among the students in the archdiocesan school system.[10] Two years later, a friend offered the use of a circus elephant for the annual event. According to one account, Sabu "freely joined in the fun, performing all the tricks trained elephants do." He stood on his head, reared up on his hind legs, laid down and saluted the children. Understandably, the elephant "seemed more interested in nodding to the kids than to the adults. After all, he is a very young elephant."[11]

A reporter describing the Cardinal's Christmas Party in 1968, said that McIntyre's "clear, soft, and kindly voice expressed the true sentiments of Christmas, and why they were all there. He pointed out that they would share a wonderful party themselves, but they would help poorer children and parents who could not be present." The event made it possible to assist with food and gifts for 14,000 poor children and parents throughout California's southland. and for the 200 orphans present, it was a "never-to-be-forgotten event in the true spirit of Christmas - a giant birthday party for Baby Jesus."[12] A lifelong friend of the cardinal said that one time he was criticized for spending an inordinate amount of time preparing and planning for the annual event. It didn't faze McIntyre who replied: "even cardinals like a party, especially one for poor kids."

COMMUNITY DINNERS

McIntyre was one of the first to use the concept of "community dinners" as fund raisers. As early as 1952, he sponsored the first such affair in Los Angeles, the proceeds of which went to Saint John's Hospital in Santa Monica. It was a tremendous success, bringing in $106,107.[13] The idea was that each year, the funds would be earmarked by the archbishop to a hospital of his choosing. Among those lending their names to this project in the early years were Irene Dunne, Louis B. Mayer, Spencer Tracy, Hernando Courtright, Charles Skouras, Willard Keith and Shirley Burden. Tickets went for $250 each, an unheard of amount in those days. Yet, they were consistently profitable, due mostly to the personal involvement of McIntyre.

Knowing that famous people are natural "drawing cards" for such events, the cardinal always tried to get prominent persons involved in his charitable affairs. In 1968, he had extracted promises from Vice President Hubert Humphrey and presidential candidate Richard M. Nixon that the winner of their campaign for the White House would appear in Los Angeles on December 5th for the Community Dinner on behalf of Santa Marta Hospital. Shortly after Nixon's victory, it was announced that he would fulfill his pledge. He journeyed to Los Angeles for the fund-raising dinner at the Century Plaza Hotel. Before going there, he and McIntyre toured the tiny ten bed facility, where he was greeted by Sister Mary Lopez, a Mexican-born Daughter of Saint Joseph and her small staff.[14] At the dinner, both Nixon and McIntyre addressed the 1,400 guests where sponsors had hoped to raise $1 million for a new fifty bed hospital-clinic. During the dinner, Daniel Donohue electrified the audience by

The Cardinal's Christmas Party became an annual event throughout the McIntyre years.

The Cardinal's Community Dinner

Thursday, December 5, 1968

THE CENTURY PLAZA HOTEL
LOS ANGELES BALLROOM

Reception — California Lounge
7:00 P.M.

Black Tie

537

Cardinal attends dedication of a plaque erected in his honor at the Los Angeles Memorial Coliseum in 1966.

Prince Juan Carlos of Spain and his wife, Sophia, visited Los Angeles, where they were greeted by Cardinal McIntyre.

538

announcing that the Dan Murphy Foundation would contribute an additional $2.5 million for the envisioned project.[15]

Cardinal McIntyre thanked the gathering for its magnificent support for a new Santa Marta. He described it as typical of charity in America. "The kindness of a neighbor, assistance in time of trial, service in time of distress, aid when in difficulty, food when hungry, consolation when distraught, have all been supplied by individual and organized effort in our beloved United States. Surely, we need no further testimony of God's recognition of our charity than the fact that we are a people blessed with the Providence of God."[16]

Anxious as he was to support hospitals and any other Catholic charity in the archdiocese, McIntyre had a keen sense of justice and he was always exceedingly careful that funds be used for the intended purposes. An example would be the projected Mercy Hospital at Monterey Park which was to be opened by the Sisters of Mercy of Canada. For many reasons, the project became embroiled in complicated obstacles, civic and private, and was eventually abandoned. Contributions already made to the proposed hospital had been kept intact by McIntyre who wrote to each donor offering to return them. Inasmuch as the hospital had been envisioned as an expansion of Santa Marta Clinic, he did suggest that donors might wish to have "their original donation applied to the continuance of Santa Marta Clinic" but, if not, they could ask for its return.[17]

THE A.C.C.W.

Among the many organizations established in Los Angeles, none was more favored and useful than the Archdiocesan Council of Catholic Women which traces its roots back to the 1920s. In an address to a national meeting of the broader National Council of Catholic Women held at Fresno in April, 1953, McIntyre praised their work for the Church, noting that "the organization found its reason for being in the free adherence to the fixed principles of life represented in the law of God."

LOS ANGELES: FASTEST GROWING SEE

Following are comparative statistics from the *Official Catholic Directory, 1948* and *1968* for ten of the largest ecclesial jurisdictions in the United States:

		1948	1968	Increase
1.	Los Angeles	625,000	1,662,242	165%
2.	Newark	873.367	1,637,634	85%
3.	Detroit	900,000	1,548,594	72%
4.	New York	1,183,417	1,870,000	58%
5.	Boston	1,242,503	1,871,408	50%
6.	Buffalo	637,565	937,567	47%
7.	Brooklyn	1,153,467	1,551,264	34%
8.	Chicago	1,755,868	2,342,000	33%
9.	Philadelphia	1,011,064	1,353,024	33%
10.	Pittsburgh	760,687	926,876	21%

He stressed that members derived their strength from the fact that they were "at one in the acceptance of the truth of our Lord and Savior, Jesus Christ."[18]

In an article for *Confraternity Notes*, Anne Heffernan stated that the objectives of the A.C.C.W. were "to carry out specific work entrusted by Ordinary of the Archdiocese of Los Angeles, to cooperate with archdiocesan moderators and directors and to implement approved archdiocesan programs through standing committees." An annual conference was held each year at which upwards of 1,600 women gathered to hear speakers and address problems and challenges facing the greater Catholic community. The role of the A.C.C.W. was that of "cooperating with" rather than replacing existing structures in the archdiocese.[19]

McIntyre used the A.C.C.W. as a means of linking together other activities and over the years he enlisted their assistance in a host of activities such as the annual crusades for *The Tidings*, efforts to remove Catholic schools from the tax rolls, opposition to Federal Aid to education that would deny equal benefits to Catholics, the encouragement of Mary's Hour and the establishing of Mission Circles for support of the lay missionary program.

Late in 1957, McIntyre suggested to the A.C.C.W. leadership that they launch a monthly newsletter, a project that began the following January with publication of the initial copy of *The ACCW Newsletter*. In the very first issue, McIntyre asked members to continue their apostolate of providing "a strong bond of spiritual accord that will merit God's blessings and the protection of our Blessed Lady."[20] The cardinal appointed a chaplain for the organization and he met personally with him prior to gatherings of the A.C.C.W.'s executive board. Each parish was encouraged to establish a branch so that the network could be activated in moments through a telephone linkup throughout the archdiocese.

Over the years, Cardinal McIntyre became increasingly displeased with the policies of the National Council of Catholic Women and, after a long series of negotiations, he encouraged the local A.C.C.W. to withdraw its affiliation. On August 8, 1958, a majority of those on the executive board voted to comply with the cardinal's advice. The Los Angeles organization had long been a dissentient voice on a number of national issues, including the N.C.C.W.'s views on pre-occupation with the United Nations, UNICEF, SFO and other similar agencies. Especially irritating to McIntyre were statements by the N.C.C.W. on the Bricker Amendment, the promotion of the Freedom Agenda, Radio Free Europe, the Catholic Association for International Peace, the sale of UNICEF anti Christmas cards, endorsement of the Genocide Convention and other issues that were misleading, if not erroneous.

In their letter of withdrawal, the ladies protested what they considered a "soft approach on Communism" and N.C.C.W.'s "silence concerning the present grave evils of secularism, materialism and atheistic Communism in our midst." They also complained about the "absence of a strong positive program of Catholic Action, the omission of an alert on discrimination in all articles on Federal Aid to Education, silence about UNESCO's proposed new treaty known as the Convention Against Discrimination in Education" and other positions that were "artfully maneuvered" through the last national convention with little or no discussion.[21]

Interestingly, the Los Angeles A.C.C.W. not only survived its breakoff from the national organization, but thrived and grew to become one of the leading Catholic organizations in the archdiocese. Local authorities pointed to the A.C.C.W. as an example of how decentralization often strengthens rather than lessens the effectiveness of religious agencies.

Another Los Angeles women's group attempting to counteract the Communist threat to world peace through an activation of the social encyclicals was the Christines. Established in December, 1949, their aim was that of striving to contribute "to the Christianization of the environment by bearing witness to Christ." The two main aspects of their program were *spiritually* "the development of a more mature understanding of our Catholic faith through prayer and the integration of the liturgical life of the Church into our daily lives" and, *practically* the holding of monthly meetings, regular lectures, a library and other means "to provide more Christian homes and more effective participation in parish and community life."[22] The Catholic lay organization of women quickly grew to a 900 member group. A three-fold program of prayer, study and action involved them in discussions of Catholic social theory, industrial relations, interracial relations, marriage problems, and the bitter controversy raging in Los Angeles at the time over the programs of UNESCO.

ARCHDIOCESAN SYNOD

Plans for a synod in the Archdiocese of Los Angeles, the first such legislative session in the area since June 12, 1942, were announced in the fall of 1959. In the official summons, Cardinal McIntyre defined a synod as "an assembly of the clergy convoked by the ordinary to formulate and promulgate legislation concerned with the

SYNODUS DIOECESANA

ANGELORUM IN CALIFORNIA

SEPTIMA

ACTA ATQUE STATUTA

Cardinal McIntyre instituted an archival facility for the Archdiocese of Los Angeles in 1962.

The archives for the archdiocese were originally located in the curial offices on West Ninth Street in Los Angeles.

spiritual welfare of the archdiocese."[23] Its enactments would have special relevance to the local area. The preliminary work for the synod, entrusted to several commissions appointed to study various aspects of Catholic life and practice in the archdiocese, would then be submitted to a General Commission as agenda for the formal sessions to be held in Saint Vibiana's Cathedral. McIntyre hoped that the actual synod would be ready before the spring of 1960.

In actuality, the preparatory work took a bit longer. In the fall of 1960, the cardinal officially set the invocation date for the Feast of Our Lady of Guadalupe. The solemn session followed a Pontifical Mass, at which time the new legislation for the welfare of the archdiocese was promulgated. Bishop Alden J. Bell read the decree for the opening of the Synod, after which Bishop Timothy Manning led the 700 priests present in a profession of faith. A portion of the decrees covering matters of parochial and archdiocesan administration and liturgical observance was read. January 1, 1961 was targeted as the date when the new regulations became effective.

The actual statutes, which numbered 181, specified the rules and recommendations governing the conduct of the clergy, the religious and the laity within the archdiocese in the light of contemporary conditions. The relationships between the priest and his people were defined, and the guidance was offered for enriching the spiritual life of his own soul and the souls entrusted to his ministry. Provisions were made for the pastoral care of his flock from the cradle to the grave, with regulations touching every phase of life from the rebirth in Baptism to the solemn beauty of Christian burial.

Among the synodal statutes were specific rules governing the preparation for marriage, the pastoral care of the sick and infirm, the conduct of parish schools and classes of instruction and the dissemination of Catholic literature. Fresh encouragement was given to such customs as the blessing of mothers after childbirth, the practice of daily Mass, the recitation of the Rosary and prayer for the dead in parish churches. Renewed impetus was given to the growth of parish societies such as the Holy Name, the Legion of Mary, St. Vincent de Paul, the Sodality of Our Lady and the Propagation of the Faith.[24] It was an historic and meaningful gathering. The local Catholic newspaper commented that "here was Jerusalem again, here was Nicaea and Chalcedon and Trent, here was Christ on the slope of Galilee, transmitting His word and His power to men and women."[25]

The canonical documentation, along with the norms and decrees promulgated on the Feast of Our Lady of Guadalupe, were subsequently issued in a booklet under the title *Synodus Diocesiana*

Angelorum in California Septima which was given to all clergy and religious attached to the Archdiocese of Los Angeles. Though the publication with its "General Norms" has been superseded by mountains of regulations, directives and guidelines in subsequent years, it remains the "official canonical handbook" for the Archdiocese of Los Angeles until a future ordinary convokes and promulgates the eighth archdiocesan synod.

CHANCERY ARCHIVES

Though an archivist had been named for the old Diocese of Los Angeles-San Diego as early as 1927, Msgr. Peter Hanrahan never functioned in any other but a titular role. He later described the collection of those early days as "a mass of unarranged materials in a walk-in vault with a combination lock at the old cathedral rectory."[26] A dozen years prior to the directive from the National Conference of Catholic Bishops encouraging local ordinaries to open their archives to researchers, Cardinal McIntyre inaugurated a formal archival program for the Archdiocese of Los Angeles. In the final months of 1962, he had a new wing for that purpose added to the northeastern end of the Chancery Office. An archivist was appointed[27] and, on the following July 8,[28] the Chancery Archives were formally blessed and designated as an archdiocesan department. Elizabeth I. Dixon of the Historical Society of Southern California ventured the opinion that the archives would "eventually constitute the largest collection of ecclesiastical documents in the Western United States."[29] There was a prophetical ring to her words.

In consultation with experts, McIntyre spelled out the basic function of the Chancery Archives as that of collecting, preserving, studying and interpreting any and all documents, diaries, manuscripts, brochures, photographs and assorted historical memorabilia pertaining in any way to California's Catholic heritage. And the term "Catholic" was not meant to be restrictive, except to limit the goals within reasonable parameters.

The Chancery Archives were also intended to function as a records management system for preserving and making available curial documents and other pertinent materials essential to the effective administration of the Archdiocese of Los Angeles. As the final repository for the permanent records of the Church, the collection is now located at Mission Hills, and has become a treasure trove for historians, economists, political scientists and others.

During the ensuing years of the McIntyre regime, efforts were made to augment and catalogue the widely diversified assortment of documents, brochures, books and other historical mementos associated with the development of the Catholic Church in California's southland and, within the first decade, the initial holdings were quadrupled. The cardinal's concern for keeping an accurate record of God's dealings with His people set an outstanding precedent and provided an enviable watershed in the story of the American Church.

SAINT VIBIANA

In an attempt to enkindle interest in and devotion to Saint Vibiana, for whom his cathedral was named, McIntyre announced in mid-1949 that Vibiana's feastday would be observed on September 4th with solemn festivities. He said that "the Archconfraternity of St. Vibiana, established during the pontificate of Pope Pius IX, was being revived." There would be an archdiocesan-wide novena made in preparation for the feast in all the parishes. He suggested that priests "ask their people, in making this triduum, to add to their personal intentions the supplications for the suffering Catholic peoples who are being persecuted in the Eastern European countries under Soviet regime. These children of God are bearing the brunt of an attack on Christianity as well as Christian civilization. Let it be our prayer that they will be strengthened in their faith and have courage to withstand the ordeals forced upon them."[30] Enclosed in his letter was a newly-translated copy of the historic novena which Bishop Thaddeus Amat had introduced to the area in 1856.[31]

During each successive year, McIntyre encouraged devotional practices that included parochial novenas, visitations to Saint Vibiana's shrine and instructions about her being a role model for young people. In 1954, McIntyre said that "in the world today, many of our brothers and sisters in the faith behind the iron curtain and in the satellite countries are being seriously harassed because of their belief in God and faith in Christ and diligence in devotion to Our Lady. Some have been martyrs, but all are suffering slow martyrdom, for there is no greater persecution than in being deprived of the privilege to worship God from Whom all blessings flow. " The cardinal thought it would be appropriate, on the feast of Saint Vibiana, "to have a triduum of prayer, concluding with Mass on her feastday, asking "all the faithful to pray particularly for our suffering and persecuted brothers and sisters."[32]

McIntyre was unaware that in faraway Rome, there were forces afoot that wanted to banish Vibiana from the role bestowed upon her by Pius IX a century earlier. Anton Debevec, a research scholar working in the Roman archives of Propaganda Fide, reported that the wreath inscribed on the original tomb of Vibiana was no longer considered, if it ever was, "a sufficient proof of St. Vibiana's martyrdom" inasmuch as the same emblem had recently been found on a number of tombs belonging to pagans or non-believers. In addition, he pointed out that "no mention is made in the epitaph of her martyrdom as in the epitaphs of other martyrs." Several well-credentialed authorities confided to Debevec "privately and unofficially - that, from the point of view of Christian archeology, St. Vibiana is not a martyr."[33]

Quite fortuitously, Debevec heard a short while later that officials at the Congregation of Rites "fully acquainted with the case and the problem arising from it," had drafted a directive which they were planning to enclose "when they return the *Officia propria* recently submitted by the diocese."[34] That potentially provocative information was passed along to Bishop Alden Bell, together with the observation that Father Joannes Quasten of The Catholic University of America, when privately asked, concurred that "the discovery of the wreath is not presently regarded as evidence of martyrdom."[35] Parenthetically, about the vials of blood deposited with the other relics, it might be noted that "the Sacred Congregation of Rites will not accept their presence alone as evidence of martyrdom unless their contents have been proved by chemical analysis to be human blood.[36]

The directive, along with the approved *Officia propria* alluded to by Debevec, was returned to Cardinal McIntyre, early in August, 1962.[37] In addition to a minor revision in the text of Matins for the Feast of Saint Emidius, the Prefect of the Congregation of Rites, Arcadio Cardinal Larraona, expressed serious reservations about the continued patronage of Vibiana, noting that Pope Pius X had ordered relics discovered under similar circumstances returned to the catacombs. While displaying a willingness to discuss the matter further, the prefect stated that "it is our policy to advise each local Ordinary, in whose dioceses there is such a relic, to see to it that the pseudo-relic be prudently removed, avoiding any scandal." Cardinal Larraona then observed that such a transfer would necessarily involve an alteration in the name of the cathedral. He suggested that once the relics had been "made to disappear without any public notice," a title of the Blessed Mother might be bestowed on the cathedral.[38]

Reaction at Los Angeles was unfavorable. Cardinal McIntyre responded that the prefect had "been misinformed and inadequately acquainted with some of the circumstances" surrounding the cultus of Vibiana. He reminded Larraona, and rightly so, of the papal directives specifically ordering the erection of a cathedral in Vibiana's honor. "To attempt the removal of the relic," said the cardinal, "would occasion grave comment and be heralded throughout the United States in a fashion analogous to that of Philomena." In effect, Cardinal McIntyre flatly refused to abide by the recommendation, noting that even the non-acceptance of the vial of blood as testimony of martyrdom was far from definitive since "the remaining evidence of virginity and piety are ample for sanctity."[39] Responding that he had signed the earlier communique "as a matter of office only," the prefect expressed agreement with the Archbishop of Los Angeles "in principle" and gave assurances he would not "do anything to eliminate Saint Vibiana," but would have the matter shelved "indefinitely."[40]

Nothing more was done about the matter until after McIntyre's retirement and the telling of that story must be relegated to another time. In his eulogy for the cardinal, Archbishop Timothy Manning alluded to the Vibiana affair in this way:

> As he enters this procession of glory to the throne of God, it is proper at this time to reveal one secret about someone who meets him there. There was a time in the post Vatican era when there was an urge for demythologizing saints, desacralizing sacred memories. People like Philomena and Christopher lost their niches in the church. There was a secret letter sent to Cardinal McIntyre that Vibiana had to go. In the inimitable McIntyre manner, he wrote his mind to Rome. And she is still here. I am sure that she was at the head of the procession that brought him to heavenly glory.[41]

THE LAITY

In his first sermon delivered in Los Angeles on the occasion of his installation as archbishop, J. Francis A. McIntyre made a pointed reference to Catholic action: "As time goes on," he said, "you will find me putting forceful stress upon Catholic action, which is far different from mere Catholic activity." In an interview with a secular news magazine, the archbishop defined Catholic action in these words: "Personal sanctity, expressed in corporate action by oneself and in communion with other people." He saw it as a way of life based on the fundamental precepts and the moral and spiritual laws of Christianity as a whole and Catholicism in particular. To McIntyre, Catholic Action meant "an intensification or the application of the principles of Christ, cultivation of increased religious life among the people and by the people." McIntyre believed that religion was not something separate and apart from a person's day-by-day life, it is, instead, a part of that life, a part of the individual himself, twenty-four hours a day.[42] Throughout his years in the California southland, McIntyre encouraged every kind of lay activity. He was an avid supporter of the Legion of Mary and other groups established primarily to stimulate involvement at every level of the Church's ministry. It was a pleased McIntyre who told Father Francis J. Connell in 1957 that "the Lay Apostolate here is progressing well, thank God."[43]

FEDERATION OF LAITY

In July of 1967, David M. Thompson and several other people organized what was called the Los Angeles Association of Laymen. In a letter to prospective members, the association was described as a "viable, if embryonic entity" of Catholics "who desire to assume a responsible role in the life of the Church." It was formed as a "response to the invitation of the Council Fathers to seek ways to express that responsibility in the Los Angeles area." Ostensibly, the association would provide a means whereby the laity could "bring its knowledge and experience to bear upon the life of the Church." Interestingly, officers had already been selected by the time others were invited to join.[44]

A preliminary meeting was held at UCLA on November 12th. Dr. Fallon Evans gave a keynote address in which he outlined the objectives of the association. According to a report in the Loyola University campus newspaper, "the gathering produced considerable pledges of financial support." The initial gathering was described as "positive, and not just an angry one." David Thompson, formerly of Loyola's Development Office was elected president. Chosen as Vice president was activist Emil Seliga, a long-time protagonist of the cardinal. Details were also given about an ad that would appear in the Los Angeles *Times* outlining the purposes of the association along with membership procedures.[45]

News of the association's formation hit the secular papers on November 26th, when John Dart told his readers that "a group of Roman Catholics, quietly forming a laymen's association outside existing church structures for the last four months, surfaced this week to announce their first public meeting." Listed among the goals was the formation of a priests' senate and "trying to persuade James Francis Cardinal McIntyre to allow experimentation in ways of worship and other innovations." Thompson admitted that he had "not sought the permission of the cardinal to organize," noting that "we feel we have not only the right but the responsibility to come together to create an authentic, free and responsible lay voice and presence in the Archdiocese of Los Angeles. "Among other objectives were "social action, upgrading Catholic literature and developing meaningful programs for youth."[46]

At the first open meeting in Beverly Hills, more than 700 Catholics "applauded a speaker who urged them to make their voices heard in the decision-making processes of the Church." Dennis Landis, president of the National Association of Laymen, told the group that "the byword of religion is relevancy." He noted that Catholics in thirty-seven cities representing eighteen states had organized to "follow out their conception of the meaning of Vatican II." Landis charged that "too much control" was being exercised by the church hierarchy over priests, religious and laity in areas where that control is inimical to the mission of the Church. His remark that "we must bring Christ back to the Church" surely was not intended to endear him or the movement to the local Catholic leadership. Another speaker softened the rhetoric a bit and said that the purpose of the association was "not to throw rocks at the cardinal or anyone else. Our purpose is to take a positive approach to basic issues" noting that "if any rocks fall, it will be incidental."[47]

A reporter for a national Catholic newspaper attended the inaugural meeting of the N.A.L. and wrote that the three hour meeting "was devoted mainly to controversial topics such as race relations, poverty, liturgy, ecumenism and the training of priests and religious." He quoted one of the speakers as saying that "risk and challenge is the language of lovers. Our conflict is not with the personalities involved, but with the antiquated structure of the Church. " He also noted that there were dissenters at the meeting and some "rose to their feet to register protest and in a few cases to heckle the panelists."[48]

There were other views expressed about the gathering. One observer said that there were fewer than 325 people present, and fully a hundred of them were opposed "to the tactics of the N.A.L." He ended his marks by saying that "there may be many conclusions which can be drawn from the first public meeting of the N.A.L., but it would be absolutely incorrect to infer that, based on attendance, there is any widespread or minuscule support for this new organization."[49]

In February of 1968, the Los Angeles Association of Laymen began publication of *The Lay Voice*. In its first issue, a sidebar noted that the association had been formed "spontaneously by concerned Catholics who saw the need for all the elements of the lay community to join together as an independent and responsible voice and arm of the Church." In the lead article, which endorsed the position taken by the Immaculate Heart Sisters in their conflict with Cardinal McIntyre, readers were encouraged to send letters of support to the Cardinal Prefect of the Sacred Congregation for Religious, but noted that "great caution should be exercised in writing. Italian cardinals are even less conditioned than American cardinals to consideration of the wishes of the laity."[50]

McIntyre refused to be drawn into any confrontations with the N.A.L. He declined to answer their letters and avoided expressing himself to the press. The March meeting of the association, held in Westwood, drew only a hundred members and it soon became obvious that there was little grass roots support for the N.A.L. as a spokesman for the Catholic laity. Organizers admitted later that they doomed the movement from the outset by setting themselves up in opposition to the structured Church. The concept, a good one, would come of age at a later time when cooler minds prevailed.

Notes to the Text

1. *The Tidings*, December 23, 1949.
2. AALA, J. Francis A. McIntyre to Mr. and Mrs. John Arena, Los Angeles, November 10, 1950.
3. Los Angeles *Times*, December 16, 1950.
4. AALA, Press Release - Jack Lawson, n.p., November 15, 1951.
5. AALA, J. Francis A. McIntyre to n.n., Los Angeles, December 7, 1952.
6. Los Angeles *Examiner*, October 31, 1952.
7. AALA, Alden J. Bell to James Francis Cardinal McIntyre, Los Angeles, January 6, 1956.
8. AALA, James Francis Cardinal McIntyre to n.n., Los Angeles, January 16, 1956.
9. Los Angeles *Examiner*, December 18, 1961.
10. AALA, James Francis Cardinal McIntyre to Mrs. Ramon Stanley, Los Angeles, December 9, 1964.
11. Los Angeles *Times*, December 12, 1966.
12. *Ibid*, n.d. (1968).
13. AALA, Sr. Mary David to J. Francis Cardinal McIntyre, Santa Monica, June 23, 1952.
14. Los Angeles *Times*, December 6, 1968.
15. *Ibid*., December 7, 1968.
16. *The Tidings*, December 13, 1968.
17. AALA, James Francis Cardinal McIntyre to Donors, Los Angeles, July 3, 1961.
18. AALA, Address by James Francis Cardinal McIntyre, Fresno, April 26, 1953.
19. XXIII (November, 1965), 4.
20. I (January, 1958), 1.
21. AALA, Brochure "To Whom It May Concern," Los Angeles Council of Catholic Women, October 3, 1962.
22. *The Christine Bulletin* (November, 1958), n.p.
23. *The Tidings*, October 16, 1959.
24. *Ibid*., December 16, 1960.
25. *Ibid*.
26. Quoted in Francis J. Weber (ed.), *Dedication Ceremonies for the Archival Center* (Mission Hills, 1981), p. 5.
27. *The Tidings*, December 28, 1962.
28. *Ibid*., July 12, 1963.
29. *Newsletter. The Historical Society of Southern California* II (Fall, 1963), 4.

30. AALA, J. Francis A. McIntyre to Priests, Los Angeles, August 17, 1949.
31. The original appeared as *Novena a Santa Vibiana, Virgen y Martir, Protectura de la Diocesis de Monterey* (San Francisco, 1856).
32. AALA, James Francis Cardinal McIntyre to Priests, Los Angeles, August 19, 1954.
33. AALA, Anthony Debevec to Francis J. Weber, Rome, February 24, 1962.
34. *Ibid* , March 5, 1962.
35. AALA, Francis J. Weber to Alden J. Bell, Washington, March 8, 1962.
36. D. F. MacDaid, *Exploring the Roman Catacombs* (Dublin, 1950), Pp. 2-3.
37. AALA, Arcadio M. Larraona, C.M.F. to James Francis McIntyre, Rome, July 26, 1962.
38. AALA, *Ibid.*
39. AALA, James Francis McIntyre to Arcadio M. Larraona, C.M.F., Los Angeles, August 3, 1962.
40. AALA, Arcadio M. Larraona, C.M.F. to James Francis McIntyre, Rome, August 28, 1962.
41. *The Tidings*, July 27, 1979.
42. *Fortnight* LV (June 18, 1948), 7.
43. AALA, James Francis Cardinal McIntyre to Francis J. Connell, C.Ss.R., Los Angeles, July 9, 1957.
44. AALA, David M. Thompson to Fellow Catholics, n.d. (c. July, 1967).
45. *Loyolan*, November 20, 1967.
46. Los Angeles *Times*, November 26, 1967.
47. *Ibid.*, December 4, 1967.
48. *National Catholic Reporter*, December 13, 1967.
49. Thomas C. Rogers in the Los Angeles *Times*, December 19, 1967.
50. *The Lay Voice* I (February, 1968), 1.

26. California's Centennial

For a brief moment, on September 18, 1949, the Los Angeles Memorial Coliseum became an "open air cathedral" as Catholics in the Archdiocese of Los Angeles gathered to celebrate the centenary of California's statehood under the title "*El Camino Real de la Cruz.*" The devotional drama about the California missions unfolded on a Sunday evening in the presence of over 35,000 people in response to an invitation from Archbishop J. Francis A. McIntyre.[1]

Presented on three giant stages on the Coliseum green, the event consisted of an historic prologue depicting the founding of the City of Nuestra Señora de los Angeles, a living tableaux of the Stations of the Cross and Benediction of the Blessed Sacrament. The story of California's Catholic background and the heroic saga of the Franciscan friars were intertwined with events in the Passion of Christ written for the occasion by Father Michael Sheahan, pastor of Santa Isabel parish in downtown Los Angeles.

Nearly a dozen stars of screen and radio took part in the narration and in leading the prayers of the Stations of the Cross. They included J. F. Regis Twomey, George Murphy, Stephen McNally, Gene Lockhart, Pedro de Cordoba, MacDonald Carey, J. Carrol Nash and Rod O'Connor. Choreographer Hermes Pan directed the overall pageant.[2] Setting the early California mood was the band of Our Lady of Talpa parish, a 100 strong group of boys who played a serenade beginning at 7:20 p.m., forty minutes before the pageant began. Choral music for the evening was provided by the Roger Wagner Chorale.

Prior to the prologue, which began at precisely 8:00 p.m., the archbishop and a long procession of priests, religious and ministers entered the coliseum in procession. During the prologue, on the first stage, the audience saw friars and Indians together with Mexican settlers on the trek from San Gabriel where they raised the cross on the site of the present church of Nuestra Señora de los Angeles. This they did as part of a ceremony of thanksgiving for having been brought safely from their homes in Sonora, Mexico.

Each of the stations was portrayed in living tableau on the second stage in the center of the Coliseum. At the close of the *via crucis*, Benediction of the Blessed Sacrament turned the arena into a huge church. All lights in the stadium were turned out and thousands of candles were held by participants. The monstrance used for Benediction was the same one used in mission days by Fray Junipero Serra at San Carlos Borromeo del Carmelo. It was brought to Los Angeles for the event by Harry Downie. Donated long ago by Antonio Bucareli, Viceroy of New Spain, the monstrance was and is among the great historic treasures of California.

Following Benediction, the event was brought to a close with the singing of the *Star Spangled Banner* and the hymn, *Holy God, We Praise Thy Name*. Members of the Catholic Youth Federation ushered the event. A small booklet was issued containing the prayers used for the celebration. Each person was also provided with a candle. The whole event was patterned after one which Saint Leonard of Port Maurice performed in the Coliseum at Rome on December 27, 1750, to mark the jubilee inaugurated that year by the Holy Father. The local Catholic newspaper account described the event in great detail, concluding with the observation "What an example these early missionaries have left for us."[3] Truly they were prophets in their own right.

THE CARDINAL AND UFOS

Nothing intrigues people more than UFOs and/or Flying Saucers which dart in and out of contemporary annals. Even churchmen occasionally figure into such scenarios. Over the years, several requests for information have been made about the late James Francis Cardinal McIntyre and his purported involvement in an incident that originally occurred in 1947.

In a book by Charles Berlitz and William L. Moore, entitled *The Roswell Incident*, it is stated that on the evening of July 2, 1947, "what appeared to be a flying saucer passed over Roswell heading northwest at a high rate of speed." It was struck by a lighting bolt and suffered severe onboard damage.[4] It managed to stay airborne long enough to get over the mountains before crashing violently in an area west of Socorro known as the Plains of San Agustin. Military officials quickly sequestered the wreckage and removed it into a security facility at Edward's Air Force Base. Only top governmental personnel were allowed to view or study the wreckage.

In April of 1954, Meade Layne, Director of the Borderland Research Associates, received a letter from Gerald Light of Los

Angeles who said that he had spent some forty-eight hours at Edwards Air Force Base in the company of three other men, Franklin Allen of the Hearst newspaper chain, Edwin Nourse of the Brookings Institute and Bishop MacIntyre (sic) of Los Angeles. Here is what he reported: "We were allowed to enter the restricted area . . . During my two days visit, I saw five separate and distinct types of aircraft being studied and handled by our air force officials with the assistance and permission of The Etherians! I have no words to express my reaction." According to Light, President Eisenhower had been spirited over to Muroc one night during a visit to Palm Springs. He felt that Ike would eventually "go directly to the people via radio and television" about the incident.[5]

Subsequently, Senator Barry Goldwater got involved in the story. While enroute to California, in the early 1960s, he stopped at Wright-Patterson and inquired about the "Blue Room" where the UFO artifacts, photographs and exhibits were stored. When later asked about the matter, Goldwater did not deny it, rather he said that he could not "believe that we are the only planet that has life on it."[6] Apart from the details of the purported crash and its cover-up, was Cardinal McIntyre ever personally involved? We know that he visited Edwards Air Force Base several times, once in November of 1956, when he confirmed about fifty military people.[7]

Was he there during the week of April 12-16, 1954, as alleged by Gerald Light? Not according to entries in his *Standard Daily Journal*. It was Holy Week and the cardinal was busy with office appointments at the Chancery and liturgical ceremonies at the Cathedral. After searching through all of McIntyre's papers, there is no evidence that would lend the slightest credence to the story of Gerald Light. Evidence can often be interpreted in diverse ways, but lack of evidence lends only to conjecture.

BIRTHDAY CELEBRATIONS

Those who wanted, expected or even suggested that James Francis Cardinal McIntyre would retire on June 25, 1961, his seventy-fifth birthday, weren't very well acquainted with the Archbishop of Los Angeles. Those who did know him would not have been surprised that he remained at the helm for almost another decade, long after most of his detractors were themselves retired from the local scene or forgotten by once prominent newspaper pundits.

In an interview with McIntyre on his seventy-fifth birthday, James Bennett found him to be "as vital and intent on his role in the Catholic Church as when he entered the priesthood forty years ago." He said that "the gracious and kindly prelate showed no signs of slackening the pace which has brought him from a successful place in the business world to his current position." McIntyre had no plans for his birthday itself, except delivering the invocation at the official opening of Los Angeles' new jet-age International Airport.[8]

Five years later, when the cardinal observed the twenty-fifth anniversary of his consecration as a bishop, Pope Paul VI sent a telegram in which he stated that "He who alone is all-good, has been mindful of you, and has adorned you with many heavenly benefits through a considerable length of time." The Holy Father expressed his "best wishes, highest regards and most sincere congratulations for the excellent pastoral ministry which you have exercised as Auxiliary Bishop and later Coadjutor Archbishop of New York, and now for almost twenty-one years as the Ordinary of the excellent and flourishing Archdiocese of Los Angeles."[9]

Actual observance of McIntyre's jubilee was postponed to coincide with the dedication of Saint John's College the following June. It was then that "California's and the west's most distinguished citizen for the past 18 years, Cardinal McIntyre will have been 45 years a priest and 25 years a bishop."[10] The ceremony at Camarillo, attended by two cardinals, thirty archbishops and bishops and hundreds of prominent Catholic lay people, was among the most impressive in California's annals. In a toast to the cardinal, Sir Daniel Donohue said that "it is our firm conviction that you have brought, and continue to bring, constant luster to the priesthood and to the hierarchy of the Church in America."[11] Jose Cardinal Garibi y Rivera of Guadalajara eloquently enumerated the many blessings Mexican-Americans in California had received through McIntyre's intervention. A prominent national Catholic newspaper noted that "birthdays and anniversaries most often are marked by gifts to the celebrant . . . whereas Cardinal McIntyre, in a typical gesture, reversed the procedure"[12] by giving back the check for $250,000 presented by the people of the archdiocese, as his contribution for the erection of the seminary chapel which was thereafter given the patronage of Saint James. Later McIntyre was honored with a white-tie dinner in the California Club. That affair, criticized by some as being "too magnificent"[13] elicited an interesting comment from L. J. Kolitsch that the cardinal surely "is a capable, efficient, kind, prudent and charitable man" who had spent most of the educational funds "to erect high schools in impoverished neighborhoods." He pointed out an ironic note that once "while McIntyre's offices were being picketed by alleged Catholics, he was presiding at the funeral of a poor Negro lady in Watts."[14] And that observation was true!

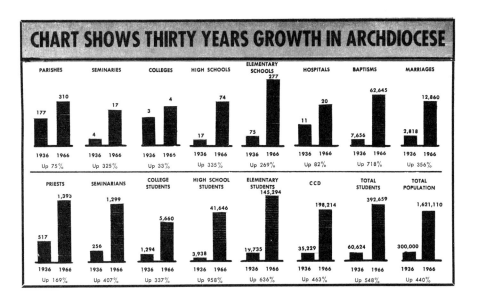

CHART SHOWS THIRTY YEARS GROWTH IN ARCHDIOCESE

PARISHES	SEMINARIES	COLLEGES	HIGH SCHOOLS	ELEMENTARY SCHOOLS	HOSPITALS	BAPTISMS	MARRIAGES
177 / 310	4 / 17	3 / 4	17 / 74	75 / 277	11 / 20	7,656 / 62,645	2,818 / 12,860
1936 1966	1936 1966	1936 1965	1936 1966	1936 1966	1936 1966	1936 1966	1936 1966
Up 75%	Up 325%	Up 33%	Up 335%	Up 269%	Up 82%	Up 718%	Up 356%

PRIESTS	SEMINARIANS	COLLEGE STUDENTS	HIGH SCHOOL STUDENTS	ELEMENTARY STUDENTS	CCD	TOTAL STUDENTS	TOTAL POPULATION
517 / 1,393	256 / 1,299	1,294 / 5,660	3,938 / 41,646	19,735 / 145,294	35,229 / 198,214	60,624 / 392,659	300,000 / 1,621,110
1936 1966	1936 1966	1936 1966	1936 1966	1936 1966	1936 1966	1936 1966	1936 1966
Up 169%	Up 407%	Up 337%	Up 958%	Up 636%	Up 463%	Up 548%	Up 440%

STATISTICS ON ARCHDIOCESE FOR THE YEAR 1966

AREA TOTALS	Los Angeles County	Los Angeles City*	Orange County	Ventura County	Santa Barbara County
313 PARISHES	249	(99)	37	14	13
Population: 1,621,101					
81 HIGH SCHOOLS	65	(27)	6	6	4
Enrollment: 41,839	36,021	(15,441)	3,494	1,246	1,078
285 ELEMENTARY SCHOOLS	228	(113)	34	12	11
Enrollment: 143,596	116,086	(52,617)	19,210	4,723	3,577
19 GENERAL HOSPITALS	14	(3)	2	1	2
Patients treated: 656,967	470,455	(60,544)	114,536	36,701	35,275
POPULATION:					
1,621,101 Catholics	1,295,655	(370,702)	218,593	60,224	46,629
Total Population					
8,716,672	7,007,400	(2,782,900)	1,174,600	311,100	243,600

*L.A. City figures are included in total for L.A. County

The Los Angeles City Council joined in according "the highest accolades for distinguished service" to the cardinal who, they proclaimed, was "recognized throughout the Catholic world as a great spiritual leader and courageous initiator of projects whose dynamism and benefits bring an excellence and uplift to the culture and character of the whole community."[15] A lengthy essay on "The Shepherd and His Flock" appeared in *The Tidings* on July 1, 1966 wherein it was noted that in the preceding eighteen years, the Catholic population of Los Angeles had increased by 1,000,000 persons - a gain of 159%. "Confronting the surging, eddying tide of migration has been the work here of James Francis Cardinal McIntyre." Noting that the Church in Los Angeles was a "missionary Church," the account went on to say that "St. Paul had Antioch and Corinth, Ephesus and Tarsus. Here there are Azusa and Covina, Encino and Torrance. Here is a Church of 135 cities and towns in coast and desert and island. The distance from Athens to Corinth is approximately the same as from Long Beach to Santa Barbara; and Antioch to Tarsus is the same as Santa Maria to San Juan Capistrano. As Paul faced the problems of numbers, so too the Church in Los Angeles faces sheer numbers because of the historical circumstances of migration." The essay continued:

Since the migration began after World War II, 1,000 Catholics a week continue arriving in Los Angeles. Unlike Paul's Christians, these are not converts but old Catholics knowing the settled Christian communities of the East and Midwest and wanting the same here before the first grass roots itself on the freshly bulldozed California soil of their new homes still flagged with realtors' signs.

Demographers say that the population rise in the Southland will not crest until 1980 when there will be a solid megalopolis from Santa Barbara south to the Mexican border. A man who makes decisions in Southern California today must think 20 years ahead of himself - to start with.

Every morning the bells of Cardinal McIntyre's cathedral on skid row toll the *Angelus* in downtown's acid dawn. They begin a new day in which the paramount fact confronting the Chief Pastor of one of the world's largest cities is that the population is yet spiraling. Pastorally, this is one of the principal facts of life in Southern California.

Every year the Archdiocese of Los Angeles is increasing by 55,000 persons. It is as if every year for the past 18 years all the Catholics of the diocese of Lincoln, Nebraska arrived here - but without their priests, or Sisters, or churches, or schools, or hospitals or other facilities.

What they do bring, however is a desire and a determination to establish for themselves the fullness of the church in their new homes, whether these be stuccos in the endless tracts in former orange groves, "view homes" literally on stilts pinioned onto hillsides, executive homes on "rice paddy" terraces, $29-a-month apartments in city housing projects, or creaky frames in the old neighborhoods. This desire for clothing their lives in the fabric of their faith translates for people and their leaders into willing work, under pressure and permanent overtime. In the divine economy there are no time clocks.

Mclntyre's eightieth birthday occasioned a number of interviews, among them one which appeared in a monthly magazine published by the Mayor's International Visitors Council. Therein the cardinal was described as "a man of iron will, with a delightful touch of Irish wit and charm. " He was quoted as saying that "religion has been a prime factor in the growth and development of this city and its surrounding communities. This metropolis is inhabited by a God loving and God fearing populace. To them, religion is an integral part of their lives. It is the source of their strength that will always help in difficult times." After citing some historical statistics, the interviewer concluded by noting that "one of the state's pioneers lives today. His name is James Francis McIntyre and he oversees the spiritual welfare of the fastest growing Catholic population in America. He will always be controversial because he is outspoken and keeps his views in the open. He would not want it any other way."[16]

SACRAMENTAL CENSUS - ARCHDIOCESE OF LOS ANGELES

Year	Infant Baptisms	Converts	Marriages	Confirmations	Catholic Population
1948	26,149	1,987	7,491		690,000
1949	22,870	2,538	6,380		832,375
1950	29,515	3,338	7,464		832,500
1951	32,345	3,291	8,172		835,000
1952	33,760	3,211	7,477		942,000
1953	35,742	3,829	8,024		934,370
1954	41,774	4,257	8,841	18,923	997,770
1955	44,442	4,333	8,555	16,516	1,075,000
1956	47,050	4,581	9,325	20,457	1,112,358
1957	49,885	4,636	9,588	20,439	1,197,357
1958	52,485	4,600	9,356	21,612	1,243,511
1959	53,662	4,730	9,727	25,364	1,297,584
1960	56,023	4,664	10,061	29,856	1,348,104
1961	57,882	4,555	10,458	29,036	1,421,478
1962	60,390	4,640	10,617	32,732	1,477,408
1963	60,055	4,985	11,942	35,839	1,532,411
1964	62,275	5,317	12,598	30,382	1,581,015
1965	62,645	4,981	12,860	38,526	1,621,101
1966	58,565	4,910	13,126	38,454	1,640,167
1967	57,052	4,495	13,652	33,485	1,662,242
1968	56,503	3,903	15,058	36,525	1,727,161
1969	60,481	3,663	15,889	37,514	1,707,605
1970	62,382	3,226	15,574	32,851	1,743,164

THE YAKIMA PROBLEM

Possessed of a universal vision of the Church, McIntyre always looked beyond the confines of his own jurisdiction, not in quest of control or influence but in the sense of service and public relations. Early in 1968, the Diocese of Yakima found itself on the brink of financial disaster. It all came to light when Bishop Joseph P. Dougherty arranged to have Price Waterhouse and Company install a new accounting system in his diocese. In the process of its work, the firm discovered that a fundamental error had been made in the preparation of the consolidated balance sheet. While the initial amount of money involved was negligible, it grew to significant proportions over the fifteen years between 1953 and 1968. When the matter was brought to his attention, James Francis Cardinal McIntyre began immediately to arrange for funds to sustain the diocese until plans could be formulated to care for the overall situation. McIntyre, a practitioner of collegiality long before that term was popularized at Vatican Council II, sent a memorandum to all the bishops in the western part of the nation, apprising them of the problem and explaining that "the financial status of Yakima is demanding of substantial and prompt assistance." He said the matter was "of vital importance not only to those directly concerned, but of equal, if not greater importance, to other dioceses and the general credit of the Church." The cardinal did not suggest a "loan" because "the resources of the diocese did not justify the making of long term loans at the time" because there was no likelihood of repayment. He then outlined a schedule of payments that needed to be met over ensuing months.[17]

Msgr. Benjamin G. Hawkes was sent to Yakima to make a cursory study of the problem and from there, he flew to Washington to alert the Apostolic Delegate of the magnitude of Yakima's indebtedness. Archbishop Luigi Raimondi thanked McIntyre for his "great understanding and wonderful generosity" towards what was obviously a major threat to the American Church.

On May 28th, McIntyre told the Apostolic Delegate that Yakima appeared to have obligations approximating nine million dollars. He attributed "the cause of the whole trouble" to a "faulty statement of assets and liabilities upon which the loans were obtained." The mistake was including diocesan assets without including the corresponding liabilities. " McIntyre said that the problem was intensified when Bishop Dougherty called a meeting of creditors and issued a corrected statement which, in turn, caused some of the lenders to refuse renewal. The cardinal had learned from Hawkes that the pastors of Yakima were "somewhat acquainted with the situation," but were "not sympathetic to a possible campaign or appeal for capital funds. McIntyre felt that "the image of the bishop" had suffered and "the net result is critical." The cardinal had spoken extensively with Archbishop Joseph McGucken of San Francisco and the two of them were willing to act as substitute creditors for Yakima in the loans aggregating two and a half million dollars. He also felt that the Archbishop of Seattle would subscribe $100,000. Finally he agreed to petition the other dioceses of the West Coast to contribute to a fund that would enable Yakima to meet its obligations for the rest of the calendar year. McIntyre said that the obligations assumed by Los Angeles and San Francisco would not be "written off" because, if those figures appeared on statements for the diocese of Yakima, bankers would mitigate their credit offerings. He concluded by expressing a desire that some authority figure be put in place at Yakima who would gain the respect of creditors and others involved in the recovery process. None of Yakima's "existing staff" possessed those qualities."[18]

On June 4, 1968, McIntyre sent out a formal plea for assistance to the other bishops. He reiterated the basic facts and admitted that the scenario was "embarrassing and frustrating." He underscored that the problem was greater than Yakima for it "indirectly involves the credit of all Catholic dioceses now engaged in financing through similar methods." Aware that some of the areas were already hard-pressed financially, McIntyre wanted "all the bishops to participate even if their contributions were nominal." He pointed out that "the united response of the bishops in assisting this situation will be of monumental effect, Vatican II in action, and will establish the spirit that represents the basis of our credit."[19]

Response was encouraging, especially when bishops beyond the west coast were also solicited. By December, Bishop Dougherty reported back that the appeal had brought back the Diocese of Yakima "to the turning point where it appears now there is a definite hope that the crisis is within range of being managed." Dougherty enumerated the returns to McIntyre's plea:

May	San Francisco	243,500.00
June	Los Angeles	234,336.50
	Seattle	100,000.00
	San Diego	5,000.00
	Baker	2,500.00
	Fresno	5,000 00
July	Spokane	50,000.00
	Monterey	10,000.00
	Tucson	10,000.00
August	Chicago	50,000.00
	Salt Lake	10,000.00
	Reno	25,000.00
September	Boise	20,000.00
	Baker	5,000.00
	Santa Rosa	25,000.00
	Stockton	20,000.00
	Fresno	1,500.00
	Monterey	5,000.00
	ABCM	200,000.00
November	ABCM	300,000.00
	Helena	10,000.00
December	Sacramento	25,000.00

$ 1,356,836.50

Substitution of credit by Archdioceses
of Los Angeles and San Francisco to   2,400,000.00
cover A. G. Becker & Company loan

$ 3,756,836.50[20]

    Early in 1969, the Holy Father accepted the resignation of Bishop Dougherty and a new administrative team was appointed to take over the continuance of the recovery.[21] Included in that program were a series of stipulations drawn up by McIntyre which included installation of a new accounting system, extensive changes of parochial personnel, suspension of a number of diocesan institutions (such as the seminary, a radio station and a newspaper) and a moratorium on capital expenditure. The uncompromising, all-embracing austerity program remained in place for a number of years.[22]

    In this and many other situations affecting the Church in the west, McIntyre unhesitatingly offered his services and those of his chancery staff. Bishop Timothy Manning of Fresno wrote to say that it was "so typical of your magnanimous heart to act as you have done in the Yakima crisis. So much of your life must forever be hid under a bushel!"[23]

ARCHIEPISCOPAL RESIDENCE

Upon his arrival in Los Angeles, McIntyre took up residence in the official archiepiscopal mansion that had been purchased by his predecessor from King Gillette in 1927. Though he never liked living in the fashionable Fremont Place, the archbishop made the most of it. As he once remarked, "there isn't much in the way of alternatives." The excess cubic footage of the residence was a challenge to McIntyre's penchant for getting the most out of a capital investment. He converted several of the large rooms on the second floor into meeting places for the Board of Consultors and other groups. Often, in the afternoons, the home was used for charity teas and similar affairs.

He retained the staff who had worked for Archbishop John J. Cantwell. Mary Boyle was the housekeeper and cook and Alex Navarro doubled as gardener and chauffeur. In the early days, the archbishop frequently drove his own car, much to the detriment of the already crowded streets. McIntyre never cared about fancy cuisine and plain, good food became the staple. Auxiliary Bishop Timothy Manning lived at Fremont Place, along with the archbishop's secretary. Ecclesial visitors were always welcome and many had their own keys to the front door. Daily Mass was offered for the benefit of local neighbors. McIntyre liked to tell visitors that the altar in the chapel was the one used by Eugenio Cardinal Pacelli when he stayed at Fremont Place in 1936.

In his earlier years, McIntyre tried to inaugurate an Easter egg hunt on the front lawn and it was only when neighbors lodged a formal protest that he decided against continuing the practice. During his New York days, there were no green lawns and, above all the other accouterments of the mansion, none was more enjoyable to McIntyre than the luxuriant grounds. From his earliest days in Los Angeles, McIntyre had wanted to live in surroundings like those at Saint Patrick's Cathedral in New York, where there were always seven or eight priests in residence. He liked the notion of participating at Sunday Masses and hearing confessions, practices for which he was famous in New York. As it was, he often slipped out on a Saturday afternoon to a neighboring parish to hear confessions, explaining that a priest who doesn't regularly hear confessions loses contact with the reality of contemporary Catholic life.

When plans were being made for the new Saint Basil's Church on Wilshire Boulevard, McIntyre seized the opportunity of having his residence included in the overall plans. When specifications for the rectory were made, two simple rooms were designated for his use

Archiepiscopal Residence at #100 Fremont Place in Los Angeles. This was formerly the home of King Gillette.

Gathering at Fremont Place of archbishops and bishops attending the reception of newly-proclaimed, James Francis Cardinal McIntyre, 1953.

and that of his secretary. By that time, Bishop Manning had assumed a parochial appointment and most of his inherited staff had died or were retired. In April of 1969, the local Catholic paper announced that Cardinal McIntyre "had moved his place of residence to the new St. Basil's rectory at Wilshire Boulevard and Kingsley Drive." McIntyre said that the move would "provide an opportunity to share a broader and more intimate form of community life with his brother priests as well as allow him to maintain closer contact with parish life."[24]

McIntyre conducted a survey among his advisors about the future of the mansion at Fremont Place and the majority asked felt that it should be sold. It was, in fact, first rented to and then sold to Miss Pat Barham. The mansion was subsequently redecorated and made into one of the more fashionable homes in Los Angeles.

Notes to the Text

1. AALA, J. Francis A. McIntyre to Priests, Los Angeles, September 7, 1949.
2. *The Tidings*, September 16, 1949.
3. *Ibid.*, September 23, 1949.
4. (New York, 1962), p. 89.
5. *Ibid.*, p. 116.
6. AALA, Barry Goldwater to Lee M. Graham, Washington, D.C., April 11, 1979.
7. AALA, James Francis Cardinal McIntyre to Aloysius Willinger, C.Ss.R., Los Angeles, November 5, 1956.
8. Los Angeles *Herald Examiner*, June 24, 1961.
9. AALA, Pope Paul VI to James Francis Cardinal McIntyre, Vatican City, January 20, 1966.
10. Idaho *Register*, June 24, 1966.
11. Los Angeles *Herald Examiner*, June 26, 1966.
12. *The Wanderer*, July 21, 1966.
13. *National Catholic Reporter*, July 13, 1966.
14. Green Bay *Register*, August 26, 1966.
15. *The Tidings*, July 1, 1966.
16. Rita Walpole, "Pastor of Granite," *Los Angeles Speaks* (Fall, 1965), p. 50.
17. AALA, James Francis Cardinal McIntyre Memorandum, Los Angeles, May 22, 1968.
18. AALA, James Francis Cardinal McIntyre to Luigi Raimondi, Los Angeles, May 28, 1968.
19. AALA, James Francis Cardinal McIntyre to Bishops, Los Angeles, June 4, 1968.
20. AALA, Joseph P. Dougherty to James Francis Cardinal McIntyre, Yakima, December 20, 1968.
21. AALA, Luigi Raimondi to James Francis Cardinal McIntyre, Washington, D.C., February 1, 1969.
22. AALA, Cornelius M. Power to Timothy Manning, Yakima, March 20, 1974.
23. AALA, Timothy Manning to James Francis Cardinal McIntyre, Fresno, June 6, 1968.
24. *The Tidings*, April 25, 1969.

27. The Critics

J ames Francis Cardinal McIntyre was not without his critics, both within and without the Church. Beyond the usual clerical gossip, which is traditionally and invariably anti-incumbent, there were those who didn't like McIntyre or didn't agree with certain of his policies.

McIntyre never minded honest differences of opinion, unless he felt that they touched upon or impugned the "fabric" of the Church or its magisterial teaching. He encouraged his Board of Consultors to openly discuss the pros and cons of issues brought to their attention. His favorite and most valued advisor, Msgr. William North, challenged him on many occasions and McIntyre would often ask him to stop by his office or home for further discussions. That North remained close to McIntyre is obvious from his appearance on at least two of the cardinal's *ternas*.

GEORGE DUNNE

Jesuit Father George H. Dunne, described on the jacket of his autobiography as a missionary, social activist and scholar, first encountered McIntyre in New York where the then chancellor had reportedly "muzzled" him for threatening to sue the New York *Post* for libel. In later years, McIntyre, by then Archbishop of Los Angeles, refused to allow Dunne to give a lecture in Hollywood on the role of the theater as an agent for social change. Nor did he want Dunne's controversial production, *Trial by Fire*, a documentary interracial play, to be performed under the auspices of the Catholic Theater Guild. Though he sympathized with efforts to do away with the evils of racism, McIntyre quarreled with the confrontational tactics that characterized Dunne's approach to the subject.

In any event, Father Dunne, who was probably "exiled" from more places in the United States and Europe than any of his Jesuit contemporaries, enlivened his memoirs with the observation that "McIntyre was not only mean-spirited and insensitive, he was also appallingly ignorant."[1] When informed of Dunne's comment, first contained in a letter to Msgr. Benjamin G. Hawkes, the cardinal smiled and responded that Dunne was "only two-thirds correct, which is pretty good for George Dunne."[2]

JOHN TRACY ELLIS

John Tracy Ellis's distaste for Francis Cardinal Spellman spilled over to his protege at Los Angeles. He once referred to McIntyre as "notoriously short-tempered and often prone to angry outbursts about matters on which he was less than well informed." Yet, Ellis admitted that there was another side to "this handsome and impressive-looking prelate," noting that "when McIntyre was made a bishop in 1940, no one was louder in praise of the appointment than Fulton Sheen. Thus as is the case of so many others there was here a mixed picture of dark spots which, of course, received the publicity, while the sympathetic actions towards those in trouble went unnoticed." He mentioned, as an example, McIntyre's "personally taking night calls from skid row in Los Angeles during his years as Archbishop there."

While speaking about the close ties between Spellman and McIntyre, Ellis took care to note that "the Archbishop of Los Angeles remained his own man." He recalled, for instance, that when the visit of Nikita Khrushchev to the United States was being planned, the White House made known its uneasiness lest the American cardinals should spark an outcry against the Russian premier's presence. President Dwight Eisenhower sent a State Department official to intercede with Spellman who promised to use his influence. But "as for Los Angeles," he cautioned "you had better speak to him yourself."

During the summer of 1960, when Ellis was teaching at Mount Saint Mary's College in Los Angeles, he was invited to dinner at 100 Fremont Place and from that pleasant encounter Ellis recalled only the "cardinal's impatience with the tardy pace of the *New Catholic Encyclopedia*," an issue about which the two agreed fully.[3]

HANS KÜNG

Early in January of 1963, following the initial session of Vatican Council II, the Jesuits at Loyola University asked the cardinal if Father Hans Küng, a Swiss theologian and a *peritus* at the council, might deliver a public lecture on their campus. McIntyre had earlier read Küng's work on *The Council, Reform and Reunion* and suggested that the editor of *The Tidings* publish a review of the book in the issue of May 4, 1962. In referring to that incident, the editor later recalled the "informative and favorable review," noting that Küng's "name and his views are no strangers to our pages or to our readers."[4] Despite his own positive impressions of the book and its author, McIntyre was apprehensive about allowing Küng to speak to impressionable students whose exposure to philosophy and theology was limited and far from mature.

The cardinal finally agreed, after prodding by the university's chancellor, to allow Küng the opportunity of meeting with the faculty, provided they not engage the students in the discussions. When the lecture took place at Loyola's Saint Robert Hall, a number of young people from the university picketed outside, in protest for not being invited to the presentation.

The talk itself was fairly innocuous. A memorandum describing the event, attributed to "one of our prelates ... a distinguished scholar," said that about 300 persons attended. Father Küng was described as a "rather naive, disarming youth" whose "gentleness of manner presented a striking contrast to the strong and aggressive content of his hour-and-a-half long speech." Küng stated that, despite the grim external picture, the inmost life of the Church is the home of freedom - the freedom of the sons of God." He specifically attacked the Index of Forbidden Books and "with a touch of humor linked its inception to the most unworthy Popes of the Renaissance period." He called for abolition of the *imprimatur* legislation and for greater freedom of thought and expression in the Church. His structural presentation was ecumenical "in the sense that he accommodated himself to Lutheran concepts to some degree." The observer concluded by saying that "there is no doubt that Father Küng is a good and zealous priest. He seems to have none of the aggressive stubbornness that might lead him into trouble."[5]

At this juncture, Küng was invited to give a lecture at nearby UCLA on April 3, as part of the distinguished Speaker's Program on the "Positive Results of the First Session of the Second Vatican Council." Küng expressed a willingness to come, provided he could get authorization from the Los Angeles Chancery. When he called for verbal permission, he was reminded of the provisions of *Exsul Familia* requiring that such requests be in writing. He immediately sent an airmail, special delivery letter to McIntyre.

Küng assured the cardinal that his address "would be a positive contribution for an understanding of the Council and of the important desires of the Church today."[6] McIntyre responded that "the extreme shortness of intervening time, which you mention, does not admit of our arranging for the necessary clearance, in accordance with Canon 1341."[7] In a private memorandum, McIntyre questioned the sincerity of officials at UCLA, noting that they "had no interest whatsoever in religion and the only reason they would invite Fr. Küng is because it would stimulate controversy."[8]

After hearing that Father Küng had not been approved to speak, the Los Angeles *Times* lamented that "the only scheduled public speech here by a controversial Catholic scholar" had been canceled. According to their sources, which went unconfirmed, Father Küng, contacted by telephone in San Francisco, called "for an end to church censorship and Roman inquisitorial proceedings against its own clergy."[9] The editor of *The Tidings* believed "that Father Hans Küng deserves an apology. One of our local daily newspapers on Tuesday carried a story to the effect that a talk scheduled here by Father Küng had been canceled by the authorities of this Archdiocese. This was an unfortunate and maladroit way of describing a situation which was much less intriguing than it was made to appear. The simple fact of the matter is that no scheduled talk was canceled. None was actually scheduled." The editorial went on to proclaim that Father Küng was "a scholar of international repute, and in good ecclesiastical standing. To imply, even indirectly, that he is under disapproval of Church authorities is to violate the basic standards of justice as well as charity."[10]

Edgar A. Jones, Professor of Law at UCLA, reacted angrily and enlisted eleven others to sign a letter which expressed distress "at the implications of your editorial." He repeated the chronology of the incident and then charged that the refusal to welcome Küng was "an invasion of the academic integrity of Loyola." He wanted a fuller explanation, noting that he had vainly tried "to visualize" the procedure used for approving such requests. He facetiously wondered if the documents in question "are illuminated in the manner of monks in medieval gold script." Jones felt that the non-appearance of Küng "reflects the loss of a substantial opportunity for an ecumenical encounter on the campus of one of the great secular universities of the world."[11] Another letter, signed by twelve people, concluded by hoping "that many of the laity and clergy will now turn, and with serious attention, to Father Küng's books for a scholarly discussion of, among many other compelling topics, the abuses of authority."[12]

The Catholic press took up the story with gusto, repeating Jones' charges that McIntyre seemed "more interested in concealing than in displaying Father Hans Küng in Southern California." Thomas Francis Ritt was quoted as saying that "it is now obvious that archdiocesan officials in Los Angeles canceled a scheduled talk of Father Küng at UCLA."[13]

Archbishop Joseph T. McGucken wrote from San Francisco where Küng's lectures were "greeted with great applause," to say that one of his priests, a seminary classmate of Küng's, "was alarmed because he felt that the line of reasoning he followed was exactly the same line of reasoning on behalf of freedom that was expressed by Doellenger at the First Vatican Council."[14]

In retrospect, Küng's popularity in the early 1960s may be slightly overstated. Many of his fellow theologians were less than enamored with the "erratic spirit of boldness" which characterized his earlier writing. One observer, while endorsing his ecumenical spirit, pointed out that "in dealing with our separated brethren, we must be completely sincere, not simply leaving unsaid what is unpleasant, not simply stressing things on which we agree, hoping thereby that the points of disagreement will somehow dissolve in good fellowship. If there is to be dialogue, it must include the points of disagreement, but in charity. The policy of the 'open door' is a happy one, but that of a 'swinging door' would insult the intellectual integrity of our separated brethren."[15]

McIntyre had been impressed by Küng's presence at the Vatican Council as the theologian for the Bishop of Rottenberg and there is no evidence to indicate that the Archbishop of Los Angeles had any less than a sincere respect for his writings. In fact, he would likely have agreed that Küng was "emphatic in his declaration of loyalty to the Church" and "nowhere near the Church's periphery, but in the center."[16]

There is no denying that McIntyre's unwillingness to allow Küng to speak at UCLA "makes all too-believable the rumors of other instances of suppression which circulate among Catholics and non Catholics alike in the Southern California area."[17] Time has a way of smoothing out and paving over the cracks and crevices of human behavior. Regarding Küng's appearance at UCLA, the man once described as "the formidable champion of the *status quo* at the council"[18] had been alerted by Roman authorities that Küng's appearances in the United States were in violation of an instruction by Giuseppe Cardinal Pizzardo and that the Sacred Congregation of Seminaries and Universities was about to issue a decree to that effect to the rectors of Catholic universities.[19]

McIntyre's refusal to disclose his reasons for not approving Küng's lecture at UCLA was, in reality, an attempt to protect the Swiss theologian from further embarrassment. Perhaps that explains why Küng never spoke publicly about events at Los Angeles, except to say that it came as no surprise that "in the midst of the great consensus in favor of my lectures there should have been isolated notes of criticism." That he wanted the chapter on the incident closed is evident from Küng's remarks that he "was particularly gratified, after certain difficulties had occurred, at the high praise I received in *The Tidings* of the Archdiocese of Los Angeles."[20]

ARCHBISHOP THOMAS ROBERTS, SJ

The one-time Archbishop of Bombay, Archbishop Thomas d'Esterre Roberts, was once referred to by *Time* magazine as being "an independent spirit who feels free to put churchly propositions up to the measure of his own reason."[21] He was a prelate in good standing who spent much of his retirement lecturing, writing and battling for causes unpopular with many members of the ecclesial hierarchy.

In any event, when it was reported that Roberts had planned to include Los Angeles on his lecture tour, in mid 1964, James Francis Cardinal McIntyre wrote him a polite, but direct letter saying "such a visit at this particular time would not be opportune." He pointed out that "visitors from abroad have been speaking at some of our colleges in California recently, some of them prelates, and the result has been much confusion."[22] Roberts had earlier written McIntyre for permission to speak, but their letters crossed in the mail. In his missive, Roberts had said he wanted to speak on *Pacem in Terris* to the San Fernando Interfaith Committee and the American Friends Service Committee.[23]

After receiving McIntyre's letter, forwarded from London to Seattle, Roberts sent his "grateful thanks," explaining that his tour had been arranged chiefly by non-Catholic bodies "anxious to increase yet further the impact for peace." That made it difficult "for me to give timely notice of arrangements made locally; that is why I have sometimes asked that such details be proposed by my sponsors with the proviso . . . that I accepted in advance any restrictions, whether absolute or partial."[24]

Before receiving Roberts' letter, McIntyre wrote again saying that he had heard that the archbishop was planning a speech under the auspices of the Pomona Fair Housing Council. He said that "since this is a controversial subject, and of a political character at the present time, and since the Archdiocese of Los Angeles has elected to maintain its practice of not participating in political discussions, our attitude has been one of neutrality." In that light McIntyre felt that Roberts' speech would be "embarrassing to us because of lack of familiarity with local conditions."[25]

One of the sponsoring agencies released the correspondence to the press and, on July 18, the Los Angeles *Times* reported that Roberts had "been denied permission by the Roman Catholic Chancery to speak in the Los Angeles Archdiocesan area."

In his traditional style, Roberts took the rebuke gracefully, telling *Time* magazine that "Cardinal McIntyre is in charge and is entitled to his own views as to what is expedient and what isn't." Commenting on the incident, *Time* writers noted that Roberts "stands at the outer periphery of the church's policy makers. He is not a methodical reformer, a dynamic organizer, but a prelate who says aloud what others may think in silence, who raises critical but often embarrassing questions for debate. Like Socrates, he feels that it is sufficient for a thoughtful man to be a gadfly."[26]

FATHER PHILLIP BERRYMAN

In February of 1965, Father Phillip Berryman, curate at a parish in Pasadena, asked for a leave of absence from the Archdiocese of Los Angeles in order to work as a missionary in Panama. At the time, it was agreed that he would leave in the springtime when the annual transfers of the clergy were customarily scheduled.

On the Sunday before the public announcement of his departure, Berryman took the occasion to lecture the predominantly white parishioners at Saint Philip's church on the subject of racial relations. The sermon was, according to Berryman, "moderate and doctrinal," as the text subsequently released to the press confirmed.[27]

A number of parishioners, claiming that the tone of the talk had been substantially toned down before its release in printed form, complained to the pastor, Msgr. William E. North who, in turn, directed Berryman not to speak at the rest of the Sunday Masses. Two days later, when Berryman's already agreed upon transfer was made public, Roger P. Kuhn, a spokesman for CURE, charged that the priest had been removed "for speaking out on racial matters,"[28] something the local newspapers were happy to report.

That accusation was vehemently denied by Auxiliary Bishop Timothy Manning who pointed out that "we had twenty-five or so routine transfers this week" which he termed as an "ordinary part of the administration of this archdiocese." Msgr. North was equally as forceful in denouncing the allegation, labeling the growing hubbub over the matter as "ridiculous." He said "my people aren't red necked, semi-literates or white supremacists."[29]

North suggested that Berryman's homily was not based, as it should have been, on the scriptural readings of the day. Nor did North think the subject matter was at all in keeping with Mother's Day which fell on the day in question. To the latter observation, Berryman responded that he thought it was indeed appropriate

Before and after his elevation to the cardinalate, McIntyre enjoyed visiting the patients at Saint Ann's Home for the Aged.

Cardinal joins novices in inspecting a new addition to a convent.

inasmuch as "his mother shared his convictions on the plight of the Negroes."[30]

When the issue faded from the Catholic press, Berryman gave an interview to George S. Mitrovich of the *Christian Century* who immediately came to his defense, calling him "a reluctant but resourceful reformer." Mitrovich, who was a newcomer to the Los Angeles scene, proclaimed authoritatively "the prevailing political persuasion among the hierarchy of the Archdiocese of Los Angeles, following the lead of Cardinal McIntyre, is far to the radical right. Consequently efforts by organizations dedicated to striving for racial justice are anathema in the archdiocese and have long been suppressed." That interview did bring to light one insight, consistently denied by pundits, that "the press, since the incident involving Fr. William DuBay has been on the alert for similar stories involving the Archdiocese of Los Angeles."[31]

Father Berryman worked for some years in Panama and subsequently left the ministry. The evidence indicates that Berryman simply used the occasion of his voluntary departure as a means of publicly expressing personal displeasure with the views of James Francis Cardinal McIntyre.

FATHER JOHN V. COFFIELD

One of the oldest ecclesial truisms says that "saints are difficult to know and impossible to live with," much like the prophets of the old covenant. Father John V. Coffield surely falls into that fairly exclusive category of "local saints." "Widely respected in Los Angeles as a longtime pastor ... and devoted to youth work and urban renewal,"[32] Coffield disavowed the tactics of CURE and William H. DuBay, but he had his own mind-set on racial and other matters that rather consistently caused embarrassment to Chancery officials. He was known as a "charter" member of the C.C.C. (Cardinal's Carpet Club) and was a regular visitor to the curial offices on West 9th Street in Los Angeles, where attempts to refocus his intemperate zeal proved unsuccessful.

To make matters worse, Father Coffield possessed no administrative ability. While never accused directly of misappropriating funds, he was frequently scolded for his failure to keep the proper financial records for his parish of the Ascension in Los Angeles. On more than one occasion, for example, he purchased property without permission and then registered it in his own name, both of which procedures were canonically verboten. Coffield was also reported to have purchased "an old bus to transport youngsters to beaches on weekends."[33] Kind, gentle and saintly man that he was, John V. Coffield had been a loose cannon for many years.

Matters reached an impasse in December of 1964, when Coffield announced that he was going into a "self-imposed exile ... as the strongest protest I can make" to Cardinal McIntyre.[34] In a farewell statement to his parishioners, the priest said that he had been ordered to take a five month "enforced vacation" because of his remarks about the controversial Fair Housing Initiative that was then on the California ballot. Nobody disbelieved Coffield when he said "I deeply love the Church that is trying to silence me."[35]

The forty-nine year old priest decided to spend his exile in the "Windy City," where he would take classes at the University of Chicago. Typically, Coffield never bothered checking with officials in the Archdiocese of Chicago.[36] When asked about Coffield's status, Auxiliary Bishop Cletus O'Donnell said that "Church rules would not permit Father Coffield to be given an official job in Chicago."[37] Meanwhile, back in Los Angeles it was announced that "no administrative discipline would be imposed on Father Coffield and that his request for a leave of absence went through regular processes."[38]

Father Coffield told reporters that he would be living at Saint Carthage parish and engaging in the activities of the Inter American Co-operative Institute, a Catholic agency for fostering better standards of living for Latin Americans through self-help programs. That work pleased the priest who said the "plight of minority groups . . . is the most critical in the world today. " He felt that "it is a priest's job to keep in touch with these people and teach them love so that they may go out and be strong witnesses for Christ."[39]

Archdiocesan officials in Chicago, "not overly joyous about his living there," were careful to point out that Coffield would not be given any official position or assignment. "He is still responsible to the people in Los Angeles and he will have no status here."[40] For his part, Coffield found the area "the most wonderful in the world," noting that priests "are actively working to improve inter-cultural relations and conditions of underprivileged people."[41]

Besides a few news accounts in the local papers, Coffield's departure from Los Angeles didn't receive extensive coverage. With the exception of the *National Catholic Reporter*, who gave it first page attention,[42] the episode was hardly noticed. A childhood chum, Father John Doran, wrote "an open letter to Fr. Coffield" in which he disagreed strongly with the manner in which his friend had handled the dissent: "Because your Cardinal does not choose the same means to pursue this cause of yours, you are condemning him. In this, I think you are wrong." While basically agreeing with

Coffield's viewpoint, Doran said that "when you take the family problems to the press and to the air waves to attack your father before the world, I will not go along." He said that "you will, indeed, be a hero to many ... but your heroism is purchased by a public attack upon a Cardinal ... at a price you had no right to pay."[43]

Msgr. S. J. Adamo took a slightly different approach, noting that he admired heroes, even foolish ones. But he felt that this "zealous priest had demonstrated that sincerity is no substitute for wisdom. What he did was exciting, incredible and futile. He made the Cardinal too black, himself the knight in white armor. Ultimately, he hurt rather than helped the cause of racial justice in California."[44]

Within a few months after his arrival, curial officials in Chicago began feeling the pressure of Coffield's presence. Though there had been a previous understanding that he "would restrict his speaking activities in Chicago," there were "differing views in the extent of the ban." In any event, Chancellor Francis W. Byrne felt obliged to cancel two talks scheduled by the priest late in January of 1965. Byrne would say no more than "it was best for Father Coffield to remain silent in Chicago."[45]

In the months and years after that rebuke, Father Coffield remained in Chicago and abided by the directive against any additional statements, working as a follower of Saul David Alinsky, the radical teacher of community organizing. In September of 1968, he ended his "exile" and returned to Los Angeles. When asked at a press conference why he had returned, Coffield said that he felt "the cardinal is much more open on racial matters than was the case four years ago" and he also admitted that "my own understanding has grown in that time."[46] He said he would devote himself to assisting Cesar Chavez and his grape pickers in their struggle for dignity and justice.

Coffield was eventually reconciled with Cardinal McIntyre and, in 1969, became pastor of Our Lady of Guadalupe parish in Santa Ana. Through the 1980s and after, he served at a small, predominantly Hispanic parish in a poverty pocket of Capistrano Beach in the Diocese of Orange. His "ministry of good deeds was accomplished quietly"[47] among the populace attached to San Felipe de Jesus. He was made a prelate of honor in April of 1981.

"THE NEW AMERICAN CATHOLIC"

During the middle months of 1968, the "sharpest collision to date between the progressive and conservative elements in the Roman Catholic Church"[48] played out in the press when the then elderly

James Francis Cardinal McIntyre (83) publicly took to task the youngish Bishop James F. Shannon (47) for the latter's role as narrator for an unauthorized television documentary. During a brief visit to Southern California in early 1966, Bishop Shannon was asked by an old friend, Dr. Richard Gilman, to address members of the student body at Occidental College about Vatican Council II. Knowing James Francis Cardinal McIntyre's hesitancy about having outside speakers in the Archdiocese of Los Angeles, Shannon wrote, asking permission to accept the invitation. McIntyre responded favorably, saying that "our policy has been entirely dictated by *exul familia*."[49] Observing that it was a violation of that instruction that occasioned the controversy with (Hans) Küng and others, he noted that the earlier incident had "given us a reputation for rigidity." McIntyre also told Shannon that he discouraged public lectures on the subject of birth control or political issues, especially those that border on racial problems.[50]

Summaries of the lectures given by Shannon at Occidental were subsequently given to McIntyre. The only markings on those pages are two penciled question marks on the final lecture about the "delay between the enactment and implementing of the (council's) decrees" and a reference to "people who hold to the old ways."[51] McIntyre appears to have sustained a cordial relationship with Shannon until 1968, when the Auxiliary Bishop of Saint Paul-Minneapolis narrated a controversial NBC television special on "The New American Catholic."

Shortly after the program aired, on June 21, 1968, McIntyre issued a strongly worded statement in which he dismissed "The New American Catholic" as "purely a summary of individual interpretation with a misleading title." He insisted that "the program in no way represented the Catholic Church or the National Council of Catholic Bishops in the United States."[52] Nor was Bishop Shannon "speaking for the people of God." McIntyre said that "the participation of Bishop Shannon and Bishop Victor J. Reed of Oklahoma City-Tulsa was purely personal."[53]

Cardinal McIntyre also criticized the presentation because of "certain sections of the Sacrifice of the Mass enacted in the program were grossly lacking in observance of liturgical rules, in reverence and respect." He added that the "opinions and ideas were also not in accord with Pope Paul VI's pronouncements on celibacy nor with the directives issued by the Congregation for Religious."[54]

Writing in the Los Angeles *Times*, John Dart expressed an opposite view, feeling that the program "captured superbly" what he termed "the excitement and spirituality of the moves for meaningful changes in the Catholic Church," and he maintained that the choice of Bishop Shannon for narrator "couldn't have been better."[55] Stuart Schulberg, producer of the show, said that "quite clearly neither Bishop Shannon nor Bishop Reed was identified as an official spokesman for the Church." He said that "the program was devoted to a renewal in the Church, not to conflict within it. No effort was made on Bishop Shannon's part, nor on ours, to depict Roman Catholicism in general." In reply to McIntyre's charge that the title was misleading, Schulberg said that "we had hoped that the title would state exactly what the program was about. We did not say that all Catholics accepted the new trends, nor how many did - we have never played the numbers game."[56]

On June 24, McIntyre sent a letter to Archbishop John Dearden, President of the National Conference of Catholic Bishops, to the bishops of California, to all the nation's archbishops and to the Apostolic Delegate in which he bluntly and frankly objected to Shannon's role as a narrator for the NBC telecast. He requested that his complaint be included on the agenda for the forty bishops who were scheduled to meet in Washington, D.C. as the administrative arm of the NCCB on September 17th. When asked for a copy of his complaint by Shannon,[57] McIntyre complied, noting that "I have no apology for my letters or my actions, including the motion I made at the recent meeting of the Administrative Board. I view this as of primary importance for the good of the Church, and I regret if the individuals involved feel disturbed." He felt impelled to speak out in his role as the spiritual shepherd "for over a million people witnessing the program."[58]

McIntyre's intervention to the assembled bishops is here reproduced in its entirety:

> In the recent past, there has appeared on one of our most prominent television stations a program entitled "The New American Catholic".
>
> A few months later, this program was repeated with some rearrangements and the inclusion, without specified connection, of a formal speech made on an extraneous public occasion by Cardinal O'Boyle. I understand the Cardinal was not consulted regarding the appropriation of this speech for this program.
>
> In both presentations, two bishops, who are members of this body, actively participated, thus giving the definite impression that they advocated the idea of "The New American Catholic" and the presentation, as portrayed, had the approval of the Church in the United States.
>
> The very title of the presentation and the manner in which the speeches were treated gave the strongest indication and intimations of an incipient schism in the

Church. Two of the more prominent topics were the place of authority in the Church and the presentation of scenes from a so called "underground Mass" that was entirely in contrast to the regulations of the official tribunal on the liturgy. The portrayal of an "underground Mass" was scandalous as to place, circumstance and practice.

These appraisals are based on observations of several bishops and many of the laity. I would be shocked indeed if most of the bishops here who witnessed the showing on either occasion did not receive similar reactions to those expressed.

Other topics presented as controversial were the subject of celibacy and the rule of religious communities.

Therefore, I hereby make a motion that in the minutes of this meeting, there be recorded a statement that these programs were not authorized by this body; that the content and the portent of these programs had not the sanction, the approval or the recommendation of this body. The purpose of so recording this statement will enable response of a decisive nature if press or periodical references are made to these programs. It is hoped indeed that there will be no repetition of the program under the same circumstances.

It would seem that our laity are entitled to an expression from this body to a program that was heard by millions of people which implied and described a situation which is not general, not accredited and which is not officially approved.[59]

There was never any official disclosure as to what the administrative board did or didn't do in reply to McIntyre's charges. In the *National Catholic Reporter*, two scenarios were proposed: "One is that the board took formal note and imposed a mild censure on Bishop Shannon;" another version is "that there was no vote and that most those who expressed an opinion were on Bishop Shannon's side rather than the cardinal's." But the commentator had to admit that "Nothing is known for certain."[60] Shannon did say that he couldn't speak about the matter and there is no evidence that the cardinal ever divulged the decision.[61] McIntyre had earlier told Shannon that he regretted his viewpoint was "in disagreement with your thinking." And he said that he was perfectly willing to accept the judgment of the bishops of the country in this matter."[62]

Shannon's backers weren't as anxious to put the matter aside. The NCR regretted that the "intelligent, open, informed" Shannon "who happens to be a leading advocate of a more open Church, is now chief episcopal victim of the closed-Church mentality."[63] Writing in *Ave Maria*, Father John Sheedy, who regarded Shannon as "the most effective apologist the American hierarchy has had during the years," decried the fact that the action of the bishops "darkened the cloud over Bishop Shannon's" head. He also criticized Archbishop Dearden who, as chairman, "could have found a parliamentary method of disposing" of the charges.[64] Father John Joyce, writing in the Oklahoma *Courier*, also fussed at Dearden for "not exercising any strong leadership" in the matter. What both commentators failed to mention was that a "parliamentary" solution would have been no solution at all.[65]

Later that year, George and Gerry Sell launched a letter-writing campaign, asking people to express their support to Shannon, to their own bishops and to the Sells directly so they could tabulate the volume of response.[66] When Shannon heard that they had received 700 replies, he "disclaimed all of the gestures of support" and noted that "there is a tendency among my friends to overreact." Shannon wisely pointed out that his supporters were "signing a blank check in my favor against the cardinal" which he thought was unwise because "they don't know the issue or the particulars."[67] Obviously, Shannon knew more than he could or would say.

The issue gradually lost its momentum in the press until early in 1969, when Bishop Shannon asked for and received a leave of absence from his episcopal duties in Minneapolis to do research at Saint John's, a non-denominational college in Santa Fe, New Mexico. On May 28, Religion editor Willmer Thorkelson wrote in the Minneapolis *Star* that "Bishop Shannon had resigned after writing to the Pope to express his disagreement with the papal encyclical on birth control." When asked the next day to comment on the report, Shannon said he would "neither affirm nor deny any report about resignation."[68] He said that in fairness to his superiors, he could not discuss the issue because "it involves confidential correspondence over a period of some time." A few days later, the NC News Service told its affiliates that the report in the *Star* was basically true. It reported that Shannon had received a "high-level letter from the Holy See" urging him to reconsider the problem "prayerfully and thoughtfully."[69] Shannon was back on the front page of the next issue of the *National Catholic Reporter*, where his canonical status was described as being "in doubt."[70] There were the usual denials from the Saint Paul-Minneapolis Chancery along with a variety of interpretations, none of which even hinted at what eventually was disclosed as the basic problem.

Dale Francis, a columnist for *Twin Circle*, noted that the overwhelming majority of the Catholic press had taken positions strongly supporting Shannon in his conflict with McIntyre, but he berated such papers as the Brooklyn *Tablet* for implying that the Church was forcing Shannon out. "The truth is," he said, "that the Church didn't reject Shannon, Bishop Shannon rejected the Church."[71]

The pieces of the puzzle about the bishop's behavior began falling in place early in August of 1969, when he abruptly announced he had "married Mrs. Ruth Wilkinson in a Protestant ceremony"[72] at the First Christian Church in Endicott, New York, thus becoming "the first Roman Catholic bishop in U.S. history to defy Church law by taking a wife."[73] A few days later, in an interview published by the New York *Times*, Shannon said that he "felt unable to cope or to manage within the ecclesiastical system in which I was being asked to function."[74]

Shannon also disclosed, for the first time, that at the celebrated meeting of the Administrative Board for the National Conference of Catholic Bishops, the board had approved a resolution critical of his role in the now famous television documentary on "The New American Catholic." He said that the vote had come as "an enormous surprise to him" and was even more painful "because it revealed that he did not have the confidence of his own local superiors, Archbishop Leo Binz and Coadjutor Archbishop Leo C. Byrne."[75]

Shannon also revealed that he had been told "on the soundest authority" that he had been nominated and endorsed to be an ordinary (residential bishop) of a diocese and that the appointment had been prevented by Cardinal McIntyre,[76] a charge that McIntyre labeled as "ridiculous."[77] Clearly Shannon had been misinformed on that matter. As an insider, Shannon knew full well that neither McIntyre nor any other American bishop exercised a veto over Roman appointments. The process for selecting bishops was specifically structured to avoid such interventions. McIntyre may have been asked about such an appointment, and there is no evidence to support that conjecture, but he could not have unilaterally blocked it.

Probably the most accurate explanation for Shannon's departure from the ministry was one that appeared in *Newsweek* magazine. It quoted an irreverent Vatican official who had spent a good deal of time counseling priests: "It's the same old pattern. First, they come and complain about the Church's structure, then they say they can't accept the Pope's teaching on birth control. I let them talk for a while and then I say: OK, chum, what's her name?"[78]

Understandably Shannon's friends and supporters were shocked and appalled at their hero. Bernard Casserly, writing in the *Catholic Bulletin*, said that "willingly or not, Bishop Shannon has provided fuel for a large credibility gap about the Church he served well for so long. If a bishop charged with responsibility for proclaiming Word of God cannot follow the rules of his Church, how can it be expected of the least of us?"[79] John Reedy, editor of *Ave Maria*, said that "the news of his marriage was for me almost unbelievable." His decision "left me stunned and bewildered, hunting blindly for a familiar point of reference." Reedy went on to say that Shannon's decision "will taint all the causes and values for which he worked," because "he has rejected his ecclesiastical commitment."[80] Even writers for *Time* magazine were dismayed that "one of Roman Catholicism's most articulate and progressive shepherds in the U. S. has been abruptly estranged from his flock."[81]

Shannon realized that his decision to marry had supplied ammunition to opponents of reform in the Church. "What hurts me most," he told columnist Kenneth L. Woodward, "is that I've left some people high and dry who counted on my leadership. But, in truth, my leadership was almost completely eroded. Psychologically, I was running out of gas."[82]

What totally escaped reporters, commentators and even Shannon was that the vote of the bishops went against Shannon not so much because of the program's content but because his participation was interpreted by many viewers as representing an official position of the American hierarchy. In other words, Shannon misused his office as a bishop, something that members of the episcopal college, even Shannon's closest friends, could not countenance. In that sense then, McIntyre's bringing this matter to the attention of the National Conference was right for the wrong reason. McIntyre called Shannon to account for what he said, but Shannon was censured for what he did.

JOHN L. McKENZIE. S.J.

Another one of McIntyre's outspoken critics was Father John L. McKenzie, Professor of Old Testament theology at De Paul University and one-time President of the Catholic Biblical Association. In his Q.E.D. series for *The Critic*, after noting that "any bishop who gets my finger in his eye will gain stature with the majority of his colleagues and with Roman prelates," the Jesuit scholar recalled a recent visit to Los Angeles. There some friends reported that the cardinal, during the annual priests' retreat, said that "whenever he ran into a theological question he consulted the notes he had taken in the seminary forty-four years earlier. They were, he said, as good now as they were then." McKenzie feared that on that score McIntyre "may have been right."

McKenzie observed that "by the same principle, he could use *Standard & Poor, 1927*, as a guide for investments. That was a good year, and the figures are just as true now as they were then." In the Jesuit's view, McIntyre had served the Church well "by not saying much about Catholic doctrine during his career; this is a service because he knows little about Catholic doctrine and has little interest in it." Nonetheless, it bothered McKenzie that "this theological illiterate should have been an official teacher of Catholic doctrine for more than twenty years." He concluded his reflections on His Eminence of Los Angeles by saying that he wouldn't have trusted McIntyre "to lay a two dollar bet with the neighborhood bookie without getting the names of the horses mixed up."[83]

In 1985, the author wrote McKenzie, asking if the passage of time had caused him to mellow in his views about McIntyre. He responded that "the judgment of history is not moved by an uncritical benevolence or by fallacious adages. My own judgment, which may be in error and is disputable and is not formed on all the evidence, has grown no kinder in fifteen years." He still believed that "the late James Francis Cardinal McIntyre was an evil man." McKenzie regretted that "I cannot show more of the mellowness which might make me more attractive."[84]

JOHN GREGORY DUNNE

Though it was not specifically critical of individuals, John Gregory Dunne's book, *True Confessions*,[85] purports to be a story of the Archdiocese of Los Angeles under the administration of thinly disguised James Francis Cardinal McIntyre and Monsignor Benjamin G. Hawkes. The author's first novel illuminates Los Angeles and, according to a reviewer in a local newspaper, it is "one of those books you recommend when someone asks you what to read to get a sense of life there." Des Spellacy is "a comer in the church, serving as chancellor - and heir-apparent-to an aging but politically acute cardinal." Much of Monsignor Spellacy's time is spent in intricate political maneuvering within the church; and then there are the pleasant golfing afternoons with rich contributors and contractors who interact with both church and state and whose corruption is a matter of spiritual concern. Set in a place too often known only for its Hollywood parties and taco stands, that alone is worth the price on the jacket ($9.95).[86] Critically, the book's qualities as entertainment reaches for something more.

Father Andrew Greeley, who admitted that he was "disinclined to speak much in defense of Cardinal McIntyre's Los Angeles." said that the book "is not satire. It is not caricature, it is not irony; it is vulgar obscenity, indeed the most gratuitously and incessantly vulgar book I have read in a long, long time." He notes that the "Irish characters in it, civil and ecclesiastical, are without exception venal, corrupt, obsessed, sick, hypercritical and disgusting." Greeley concluded his remarks by saying that "the Irish are very honest people. They seldom speak well of one another."[87]

If unkind observations are measured by the dignity of their source, then the harshest commentary about James Francis Cardinal McIntyre was that written into his diary by Archbishop Paul J. Hallinan of Atlanta on October 16, 1962. He characterized McIntyre as "absolutely stupid,"[88] an opinion apparently based on the cardinal's impassioned defense of Latin at Vatican Council II. Another writer, this one admitting that the cardinal was "hardly a theoretician on matters liturgical, or even a good debater on the subject," rebutted Hallinan by pointing out that McIntyre "was far from stupid, not this man who turned Los Angeles into one of the major sees in the country."[89]

There were rebellions of one kind or another at almost every level of society in the 1960s, and the clergy was not spared.[90] Though it received the lion's share of public attention in the media, the Archdiocese of Los Angeles was not alone in having its disgruntled priests and laity. In almost every case, press coverage of the incidents magnified and complicated the original problem.

Notes to the Text

1. *King's Pawn. The Memoirs of George H. Dunne, S.J.* (Chicago, 1990), p. 211.
2. AALA, Statement by James Francis Cardinal McIntyre, Los Angeles, undated.
3. John Tracy Ellis, *Catholic Bishops. A Memoir* (Wilmington, Delaware 1983), pp. 92-102.
4. *The Tidings*, April 5, 1963.
5. AALA, Unsigned Memorandum, April 5, 1963.
6. AALA, Fr. Hans Küng to James Francis Cardinal McIntyre, Spokane, March 28, 1963.
7. AALA, James Francis Cardinal McIntyre to Fr. Hans Küng, Los Angeles, March 30, 1963
8. AALA, James Francis Cardinal McIntyre to Apostolic Delegate, Los Angeles, March 31, 1963
9. April 2, 1963.
10. April 5, 1963.
11. AALA, Edgar A. Jones *et al.* to *The Tidings*, Los Angeles, April 8, 1963.
12. AALA, A Public Statement, Los Angeles, April 19, 1963.
13. Georgia *Bulletin*, April 25, 1963.
14. AALA, Joseph T. McGucken to James Francis Cardinal McIntyre, San Francisco, April 8, 1963
15. Regis N. Barnes, O.S.B., *"Quo Vadis* Hans Küng?" *The Voice of the Church* VII (April, 1963), 3.
16. Xavier Rynne in the Los Angeles *Times*, October 12, 1975..
17. A. V. Krebs, Jr., "A Church of Silence," LXXX *Commonweal* (July 10, 1964), 473.
18. Xavier Rynne, *op cit.*
19. AALA, Joseph Cardinal Pizzardo to the Rectors of Catholic Universities, Rome, May 30, 1963.
20. "A Word of Thanks," *America* LVII (June 8, 1963), 828.
21. LXXXIV (July 31, 1964), 54.
22. AALA, James Francis Cardinal McIntyre to Thomas Roberts, S.J., Los Angeles, June 11, 1964.
23. AALA, Thomas Roberts, S.J. to James Francis Cardinal McIntyre, Spokane, January 23, 1964.
24. *Ibid.*, Spokane, July 7, 1964.
25. AALA James Francis Cardinal McIntyre to Thomas Roberts, S.J., Los Angeles, July 8, 1964.
26. LXXXIV (July 31, 1964), 54.

27. *National Catholic Reporter*, May 19, 1965.
28. Los Angeles *Times*, May 15, 1965.
29. Pasadena *Star News*, May 14, 1965.
30. George S. Mitrovich, "Punishment of a Priest," *Christian Century* LXXXII (June 16, 1965).
31. *Ibid.*
32. *Time* LXXXV (January 8, 1965), 36.
33. *Newsweek* LXV (January 11, 1965), 57.
34. Washington, D.C. *Evening Star*, December 28, 1964.
35. Los Angeles *Times*, December 28, 1964.
36. Chicago *Daily News*, December 29, 1964.
37. Washington, D.C. *Post*, December 29, 1964.
38. Los Angeles *Times*, December 29, 1964.
39. Chicago *Daily News*, December 30, 1964.
40. Los Angeles *Times*, January 7, 1965.
41. Los Angeles *Herald-Examiner*, December 30, 1964.
42. January 6, 1965.
43. Texas *Catholic Herald*, January 7, 1965.
44. Camden *Star Herald*, January 8, 1965.
45. *National Catholic Reporter*, January 20, 1965.
46. Los Angeles *Times*, September 6, 1968.
47. *Ibid.*, June 15, 1991.
48. Los Angeles *Times*, August 24, 1969.
49. AALA, James F. Shannon to James Francis Cardinal McIntyre, Saint Paul, March 20, 1966.
50. AALA, James Francis Cardinal McIntyre to James F. Shannon, Los Angeles, March 29, 1966.
51. AALA, Summary of Final Lecture, October 25, 1966.
52. Los Angeles *Times*, June 23, 1968.
53. *National Catholic Reporter*, July 3, 1968.
54. AALA, NCWC News Service release, June 22, 1968.
55. Los Angeles *Times*, June 22, 1968.
56. *National Catholic Reporter*, July 3, 1968.
57. AALA, James F. Shannon to James Francis Cardinal McIntyre, Minneapolis, September 19, 1968.
58. AALA James Francis Cardinal McIntyre to James F. Shannon, Los Angeles, September 24, 1968.
59. AALA, Memorandum to Administrative Board, NCWC, on "The New American Catholic," n.d.
60. *National Catholic Reporter*, October 2, 1968.
61. Michigan *Catholic*, September 26, 1968.
62. AALA, James Francis Cardinal McIntyre to James F. Shannon, Los Angeles, September 24, 1968.
63. *National Catholic Reporter*, October 2, 1968.
64. October 19, 1968.

65. September 27, 1968.
66. *National Catholic Reporter*, October 2, 1968.
67. *National Catholic Register*, November 3, 1968.
68. Los Angeles *Times*, May 29, 1969.
69. Release dated May 31, 1969.
70. June 4, 1969.
71. June 22, 1969.
72. AALA, NC News Service, August 11, 1969.
73. *Newsweek* LXXIV (August 25, 1969), 76.
74. August 20, 1969.
75. *National Catholic Reporter*, August 20, 1969.
76. New York *Times*, August 20, 1969.
77. *National Catholic Reporter*, August 27, 1969.
78. LXXIV (August 25, 1969), 76.
79. August 15, 1969.
80. CX (August 23, 1969), 3.
81. XCIX (August 22, 1969), 94.
82. *Newsweek* LXXIV (August 25, 1969), 76.
83. *The Critic* XXIX (July-August, 1971), 8-9.
84. AALA, John L. McKenzie to Francis J. Weber, Claremont, January 22, 1985.
85. (New York, 1977).
86. Lawrence S. Dietz, "Book Review" in the Los Angeles *Times*, October 16, 1977.
87. AALA, Unidentified news clipping, dated December, 1977.
88. Thomas J. Shelley, *Paul J. Hallinan. First Archbishop of Atlanta* (Wilmington, 1989), 319.
89. George A. Kelley, *The Battle for the American Church Revisited* (San Francisco, 1995), p. 69.
90. Among the other clerical outriders who ran afoul of their bishops or religious superiors in the United States during those tumultuous years were Fathers Daniel Berrigan, S.J., Phillip Berrigan, S.S.J., J. Clement Burns, O.P., Gommar De Paux (Baltimore), Michael Garvin (Philadelphia), James E. Groppi (Milwaukee), Bonaventure O'Brien, O.F.M. and Maurice Ouillet, S.V.D. Two others put their views into print; Elwood Kaiser referred to McIntyre as "a simple, honest, straightforward man who was called the sixteenth century fox by his more progressive priests." *Hollywood Priest* (New York, 1991), p. 176 and finally Robert G. Hoyt who wrote about "Baffled Bishops" in *Harper's Magazine* CCXXXXIII (October, 1971), to the effect that McIntyre was known as "the old curmudgeon of Los Angeles."

28. *An Incident of Violence*

L os Angeles is truly a unique place. Where else could a major
church break-in be filmed live on television? Christmas Eve,
1969, was the time and Saint Basil's Catholic Church in the mid-
Wilshire area was the place.

In a press release, issued on December 4, 1969, *Catolicos Por La
Raza*, a coalition of Mexican-American Catholics working within the
framework of the Congress of Mexican-American unity, wrote a
letter to James Francis Cardinal McIntyre in which they advocated
"the return of the Catholic Church to the oppressed Chicano
community." The letter complained that Mexican-Americans "lived
in *barrios*, have received on the average an eighth grade education
in the United States and are treated as beasts of burden for the
betterment of agribusiness. Paradoxically," they charged, "the
Catholic Church is one of the richest and most powerful institutions
in the world and the United States."[1]

On December 18, Cardinal McIntyre agreed to meet with a
delegation of four spokesmen. About thirty members showed up
and forced their way into his office, brushing aside a secretary and
several other laymen who worked at the Chancery. The cardinal
attempted to talk with the group which shouted at him for about
fifteen minutes before departing.[2]

Shortly after their meeting, the leadership of *Catolicos Por La
Raza* decided to go public, noting that "we are left with no choice
but to publicly demand that the Catholic institutions in Los
Angeles practice what they preach and channel their tremendous
spiritual and economic power to meet the needs of their most
faithful servants." Then came the not-so-veiled threat that "we
shall enforce our demands with whatever spiritual and physical
powers we possess even if it means we must be jailed."

In a letter to its members, the Congress of Mexican-American
Unity, told how, on December 7, approximately 350 Chicanos
"gathered for a significant and successful demonstration at the
multi-million dollar residence of Cardinal McYntire (sic), Saint
Basil's Catholic Church on Wilshire Boulevard."[3] McIntyre reported
the incident to Archbishop Luigi Raimondi, the Apostolic Delegate,
noting that "the spark plug of the group" appeared to have been
former Maryknoller Father Blase A. Bonpane, assisted by another
former priest from Chicago, Andrew Gallegos.[4]

Saint Basil's Church in the mid-Wilshire district was hailed as one of the most distinctive in the nation.

CATOLICOS POR LA RAZA
CPLR

BAUTISMO DE FUEGO
ST.BASIL'S CHURCH
SEPT.13 IIAM

Sometime during the ensuing week, *Catolicos de la Raza* began distributing pamphlets calling for members and friends to "attend a Midnight Mass with the poor on the steps of the rich" at Saint Basil's Church on Wilshire Boulevard. One of the pamphlets contended that their group was "representative of all areas of the community: clergy, religious and laity." It listed as their primary objective having "the Church relate to the tremendous needs of the people." It then quoted (out of context) a remark of Cesar Chavez that "we do not want more cathedrals; but ask the Catholic Church to sacrifice with the people for social change." After all, the wording went, "to be oblivious to the needs of the poor is to be responsible for their poverty. The Church must now account for its lack of responsibility to the poor people of the *barrios*."[5]

After seeing the pamphlets, which were circulated throughout the city, Msgr. Benjamin G. Hawkes, Pastor of Saint Basil's, added a contingency of security officers to his group of ushers. Then he notified the police. Shortly after the beginning of the midnight service, "a chanting, club-swinging mob of 200 demonstrators burst into St. Basil's ... briefly interrupting the Christmas Midnight Mass at which James Francis Cardinal McIntyre was presiding."[6] The heavy glass outer doors of the church were smashed and several members of the congregation were injured as they joined in repulsing the intruders.

Police called for reinforcements as soon as the disturbance erupted and a tactical alert was issued at 12:30 p.m. Order was soon restored and services inside the church continued. One police officer was injured and three civilians were taken to Central Receiving Hospital. When peace had finally been restored, Cardinal McIntyre apologized to the regular worshipers and those watching on television, comparing the protest group to the "rabble that gathered at the foot of the Cross when Christ died. And in the spirit of Christ," he added, "we can only say: 'Father, forgive them, they know not what they do!'"[7]

Father Blase Bonpane, who had been suspended "after a stormy career in Guatemala," had earlier offered Mass on the steps of the church, warning in his homily that "the disturbance will be a continuing thing."[8] He said that Saint Basil's Church had "become a symbol of the affluence of the Catholic Church in this area," he noted that "the Chicanos feel they have been short-changed by the institutional Church, that it must proclaim something of the message of Jesus, which had to do with poverty and not $3 million structures."[9]

Oscar Acosta,[10] a Mexican-American lawyer and spokesman for *Catolicos Por La Raza*, blamed the sheriff's deputies and police for provoking the disturbance. He charged that his people were told they could enter the church "so long as we did not bring our banners and candles in."[11] The police, on the other hand, maintained that the demonstrators hit them with picket signs and threw objects at them, a charge denied by the demonstrators. The deputies said no one was being admitted because services were already in progress and the church was filled to capacity.

Former Los Angeles Police Chief Tom Reddin, by then a newscaster, had a KTLA-TV team at the church for the Mass. He was quoted as saying that the militants had aimed at "extortion" under threat of disrupting a church service and he reminded people that "disrupting a religious service is a crime."[12]

Less than twelve hours after the midnight fracas, another group of protesters arrived at the church. In contrast to the earlier outburst, the picketing was peaceful, except for two minor incidents and, this time, the demonstrators dispersed when one of their leaders urged them to avoid further confrontations.[13]

Friction remained at fever pitch for several days. On Monday, December 29, another protest took place, this one orchestrated in a parking lot across the street from Saint Basil's Church. Some 200 placard-carrying pickets attended a Mass offered there by Bishop Antulio Parrilla-Bonilla, S.J., former Auxiliary of Caguas, Puerto Rico, resident of San Juan, Puerto Rico, and assisted by Father Mark Day, O.F.M., a Franciscan who told reporters that he was chaplain to Cesar Chavez. Parilla-Bonilla, assuring the gathering that he was "totally in support of the Chicano cause," said "this Mass is not a Mass of confrontation. It is a Mass of solidarity. It is a Mass of love."[14] Parilla-Bonilla was an interesting person. Claiming to be associated with the University of Puerto Rico, he said he was "in good standing with the Holy See" and had received permission from the Pope to preach the Gospel "to the poor people of his race."[15] Parrilla-Bonilla was touring the United States under the sponsorship of an organization called Clergy and Laymen Concerned about Vietnam.[16]

John Dart, religion writer for the Los Angeles *Times*, used his weekly column to outline the accomplishments of James Francis Cardinal McIntyre in the Hispanic community. After recalling that McIntyre had said that "his first commission in Los Angeles was to serve and serve well, the Mexican people," Dart outlined the Church's educational programs and welfare outreaches, concluding with the observation that "the differences between archdiocesan leaders and church reformers are mostly philosophical."[17] Dart quoted Auxiliary Bishop William R. Johnson, director of Catholic Charities, to the effect that during the preceding six years, more than $13 million from affluent areas had been transferred to poorer parishes by the Archdiocese of Los Angeles.

There were numerous reactions among all levels of society to the Christmas event. "Shock and pain" were the words used by Nelson J. Baldo, president of the Southern California Chapter, Knights of Columbus. Baldo said that the disgraceful display was especially painful "in that it happened on Christmas" and that it "interfered with the congregation's fundamental right of practicing their religion."[18]

The first response to the incident by ecclesial officials took place on Sunday, December 28th, when Father John Urban, a resident priest at Saint Basil's, preached at all the Masses on how "persecution, prejudice and hatred have marred the otherwise noble efforts of humanity to aim for the stars and become a little less than the angels." He said that the "bizarre events of our Christmas day are abundant proof of the dichotomy which exists between peaceful men of goodwill and those who have espoused a philosophy of turmoil." Such people, he suggested, refuse to accept honest efforts to correct ills within the framework of orderly process. "They discount as irrelevant the fact that the Catholic Archdiocese of Los Angeles, at no cost to the citizenry, supports a vast educational, medical and social welfare program for the Mexican-American community." And he pointed out that the funds for these services were being provided by people of goodwill in all areas of the archdiocese. He concluded by reminding his listeners that "irresponsible revolutionaries cannot pretend to represent the Latin community."[19]

Msgr. Patrick Roche, editor of *The Tidings*, weighed into the scene with a masterful editorial about "Facts vs. Protests." After decrying that Christmas Eve "should be selected as the occasion of a wild and violent demonstration at the doors" of a church, Roche said that "somehow the event is symbolic of the undisciplined, irrational and anarchistic pattern of our age." Then he pointed out that the first seventeen schools erected by the Youth Education Fund were built on the East side of Los Angeles. And he went on to observe that "through the years, the work has progressed to the point where there is no Mexican-American parish which does not have its own parish school and regional high school." Throughout the Archdiocese of Los Angeles, "we witness the people of God sharing their goods with their neighbors and friends, quietly, efficiently and effectively." Roche concluded by recalling that "in early December, the officials of these organizations offered to meet with a committee of newly-blown dissenters to explain the program and invite suggestions." But "the offer was ignored."[20]

There were other clerical reactions on the local scene. Father Luis Pienado, S.J., who was raised in East Los Angeles, was visiting relatives in Los Angeles at the time. He was "dismayed by the militants' protest against the Church" and worried that the leaders of the protest may advocate socialism or communism. He thought that "the Chicanos should be alerted to the possible political motivations of their leaders."[21] Father Thomas Hayes who had worked twenty-three years on the east side, said that he would like to think "that *Catolicos Por La Raza* may learn the truth about the history of the Catholic Church in East Los Angeles, and this truth will free them from error and unjustified bitterness, and that they may use their youthful energy to tackle some of the real problems rather than to create imaginary ones."[22]

Father Luis Valbuena, a dynamic and highly-respected Oblate priest, told his people that he was strongly tempted to apologize to Cardinal McIntyre for the recent tactics of local militants. He reminded his audience that "only a year ago, the Spanish government had honored the Cardinal for the prelate's outstanding service on behalf of the Spanish-speaking of the archdiocese."[23]

With the spectre of imprisonment facing certain of the Christmas Eve demonstrators, Richard Cruz, a spokesman for *Catolicos Por La Raza*, offered a formal apology to the cardinal.[24] In response to a letter from Cruz, His Eminence of Los Angeles pointed out that "you as a law student know criminal charges are not brought by individuals who are wronged by criminal acts or by organizations such as the Church." Charges are lodged by "the appropriate officers of the government on behalf of all of the people." He observed that "the outbreak which led to these charges put in great fear and danger the faithful who gathered to celebrate the First Mass of Christmas. Those who violated the law must answer for any crimes they may have committed against the people of this state."

Noting that he was "completely disposed to hear with sympathy your petition for forgiveness ... for this regrettable occurrence," he reminded Cruz that true sorrow carries with it the intention of amending a wrongful course of conduct. McIntyre concluded his letter, which was released to the press, with these words:

> We sincerely hope that this occurrence will be a lesson to all of us about the danger of setting in action forces which we cannot control. Enemies of our beloved Mexican-American citizens are also enemies of our faith and country and constantly seek to use the innocent and the unwary to further their hidden aims. Historically, our enemies attempt to put a wedge between our people and the loyalty they have to the leaders of their faith. We ask that you consider these factors in future activities.[25]

A few days later, Richard Cruz led a group of about seventy-five supporters to Saint Basil's Church, where they attended Mass and ended a fast in support of their convictions. Cruz observed that "we are Catholics and we are going to end our fast by attending Mass in a Catholic church." Inside, they "were courteously shown seats by ushers."[26]

Significantly, the actions of *Catolicos Por La Raza* did not generate any enthusiasm among the Mexican-American people in California's southland. During the first week in January of 1970, Cardinal McIntyre received a letter from a number of people on the east side of Los Angeles, including officials of the Holy Name Society, the Legion of Mary and Cursillo groups repudiating the activities "recently sponsored by a small dissident group." The letter reiterated the loyalty and devotion of Mexican-American people to the Church and its leadership. It said that "the Church has always resisted attacks of the enemy and always has known its foes. In this case, the enemies are not the Mexican people of Los Angeles nor the true Catholics who feel the pain of the Church at the outrages perpetrated with premeditated organization and planned by its enemies." The letter concluded by saying that "we Catholics do not fight against the Church. We are peaceful. We love peace and order. And if sometimes we have to fight, we do it against the enemies of the Holy Church."[27]

On January 11, some 800 persons gathered at the Old Plaza Church of Our Lady of the Angels for a special Mass of reparation for the disturbance caused by militants on Christmas Eve. Father Dominic Fonseca, C.M.F., preached an eloquent homily in which he said "we are not Catholic if we profane Catholic altars." He went on to affirm that "We love God, His Church and the authority instituted by Jesus Christ and represented in His Church."[28]

With his retirement, on January 21st, James Francis Cardinal McIntyre's involvement with *Catolicos Por La Raza* was terminated. The story of the trial and conviction of the demonstrators belongs to another book.

While Oscar Acosta maintained that St. Basil's was chosen for the Christmas Eve protest in 1969 because it was "where Cardinal McIntyre would be,"[29] other spokesmen for *Catolicos Por La Raza* said it was because the church was "a new $3 million structure that graphically illustrates the misappropriation of funds which should be devoted to the poor and to social justice."[30] Sam Kushner, writing in *People's World*, went a step further and said that the church "which cost more than $3 million" stands to many Chicanos "as a symbol of money for cathedrals that could better be used for the poor."[31]

600

Perhaps, as an afterthought to the turmoil mentioned above, something should be said about the church-rectory-hall complex erected in 1967-1968 under the patronage of Saint Basil. After all, there were others, even among the clergy, who resented and belittled the erection of what was probably the most expensive Catholic edifice in Los Angeles.

Shortly after arriving as pastor in 1949, Msgr. Henry Gross became aware that a replacement was sorely needed for the wooden house-of-worship that had served the area for three decades. The earlier building, which had burned three times, was eminently worthy of retirement. On November 15, 1952, Gross sent a letter to parishioners outlining plans for a new parochial complex. He had already begun collecting funds for additional property and, by 1965, had acquired and paid for ten choice lots for his envisioned 40,000 square foot combination church-rectory-hall which would be built between Kingsley Drive and Harvard on the north side of Wilshire Boulevard.

Though often referred to in the press as being "located in an area of high rise apartments and expensive homes populated by affluent residents,"[32] the parish in reality had deteriorated considerably and, by the 1960s, was a low-middle income community. Msgr. Benjamin G. Hawkes, who would become the canonical pastor in 1969, agreed to raise the necessary pledges through a series of private subscriptions. No archdiocesan funds and very little parochial moneys were used in the project. So successful was the low-keyed drive that upwards of a million surplus dollars was diverted into an endowment for future parochial use.

There were all sorts of guesstimates circulated about the costs of the stylistic new church. Mike Davis, for example, said that the "showcase residence church on a ritzy stretch of Wilshire Boulevard" cost $4 million![33] Other figures were even more preposterous. The local press kept using the amount of $3 million which somehow had crept into their morgue files. The actual cost, excluding the property purchased by the parish over a thirty-year period, was $2,516,162.[34] For an architecturally stunning and innovative church seating 1,000 people, a commodious rectory housing ten priests and a spacious parish hall, that figure appears to have been eminently reasonable.[35]

To have denied the parishioners and their pastor permission for using funds raised specifically for their new church-rectory-hall complex would have been a gross violation of canonical legislation and totally outside the American tradition of free expression.

And there were other considerations. John W. Scannell, writing in a "Reader's Forum" told readers of the Los Angeles *Herald-Examiner* that "If St. Basil's cost was three million - probably an exaggeration - where did the money go? Not a penny, certainly, to Cardinal McIntyre. At least 60 percent went into the pockets of the laborers who toiled in the actual construction of the building. Perhaps 25 per cent went for the building materials and likely 80 per cent of that was paid to workers. Perhaps, the remaining 15 per cent went to the artists in beautifying the church; again, workers well-paid for their artistry." He concluded by saying that "thousands of people were benefited in a financial way and the entire community was assisted economically. Undoubtedly, hundreds of our wonderful Mexican-Americans themselves were helped by the paychecks received from the project."[36]

Notes to the Text

1. AALA, Brochure, December, 1969.
2. Oakland *Catholic Voice*, December 31, 1969.
3. AALA, Circular Letter, Los Angeles, December 15, 1969.
4. AALA, J. Francis A. McIntyre to Luigi Raimondi, Los Angeles, December 9, 1969.
5. AALA, three undated pamphlets.
6. Los Angeles *Times*, December 25, 1969.
7. Los Angeles *Herald-Examiner*, December 26, 1969.
8. Steubenville *Register*, January 11, 1970. An article in *People's World* (January 3, 1970) said that at the "unusual Mass" by Bonpane "tortillas replaced the original wafers."
9. Los Angeles *Times*, December 27, 1969.
10. Oscar Zeta Acosta (1935-1974) published his rambling and questionably factual memoirs about the event in 1973 under the title *The Revolt of the Cockroach People*. The book was re-issued fifteen years later with an introduction by Hunter Thompson.
11. Los Angeles *Times*, December 26, 1969.
12. Quoted in *The Tidings*, January 2, 1970.
13. Los Angeles *Times*, December 26, 1969.
14. Los Angeles *Herald-Examiner*, December 29, 1969.
15. Los Angeles *Times*, December 29, 1969.
16. *Ibid.*, January 31, 1969.
17 *Ibid.*
18. AALA, Nelson J. Baldo to James Francis Cardinal McIntyre, Los Angeles, December 30, 1969.
19. Reproduced in *The Tidings*, January 2, 1970.
20. *Ibid.*, January 2, 1970.
21. Los Angeles *Herald-Examiner*, January 4, 1970.
22. *The Tidings*, January 23, 1970.
23. *Ibid.*, January 30, 1970.
24. AALA Richard Cruz to James Francis Cardinal McIntyre, Los Angeles, December 26, 1969.
25. *The Tidings*, January 2, 1970.
26. Los Angeles *Times* January 5, 1970.
27. Reproduced in *The Tidings*, January 9, 1970.
28. *Ibid.*, January 16, 1970.
29. Los Angeles *Times*, December 26, 1969.
30. *Ibid.*, December 29, 1969.
31. January 3, 1970.
32. Davenport *Catholic Messenger*, January 8, 1970.

33. *City of Quartz* (New York, 1990), p. 334.
34. AALA, Council Minutes, January 18, 1967, p. 1367.
35. For an historical and architectural description of the church, see Francis J. Weber, *Christ on Wilshire Boulevard* (Los Angeles, 1969).
36. December 31, 1969.

29. McIntyre and the Press

During the years James Francis Cardinal McIntyre was not without his critics. Prior to Vatican Council II, he enjoyed a better than average press. All of that changed in the mid 1960s, when journalists within and without the Catholic Church began taking themselves and their opinions more seriously, maybe even too seriously.

Among the dozens of feature articles written about the cardinal over the years, some were more memorable than others. A sampling of the more significant essays, arranged here chronologically, demonstrates a wide spectrum of opinion and innuendo, much of it critical, some of it commendatory but none of it indifferent. Truly important people are loved or hated, never ignored.

In a feature about the "Private Life of a Catholic Cardinal" for the *Saturday Evening Post*, Jack Alexander said that "by any standard, James Francis Cardinal McIntyre, a sixty-seven year old citizen of California transplanted from New York, qualifies as an exceptional man, having won distinction in two callings not considered to be closely related."

Describing McIntyre as "a tall, courtly and rather handsome man," he noted that the cardinal is amply endowed with the everyday politeness that he was taught during his childhood. He is easily approachable, and when a visitor arrives the cardinal grabs his brief case or whatever else he is burdened with and helps him off with his coat with easy deference." He described the cardinal "as neat-minded" and a person irritated by slipshod work. "He can pull the rug out from under an offending priest with a maximum of compassion. As disciplinarian he is demanding but fair."

When propelled from New York to Los Angeles, "the cross county shift fused a remarkable man with a remarkable community and the fusion produced some remarkable results." The four county archdiocese was suffering from advanced growth pains. "Its facilities for worship and education were suffering from the same appalling time lag that afflicted transportation and related services and for the same reasons, the never-ending stream of migrants from the east.

McIntyre inaugurated a building program, "probably the biggest of its kind ever attempted." Scores of churches and schools were built and even more were renovated. The total expenditure for all of this came to a staggering $15,000,000, "an upsetting sum for most archbishops, or almost anyone else, as most of it was in the form of debt." But "the figures held no terror for McIntyre" who was always at home with financial challenges. McIntyre was described as "an implacable foe of progressive education, holding it to be a vicious movement which seeks by teaching moral relativism, to destroy the most elementary moral standards." The author concludes by comparing Fray Junipero Serra and James Francis Cardinal McIntyre. "As builders and adoptive Californians, they would have understood each other without hesitation."[1]

In an effort to call attention to what they termed "an extraordinary situation," the editors of *The Commonweal* published a "special issue" on July 10, 1964, about "Catholicism in Los Angeles." Two essays, one by freelance writer A. V. Krebs, Jr., and the other by associate editor John Leo, concentrated on supposed scandals which have "no place in Los Angeles or anywhere in the American Church."

After acknowledging McIntyre's accomplishments in the field of education and missionary outreach, Krebs said that "the success of these programs is in contrast with some underlying realities of Catholic life in the archdiocese, realities which have caused the Church in Los Angeles to be called by some a "Church of Silence."

While complaining that getting "a clear picture of the archdiocese is not an easy task" because "a fear of reprisal closes many mouths," he said that "there exists in Southern California today a multitude of religiously-orientated "particularlists, ultranationalistic and so-called anti-Communist organizations," all of which he ascribed to McIntyre. An inordinately large part of the essay is devoted to decrying the Cardinal Mindszenty Foundation, the Christian Resistance Movement and San Diego Catholics for Better Libraries, none of which operated under the archdiocesan umbrella or were even recognized by McIntyre. Criticizing the ultra-nationalistic tone of "Headlines and Deadlines," a column by George N. Kramer that appeared weekly in *The Tidings*, he was especially upset by a ten inch, seven column advertisement for the Schick Safety Razor Company which appeared opposite Kramer's column.

Though he admitted that "archdiocesan officials including Cardinal McIntyre have denied that such 'particularist' groups or *The Tidings* reflect their political views," he noticed that in the chancery parking lot "nearly every car" portrayed signs proclaiming that "the John Birch Society is not a Secret Society," "the Only Ism is Americanism" or "Stamp Out CommUNism."

Krebs also observed that "the United Nations is repeatedly branded by Southern California groups as subversive and a threat to American freedom" and that the most prominent of those groups in Los Angeles opposing the United Nations at the time was the Archdiocesan Council of Catholic Women. Noting that the Los Angeles group was no longer affiliated with the National Council of Catholic Women, Krebs charged their reason for withdrawal from the parent group was "the NCCW bias, slant and pre-occupation with the UNICEP, UNESCO, WHO and other specialized agencies of the U.N."

Then he faulted McIntyre for not taking a stand in the dispute between the Christines and the American Public Relations Forum. When given a nineteen point statement listing "acts of intimidation" to which the membership of the APRF had been subjected, McIntyre replied that "lay Catholics were free to follow the dictates of their own consciences in political affairs, notwithstanding what position other laymen or clergymen might take." Precisely why that bothered Krebs is unclear.

Krebs also thought that McIntyre came down too heavily on UNESCO. In fact, the cardinal's displeasure with UNESCO was well known and shared by many other ecclesial leaders, both Catholic and non-Catholic. He reported that on March 6, 1953,[2] McIntyre had addressed the Bond Club, an organization of investment brokers, complaining about "the attempt by a powerful minority to impose on American schools a new philosophy which admits no responsibility toward the principles on which this nation was founded." McIntyre was especially irritated at the National Education Association for its support of UNESCO and he made no secret of his view that the philosophy then espoused by UNESCO was "destructive because it attempts to supplant the patriotic and loyal spirit of American Citizenry with a world viewpoint that ignores what is proximate for that which is remote - and dubious at least." When Krebs inquired of Msgr. William North, editor of *The Tidings*, why the NEA was singled out by the cardinal, North responded in his usual outspoken way that the NEA contains "a clique ... bent on the complete secularization of the country's schools." He pointed out that the stated objectives of UNESCO "are not the laws of the land, they are merely attempts by a crackpot secular group to substitute secularism for our Judeo Christian heritage." North went a step further, when asked who belonged to this "crackpot" group, by identifying Eleanor Roosevelt and "the Russian delegates." Krebs protested that the passage of years had done little to assuage McIntyre's views about the NEA. And what was worse, according to Krebs, was that McIntyre's conservatism had "taken on other dimensions."

Throughout the article, Krebs liberally quoted "members of the archdiocesan clergy" without ever mentioning any by name, a

practice that calls into question the very substance of his accusations. An example would be his contention that there were two
unwritten rules for the clergy: "no interfaith activity and do not
disturb the faithful's consciences on racial problems." He repeated
the totally unfounded contention that "Catholic magazines such as
Ave Maria, Way, Worship, America and *Commonweal* are considered
dangerous at the seminary. The latter two are kept in the reserve
stacks of the seminary library and can be obtained only through the
permission of the seminary rector or through written permission
from the Los Angeles Chancery Office." He added the equally
unsubstantiated charge that McIntyre, after a visit to the seminary,
had "demanded of the seminarians and soon-to-be-ordained priests
a signed oath of absolute obedience to him."

The author objected to the lack of welcome for Father Hans Kung,
the supposed refusal of the Church on the local scene in the case of
racial justice and McIntyre's contention that a striving for interracial justice should be rendered quietly, consistently and as a
normal aspect of parish life among our people. There were other
points on which the writer disagreed with His Eminence of Los
Angeles, none of which justified the term of "scandal" or the charge
that "Los Angeles constituted a Church unto itself."[3] Though the
article was laced with factual errors, misrepresentations and
quotations taken out of context, it was unfortunately accepted in
many quarters as an authentic portrayal of the McIntyre regime in
Los Angeles. Most assuredly, it was not that at all.

In the second of the *Commonweal* articles, John Leo took up the
torch by referring to the "glittering repertoire of atrocity stories
about life under Cardinal McIntyre," repeating such oft-heard
charges that encyclicals were "suppressed" (they were on sale across
the street from the chancery), that *America* and the *Commonweal*
were "barred from the churches" (untrue), that priests were not
allowed to be A.A. chaplains (false), that "dialogue Masses are
forbidden," (they were, in fact, celebrated weekly at the major
seminary), that "Newman work was discouraged," (the archdiocese
had a full-time priest in that apostolate) and on and on.

Then he launched into his version of "the DuBay case" which,
except for emphasis, was chronologically accurate. He felt that the
young priest's tactics were ill-conceived, noting that "Father DuBay
is one of the slow learners" while grudgingly admitting "whatever
his inflexibility on issues, Cardinal McIntyre has a reputation for
being fatherly to priests in trouble." Leo correctly observed that
contrary to expectations, the episode "failed to polarize opposition
to the Cardinal on the race issue." For a number of reasons, the
majority of sympathetic "clergy appear to have debarked from

Father DuBay's train at one stop or another. Most of the pastors," he said, "opposed the whole thing. They think DuBay is a young whippersnapper who deserves everything he's going to get. Few thought that DuBay made an important contribution." But a prophet Leo was not. His prediction that "eruptions like Father DuBay's - battles fought on short notice with no hope of winning - will become more inevitable, and possibly will become more frequent." Though there was little new in Leo's story, it was, in balance, a far more effective presentation than its companion piece. One commentator, after reading the essays, wondered whether they needed to be written, much less published, in a national Catholic journal.

"It was true," as Robert Blair Kaiser wrote, that Cardinal McIntyre was among the "kindest of men." He invited Kaiser to his home in Fremont Place for a long chat in 1961, and he was always cordial to the writer in Rome,[4] even after he "had written critically about his resistance to change."

Early in 1964, Kaiser, in his role as the Roman correspondent for Time, Inc., wrote a lengthy article for *Los Angeles Magazine* on "The McIntyre Controversy" in which he endeavored to explain the conflicts "between a revered cardinal and a new breed of priests and laity. " Of all the accounts compiled during those hectic times, the lease offensive is that by Blair, a former Jesuit scholastic who had a better understanding of McIntyre than most others.

Blair portrayed the cardinal as a "brick and mortar pastor" whose genius as a builder of churches, schools, convents and hospitals, although quite necessary to the booming counties of Southern California, helped contribute to his own obsolescence. While noting that "measured by all the old standards, McIntyre would have stood tall," he opined that the cardinal had been caught up in Pope John XXIII's revolution. In his view, McIntyre hadn't changed, but the Catholic world had, leaving His Eminence of Los Angeles as something of "a dinosaur in the middle of the 20th century."

In some respects that portrayal was accurate. Yet, interestingly enough, few of the new breed, "a young, radical lot, generous with the poor and suffering, and terribly harsh in their judgments of superiors," seemed personally severe toward Cardinal McIntyre, feeling as one pastor put it, that the cardinal was "a holy man, sincere in his convictions that he is defending the faith by resisting the changes of reformers." Blair saw the conflicts in Los Angeles as "a battle of good men, earnest people, few in number." He pointed out that "as long as Church and society grow, problems will change and new solutions will be demanded. Today's New Breed may be part of tomorrow's Old Guard and the conflicts between the two in the future may well be much more highly sophisticated."[5]

Among the attacks made on James Francis Cardinal McIntyre during his tenure as Archbishop of Los Angeles, none was more virulent than the one mounted by Edward M. Keating, an attorney and investor who lived in Atherton, California. Keating was the founder and publisher of *Ramparts* magazine, which described itself as a "Catholic Layman's Journal" which had been published five times yearly since 1961.[6] During its earliest years, *Ramparts* published articles on such topics as the quality of Jesuit university education, the treatment of black Catholics and the influence of the John Birch Society on the Church.

In mid-1964, Keating, a graduate of Stanford University, had just signed a contract with Random House for a book entitled *The Scandal of Silence*. As a publicity gimmick for his soon-to be-released book, Keating orchestrated a press conference at the Sheraton Palace Hotel in San Francisco for June 10, 1964 in which an unnamed Catholic priest gave "a precedent-shattering interview" about "Cardinal McIntyre's racial policies" or the lack thereof.[7]

Accusations were made that McIntyre had "failed to speak out on the race issue and against the initiative to repeal the Rumford Housing Act." Keating charged that "many Catholic priests in California are afraid to denounce the sin of racism from their pulpits because their superiors shy away from the ticklish subject."[8] On and on the charges went. Almost immediately, Father Eugene A. Boyle, chaplain of the Interracial Council for the Archdiocese of San Francisco, denied the validity of the charges. He noted that "Keating has failed to accept a single invitation to the many conferences on religion and race which the archdiocese has sponsored."[9]

For unknown reasons, Keating never joined forces with Father William H. DuBay, and he assured the Los Angeles *Times* that the Los Angeles priest was *not* the unnamed cleric[10] who made the charges in San Francisco. Yet Keating used DuBay for his own purposes, saying that "as long as McIntyre is cardinal, no priest will ever dare say anything critical on any subject in his archdiocese."[11] Keating devoted the major portion of the Summer, 1964 issue of *Ramparts* to the subject, reserving his own editorial to commenting on the "tyranny in Los Angeles":

> The DuBay case is only the beginning; others will follow, taking the same course he took, until such time as the Church ends its rigid authoritarianism and absolute paternalism that treats everyone less than a bishop as an object rather than a person...[12]

The reception of Keating's charges, never answered directly by the Archdiocese of Los Angeles or its archbishop, was unusually quiet. Only *America* ventured into the fray by wondering if "there is a place in the Catholic body politic for a publication whose sole ambition seems to be to slay clerical dragons." After all, it was observed, it is one thing for people to voice their grief publicly over what they regard as lamentable clerical leadership and quite another to make dissent "an end in itself."[13] As a matter of fact, ever-so-gradually, Keating had moved his journal beyond its original orientation. Though referred to by the New York *Times* as a journal "edited for lay Catholics," its publisher proclaimed in at least one advertisement that "we certainly *were* a Catholic magazine,"[14] at least until 1964.

In an earlier issue, there was another major feature story, this one about Cardinal McIntyre whom the editor characterized as "a McKinley conservative who has often expressed his dissatisfaction with the United Nations."[15] The body of the magazine was devoted to attacking Barry Goldwater, then running for president and the cardinal of Los Angeles. One article was particularly offensive. Just as the fathers of Vatican Council II were reporting on a document stating that "freedom of conscience is a natural right," *Ramparts* set itself up as McIntyre's conscience. Page forty-three presented a double exposure picture of McIntyre and, within a balloon, *Ramparts* gives its version of what the cardinal's conscience was saying to him, along with the cardinal's response.

Father John Doran, in an essay on "The Charity of Criticism," said he had no quarrel with the magazine criticizing McIntyre, but he did "propose that those who present their publications as 'Catholic' should practice the Catholic virtues of charity and justice."[16] Val King reported that he was at home enjoying a musical program over KPEN when he was "jolted to hear a commercial charging Cardinal McIntyre with an iron fisted administration," the gruesome details of which would be explained to those subscribing to *Ramparts*. While acknowledging that the editor was seeking subscribers, King wondered if it was necessary "to stand the Church on its head to get attention." He concluded by terming the unseemly appeal for subscribers as "evidence of impatient immaturity."[17]

An editorial in the *Catholic Star Herald* said that "it seems that the editor, Edward Keating, has embarked on a personal crusade to destroy Cardinal McIntyre. He has outdone the extremist writings of the John Birch Society and has penned comments so virulent that they can only be excused on the grounds of hysteria or some form of monomania." The writer said that "we don't agree with Cardinal McIntyre's views, but we do give him credit for being honestly and sincerely mistaken. Keating's attacks on the cardinal seem obviously based on a conviction that the cardinal is a malevolent man. We must confess that the only hint of malevolence we have discovered in this incredible and indecent attack on Cardinal McIntyre has been in the pages of *Ramparts*."[18]

The editor of the Boston *Pilot* characterized the attack as "disastrous." It was a "puerile and frenetic attack on Cardinal McIntyre, contrived with mockery and a total lack of human respect. Venturing far beyond the bounds of intelligent controversy and difference, *Ramparts* lost whatever title it had to our attention."[19] Gerald E. Sherry, writing in Atlanta's *Bulletin* said he thought that "the most disgraceful part of the *Ramparts* issue is its bitter attack on James Francis Cardinal McIntyre, Archbishop of Los Angeles. It was an unforgivable piece of writing and is more reminiscent of yellow journalism than Catholic culture. There is justification for disagreeing with some of the views and positions of Catholic leaders in the Los Angeles area - but at no time can we ever stoop to public mockery of our priests and bishops."[20]

Writing from "the Editor's desk" at *Ave Maria* magazine, John Reedy agreed with the judgment of many other Catholic periodicals: "In its crude use of hate-smear techniques, *Ramparts* has lost its right to be taken seriously by readers who search for truth and objectivity."[21] S. I. Adamo suggested that a "Be Kind to Hierarchy Week" be instituted, noting that "we may be frank and forthright but never damning or bullyragging."[22]

Either Keating didn't read the Catholic press or he didn't care about its reaction. In any event, he inserted an ad in the *National Catholic Reporter* for late 1964 in which Cardinal McIntyre was portrayed beneath the label *Sic Semper Tyrannis*.[23] There was even objection to that. In the Albany *Evangelist* the editor said "the sword of extremism is a dangerous weapon. " Noting that extremism was not exclusively a characteristic of the right, he pointed out that "liberalism with a vengeance can be just as destructive of the social fabric as the tactics of the radical right." He termed the ad as hardly a boost to the liberal cause.[24]

Keating's book, *The Scandal of Silence* released by Random House in early 1965, was advertised as "a laymen's powerful critique of the Catholic Church in America." Therein he offered his "frank and sweeping" appraisal of the Church as he saw it. Ever the campaigner, Keating "calls for changes of mood and emphasis, for more heroism on the line, for better education especially in the seminaries and growing relationships with other churches and groups, and generally for the broad and open-air policy that Pope John XXIII called *aggiornamento.*"[25]

Especially aggravating to the author was what he called "the tradition of lay silence" in the Church. "The greatest obstacle to free speech is psychological, but breaking the silence is like breaking down an enormous wall, unaided by anything except the belief that the wall must come down." Keating believed that to be the "true significance" of his book. Like many authors, Keating utilized chapters of his book in *Ramparts,* hoping thereby to stimulate interest in his volume.

The book, written in the same style as *Ramparts,* was referred to as a "collection of fantastic generalizations and dreadful clichés that is safe from parody because it is beyond it." John Leo, a fellow liberal, said that the book "really has to be seen to be believed." It is "so embarrassing that one can only stare at the publisher in wonderment at his reasons for perpetrating it." Leo concluded his observations with this question: "What has happened to good old Bennett Cerf?"[26]

Keating also appeared occasionally in other forums. In a radio discussion with John Leo, Keating came across as a "personal" and "highly motivated fellow" but Leo felt that "he trades only in comic generalizations." If an opponent introduces a contrary fact into the conversation, "he just replies with another two-megaton generalization, more vehement and ever-more cosmic ... a chronic case of rhetorical overkill."[27]

Keating's final public assault against Cardinal McIntyre and his policies in the Archdiocese of Los Angeles was made on July 17, 1965, in a half hour interview aired on KNBC-TV.[28] Keating's flamboyant statements to Bill Brown and Jack Latham that "Cardinal McIntyre and his underlings in this archdiocese have simply disobeyed the teachings of the Church and the promulgations of the American bishops" unleashed a firestorm of complaints into the Burbank offices of Channel 4. In a customary reply, Thomas C. McCray repeated the ageless media dictum that "through constructive criticism or commendation, we are better able to evaluate our efforts to serve the community."[29]

Edward M. Keating could best be described as a Catholic muckraker who peaked early in his journalistic career. He was a man who allowed for two views - his and the wrong one. Whatever his original objectives for the Church, Keating self destructed, leaving many undeserved scars on the ecclesial fabric of Los Angeles.

In a major story on the "new anguish of American Catholicism, Edward R. F. Sheehan wrote a feature article for the *Saturday*

Cardinal McIntyre greets Eamon de Valera, President of Ireland, to Los Angeles.

Few important people visited Los Angeles without paying their respects to Cardinal McIntyre, including West Germany Chancellor, Konrad Adenauer.

Attorney General Patrick (Edmund G.) Brown was a close friend of the cardinal. He later became governor as did his son, Jerry.

Few people amassed a greater number of proclamations than did James Francis Cardinal McIntyre. Here Mayor Sam Yorty is presenting His Eminence with one of the many.

McIntyre knew most of the Hollywood luminaries. Here he speaks with Cecil B. DeMille and Rabbi Edgar Magnin.

Evening Post which appeared at the newsstands on November 28, 1964. The "monumental, searching and reverent report," ten months in the making, told how "in seminaries, convents, colleges - even in bishops' chanceries" a bold new generation was struggling to break with the imbred past in order "to bring the Church to grips with modern society."[30]

Sheehan journeyed to Los Angeles, "the scene of the American Church's most controversial cardinal," where he found the indomitable J. Francis A. McIntyre still very much in charge. Sheehan credited McIntyre with being "a financial wizard," who had "deployed his talents to great advantage in the swift expansion of his archdiocese." Acknowledging that McIntyre was "a kind and fatherly man," the author related a story told by "a distinguished Catholic scholar" in which the cardinal happened to overhear one of the priests who shared his residence complaining about being awakened at all hours of the night to answer emergency calls on Skid Row. His Eminence quietly arranged to have all such calls transferred to his own bedroom and for some time after that, it was the cardinal himself who carried sacramental consolation to the derelicts of Los Angeles in the middle of the night. That story, by the way, is correct. It was only after becoming a cardinal that McIntyre was convinced that his driving abilities, learned only after he came to Los Angeles, were hazardous.

After the usual pleasantries, Sheehan said that "paradoxically McIntyre's archdiocesan policies failed to reflect his personal benevolence." He said that it wasn't enough to say that McIntyre was a conservative, he was "a reactionary." Sheehan characterized his hour and a half interview with the cardinal as "a memorable experience." McIntyre exuded "a sort of irascible charm. A rather handsome man who appears considerably more youthful than 78, he has a way of puckering up his lower lip when he has finished making an important point, a mannerism almost endearing." The writer said that the cardinal had three principal preoccupations: the godlessness of the public school system, the godliness of the United States Supreme Court and the supremacy of the natural law.

Though he had been warned by "a number of people" to refrain from mentioning the race questions, McIntyre himself brought up the issue. The cardinal assured Sheehan that "all our institutions are integrated. All our seminarians are taught Spanish, so that when they become priests, they can serve our Mexicans." He noted that there were 700,000 Mexican-Americans in the archdiocese. "We have built schools for them - and for Negroes, too, and these schools have given them cultural accomplishments and civic advancement. These people need education, and we are giving it to them."

Sheehan reported that shortly after his arrival in Los Angeles, he met with "a number" of priests "clandestinely in my rooms" at the hotel. He went on to say it is well known that "the cardinal has reprimanded several of his priests for preaching from the pulpit about racial injustice." He argued that the problem was political and not moral. Then came the tale about the C.C.C. (Cardinal's Carpet Club) which was reserved for those who had preached on such forbidden subjects as "liturgical reform, ecumenism or psychiatry." He concluded by complaining that "The Tidings ... continues to publish undisguised John Birch Society propaganda."

Though he covered a lot of bases in Los Angeles, Sheehan interviewed no more than half a dozen priests, if that many. His impressions of the archdiocese were more folklorish than accurate, causing one venerable cleric to observe that "97% of a bishop's problem are caused by 3% of his priests. Sheehan's genius was searching out that 3%."

There were others who felt that the Sheehan treatise was wide of the mark. Father Joseph McGroarty said that what the writer digested from "his mountain of memoranda amounts to more slag than ore. Far from being the reverent thing the editors say it is, his report is a monumental heap of half truths, contradictions, innuendo, generalization, oversimplification, sensationalism, gossip and supposition." He was especially critical of those "exposures" founded on the "testimony of unidentified, though supposedly reliable, informants." He concluded by saying that "if you happened to have a taste for accounts of unsubstantiated ecclesiastical intrigue, the *Post* expose is not to be missed."[31]

No less a figure than Richard Cardinal Cushing warned that some "freewheeling commentators are using the second Vatican Council's approach to the modern world as a 'freeway' to overrun the Roman Catholic Church with criticism." Without mentioning the article or the author by name, His Eminence of Boston clearly indicated to a meeting of the National Catholic Educational Association at Emmanuel College that his remarks were directed at Sheehan, who once served him as an altar boy. Cushing said that "he has a facility for writing and a nice personality but he would go places if he took a positive approach to the Church rather than rehashing everything critical that's been said before."[32]

Near the end of McIntyre's tenure, novelist Kenneth Lamott wrote an article for *Horizon, A Magazine of the Arts* which he based on extensive interviews with a former priest, Daniel Delaney. He portrayed the southland's "underground" Church against the background of two million communicants worshipping in 312 parishes in the "most conservative, unyielding and monolithic archdiocese in the country."[33]

Lamott resisted blaming McIntyre, "the most tradition-bound archbishop in the country," for the supposed ecclesial ills of the time, saying that it was "tempting to attribute the intransigence of the official Church in Los Angeles to the personality of His Eminence James Francis Cardinal McIntyre." Though he felt that the Los Angeles archdiocese had shown no friendliness toward change since the beginning of the Vatican Council, the author admitted that "even those people who have confronted the establishment most directly are remarkably free of bitterness toward Cardinal McIntyre." He said that "this lack of hostility" stemmed not out of love or reverence for the cardinal but from their belief that the problem reflected "the inbuilt prejudices of the entire ecclesiastical organization and of the community it serves." While acknowledging that there was no "question that the archdiocese had prospered" under McIntyre's leadership, the author appears to attribute whatever immobility existed to the entire local populace, an accusation that remained unsubstantiated.

Perhaps the cruelest and most inaccurate feature story involving Cardinal McIntyre came after his retirement when Nolan Davis, a feature writer for *West*, the Sunday magazine of the Los Angeles *Times*, published an essay entitled "The Archbishop in Motion."[34] The ostensible purpose of the writer was to delineate the character of Archbishop Timothy Manning, the tenor of his daily life, his rich insights and the spiritual life of the archdiocese. To some degree, that purpose was accomplished. But for reasons of his own, Davis felt impelled to embellish his story with a tapestry of inaccuracies, slanders and misconceptions about McIntyre.

He began by quoting Father Rocco Caporale, a visiting Italian Jesuit, who alleged that "priests in the Los Angeles Archdiocese worked in an atmosphere of sheer terror "during the McIntyre days. "Dubbed everything from 'the bookkeeper' to 'His Emptiness,' McIntyre concentrated on the Church's physical layout in the four counties of the diocese, tripling its seminaries, doubling its congregations and nearly doubling its schools." McIntyre was characterized as being "autocratic and impetuous," a man "increasingly alienated from the poor, the liberal, the black and the brown, as well as the more progressive priests and nuns." Davis said that "McIntyre outlived his time, a time when priests and laymen alike accepted the precepts of their bishop unquestioningly."

It was he who began what was later repeated as factual in books[35] that "McIntyre maintained a highly effective spy network," sending "priests and monsignors and others faithful to him in disguise into the homes of underground Catholics, armed with tape recorders." He even told how "one priest, a favorite on the underground circuit, worked right under the cardinal's nose and made his appointments to say home Masses from a confessional in the cathedral itself."

The swipe at McIntyre did not go unnoticed. An editorial in *The Tidings* wondered why Davis needed to drag "out every tired and sick tale which has wagged tongues and titillated the fancies of the idle rumor-mongers of our day." It charged that some of them were "so laughable that they border on the hysterical; some of them are so vicious that they defy definition." On the contrary, the 1,700,000 Catholics in the Archdiocese of Los Angeles "give the final answer to those who rake the muck-heaps of petulant discontent. They have come to know and love a man possessed of deep faith, a positive instinct for justice and truth and an abiding allegiance to Christ's Church and Christ's Vicar on earth."[36]

Gentle person that he always was, Archbishop Manning was furious about the article and the next day addressed an open letter to Otis Chandler, editor of the Los Angeles *Times*. Manning found it reprehensible that the occasion had been "employed to launch a totally unsympathetic and distorted attack on the stewardship of James Francis Cardinal McIntyre, my predecessor in this office and now retired." Manning said he had esteemed McIntyre since 1948 as "a model churchman, a priestly priest and a warm and personal friend," an esteem shared by "the vast body of priests, religious and laity whom he has served. " He termed the references to McIntyre as being developed "upon innuendoes, rather than the truth, gossip rather than the facts, rumor rather than reality." In conclusion, he felt that the Los Angeles *Times*, "in publishing such material" had done "an injustice to a great citizen of this community, and to the loyal people whom he faithfully shepherded for over twenty years."[37]

Manning's complaint was also published in the April 16th issue of *West* magazine. The editor noted that the Davis article had occasioned "an avalanche of mail," some of which had been and would be published by the paper. Davis himself answered the complaint, claiming that "the facts and figures are corroborated by the files of *The Times* itself as well as by my own research."

In a sampling of the letters of protest, Gerald Sherry, no fan of McIntyre's, deplored the article and denounced "the underlying acumination and spinosity" in references to McIntyre. He thought that "it was sad to see a responsible writer playing one person off against another, with shades of a James Bond movie." Despite his often unpopular views, Cardinal McIntyre has always been a priest among the people, and his concerns have always centered on the needs of the poor and the needy."[38] In other responses, Gilbert Darwinite described the attack of McIntyre as "vicious" and Mrs. Louis J. Paradiso said that "this great and good man has suffered silently and with dignity the stings and stabs of immature personalities who seem to be willing to set aside all Christian charity and temperance in their quest for publicity."[39]

Notes to the Text

1. *Saturday Evening Post* CCXXVI (September 12, 1953), 21-29, 85-88.
2. The writer was confused about this date. McIntyre did *not* address the Bond Club on that day or any day close by.
3. LXXX, 463-482.
4. See this writer's review of Blair's *Pope, Council and World in the Homiletic and Pastoral Review* LXIV (October, 1963), 85-87.
5. VIII (August, 1964) 28-31, 56.
6. Ramparts continued publication until the early 1970s.
7. Press Release, *Ramparts* magazine, June 10, 1964.
8. Los Angeles *Herald-Examiner* June 11, 1964.
9. *Ibid.* Also see *The Monitor* June 19, 1964 and the London *Tablet* July 4, 1964.
10. In a telephone conversation with Keating on July 15, 1994, he confirmed this writer's suspicion that the unnamed priest was indeed Father William H. DuBay.
11. Los Angeles *Times,* June 20, 1964.
12. *Ramparts* III (October, 1964), 6.
13. CXI (September 19, 1964), 282.
14. IV (December, 1965), end paper.
15. III (November, 1964).
16. *The Catholic Commentator,* October 9, 1964.
17. *The Monitor,* October 15, 1964.
18. October 16, 1964.
19. October 17, 1964.
20. October 29, 1964.
21. C (November 7, 1964).
22. January 29, 1965.
23. Keating wasn't much of a Latin scholar. Tyrannus was the word he wanted.
24. October 22, 1964.
25. AALA, Press Release, Menlo Park, April, 1965.
26. *National Catholic Reporter,* May 5, 1965.
27. Ibid. The editor of *Commonweal* told his readers, early in 1927, that *"Ramparts* magazine is up for sale." LXXXV (January 27, 1967), 440.
28. AALA, Transcription of News Conference #117 with Edward M. Keating.
29. AALA, Thomas C. McCray to K. Downey, Burbank, August 11, 1965.

29. AALA, Thomas C. McCray to K. Downey, Burbank, August 11, 1965.
30. "Not Peace, But the Sword," CCXXXVII (November 28, 1964).
31. Brooklyn *Tablet*, December 13, 1964.
32. Quoted in *The Tidings*, December 11, 1964.
33. XII (Winter, 1970), 68-72.
34. March 12, 1972.
35. See for example Kay Alexander, *California Catholicism* (Santa Barbara, 1993), p. 72.
36. March 17, 1972.
37. AALA, Timothy Manning to Otis Chandler, Los Angeles, March 15, 1972.
38. Los Angeles *Times*, March 22, 1972.
39. *Ibid.*, April 23, 1972.

30. Patriotism and Communism

With the outbreak of the Korean War, McIntyre wrote to his priests saying that "the apprehension occasioned by the current confusion and hostilities in the East, joined to the trend of world conflict, makes us realize that our peace has been encroached." He asked them to join with their congregations in raising their "hearts and voices in prayer, petitioning the unfathomable mercy of God to divert us from conflict and restore concord amongst all men."[1]

In a letter to his people in the fall of 1950, McIntyre recalled that "for many years we have been declaring the potential dangers of the Communist regime and activities." In order to refresh Catholics in the rationale for such opposition, he asked that sermons be preached on the subject for four consecutive Sundays. And, because he looked upon prayer as the ultimate weapon, he urged that Catholics throughout the archdiocese recite the rosary daily during the month of October "for the welfare of our boys in Korea, for the restoration of peace and the rejection of communism." He especially recommended that the rosary be recited by the family as a group."[2]

When McIntyre was made a cardinal, a local religion editor wrote that "Americans of all faiths liked his outspoken patriotism. He never hesitated to state unequivocally that in international affairs, his country came first with him."[3] Several years later, he wrote a moving letter about "our suffering brethren in the Church of Silence." He said that "we look to the lands where there is no peace, and are startled at the direful conditions prevailing. Multitudes are under the dominion of Godless governments and excluded from the consolations of the religion which expresses their abiding belief in God. Eternal damnation consists in being excluded from the Vision of God in Heaven; the greatest loss in our earthly life is to be excluded from the freedom to worship Him in a fitting manner, and to be deprived of the spiritual consolations that flow from the sacramental life of the Church. By our prayers and penances on this particular day, we must importune Heaven to shatter the chains that bind the imprisoned Church, to grant fortitude for those enduring the white martyrdom of persecution, and that the mercy of God might fall in forgiveness on those who persecute them for 'they know not what they do.'"[4]

On May 20, 1953, the cardinal spoke before the Jonathan Club Army-Navy Group about the "threat from within." He noted that "we are shocked when a professor, or an educator here, and a statesman or public servant there, is revealed as sharing the philosophy of Communism." He went on to observe that the "erroneous philosophy of Hegel, of Marx, of Nietzsche reflected in John Dewey and his perpetuated school is basically the same philosophy that motivates Communism. The substantial and primary difference in this philosophy and the philosophy of the Founding Fathers of our United States is in the denial of the divinity and the rejection of religion. In the new philosophy, the state is enshrouded with divinity. All rights and privileges proceed only from the state and are directed to the state. Divinity itself is ignored."

McIntyre said that "it has been left to our time, to the courts and the educators of our day, stimulated and dominated by the false philosophy that has found deep root amongst us, to deny the traditions and the history of time, which have been founded and prospered under God. The student of history soon discovers that the violation of divine law, human law, the law of the sea and the law of the land has ever begot war and desolation. There is no more striking example of the hand of God punishing the violation of His law, the laws of justice and morality than is recorded in the Old Testament." He concluded with "the threat to our liberty, our country, our culture, democracy is within us. We are literally affected by a malignant disease. The enemy is not alone from without. Further, it may be from within ourselves. If man today is not thinking in the terms of a Divine Providence ruling over us - if man's morality is not in accordance with the Commandments of God - the laws of justice and equity, - if man's judgments are based on variable and expedient values rather than on the fixed and permanent verities - then man is fooling himself if he seeks or looks for peace. He is pulling from beneath his feet the carpet on which he stands. He is destined to disappointment. Let him look to tradition and history instead and realize that it is God in Heaven Who rules the world and not the Kremlin. The selection is God or the Kremlin. Take your choice."[5]

McIntyre's frequent and outspoken views about the evils of communism were always in touch with reality. He was tremendously upset when some unnamed curial official in Rome released a statement directing that priests not be members of Rotary International, suggesting that the society was in cahoots with masonry and communism. Bishop Aloysius J. Willinger had written to McIntyre pointing out that in many areas of the world Rotary had been immensely successful in counteracting the influence of masonry. Willinger was irked that Roman officials had not discussed the

626

issue with American bishops before taking action.[6] McIntyre agreed
and said that "it is very unfortunate that this news has been
handled so badly in the American press." He observed that while he
didn't favor priests joining Rotary, he saw "no objection to them
giving a talk now and then." He saw no objection, whatsoever "for
the laity belonging to the organization," noting that his knowledge
of Rotary indicated "that it is purely an organization to promote
business friendships and general good feelings on the business
level."[7] The record indicates that McIntyre himself gave several
talks to Rotary Clubs over the years. He later released a statement
to the press saying that "there is no reason to caution the faithful
against membership" in Rotary and, he went even further, declaring
that "the recent comments of the Congregation have no application"
in the United States.[8] His response probably irritated Roman
officials, but none ever challenged him on the issue.

On another occasion, McIntyre told his priests that "we are made
the more conscious of the millions of people in the Satellite countries
and behind the Iron Curtain who are poignantly carrying the cross
of persecution." He urged that "as an act of reparation for the
offenders, and in supplication to Our Divine Saviour for strength
and perseverance for the distressed and distraught of Europe and
Asia. "We earnestly suggest that in every parish on Passion
Sunday, there is a Holy Hour, or some special devotions for the
intentions of our persecuted brethren of the household of the faith."[9]

Throughout his many years in Los Angeles, Cardinal McIntyre
used every opportunity for speaking out on the evils of communism,
emphasizing always that it was a philosophy that left God out of
its priorities. Opposed as he was to the economical deficiencies of
communism, they paled when compared to its Godless nature.

PATRIOTISM

McIntyre often said that whether people looked to the first
Charter of Virginia, to the Charter of New England, to the Charter
of Massachusetts, to the Fundamental Orders of Connecticut, the
same objective was present: a Christian land governed by Christian
principles. The Bible itself permeates the Bill of Rights. Freedom of
worship, expression, assembly, petition, the dignity of the
individual, the sanctity of the home, equal justice under law, and
the reservation of powers to the people were embodiments of the
Christian religion. These were among his core beliefs and he felt
that most Americans agreed on that point.

Speaking at a Forum on Juvenile Delinquency sponsored by the Holy Name Society at its Seventh National Convention in New Orleans in mid-October, 1959, Cardinal McIntyre charged that the removal of "patriotism, philosophy and the natural law of right and wrong from the American scene" by proponents of progressive education was a major cause of delinquency among young people. "Modern education is fast developing an incapacity to acknowledge and practice the positive life that flows from the observance of the natural and divine law." He said that "removal of the teachings of God" was also preventing America from being a free country because the law of God is a truth and without truth we are not free." McIntyre concluded his remarks by saying that "it's up to everyone in this country to force educational leaders to recognize the importance of teaching the true authority of God in schools." And he pointed out that such teachings could be generic enough to avoid denominational criticism.[10]

Cardinal McIntyre was a self-professed patriot and he had no apologies for his love of country. He decried the fact that youngsters were "not taught patriotism in school" or even "the recognition of God, the creator, as were taught in our time." It upset him that the so-called "educational modernists" deliberately strove to separate God from patriotism - to separate God from country. McIntyre vividly recalled how he and others "were thrilled as we sang in unison patriotic hymns of our land, all of which, like the authentic and traditional documents of the Founding Fathers were based upon the recognition of God's existence."[11] The cardinal was not alone in his views. In January of 1960, when he gave the invocation for a luncheon honoring the National Commander of the American Legion, the organization was swamped by those wanting reprints. There he had lamented "the present day vagueness of patriotism as we envision its vanishing qualities of deep faith, of true loyalty, of devoted sacrifice, under the benign bondage of brotherly love." He went on to note that acts of patriotism support, sustain and advocate "the honesty, the integrity and the loyalty that constitute the precious heritage of service to our beloved United States."[12]

While encouraging priests and others to readily comply when asked to give invocations and dedicatory prayers, the cardinal did not feel that taking an active part in politics was advisable for the clergy. In response to a query from the Apostolic Delegate to the United States, McIntyre said that "the participation as manifested in Selma and other cities of the south and north" were, in his opinion, "entirely reprehensible." He agreed with the Archbishop of Mobile that "priests, religious and sisters had no place in Selma and should have stayed home and attended to their own business."

He didn't agree that involvement in such demonstrations by the clergy was in any way "patriotic" since he felt that remedies for racial wrongs could best be obtained in other channels.[13] Nor did McIntyre allow his name to be used in even worthwhile political pursuits. In 1950, for example, when approached by Dr. James Fifield and Rabbi Edgar Magnin to join in sponsoring a luncheon protesting the petition for recalling Mayor Fletcher Bowron. He replied that it has been the policy of his predecessor and had been his policy "since I came here and for years in New York, to abstain from any political interference." And, though he agreed with Fifield and Magnin on the issue itself, he adamantly refused to take a public stance because he felt that the matter was political.[14]

Though he was a registered Democrat throughout his life, the cardinal never disclosed that fact to anyone, at least publicly. When it came to the privacy of the polling booth, he rarely tipped his hand by expressing his personal preferences. He was never known to miss an election and he spoke out eloquently and loudly about the rights and duties of Catholics in the arena of public expression. An example of his belief in the American system of government came in 1960 when the question of a Catholic running for president was raised and widely discussed. In one of the few first page editorials he ever wrote for *The Tidings*, McIntyre revealed his thinking on what became a matter of intense conversation around the nation.

> Throughout the years of our history, the people have elected men of all shades of denominational belief, and committed to them the highest and most respected public authority - to the judiciary, from the lowest to the highest courts; to the administrative branches of the government, in all its divisions; to the legislative halls of our nation wherein are made the laws of man based on the natural law of God. In all these selections, choice has been made without discrimination as to religious creed.
>
> To the highest administrative posts in the nation, elections and selections have been made on the basis of the individual integrity and with adherence to known and fundamental principles, policies and truths, and all this without prejudice because of religious affiliation.
>
> Since, therefore, men of all religious affiliations have administered, and administered well, responsible public office, is it not a manifestation of an un-American spirit to raise the question in this late day that religious affiliation disqualifies any citizen of integrity, and honesty, and

ability for any office within the gift of the American people, or the appointive agent of duly established authority? Every public office of trust has its relative responsibility. All authority basically comes from God, and the authority imposed in any public service begets an obligation to its source in the exercise of that authority, namely, God. This obligation is universal, as is the law of God universal, and binding upon all creatures. We are a nation governed and functioning under God.

Therefore, historically, philosophically and constitutionally, the eligibility of a candidate for public office has not been determined by religious affiliation. To do so now is un-American.[15]

McIntyre's editorial was reprinted in newspapers around the country. Bill Becker, writing in the New York *Times*, reported that "the Roman Catholic Archbishop of Los Angeles said Friday that it is un-American to raise the question of a political candidate's religious affiliation." While noting that the editorial made no mention of a particular candidate, "Senator John F. Kennedy of Massachusetts, candidate for the Democratic nomination for president, is a Roman Catholic."[16] The Los Angeles *Times* quoted McIntyre as saying that "the question of a political candidate's religious affiliation is contrary to American tradition,"[17] reprinted the entire editorial without any further comment, something they rarely did.

DEMOCRATIC NATIONAL CONVENTION

It was indeed appropriate that the convention which nominated John F. Kennedy be held in Los Angeles, where the archbishop was a longtime friend of the Kennedys. Joseph and Rose Kennedy, their four boys and other members of the family had attended McIntyre's ordination as a bishop in New York. Their link with McIntyre had endured over the years.

There is no evidence that the Kennedy people were involved in inviting the cardinal to give the invocation at the opening of the convention, though it was and is traditional that the local Catholic bishop be included among those asked to participate in the proceedings. In any event, McIntyre's invocation was given at the opening session on July 11, 1960. It is here reproduced in its entirety because it reveals much about the cardinal's convictions regarding the commonweal.

Cardinal McIntyre delivers the invocation for the Democratic National Convention, in 1960, at which John F. Kennedy was nominated for presidency.

631

His Eminence
of
Los Angeles

Fifty Priestly
Years
1921-1971

O Almighty God, You anointed Your only Son High Priest of the new and eternal covenant. With wisdom and love You planned that this one priesthood should continue in the Church. Christ gives the dignity of a royal priesthood to the people He has made His Own. From these, with a father's love, He chooses men to share in His sacred ministry by the laying on of hands. He appoints them to renew, in His name, the sacrifice of our redemption as they set before Your family His paschal meal. He calls them to lead Your holy people in love, nourish them by Your word and strengthen them through the sacraments. Father, they are to give their lives in Your service and for the salvation of Your people as they strive to grow in the likeness of Christ and honor You by their courageous witness of faith and love. From among this priestly family, **James Francis Cardinal McIntyre** embarks upon the second half century of his sacerdotal ministry. We pray that Our Lady of the Angels, whose name graces this portion of the vineyard, may continue to bless the retired Archbishop of Los Angeles and his labors on behalf of the People of God. This we ask through Jesus Christ, Your Son, our Lord. Amen.

On this the eleventh day of July in the year of Our Lord nineteen hundred and sixty, here in the fair city of Our Lady of the Angels, assembled in convention, are the delegates of the Democratic Party of the United States of America. The primary purpose of this conclave is to select the candidate that this Party will present to the consideration of the electorate, next November, for the supreme office of president of our country.

We are a nation founded and functioning in the declared recognition of the existence of a Supreme Being Who is our creator and the source of all human rights. We are ever aware of God's providence and protection over the life we live. In all our undertakings we are dependent on His divine assistance.

It is therefore appropriate and proper, it is right and just and salutary, that we inaugurate the deliberations of this immensely important proceeding by invoking God's wisdom and guidance. The honorable delegates of this Convention function in a representative capacity. They will exercise a delegated power as they cast their votes for the candidates presented.

This power comes to them by procedural selection. While it comes with more or less specific instructions or expressions or preference, this power in reality draws its origin from the source of all power, from Almighty God. There is no power but from God, and those that are appointed by God.

Civil authority comes from God. We know this not so much by revelation or positive instruction as by the self-evident fact that God is the Author of nature, and man's social nature requires that civil authority be established and obeyed.

What nature absolutely requires, that God commands. What nature absolutely rejects as incompatible with man's well-being, that God forbids. Hence it is that all just authority comes from God. God binds people in conscience to observe the rule of the State within the sphere of its competence. Thus the exercise of delegated authority is governed by the demands of conscience and by the laws of nature and of nature's God.

Let us be mindful further that in the fulfillment of the responsibility imposed by the exercise of authority, God in His great mercy and providence supplies the special gifts and guidance necessary to conduct that responsibility in justice, integrity and charity. Thus the promise of divine assistance overshadows your actions and awaits your cooperation.

The history of our beloved land gives testimony to the guidance and protection which God has always furnished to our country's leaders. Confidence in His continued blessing should give you assurance as you approach your present responsibility .

The grave importance of this moment is obvious. This gravity emphasizes the responsibility which you bear. It is a responsibility which is shared by millions of our fellow Americans as they follow your deliberations with intense interest and concern.

As your spokesman and theirs, I know that I express the impulses of all our minds and hearts, as we lift them with supplication to Almighty God in fervent petition that His divine wisdom will prevail in your decisions, and that His manifold blessings will ever remain with you abundantly.[18]

McIntyre received an avalanche of commendatory mail from all over the United States when his invocation was broadcast at prime time. One of the most interesting came from the Auxiliary Bishop of Saint Paul, Leonard P. Cowley, who said that it was the first "fan letter he had ever written." He applauded the invocation, noting that "your brother in the College, John Henry Newman, would have been specially proud because of his fear that theology has been separated from, and unrelated to its role as queen of the other sciences." Cowley felt that the cardinal had stated "in a very persuasive way that Almighty God and His authority are too easily forgotten in political pursuits."[19]

UNITED NATIONS

The widespread perception that Cardinal McIntyre advocated or called for boycotting or withdrawing from the United Nations is simply untrue. He was indeed cautious and suspicious about certain activities of the UN, but like most churchmen of his time, he saw it as "the last best hope of a world plunging madly to its own destruction." An editorial in *The Tidings* pretty much reflected his own views when it stated that initial misgivings and vigorous criticisms of the secular spirit of the UN "do not imply condemnation." The cardinal told Catholics to be ever vigilant, alert and courageous in their views of the UN, not allowing enthusiasm to run away with their judgment nor criticism cloud their hopes.[20]

As a matter of fact, before he came to Los Angeles, McIntyre had extensive dealings with members of the United Nations in New York. One newspaper showed him greeting Russia's Deputy Foreign Minister Andrei Vishinsky at Saint Patrick's Cathedral where members had gone "to invoke divine guidance upon the deliberations of the UN Assembly" in October of 1946.[21] That he was recognized as a strong voice was evident in mid-1950 when his call for the admission of Spain to the United Nations made the first page of newspapers throughout the country. He was reported as having "paid tribute to Franco for taking the bull by the horns and meeting the Communist issue in Spain candidly, courageously and victoriously." McIntyre used that occasion to express his chagrin "over the misapprehension current in America over religious freedom in Spain."[22]

McIntyre was often critical of the United Nations, especially over its failure at promoting peace. "After three years of discussion, its Bill of Rights persists in omitting God and recognizing God's law."[23] In another context, he said that the "avoidance of divine guidance in the UN and the elimination of the Commandments as a norm of peace proposals" was further evidence of that organization's "departure from principle."[24]

While there were other aspects of the UN that irritated McIntyre, none so occupied his attention as that dealing with the educational programs of UNESCO. McIntyre was not alone in expressing reservations about UNESCO. Representative John T. Wood, to cite one example, gave a speech to the United States House of Representatives in which he called UNESCO "the greatest subversive plot in history." He told his colleagues that it was his sincere hope "that every parent of every child in America may be able to read the inroads that this infamous plot has already made in the educational system of America."[25] Richard Pattee, a former executive with the Department of State, said that "the public was apprised some weeks ago regarding the UNESCO project for a world history that it is to fuse and merge the whole history of humankind to the end that the common denominators will be emphasized rather than the particular characteristics of each people or nation." He said that he had always "had the greatest reservations about that kind of culture produced by government edict," noting that "as is usual in these cases, non-Catholic and what is far more significant, non-Christian thinking is overwhelmingly represented while the thought that is fundamental to the whole development of the West is scarcely there at all."[26]

In a letter to his old friend, Paul G. Hoffman, President of the Ford Foundation, McIntyre said that "it seems to be a system of education that ignores principles, traditions and standards of long time duration, as well as experience. But what bothered McIntyre more was that "God is not mentioned in this system of education. Neither is religion. The commandments given to Moses are waived, as is the Sermon of Christ on the Mount. The existence of Christ, even as an historical figure, is omitted." He wondered whether education could be "complete without a knowledge and consideration of Christianity and its founder, Jesus Christ, and its influence upon all civilization."[27] In another letter, the cardinal felt that the educational program of UNESCO was a system "that would substitute the traditional education in America. It is godless, and therefore, by omission, atheistic. In this system, the whole concept of Christian civilization would be eliminated - again by omission. The effect of Christianity on the history of civilization would be regarded as *nil*. Furthermore, UNESCO rather plays down the Constitution and the Bill of Rights and upholds the Bill of Human Rights of the United Nations. There is no recognition of Washington, or Lincoln or Jefferson."[28]

That theme was repeated in an editorial published by *The Tidings* which wondered why the nation was rhapsodizing over the latest lucubrations of Julian Huxley. "The first world head of UNESCO wants a new religion based on scientific knowledge. He thinks the well-marked revival of Christianity will wane because its supernatural theology and its absolutes invalidate its claims to be a universal system." It went on to state that "Catholics are educated from childhood to consider all men of whatever area, nation or color as creatures and images of God, redeemed by Christ and called to an eternal destiny. There is no other human group which offers such favorable presuppositions in breadth and depth of international understanding."[29] To the argument that prior to his election to the papacy as John XXIII, Angelo Cardinal Roncalli, then nuncio in Paris, had been named a papal representative to UNESCO, McIntyre countered that he was "only an observer and had very little time to observe before he was made a cardinal and transferred to the patriarchate of Venice."[30]

During his tour of Ireland, in the fall of 1954, McIntyre voiced criticism of the United Nations for "ignoring God in its delibera-tions." In an address to the monks of the Cistercian Abbey of Mount Melleray, he said that "The different nations of the world are supposed to be gathered together in unity, but, as you know, they leave out God and leave out the celestial nation, Heaven, the main guide of life, and consequently we have no peace. No matter how united we may be, if we leave out God we are isolated." He went on to say that "If the world could only have an appreciation of life as you see it and live it in Ireland, you would not have any need for the United Nations."[31]

Discussions about the UNESCO's policy on education dragged on for some years. In June of 1955, the editor of *The Tidings* once again reminded his readers that while "we confess to some original strictures on UNESCO and even to some continuing reservations," such as its World History project and a "pervading secularism which could sadly stifle an experiment noble in purpose, " no one at Los Angeles had publicly or otherwise dubbed UNESCO as "the tool of the Kremlin." He concluded by observing that "responsible criticism has proved a greater blessing for UNESCO than careless adulation."[32]

In an address to the Saint Vincent de Paul Society, McIntyre said that the proposal to adopt the educational program of UNESCO "would compel this country to socialize education under international control."[33] He called the resolution "discrimination of education," noting that "even the dangers of Federal aid to education fade to a shadow in the light of this measure." He said that "widespread apprehension that Federal aid will socialize the American education is confirmed by the philosophy of this UNESCO resolution passed in Paris in 1960 and now submitted to the Senate." The cardinal charged that the proposal would:

1. Substantially eliminate all local control of public education at the state or local level.
2. Would override this Federal control and make it a subsidiary to UNESCO as a world court and final international arbiter of education.
3. Would subject private education and non-tax supported, independent schools and colleges to rigid restriction and conformity with respect to plan, staff, curriculum and policy.

"In other words," he said, "it would do away with freedom in education. Such a policy is opposed to the traditional American principal of freedom in education as guaranteed and determined by local authority."[34]

George R. Hearst agreed with the cardinal. In a long editorial on the subject, he pointed out that McIntyre's· assertion about the proposed treaty substantially eliminating "all local control of public education at state or local level" was accurate. He called on all Southern Californians "opposed to this sort of dictatorship of

637

Federal control from Washington, or of international or One World control from abroad" to flood their senators and congressmen" with letters and telegrams asking that the proposed UNESCO treaty be killed in its entirety."[35]

McIntyre felt that UNESCO was calling for "a blank check over American education," and he felt that "if the United States were to buy this convention, it would be buying a cat in a bag . . . and a very dangerous cat it would be."[36] Happily, the UNESCO program, as it was originally drafted was not overly popular among academicians, many of whom wrote privately to McIntyre commending his courage and fortitude in expressing their views as well as his own.

Notes to the Text

1. AALA, J. Francis A. McIntyre to Priests, Los Angeles, August 16, 1950.
2. AALA, J. Francis A. McIntyre to Faithful, Los Angeles, September 25, 1950.
3. Omar Garrison in the Los Angeles *Mirror*, January 17, 1953.
4. AALA, James Francis Cardinal McIntyre to Priests, Los Angeles, December 17, 1953.
5. *The Tidings*, May 22, 1953.
6. AALA, Aloysius Willinger, C.Ss.R. to J. Francis A. McIntyre, Fresno, January 15, 1951.
7. AALA, J. Francis A. McIntyre to Aloysius Willinger, C.Ss.R., Los Angeles, January 16, 1951.
8. AALA, J. Francis A. McIntyre Statement on Rotary issued on January 27, 1951.
9. AALA, James Francis Cardinal McIntyre to Priests, Los Angeles, March 31, 1954.
10. New Orleans *Times-Picayune*, October 17, 1959.
11. AALA, Address of James Francis Cardinal McIntyre at the National Federation of Catholic Alumnae, Saint Paul, August 21, 1955.
12. *The California Legionnaire* (February, 1960).
13. AALA, James Francis Cardinal McIntyre to Egidio Vagnozzi, Los Angeles, June 29, 1965.
14. AALA, Memorandum, Exchange of telephone calls, Los Angeles, January 7, 1950.
15. *The Tidings*, January 15, 1960.
16. New York *Times*, June 16, 1950.
17. Los Angeles *Times*, January 15, 1960.
18. AALA, James Francis Cardinal McIntyre Press Release, Los Angeles, July 11, 1960.
19. AALA, Leonard P. Cowley to James Francis Cardinal McIntyre, Saint Paul, n.d.
20. *The Tidings*, August 1, 1952.
21. Unidentified New York newspaper, October 28, 1946.
22. Los Angeles *Times*, July 23, 1950.
23. AALA, J. Francis A. McIntyre Address to Friendly Sons of Saint Patrick, Los Angeles, March 17, 1949.
24 *The Tidings*, May 22, 1953.
25. *Congressional Record*. Proceedings of the 82nd Congress, October 18, 1951, p. 1.

26. *The Tidings*, February 15, 1952.
27. AALA, J. Francis A. McIntyre to Paul Hoffman, Los Angeles, August 13, 1952.
28. AALA, J. Francis A. McIntyre to Thomas J. McCarthy, Los Angeles, September 17, 1952.
29. *The Tidings*, September 19, 1952.
30. AALA, James Francis Cardinal McIntyre to Edwin V. O'Hara, Los Angeles, September 12, 1953.
31. AALA, James Francis Cardinal McIntyre, Religious News Service, Release dated September 30, 1954, p. 2.
32. *The Tidings*, June 3, 1955.
33. Dallas *Times Herald*, July 17, 1961.
34. Los Angeles *Herald Express*, July 17, 1961.
35. *Ibid.*, July 28, 1961.
36. *The Tidings*, July 21, 1961.

31. Final Years

RETIREMENT

C ardinal McIntyre exhibited no hesitation or reluctance in supporting section 21 of the Decree on the Bishops' Pastoral Office in the Church which suggested that bishops who "have become less capable of fulfilling their duties properly because of the increasing burden of age or some other serious reason" should be encouraged to retire. But it was his clear understanding that the initiative would always remain with the individual, except in cases where the incumbent was physically impaired.[1] Opposed to mandatory age limitations on the grounds that they were discriminatory, he pointed out personally to Pope Paul VI that some of America's greatest ecclesial personages, including the universally-acclaimed James Cardinal Gibbons of Baltimore, had served well beyond their seventy-fifth year. The Holy Father assured McIntyre that whatever limitations might later be adopted, they would not be retroactive and would not apply to incumbents.

Over the years after Vatican Council II, there was much speculation about a possible vacancy at Los Angeles. Not a few eastern hierarchs cast a longing eye westward and at least one of the California bishops was known to have commissioned an artist to redesign his coat-of-arms to accommodate the added row of tassels used by archbishops.

The rumor mill produced a number of scenarios, some of them plausible, others quite fanciful and none accurate. An example would be the story about Archbishop William O. Brady of Saint Paul-Minneapolis who purportedly died on October 1, 1961 with a bull of appointment as coadjutor to Los Angeles in his pocket. In 1965, a news item in a leading mid-western newspaper reported that "many top Catholic churchmen" had "apparently agreed, among themselves," that the Vatican had marked the Rev. Theodore Hesburgh, President of Notre Dame University, "for extraordinary responsibilities but feel that he eventually will succeed Cardinal McIntyre as archbishop in Los Angeles."[2]

As part of the implementation process for the decrees of the council, Pope Paul VI issued a procedural directive in mid-1966 whereby "pastors" of local churches, notably bishops, were urged "to submit their resignations by the time they reach 75." The new

Cardinal McIntyre lived at Saint Basil's Rectory during his retirement.

The three Archbishops of Los Angeles: John J. Cantwell, Timothy Manning and James Francis McIntyre, 1971.

Cardinal McIntyre, flanked by Bishop John J. Ward and Coadjutor Archbishop Timothy Manning, at his golden jubilee, 1971.

Cardinal speaks at his fiftieth sacerdotal jubilee at Saint Basil's Church, 1971.

regulation was to become operative October 11th. Local pundits in California's southland conjectured that James Francis Cardinal McIntyre, then eighty years of age, "will be expected - but not required - to give up his diocese."[3] He was among the 11% of archbishops and bishops in the world who were already or would be seventy-five by the end of the year.

When he read about the directive in the Associated Press, McIntyre responded that "the statements are not wholly correct; therefore the conclusions are without foundation."[4] He declined to comment on any plans he had for retirement, much to the annoyance of reporters. Early the following year, the question of McIntyre's retirement surfaced again, and the cardinal's secretary reported that "His Eminence said this is the first he has heard of it (his rumored resignation) and it simply is not true." Msgr. Eugene Gilb further said that the cardinal was "in great health despite a recent eye operation."[5]

Though the Holy Father had personally assured McIntyre that his retirement was "open ended," there were others in Rome, apparently unaware of the pontiff's verbal concession to McIntyre, who had designs on Los Angeles. Near the end of March, 1968, an "unacknowledged source"[6] in Rome leaked to Winston Burdett, the chief European correspondent for CBS, that McIntyre had asked to retire on May 3rd. Radio station KFWB said its Rome office reportedly "was told by Vatican sources that the cardinal had submitted his resignation." Again, McIntyre was quick to squelch the report, saying that "any consideration of retirement will await my commencing to feel old."[7]

Fred Farrar, news editor at KFWB, said that his station was standing by its original story, even stating that "it had confirmed its Rome report with a Los Angeles chancery source early Sunday, before the Cardinal issued his denial." Farrar said the station re-checked with "George Armstrong, Westinghouse correspondent in Rome for the past 10 years," and that Armstrong was "puzzled" by the cardinal's denial. Armstrong said that "the resignation had been known for two days in the Vatican as fact." When asked to comment on the report, officials at NC News Service checked with sources and decided it was without foundation. They also noted that suggestions about "Cardinal McIntyre's resignation are regular rumors received in their offices."[8] Winston Burdett subsequently told this writer that he vividly remembered the incident because it caused him much personal embarrassment. He opined that the "leak" was "meant as a signal to McIntyre that certain curial members wanted him out." Burdett said that "such ploys often worked," but added that "McIntyre knew how they operated and always he kept three steps ahead of them."

In mid-1967, McIntyre was asked by the Pope Paul VI to consider the appointment of a coadjutor archbishop who would eventually succeed him as Archbishop of Los Angeles, with the understanding that the cardinal could exercise a veto over any candidate proposed by the Holy See. During the succeeding months, several (probably as many as three) names were discussed and each time, McIntyre expressed reservations. Early on, McIntyre wanted the nominee to be an experienced ordinary, as opposed to an auxiliary bishop or a senior priest. Ultimately an agreement was reached whereby Auxiliary Bishop Timothy Manning would be named to the then vacant Diocese of Fresno, with the understanding that he would eventually return to Los Angeles as coadjutor if he did well in Central California. McIntyre, who had never been close to Manning, harbored some doubts as to his administrative abilities. At the same time, the cardinal clearly appreciated the fact that no one knew more about the Archdiocese of Los Angeles, its clerical and religious personnel, its internal working and its ecclesial history than Manning. It was further stipulated that Manning would not be privy to his possible return to Los Angeles. If any problems surfaced in Fresno during Manning's tenure there, another candidate would be proposed. That this arrangement was never disclosed publicly is obvious from such spurious comments as the one by Kenneth Lamott that Manning had been "exiled to Fresno" because "his views on social issues were too liberal for the cardinal."[9]

In any event, Manning was named to Fresno, where he was installed in Saint John's Cathedral on December 15, 1967. It was during a banquet at the Elk's Hall after that ceremony that McIntyre gave the first hint of his own future. In a tribute to Bishop Aloysius J. Willinger, the cardinal jokingly said he would monitor the activities of the retiring prelate over the years ahead as a possible pattern for the final chapter of his own service to the Church.

Cardinal McIntyre was pleased with what he observed during the months of Manning's episcopate in Fresno. He was especially happy with the way the prelate handled the delicate negotiations over the grape dispute involving Cesar Chavez and the growers, much of which was engineered by a priest of the area who would himself eventually become Archbishop of Los Angeles, Father Roger M. Mahony.

During breakfast with an assemblage of priests at Saint John's Seminary, Camarillo, on June 11, 1969, McIntyre announced that

645

the Holy Father, "acting on our advice and encouragement," had named a new coadjutor archbishop for Los Angeles, "a man known and loved by everyone in this room and in the whole archdiocese, Timothy Manning." Judging from the enthusiastic and sustained applause, Manning was indeed a welcome choice. Concluding his remarks with a wink in his eye, McIntyre reminded his listeners that he was still the residential ordinary and would remain as such for the foreseeable future.

In his public statement, McIntyre said that he was "particularly grateful that the new coadjutor will be our known and sincerely revered Archbishop Timothy Manning" who had "served the Archdiocese of Los Angeles for many years and endeared himself to the hearts of clergy and people." After saying that his twenty year association with Manning had been "a rewarding experience," the cardinal felt assured "of a continuance of cooperative administration."[10] For his part, Archbishop Manning said that "his assignment is as a helper to Cardinal McIntyre. I shall try to be just that, with renewed affection and gratitude, quietly and generously." Manning said that McIntyre's "achievements and dedication are a precious legacy of the Church in Los Angeles."[11]

That McIntyre remained firmly in charge was evident from the outset. He insisted, for example, against Manning's expressed wishes, that the coadjutor take a pastoral assignment. Within a few days after the announcement, Archbishop Manning was named Pastor of Saint Brendan's parish in the mid-Wilshire district. McIntyre was convinced that bishops who did not regularly hear confessions and administer the other sacraments soon lost contact with the real world. Throughout his own life, McIntyre heard confessions at Our Lady's Chapel, Cathedral Chapel parish and other churches throughout the archdiocese on a monthly basis. He often said that his one unfulfilled priestly ambition was that of administering a parish.

Once Manning had been ensconced into office, McIntyre's reluctance to step aside was assuaged. He was especially anxious that his successor feel at home with the financial challenges then facing the archdiocese which were still in considerable debt because of the expansionary programs of the 1950s and 1960s. When Archbishop Manning asked Msgr. Benjamin G. Hawkes to remain on his staff, McIntyre felt that it was time for the transition.[12]

On January 21, 1970, the Vatican announced McIntyre's resignation "because of advanced age." The following day, the Los Angeles *Times* published the statement issued by the cardinal:

Time, in its progress, is resolute and persevering. It overcomes all obstacles and withstands the favorable and the unfavorable with success.

Its processing and its functioning amongst us are constant. It commands our attention and our consequent action.

Realizing the protracted relationship with time that has been mine, I have come to the conclusion that my experience in the realm of time has more than consumed a normal allotment, and hence I am intruding on borrowed time.

To be a borrower, even of time, has its attendant risks to all. I have decided to act upon the suggestion proposed in the recent Vatican Council and have accordingly submitted to the Holy See my resignation as Archbishop of Los Angeles.

My appreciation and gratitude, perforce, finds stimulus in the recognition of the abundant blessings received from our Divine Savior. He has bestowed these gifts through the media of a staunch, devoted and spiritual people of all ethnic origins. They will continue to share in my prayerful supplications that the most cherished graces of a merciful Lord will continue to flow through the lives of the treasured people of Los Angeles, my brothers and sisters in religion and the children of our schools.

With a heart full of gratitude and affection, I surrender my official position and commend to your graciousness my beloved successor.[13]

HIS EMINENCE OF LOS ANGELES

3339 MASSACHUSETTS AVENUE, N. W.
WASHINGTON, D. C. 20008

His Eminence
Timothy Cardinal McIntyre
Archbishop of Los Angeles
1531 West Ninth Street
Los Angeles, California 90015

Interesting philantelic memento.

648

McINTYRE'S MEMORY LIVES ON

James Francis Cardinal McIntyre captured the attention and imagination of people as did few other American ecclesial leaders of his time. For many years after his death, mail arrived daily at the Chancery Office addressed to him. An amusing example is a letter mailed by Archbishop Jean Jadot, the Apostollic Delegate, to Timothy Cardinal Manning on July 31, 1979. Manning consigned the envelope to the archives, along with a note that read: "Someday, when I am safely put away at Calvary, you might use this envelope to prove that infallibility does not extend to the Holy Father's diplomatic corps."

Pope Paul VI, in a statement released by the Los Angeles Chancery office, praised McIntyre for the way he had borne the "weighty responsibilities" associated with the area's "unprecedented growth in population, business, industry, culture and public life," added to which was "the great diversity of peoples" who had migrated to Los Angeles. The pontiff paid tribute to the "integrity of doctrine" which Cardinal McIntyre, over the past twenty years, had defended as well as his "loyalty to the teaching authority of the Church and the successor of Blessed Peter."[14] Archbishop Timothy Manning expressed his gratitude to the cardinal "for his gracious action in allowing that the destinies of the Archdiocese of Los Angeles be entrusted to me at this moment" acknowledging ever-so discreetly McIntyre's hand in his own selection. "By and large," said Manning, "the archdiocese is today what he has made it, giving it princely dimensions and knowing the agony and the anxiety of its shepherding."[15]

In its editorial for the event, the Los Angeles *Herald-Examiner* noted that during McIntyre's incumbency, parishes were increased from 221 to 318, the number of parochial schools grew from 159 to 351, seminaries for the education of priests tripled and hospitals rose from 12 to 18."[16] While recalling that McIntyre had been faulted "by some as being too conservative and set in his opinions, he never compromised his high principles and emerged unsullied from all confrontations." The editor of *The Tidings* said that "twenty-two years of the life of a man were summed up and capsuled last Wednesday when news came of the retirement of our beloved Cardinal, our chief shepherd, or, as he so likes to phrase it, our fellow priest. It is, of course, inaccurate to say that those fruitful years can be capsuled in one moment, for the history of the past and the unwound scroll of the future will serve to embellish those years with the steady glow of radiance which rightfully belongs to them."[17]

Church and civic leaders flocked to pay tribute to the retiring cardinal. Methodist Bishop Gerald Kennedy said that he had "prized very highly the friendship of Cardinal McIntyre" during his years in Los Angeles. Dr. Forrest Weir, executive director of the Southern California Council of Churches, said that through the turbulent years, he had "gained a profound respect for his dedication and single-minded service both to his Church and to this community." Rabbi Edgar Magnin, leading Jewish spokesman and spiritual leader of the Wilshire Boulevard Temple, hailed Cardinal McIntyre as "a great figure in the Church, a man who has stood for the fundamental principles of religious faith and a power for good." Mayor Sam Yorty said the archdiocese had lost "the active service and guidance of one of the world's outstanding spiritual leaders. His projects and programs have brought great benefits to the poor and minority groups and to the community in general."[18]

Even those writers of the Catholic press who had pummeted McIntyre over the years were gracious and positive. S. J. Adamo of the Camden *Star Herald* said that McIntyre's "battles were not born of a cantankerous spirit but rather a love for the truth as he saw it. According to his lights, he was utterly dedicated to the Church. Agree with him or not, no man can deny his passionate zeal for the community of the faithful."[19] F. A. Maurovich suggested that "aside from his own personal piety and unmitigated loyalty to the Pope, Cardinal McIntyre will be portrayed in history by a double image - a master builder and an immovable conservative in time of social and religious change." Yet he said that "what went unnoticed in the noise and heat of controversies was the tremendous work the Cardinal had done in establishing professionally staffed youth centers throughout the inner city. Also hardly ever mentioned is the unique lay missionary program sponsored by the archdiocese which has sent hundreds of doctors, nurses, trained technicians and catechists to developing countries."[20]

In the Brooklyn *Tablet*, McIntyre was described as "one of America's great churchmen." The editor pointed out that the cardinal had been called to meet the changes of Vatican Council II "almost a generation beyond the retirement age of most men in our society." The writer said that it was "an insult to no one to point out that neither adaptability nor the type of acumen necessary for delicate human negotiations are characteristic of octogenarians."[21] Another writer portrayed McIntyre as "simply the outstanding figure in American Catholicism during the last ten years. He was a man of true Faith and deep prudence. He was genuinely, religiously, simply loyal to the Pope, to the Faith, and to the American Catholics as a body - to the faithful."[22]

The Monitor of San Francisco, in its appraisal pointed out that McIntyre had met and overcome challenges unparalleled in American ecclesial annals.[23] Probably the most moving tribute came from the parishioners of Saint Marcellinus parish in the City of Commerce:

Thirteen years ago, three years before the City of Commerce was created, we, the Catholic people of Bandini and Rosewood Park, carried to you a request for a Catholic church in our area - a petition which you kindly received and favorably fulfilled.

We are but one tiny portion of a vast Archdiocese, the whole of which has been blessed with your prayerful guidance and fatherly support, but we feel that ours were more than just commonplace benefits.

Your Eminence established for us a parish in critical and (to others) dubious times; you came in person to bless and dedicate our church and to dine with us in joyous celebration; you presided in our sanctuary when our parish hosted the Knights of Peter Claver. On two occasions Your Eminence gave us, unasked, generous financial help, when you noticed our small parish in rather heavy debt. And these are only a few highlights of your friendly and apostolic interest.

To our clearly beloved Cardinal, God's retiring workman who need not be ashamed, and to our new, and also dearly beloved Archbishop, who takes up, not rusty, but well-burnished tools of loving service for Christ and Mary and for all the Father's children, we offer our gratitude and love."[24]

Archbishop Manning had planned that McIntyre would keep an office at the Chancery in his retirement years, but the cardinal adamantly refused the well-intentioned offer. On the contrary, he pledged never again to enter the building and he never did. Manning subsequently marveled that "when he asked to surrender the administration of this largest archdiocese in the United States largest in fact, if not on record - overnight, he could divest himself of all his attachments, all of his responsibilities, turn his back on his office and never once in ten years by word or deed reflect on the judgments of his successor."[25]

RETIREMENT YEARS

Much to everyone's dismay, James Francis Cardinal McIntyre adjusted quickly if not easily to being "retired." Being the first American member of the College of Cardinals to have that distinction, he set an admirable precedent for others. His successor often commented that "McIntyre wrote the book on how to step aside gracefully."

On the day he left the Chancery for the last time, McIntyre told his staff that he would never return. And he didn't. McIntyre refused to grant interviews, to comment publicly about ecclesial affairs or to attend liturgical events except at the express request of Manning. It was his view that even a hint of interference would not be "fair" to the one who followed him in office. He entrusted his cardinalatial insignia to the archdiocesan archives and decided against attending any further meetings of the National Conference of Catholic Bishops or the California Catholic Conference. He commented on numerous occasions that "there can be only one Archbishop of Los Angeles and his name is Timothy Manning."

McIntyre had lived at Saint Basil's rectory since 1969 when he was finally able to move out of the Fremont Place mansion purchased by his predecessor. The cardinal had resided in the rectory at Saint Patrick's Cathedral in New York City for twenty-five years and he preferred the camaraderie of a house full of priests. At Saint Basil's, his second-floor quarters consisted of a bedroom and sitting room. In the sitting room was a couch, an easy chair, a desk, a television set and a portable typewriter. On the wall over the desk was a portrait of Pope Pius XII and his class picture from Dunwoodie. Against one of the walls was a bookcase, crowded with volumes he used in preparing his daily homilies.

The only item conspicuously missing from the room was a rocking chair. Though the orientation of his life had changed radically, he soon found that his days were as crowded as ever with concern for the spiritual welfare of others. His daily horarium was crammed with the normal demands associated with the parochial ministry. He customarily rose early and was in the sacristy vested for Mass at 7:30 a.m. Unless impeded by other commitments, the cardinal offered an English public Mass on Sundays and holydays. Whenever possible, he used the option of concelebrating with one of the other priests assigned in residence at the parish. On weekdays, dressed in a plain black cassock he would spend several hours hearing confessions during the scheduled Masses. He enjoyed the pastoral role of greeting the parishioners and visitors as they arrived and left the handsome Wilshire Boulevard church. The Cardinal received his first "post-retirement" convert into the Church on May 23, 1970. "It was a happy day," recalled the tall, slender prelate, "for I was also able to confer on him the Sacrament of Confirmation."

His appointment book did not, in any way, resemble that of a "retired" archbishop. The cardinal's thirty years as an active and provocative participant in proceedings of the National Catholic Welfare Conference partially accounted for the steady stream of cardinals, archbishops, bishops and priests who dropped by his Kingsley Drive residence for counsel and advice. Though he had no secretarial staff, the cardinal responded personally to as much of his extensive correspondence as was possible. The literal "avalanche" of good wishes following his retirement indicated the esteem held for the cardinal by the 1,727,161 Catholics whom he served for twenty-two hectic years as Archbishop of Los Angeles.

The cardinal devoted a considerable amount of time to an oral history program whereby material was recorded and preserved for his biography. All his public and personal correspondence and official papers were consigned to and accessioned in the archdiocesan Chancery Archives. Those who visited the cardinal during this "epilogue" of his service to the Church in the United States were impressed by the ease with which he had bridged this last of his many transitions in a long and productive life. "To retire from a position of authority is one thing," says Cardinal McIntyre, "but to abdicate the care and concern of souls is something a priestly conscience could never endure."[26]

Though entitled to a pension of $1,000 monthly, the cardinal only wanted $400 of that amount. He would take his check across the street to the bank, change it into $1 bills and then spend the rest of the month dispensing it to people knocking at the rectory door. Father Francis Wallace, a priest who lived with the cardinal, told how bums would telephone the cardinal from the phone on the parking lot and ask for an appointment. When he appeared, they would collect their dollar bill. He had a rather extensive clientele of "down-and-outers."

A staff member of *The Tidings*, in an article for *Our Sunday Visitor*, described the role of "America's senior cardinal as a parish priest at a downtown church in Los Angeles." He told about his daily routine noting, among other things, that "like parish priests everywhere, after Mass he is out on the porch in front of the church to greet parishioners, conversing easily with businessmen from the neighboring high-rise buildings, and housewives, blessing their small children when they come along." At the age of eighty-five, McIntyre was "fulfilling a long-long ambition" of being a "parish priest." The writer quoted Archbishop Manning as saying that articles about the cardinal had always stressed his background on New York's Wall Street and his accomplishments as an administrator, but "they seldom talked about his life as a priest - which is all he ever wanted to be."[27]

GOLDEN JUBILEE

The cardinal did not want to officially celebrate his golden jubilee of priestly ordination. He hadn't been feeling well and would have preferred to keep the occasion quiet. It was only at the insistence of his successor, Archbishop Timothy Manning, that McIntyre agreed to a public Mass at Saint Basil's Church. It turned out to be a prayer-filled occasion attended by an overflow crowd of friends and well-wishers. A reporter from *The Tidings* held a leisurely morning interview with him on that occasion and found the cardinal still full of the enthusiasm that had characterized his many years as Ordinary. When asked to comment on recent developments, he replied that his "parochial experience encouraged me to believe that the spirit of God among the people will bring about a new realization of the reality of the existence of God in every day life. There is a bedrock belief in God, in His creation and in man's eternal destiny."[28]

An editorial in the same paper noted that "when James Francis Cardinal McIntyre came to us in 1948, he came to us with but one destination in mind. And that destination was the service of the flock which God had entrusted to him on this rim of the western sea, and particularly, the fatherly and pastoral care of the poor and unfortunate among us in that era of sudden population expansion and growth. That purpose and goal were almost immediately defined with his decision to channel the resources of the Church into the low-income areas of the archdiocese. Those resources were not great, but supplemented by successive appeals to the generous people of all parishes, there blossomed forth an almost instant harvest of schools, social service facilities and charitable centers for those in most need. In the years that followed, that unflagging purpose never weakened, nor did the vision ever dim. It is not necessary here to recount the dry statistics which serve to frame in luminous outline the story of skill and zeal and foresight, wonderfully sustained by the support of a vigorous and open-hearted flock who responded to the impulse of his mind and heart. But even now, without the perspective of time to give it depth, it may be said that these years form one of the great chapters of the Church's history in our land."[29]

Los Angeles county officials used McIntyre's golden jubilee as an occasion for expressing their sentiments. In a letter from Ernest Debs, joined by the other members on the Board of Supervisors, the resolution said that "Your constant efforts during your twenty-two years as Archbishop of Los Angeles on behalf of your parishioners, as evidenced by the variety of welfare and social programs directed to the needs of minority groups and parishes, have made your tenure as archbishop an outstanding example of selfless devotion to the needs of your fellowman."[30] And an editorial in the *National Catholic Register* told about the "great love for Cardinal McIntyre among the people, most particularly among those who knew him best." It noted that "here is a man who is totally dedicated, a man who has served his people with complete dedication . . . he is a man who loves Christ, who loves Christ's own Church, who loves people."[31]

In July of 1972, the cardinal journeyed to Rome for a visit with Pope Paul VI, the first since 1968. Received on the 14th, McIntyre reported that "the Holy Father looked remarkably well. His manner was most gracious and his comments were warm and affectionate toward the people of Los Angeles." He recalled that he had first met the then Msgr. Giovanni Montini in 1944 when he had flown to Rome from New York on a United States military transport for a diplomatic mission. As he was leaving, the Holy Father gave McIntyre a ceremonial pectoral cross.[32]

Occasionally McIntyre substituted for Archbishop, later Cardinal Timothy Manning. Among those events was a memorial observance for French President George Pompidou which was held at Saint Basil's Church on April 6, 1974. Almost weekly, Manning visited the cardinal, but their conversations were generally about matters other than ecclesial business. The cardinal gave advice only when pointedly asked and even then, he was reluctant. Delegations often came to pay their respects. On May 14, 1974, for example, representatives from the Association of Student Councils came to Saint Basil's, where they presented McIntyre with a colorful banner from Our Lady of Victory School.

On May 21, 1974, McIntyre celebrated the fifty-third anniversary of his ordination, a long time for one who was already thirty-five years old when he became a priest. It was also early in 1974 that McIntyre achieved the distinction of being the oldest American ever to have served in the College of Cardinals.[33]

Recalling that on leaving Rome in 1972, Pope Paul VI asked McIntyre to do three things: "to give him his prayers, to give him his affection and to come back again."[34] The cardinal decided, in 1975, to make one last pilgrimage to Rome. This time he was making his third Holy Year pilgrimage, his first having been in 1925 and the second in 1950. He recalled his initial trip to the Eternal City: "I went with Bishop John J. Dunn, Auxiliary of New York. I was secretary then to Cardinal Hayes and had responsibility for the funds of North American College." At the conclusion of his visit with the Holy Father, Paul VI said, "I will say good-bye to you for the last time."[35]

During the final conversation spoken for publication, the dean of the American hierarchy offered his views "as part of the framework for the observance of the national Bicentennial." He decried the Supreme Court's abortion decision, noting that "this nation conceived and brought forth in a spirit of reliance on God's Providence and with a clear acknowledgment of the role of God's justice in our social and personal conduct, cannot perdure in a welter of medical and legal semantics which ignore and even deny the role of God's justice in the conception and inviolability of human life itself."[36]

ILLNESS

According to Pamela Harriman, the American Ambassador to France, "to be a public figure, a leader on the world stage, you have to first of all have extra-ordinary health and physical strength." She went on to observe that she had known "many leaders and all of the greats have had an outstanding physical capacity - a capacity to endure."[37] James Francis Cardinal McIntyre certainly qualifies on that score. Except for a serious bout with pneumonia early in 1956, the cardinal enjoyed remarkably good health for the first seventy-eight years of his life. He rarely suffered even colds and his appointment books indicate almost a perfect on-the-job record.

McIntyre's first major illness received international coverage, much to his personal embarrassment. He had left Los Angeles to attend the third session of Vatican Council II, traveling by polar flight directly to the Eternal City. During the opening liturgy, presided over by Pope Paul VI, McIntyre was seated in his regular place on the third row of the cardinals' tier. Just after the consecration of the Mass, he collapsed and fell forward. Attendants, including Auxiliary Bishop John J. Ward, quickly rushed to his assistance, placed him on a mobile gurney and wheeled him to the first aid station at the rear of the basilica. The Holy Father's personal physician, Dr. Mario Fontana, gave him a shot of digitalis and directed that he be sent to the Blue Sisters Clinic on Rome's Celian Hill. Electrocardiograms taken there showed his heart functions to be normal.

The cardinal collapsed during opening of the third session of Vatican Council II.

Reaction in Rome, often described as the "great motherhouse of all rumor mills," was instantaneous, "Reports of McIntyre's death spread rapidly through the Holy See" and it was several hours before the wire services upgraded his condition to "not grave."[38] Subsequent medical reports attributed his fainting spell to "the extreme heat in St. Peter's and from the fatigue of a long non-stop flight from Los Angeles."[39] McIntyre apologized for all the inconvenience noting in a letter to Bishop Timothy Manning that "I surely indulged in the melodramatic." After describing the incident, he said that "between Dubay and this, I am becoming used to world publicity."[40]

After a few days of rest, the cardinal went back to the council chambers several times and, on September 30th, he and another priest from Los Angeles were received by the Holy Father.[41] The pontiff suggested that McIntyre return home for a prolonged rest, noting that it was almost impossible to recuperate in Rome during a conciliar session. When McIntyre arrived back in the southland, he suggested that his collapse at the Vatican Council had been "Hollywoody and dramatic, but of little consequence." He said he felt fine and would soon be back on the job full time.[42] After ten days rest in Camarillo, McIntyre resumed his usual hectic schedule. Few illnesses of churchmen had been followed as graphically by the papers. McIntyre's collapse was featured on the first page of the Los Angeles *Times* and Rome's *Daily American* and formed a feature story in the Italian magazine *L'Europeo*.[43]

About a year later, the cardinal underwent surgery at Saint Vincent's Hospital in Los Angeles for removal of bladder stones. "A Church spokesman said that he withstood the operation exceptionally well and his post-operative condition was very good, adding that there was no evidence of any malignancy."[44] He later remarked to Cardinal Spellman that "on my return from Rome, I consulted with the doctors and they discovered some bladder secretions which were thought to have a potential of trouble." He was grateful that it all went so well and noted that the "recuperation has been most fortunate."[45] He later told Cardinal Cicognani what had not been reported earlier, that the surgery also included treatment for a prostate condition. He apologized for not being able to attend the closing session of the council and said that Bishop Timothy Manning would represent him and the archdiocese. McIntyre spoke glowingly of the council which "presents to the world a tremendous accomplishment, the value of which we shall not fully realize except as the years go on."[46]

Late in December of 1966, the cardinal underwent eye surgery to correct a detached retina. Drs. Clarence and Kathryn Albaugh announced that "it was expected that His Eminence will require two to three weeks recuperation before resuming his duties."[47] What bothered the cardinal more than the operation was his enforced absence from the annual Christmas Party which he sponsored each year for the deprived youngsters of the city and its environs.

McIntyre was hospitalized early in May of 1971 for a sciatica condition. He was released for a few days to observe his fiftieth priestly anniversary and then re-admitted to the hospital for a series of tests "just to make sure everything is all right." He spent much of his time "walking up and down the corridors, visiting with doctors and other patients." Hospital authorities reported that he was just worn out, saying "it's nothing serious."[48]

The cardinal's strength remained fairly stable during the next few years until Easter of 1976. He was listening to a homily, preached at Saint Basil's Church by Archbishop Fulton J. Sheen. When the congregation arose to recite the Creed, McIntyre was unable to stand. It was thought at the time that he was "just overly tired,"[49] but a subsequent examination at Saint Vincent's Hospital revealed that he had suffered a stroke. In the earliest weeks and months, he was able to speak but gradually his condition deteriorated. Thereafter, he appeared to recognize friends, but was mostly unable to communicate.

On June 25th, he observed his ninetieth birthday at a Mass celebrated in the hospital chapel by Cardinals Timothy Manning and Patrick O'Boyle. A telegram was read from Pope Paul VI who took "this rare and outstanding occasion to congratulate you from the bottom of our hearts and to express once again the highest esteem we have for you." The Holy Father went on to say that "viewing the rich harvest resulting from your labors, you must have a great spiritual joy. In your present illness, may your spiritual joy even now be a foretaste of heavenly reward." The pontiff recalled McIntyre's "unusually close relationship with this Apostolic See, begun so long ago with our predecessor Pope Pius XII who raised you to the cardinalatial dignity."[50] At that time, he was listed in "stable condition."[51] *The Monitor*, Catholic newspaper for San Francisco, printed a tribute to the cardinal which noted that during his tenure he "was considered by some to be a controversial figure, but he withstood the storms surrounding his administration. He must be credited as the main architect of the viable and vital Church which now exists in the Southland of our State. The People of God are indebted to him. He has always been first a priest and a dedicated and fiercely loyal son of the Church - so much so that upon his retirement, he assumed the unofficial post of an Assistant Pastor at St. Basil's on Wilshire. Almost up to the time of his recent illness, he was still spending long hours in the confessional. After public Masses, he was always there to greet his parishioners. We salute Cardinal McIntyre and offer prayerful best wishes for better health and much happiness in the years to come."[52]

A year later, when McIntyre observed his ninety-first birthday, Cardinal Timothy Manning noted that "nothing in his life has equaled the resignation and patience in which he spends his remaining years. Within reach of his hand is his Breviary. It is his daily comfort." The cardinal recommended McIntyre "to the continued prayers of the people of God in Los Angeles, those whom he loved and served so well. His presence is a benediction on us all."[53]

DEATH

On July 16, 1979, the Los Angeles *Times* announced that James Francis Cardinal McIntyre, "whose 22 years as the conservative leader of the Catholic Archdiocese of Los Angeles spanned an era of great Church growth and ended in a time of change and controversy, died early today at the age of 93." His death came at 2:30 p.m. at Saint Vincent's Medical Center where he had been since suffering a stroke three years earlier. The paper observed how the "tall, erect McIntyre, retired since 1970, was hardly inactive during the years of his retirement." He lived at Saint Basil's church where, "like the parish priests there, often participated in the liturgy, heard confessions and advised potential converts."[54] The report in the Washington *Post* quoted Cardinal Manning as saying that McIntyre was "among the pivotal personalities of our time who have contributed to the greatness of Los Angeles."[55] Pope John Paul, in a cable to the United States Conference of Bishops said that "I pray that the example of his Christian simplicity and pastoral charity will be held in honor for years to come."[56]

Attending the funeral obsequies held at Saint Basil's Church on Wilshire Boulevard were Cardinals Patrick O'Boyle (Washington), John Cody (Chicago), Terence Cooke (New York), John Dearden (Detroit), Humberto Medeiros (Boston) and Lawrence Shehan (Baltimore), together with the Apostolic Delegate, a host of archbishops and bishops, city and state officials and hundreds of priests and laity. In his homily, Cardinal Manning said that "clearly and without reservation, the whole life of James Francis McIntyre was a total, passionate, selfless, sacrificing commitment of years, talents, earthly possessions, ambitions and life itself to the service of the Church. His defense of her doctrine, his insistence

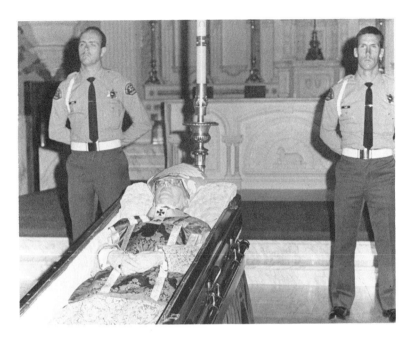

The cardinal lies in state at Saint Vibana's Cathedral.

Cardinals Huberto Medeiros, Patrick O'Boyle and Timothy Manning at Calvary Mausoleum where McIntyre was interred.

Timothy Cardinal Manning preaches at funeral of McIntyre at Saint Basil's Church.

on her discipline, his subordination to her leadership - these made up the substance of his zeal. They consumed his life."[57] Following the funeral itself, the remains of the cardinal were taken to Calvary Mausoleum, where they were entombed alongside his predecessors in the episcopal vault. At his own request, the galero which symbolized his rank as cardinal was hung from the sanctuary of Saint Basil's Church where he labored as parish priest during the last active years of his life.[58]

Among the hundreds of eulogies appearing in print after the cardinal's death, only a few can or need be mentioned here. The Los Angeles *Times*, who had been no friend of McIntyre's during his later years in Los Angeles, said that "like the church he loved and served, Cardinal James Francis McIntyre was formidable and contradictory. He was a brilliant financier whose personal life was a model of asceticism and humility, a master administrator and builder whose happiest moments were spent in the pastoral care of his people, a staunch defender of American constitutional democracy whose own archdiocese was run in an uncompromisingly authoritarian manner."[59]

The pastor of San Buenaventura Mission was quoted in the local newspaper as saying that McIntyre had been "everybody's cardinal, in much the same sense that Francis of Assisi was everybody's saint. There was no formality in his presence. The sincerity of his person, even when circumstances demanded severity, bespoke a man principled enough to have opponents, but Christlike enough to have no enemies." He went on to note that "the elasticity of his thoughts catapulted James Francis McIntyre a decade ahead of his episcopal confreres in such vitally contemporary pursuits as missionary work, inner-city renewal, qualitative educational expansion, clerical recruiting and training, radio and television communications, to mention but a few."[60]

McIntyre's successor opined that he would "surely rank among the pivotal personalities of our time who have contributed to the greatness of Los Angeles."[61] His long-time and dear friend, Rabbi Edgar Magnin, said that McIntyre was "a combination of idealist and pragmatist. He knew human nature and had a lot of common sense. He was opposed to changes that might injure the stability and traditions of the Church. He believed in the values that made America strong and respected."[62]

Archbishop John Quinn of San Francisco said that McIntyre had "written an indelible testament in the lives of the rich and poor, Hispanic and Anglo, native and immigrant, black and white, whom he loved and served with tireless energy."[63] Los Angeles Mayor Tom Bradley referred to McIntyre as "a remarkable man in that his service to the Church he loved and its people engrossed his every waking hour."[64] Dale Francis, nationally syndicated writer for Catholic newspapers, said the cardinal "was gracious but never ingratiating, he was warm but never effusive."[65] Gerard Sherry, writing for the *National Catholic Reporter*, said that McIntyre "was very human, with a deep prayer life and compassion, even for dissenters."[66]

In the final analysis, perhaps Timothy Cardinal Manning said it best when he recalled the life of his predecessor in the light of the Gospel message. Here are some excerpts:

WHEN WE COME to evaluate the measure of a man, we may not in the Church use the obligations, specifications, that are used in the secular world by the media, by political commentators. They have their own sense of values that will honor a man that has sprung from poverty to greatness, who has attained great political power, moved the destinies of peoples, or who has a public relations image. These things might have been the parameters within which James Francis McIntyre might have lived and had he done so certainly would have achieved greatness.

BUT WITHIN the framework of the Church, the values by which we measure men or women dedicated to God are Gospel values. Therefore we have to reach into the Gospel pages to find the measure of this priest and bishop. As we do, we see that Christ holds the central place in the Gospel. It is the mission of Christ that we come to proclaim and to spread the kingdom of God, and to push back the frontiers of the kingdom of Satan.

WHEN JESUS LEFT this earthly scene and the apostles in turn died in martyrdom, it was the plan of Jesus that He would create the Church, and the Church would be His extension into history, and that in the succession of the college of the twelve he would provide a college of bishops who would assume a mission, the authority of servitude of the apostles, until the end of time.

THEREFORE, when we refer to Cardinal McIntyre, and we realize his devotion to the Church, we can then understand that it was to the Church, as identified with Christ, that he brought that same passionate loyalty, that dedication, that willingness to shed his blood in defense of her doctrine, of her discipline, and of her authority. His whole priestly life was an exemplification of those passages manifested in Scripture.

WE WHO KNEW HIM and served by his side, priests and people of this diocese who were guided by him, know the intensity with which he endeavored to serve this fidelity, this loyalty to his Master, to this Church. It is impossible without the cross. Jesus invites them to take up the cross and follow Him. It is allowed that into the ministry of the servant of Christ there shall enter the dimension of the cross. That was seen in this man. We who lived with him know that even though in his serving of the people in the course of the day - meetings, encounters - there might be abrasions, assertions, strength of convictions, unyielding tenacity, yet never in all the time we have known him did he not once not end the day in the quiet of his private chapel, alone in the darkness of the night on his knees before his God. That was the priest, Father McIntyre, humble, lowly, a testing for his greatness.[67]

Notes to the Text

1. Joseph Gallagher, *The Documents of Vatican II* (New York, 1966), p. 412.
2. Chicago *Tribune*, April 17, 1965.
3. Los Angeles *Herald-Examiner*, September 3, 1966.
4. Los Angeles *Times*, September 4, 1966.
5. *Ibid.*, February 21, 1967.
6. San Fernando *Valley Times*, April 1, 1968.
7. Los Angeles *Times*, April 1, 1968.
8. Saint Louis *Review*, April 5, 1968.
9. "A Quiet Revolt," *Horizon* XII (Winter, 1970), 71.
10. *The Tidings*, June 13, 1965.
11. Los Angeles *Times*, June 12, 1965.
12. There were no deals made. The decision came spontaneously from Manning. Given the new archbishop's passive and non-directive temperament, the appointment of Msgr. Hawkes was the single wisest decision Manning made during his incumbency.
13. Los Angeles *Times*, January 21, 1970. Though he did, in fact, "surrender" his official position, McIntyre's influence remained for yet another sixteen years. In a sense there were two McIntyre regimes, the one between 1948 and 1970 and the other stretching from 1971 to 1985, a time when McIntyre continued to dominate the ecclesial scene in Southern California vicariously. There were some cosmetic changes in Manning's time. A priests' senate, an inter parochial council and a clerical personnel board were established and the new archbishop energetically supported a host of ecumenical involvements and warmly endorsed the existing Cursillo movement, but essentially the McIntyre structures remained firmly in place for a total of thirty-seven years.
14. AALA, Pope Paul VI to James Francis Cardinal McIntyre, Rome, December 25, 1969. This was later reprinted in the Los Angeles *Times*.
15. *The Tidings*, January 23, 1970.
16. January 23, 1970.
17. January 23, 1970.
18. Los Angeles *Times*, January 22, 1970.
19. January 23, 1970.
20. *Catholic Voice*, January 28, 1970.
21. January 29, 1970.

22. *Triumph* V (February, 1970), 7.
23. January 29, 1970.
24. East Los Angeles *Tribune*, February 12, 1970.
25. *The Tidings*, June 27, 1979.
26. For a more extensive account of the cardinal's retirement, see article by Francis J. Weber in the Los Angeles *Times*, August 2, 1970.
27. Alphonze Antczak in *Our Sunday Visitor*, October 24, 1971.
28. *The Tidings*, May 21, 1971.
29. *Ibid.*
30. Reprinted in *The Tidings*, May 28, 1971.
31. June 13, 1971.
32. *The Tidings*, July 28, 1972.
33. Francis J. Weber quoted in the Los Angeles *Times*, June 22, 1974.
34. *The Tidings*, July 28, 1972.
35. *Ibid*, May 16, 1975.
36. *Ibid*, May 23, 1975.
37. Quoted in the Los Angeles *Times*, November 20, 1994.
38. Los Angeles *Herald-Examiner*, September 14, 1964.
39. Los Angeles *Times*, September 15, 1964.
40. AALA, James Francis Cardinal McIntyre to Timothy Manning, Rome, no date.
41. *The Tidings*, October 9, 1964.
42. Los Angeles *Times*, October 3, 1974.
43. September 15, 1964; September 15, 1964 and XX (September 27, 1964), 12-15, 17.
44. Los Angeles *Times*, November 16, 1965.
45. AALA, James Francis Cardinal McIntyre to Francis Cardinal Spellman, Los Angeles, November 30, 1965.
46. AALA, James Francis Cardinal McIntyre to Amleto Cardinal Cicognani, Los Angeles, November 30, 1965.
47. Los Angeles *Herald-Examiner*, December 18, 1966.
48. *Ibid.*, May 24, 1971.
49. Los Angeles *Times*, May 4, 1976.
50. *The Tidings*, June 25, 1976.
51. Los Angeles *Times*, June 26, 1976.
52. *The Monitor*, July 1, 1976.
53. *The Tidings*, June 24, 1977.
54. July 16, 1979.
55. July 17, 1979.
56. Quoted in Los Angeles *Times*, July 17, 1979.
57. *The Tidings*, July 27, 1979.

58. By tradition, the *galero* is hung in the cathedral of the cardinal's archdiocese. Since McIntyre was retired at the time of his death, he didn't have a cathedral. He asked that his *galero* be hung at Saint Basil's Church.

59. July 17, 1979.

60. Ventura *Star Free Press*, July 18, 1979.

61. *The Tidings*, July 20, 1979.

62. *Bulletin of the Wilshire Boulevard Temple* LVI (July 30, 1979), n.p.

63. *The Tidings*, July 20, 1979.

64. AALA, Tom Bradley to Timothy Cardinal Manning, Los Angeles, July 18, 1979.

65. Washington, D.C. *Catholic Standard*, July 26, 1979.

66. *National Catholic Reporter*, July 27, 1979.

67. *The Tidings*, July 27, 1979.

Appendix I
Parishes Established during the Archiepiscopate of James Francis Cardinal McIntyre

PLACE	PATRONAGE	COUNTY
	1948	
Alhambra:	St. Thomas More	Los Angeles
Arcadia:	Annunciation	Los Angeles
Buena Park:	St. Pius V	Orange
Lynwood:	St. Phillip Neri	Los Angeles
Long Beach:	Our Lady of Refuge	Los Angeles
North Hollywood:	St. Jane Frances de Chantal	Los Angeles
North Hollywood:	St. Patrick	Los Angeles
	1949	
Los Angeles:	St. Jerome	Los Angeles
Compton:	St. Albert the Great	Los Angeles
Encino:	St. Cyril of Jerusalem	Los Angeles
Reseda:	St. Catherine of Siena	Los Angeles
San Clemente:	Our Lady of Fatima	Orange
	1950	
Montebello:	Our Lady of the Miraculous Medal	Los Angeles
Norwalk:	St. John of God	Los Angeles
Pacific Palisades:	Corpus Christi	Los Angeles
Pico Rivera:	St. Hilary	Los Angeles
Pico Rivera:	St. Mariana de Paredes	Los Angeles
Panorama City:	St. Genevieve	Los Angeles
	1951	
La Canada:	St. Bede the Venerable	Los Angeles
Long Beach:	St. Cornelius	Los Angeles
Whittier:	St. Gregory the Great	Los Angeles
	1952	
Los Angeles:	St. Gerard Majella	Los Angeles
	1953	
Los Angeles:	St. Anastasia	Los Angeles
Garden Grove:	St. Columban	Orange
Lakewood:	St. Pancratius	Los Angeles
Santa Barbara:	San Roque	Santa Barbara

1954

Los Angeles:	St. Camillus	Los Angeles
Bellflower:	St. Dominic Savio	Los Angeles
Burbank:	St. Francis Xavier	Los Angeles
West Covina:	St. Christopher	Los Angeles
Pacoima:	Mary Immaculate	Los Angeles
Santa Fe Springs:	St. Pius X	Los Angeles
Ventura:	Our Lady of the Assumption	Ventura

1955

Anaheim:	St. Anthony Claret	Orange
La Puente:	St. Louis of France	Los Angeles
La Crescenta:	St. James the Less	Los Angeles
Long Beach:	St. Joseph	Los Angeles
Redondo Beach:	St. Lawrence	Los Angeles
Van Nuys:	St. Bridget of Sweden	Los Angeles
Whittier:	St. Bruno	Los Angeles
Woodland Hills:	St. Mel	Los Angeles

1956

Canoga Park:	St. Joseph the Worker	Los Angeles
Downey:	St. Raymond	Los Angeles
Gardena:	Maria Regina	Los Angeles
La Mirada:	St. Paul of the Cross	Los Angeles
Pacoima:	Guardian Angel	Los Angeles
Carson:	St. Philomena	Los Angeles

1957

Los Angeles:	St. Marcellinus	Los Angeles
Los Angeles:	Our Saviour	Los Angeles
Tustin:	St. Cecilia	Orange
Sylmar:	St. Didacus	Los Angeles
Hermosa Beach:	Our Lady of Guadalupe	Los Angeles

1958

Anaheim:	St. Justin	Orange
South El Monte:	Epiphany	Los Angeles
Fullerton:	St. Philip Benizi	Orange
Glendora:	St. Dorothy	Los Angeles
Long Beach:	St. Maria Goretti	Los Angeles
La Puente:	St. Martha	Los Angeles
Los Nietos:	Our Lady of Perpetual Help	Los Angeles
Northridge:	Our Lady of Lourdes	Los Angeles
Oxnard:	Our Lady of Guadalupe	Ventura

1959

Oxnard:	St. Anthony	Ventura

1960

Costa Mesa:	St. John the Baptist	Orange
Monterey Park:	St. Thomas Aquinas	Los Angeles
Santa Ana:	Immaculate Heart of Mary	Orange
Thousand Oaks:	St. Paschal Baylon	Ventura

1961

Corona del Mar:	Our Lady, Queen of the Angels	Orange
Cypress:	St. Irenaeus	Orange
Garden Grove:	St. Callistus	Orange
Norwalk:	St. Linus	Los Angeles
Palos Verdes:	St. John Fisher	Los Angeles
Stanton:	St. Polycarp	Orange

1962

Brea:	St. Angela Merici	Orange
Santa Ana:	St. Barbara	Orange
Woodland Hills:	St. Bernardine of Siena	Los Angeles

1963

Chatsworth:	St. John Eudes	Los Angeles
Covina:	St. Louise de Marillac	Los Angeles
Granada Hills:	St. Euphrasia	Los Angeles
Orange:	St. Norbert	Orange
Orcutt: (Santa Maria)	St. Louis (de Montfort)	Santa Barbara
Oxnard:	Mary, Star of the Sea	Ventura
Pomona:	St. Madeleine Sophie Barat	Los Angeles

1964

Irwindale:	Our Lady of Guadalupe	Los Angeles
La Mirada:	Beatitudes of Our Lord	Los Angeles

1965

Fullerton:	St. Juliana Falconieri	Orange
Hacienda Heights:	St. John Vianney	Los Angeles
Huntington Beach:	St. Bonaventure	Orange
Laguna Hills:	St. Nicholas	Orange
Santa Ana:	Our Lady of the Pillar	Orange

1966

Los Angeles:	Our Lady of Victory	Los Angeles
Goleta:	St. Mark	Santa Barbara
San Pedro:	St. Peter Alcantara	Los Angeles
Saticoy:	Sacred Heart	Ventura

1969

Dana Point:	St. Edward	Orange
Newbury Park:	St. Julie Billiart	Ventura
Seal Beach:	Holy Family	Orange

Appendix II
Churches Dedicated During the Archiepiscopate of
James Francis Cardinal McIntyre

NAME	DATE	PLACE
	1948	
St. Joseph's	January 4	Santa Ana
Our Lady of Victory	January 18	Compton
St. Bernadette	April 4	Los Angeles
Holy Family	April 18	Wilmington
St. Catherine Laboure	May 30	Torrance
St. Joachim	June 13	Costa Mesa
Our Lady of Fatima	July 11	San Clemente
SS. Felicitas and Perpetua	July 18	San Marino
St. Ann's (Davis Street)	July 25	Los Angeles
St. Francis Xavier Cabrini	September 19	Los Angeles
	1949	
Our Lady of Guadalupe	January 16	Santa Ana
St. Emydius	February 6	Lynwood
St. Lawrence	April 24	Los Angeles
Our Lady of Refuge	October 30	Long Beach
St. Philip Neri	November 6	Lynwood
Our Lady of Guadalupe	December 11	Santa Ana (Gloryetta)
St. Ferdinand	December 18	San Fernando
	1950	
Our Lady of the Rosary	January 22	Paramount
St. Timothy	March 5	Los Angeles
St. Pius V	March 19	Buena Park
St. Helen	March 26	South Gate
St. Luke the Evangelist	April 16	Temple City
St. Edward	April 23	Doheny Park
St. Catherine	August 27	Avalon
Our Lady of Guadalupe	September 10	Whittier
St. Elizabeth	November 26	Van Nuys

1951

St. Theresa	January 14	Alhambra
Blessed Sacrament	February 4	Westminister
St. Cyril of Jerusalem	February 18	Encino
St. Jerome	April 8	Los Angeles
St. Ambrose	May 20	Los Angeles
Visitation	May 27	Los Angeles
St. Matthias	June 17	Huntington Park
St. Alphonsus	July 1	Los Angeles
Our Lady of Mount Carmel	July 8	Newport Beach
St. Leo	October 14	Los Angeles
St. Casimir	November 4	Los Angeles
St. Aloysius	November 18	Los Angeles
St. Genevieve	November 25	Van Nuys
St. Barnabas	December 2	Long Beach
St. Athanasius	December 16	Long Beach

1952

Holy Name	January 4	Los Angeles
Rancho San Antonio (chapel)	January 6	Chatsworth
Our Lady of the Assumption	January 13	Claremont
St. Finbar	February 10	Burbank
St. John of God	March 9	Norwalk
St. Mariana de Paredes	March 16	Pico Rivera
St. Albert the Great	May 11	Compton
St. Hilary	September 28	Pico Rivera
Incarnation	October 12	Glendale
Assumption of the Blessed Virgin Mary	November 23	Pasadena

1953

Holy Name	January 4	Los Angeles
St. Rita	March 8	Sierra Madre
St. Gregory the Great	September 13	Whittier
St. Gerard Majella	October 25	Los Angeles
St. Bede	December 13	La Canada

1954

St. Rose of Lima	January 3	Maywood
St. John of Chrysostom	February 21	Inglewood
Holy Family	May 9	Orange
St. Joseph	July 18	Placentia
Assumption	August 22	Ventura
St. Ignatius	October 24	Los Angeles

1955

St. Joan of Arc	January 30	Los Angeles
St. John Baptist de la Salle	February 20	Granada Hills
St. Pancratius	March 6	Lakewood
St. Anne	April 17	Santa Monica
St. Camillus	May 15	Los Angeles
St. Brigid	May 22	Los Angeles
Sacred Heart	July 3	Altadena
Nativity	September 25	El Monte
Immaculate Conception	October 2	Monrovia
St. Eugene	October 16	Los Angeles
St. Bernard	December 4	Bellflower

1956

St. Columban	January 15	Garden Grove
Our Lady Queen of Martyrs	April 29	Los Angeles
St. Sebastian	June 17	Santa Paula
St. Anastasia	October 14	Los Angeles
Sacred Heart	October 28	Lancaster
Our Lady of the Bright Mount	December 9	Los Angeles

1957

St. Pius X	February 24	Santa Fe Springs
St. Francis Xavier	March 24	Burbank
Our Lady of Guadalupe	March 31	La Habra
St. Dominic Savio	May 12	Bellflower
Mary Immaculate	May 19	Pacoima
St. Lawrence Martyr	May 19	South Redondo
St. Anthony	May 26	San Gabriel
St. Louis of France	May 26	Bassett
St. John the Baptist	June 2	Baldwin Park
St. Joseph	September 22	Long Beach
St. Maria Goretti	October 13	Long Beach
St. Catherine Laboure	October 27	Torrance
St. Bruno	November 24	Whittier

1958

St. Anselm	February 9	Los Angeles
St. Bridget of Sweden	March 2	Van Nuys
St. Anthony Claret	March 16	Anaheim
St. Mel	May 18	Woodland Hills
American Martyrs	June 8	Manhattan Beach
St. Augustine	June 22	Culver City
St. Paul the Apostle	June 29	Los Angeles
Ascension	September 21	Los Angeles
St. Paul of the Cross	September 28	La Mirada
Our Saviour	October 5	Los Angeles
St. Raymond	October 19	Downey
St. James the Less	November 30	La Crescenta
Maria Regina	December 7	Gardena
St. Emydius	December 21	Lynwood

1959

St. Benedict	January 11	Montebello
Santa Isabel	January 18	Los Angeles
St. Joseph's	February 15	Hawthorne
Holy Name of Mary	March 1	La Verne
St. Philomena	March 8	Carson
St. Mary of the Assumption	March 15	Santa Maria
St. Mary	April 19	Whittier
Sacred Heart	June 7	Compton
St. Phillip Benizi	August 23	Fullerton
Our Lady of Perpetual Help	August 30	Los Nietos
St. Marcellinus	September 13	Los Angeles
Epiphany	October 4	South El Monte
Our Lady of Loretto	November 1	Los Angeles
St. Stephen	November 8	Monterey Park

1960

Holy Cross	January 10	Santa Barbara
Immaculate Heart of Mary	January 17	Santa Ana
Sacred Heart	February 14	Covina
St. Timothy	February 21	Los Angeles
St. Casimir	March 20	Los Angeles
St. Justin Martyr	June 26	Anaheim
Mary Star of the Sea	August 28	San Pedro
St. Francis of Assisi	October 2	Los Angeles
St. Frances of Rome	October 9	Azusa
Our Lady of Lourdes	October 16	Northridge
St. Mary	October 23	Palmdale
St. Didacus	November 6	Sylmar

1961

Holy Family	January 8	Orange
St. Mary's Byzantine	February 12	Van Nuys
St. John the Baptist	April 9	Costa Mesa
St. Joseph the Worker	April 30	Canoga Park
St. James	June 18	Redondo Beach
Assumption	August 20	Los Angeles
St. Agnes	September 24	Los Angeles
Holy Family	October 1	Artesia
St. John Chrysostom	October 8	Inglewood
St. Charles	November 26	North Hollywood
La Purisima	December 10	Lompoc

1962

St. Bernadette	January 7	Los Angeles
Holy Trinity	April 29	San Pedro
Our Lady of Grace	May 27	Encino
Santa Rosa	September 30	San Fernando

1963

St. Christopher	January 13	West Covina
St. John Fisher	January 20	Palos Verdes
Our Lady of Perpetual Help	March 10	Newhall
St. Thomas Aquinas	August 25	Ojai
Our Lady of Refuge	November 24	Long Beach

1964

St. Pascal Baylon	January 5	Thousand Oaks
St. Boniface	January 12	Anaheim
St. Polycarp	April 19	Stanton
St. Callistus	April 21	Garden Grove
St. Irenaeus	April 26	Cypress
St. Joseph	May 24	La Puente
St. Linus	May 31	Norwalk
Our Lady of Guadalupe	June 21	Santa Ana
Our Lady of the Pillar	June 21	Santa Ana
St. Jeanne de Lestonnac	December 6	Santa Ana

1965

| San Roque | March 14 | Santa Barbara |
| Resurrection | May 16 | Los Angeles |

1966

Corpus Christi Church	January 30	Pacific Palisades
Divine Saviour	March 13	Los Angeles
St. Joachim Church	May 8	Costa Mesa
Our Lady Queen of the Angels	September 18	Corona Del Mar
St. Genevieve	September 25	Van Nuys
St. Bernardine of Siena	October 16	Woodland Hills

1967

St. Joseph Church	January 8	Carpinteria
St. Anthony Mission Church	March 19	Los Alamos
Our Lady of Fatima Church	May 28	San Clemente
St. Nicholas Church	July 9	Laguna Hills
Our Lady of Guadalupe	July 16	Los Angeles
Beatitudes of Our Lord	October 22	La Mirada

1968

Our Lady of Guadalupe	January 7	El Monte
St. Louis de Montfort	February 4	Santa Maria
St. Thomas More	February 25	Alhambra
St. Euphrasia	March 10	Granada Hills
St. Cyril of Jerusalem	March 24	Encino
St. Columban	April 21	Garden Grove
St. Cornelius	May 26	Long Beach
St. Rose of Lima	June 16	Simi
St. Columban	June 30	Los Angeles

1969

St. John Baptist de La Salle	May 11	Granada Hills
Our Lady of Miraculous Medal	May 18	Montebello
St. Joseph the Worker	June 1	Canoga Park
St. Basil Church	June 29	Los Angeles
Immaculate Conception Mission	October 5	New Cuyama
St. John Vianney Church	November 23	Hacienda Heights

1970

St. Rita Church	January 4	Sierra Madre

Appendix III
Educational Facilities Dedicated During the Archiepiscopate of James Francis Cardinal McIntyre

SCHOOL	DATE	PLACE
	1948	
St. Monica High School and Gymnasium	January 4	Santa Monica
St. Mary Magdalen	January 11	Los Angeles
Visitation	January 18	Los Angeles
St. Joan of Arc	February 22	Los Angeles
Holy Angels	March 14	Arcadia
American Martyrs	May 9	Manhattan Beach
Notre Dame High School	October 17	Sherman Oaks
Nazareth House (School)	October 24	Van Nuys
Blessed Sacrament	November 28	Westminister
Nativity	November 28	Torrance
St. Athanasius	December 19	Long Beach
	1949	
St. Anthony	January 9	Wilmar
St. Augustine	January 9	Culver City
St. Eugene	January 23	Inglewood
St. Emydius	February 6	Lynwood
Our Lady of the Valley	March 6	Canoga Park
Mother of Sorrows	March 6	Los Angeles
St. Malachy	April 3	Los Angeles
St. Vibiana Cathedral	September 18	Los Angeles
Mother of Good Counsel	September 25	Los Angeles
Our Lady of Perpetual Help	September 25	Downey
Sacred Heart	October 9	Lancaster
Sacred Heart	October 9	Pomona
St. Mark	November 27	Venice
St. Turibius	December 4	Los Angeles
St. Andrew	December 4	Pasadena
Our Lady of Loretto	December 11	Los Angeles

1950

Sacred Heart High School	January 14	Los Angeles
All Souls	February 12	Alhambra
St. Anselm	March 12	Los Angeles
Assumption	March 12	Los Angeles
St. Catherine's Academy	April 2	Anaheim
Santa Isabel	April 30	Los Angeles
St. Francis de Sales	April 30	Sherman Oaks
Bellarmine - Jefferson High	September 17	Burbank
St. Sebastian	October 1	Santa Paula
Holy Family Parish	October 29	Wilmington
St. Sebastian	October 29	Los Angeles
Mary Star of the Sea	October 29	San Pedro

1951

San Gabriel Mission High School	January 14	San Gabriel
St. Odilia	January 14	Los Angeles
St. Patrick	February 4	Los Angeles
St. Joseph	February 25	La Puente
St. Bartholomew	March 4	Long Beach
St. Luke the Evangelist	March 4	Temple City
Resurrection	March 11	Los Angeles
St. Mary	April 8	Los Angeles
Mount Carmel High School	May 17	Los Angeles
Mater Dei High School	May 20	Santa Ana
St. Victor	September 16	West Hollywood
Our Lady of Lourdes	September 23	Los Angeles
St. Lucy	October 7	Long Beach
St. Francis of Assisi	October 28	Los Angeles
Holy Trinity	November 4	San Pedro
Our Lady of Lourdes	November 11	Tujunga
St. Aloysius	November 18	Los Angeles
St. Genevieve	November 25	Van Nuys
San Antonio de Padua	December 2	Los Angeles
Junipero Serra High School	December 9	Gardena

1952

Our Lady of Peace	January 27	Sepulveda
Santa Teresita	February 3	Los Angeles
St. Benedict	February 17	Montebello
SS. Peter and Paul	February 17	Wilmington
St. Jane Frances de Chantal	February 24	North Hollywood
St. Margaret Mary Alacoque	March 16	Lomita
Santa Clara High School	April 20	Oxnard

St. Joseph High School	April 27	Pomona
Our Lady of Guadalupe (Fisher St)	April 6	Los Angeles
Our Lady of the Rosary	May 11	Sun Valley
Dolores Mission	May 11	Los Angeles
St. Hilary	September 28	Pico Rivera
Chaminade High School	October 5	West Hills
St. Francis Xavier Cabrini	October 26	Los Angeles
Assumption of the Blessed Virgin Mary	November 23	Pasadena
Notre Dame Academy	November 30	Los Angeles
St. Ferdinand	November 30	San Fernando
Our Lady of the Rosary	December 7	Paramount

1953

Mary Star of the Sea High School	January 25	San Pedro
St. Cyril	February 1	Encino
St. Rita	March 8	Sierra Madre
St. Frances of Rome	May 3	Azusa
St. John the Baptist	May 10	Baldwin Park
St. Jerome	May 17	Los Angeles
St. Patrick	May 17	North Hollywood
Our Lady of the Rosary of Talpa	May 24	Los Angeles
Our Lady of Refuge	October 18	Long Beach
St. Mark	October 25	Venice
Our Lady of Mount Carmel	December 6	Santa Ana

1954

St. John of God	March 28	Norwalk
St. Gerard Majella	October 10	Los Angeles
St. Mary Magdalen	November 6	Camarillo

1955

Sacred Heart	January 23	Covina
St. Martin of Tours	January 30	Los Angeles
San Juan Capistrano	February 27	San Juan Capistrano
Santa Rosa	March 13	San Fernando
St. Cornelius	March 20	Lakewood
Our Lady of the Miraculous Medal	May 8	Montebello
Our Lady of Mount Carmel	October 30	Santa Barbara

1956

Cantwell High School	January 25	Montebello
St. Gregory the Great	March 4	Whittier
Our Lady of Grace	April 22	Encino
Our Lady of the Assumption	September 23	Claremont
St. Thomas Aquinas	October 7	Ojai
St. Anastasia	October 14	Los Angeles
Mayfield Junior High School	November 4	Pasadena
La Salle High School	November 10	Pasadena
Providence High School	November 25	Burbank

1957

St. Christopher	January 13	West Covina
St. Pius	February 24	Santa Fe Springs
St. Francis Xavier	March 24	Burbank
Our Lady of Guadalupe	March 31	La Habra
St. Dominic Savio	May 12	Bellflower
St. Lawrence Martyr	May 19	South Redondo
St. Monica High School	May 25	Santa Monica
St. Louis of France	May 26	Bassett
Santa Clara	December 1	Oxnard

1958

La Purisima	January 12	Lompoc
Bishop Montgomery High School	February 23	Torrance

1959

Servite High School	February 12	Anaheim
Bishop Mora High School	April 26	Los Angeles
St. Bernard High School	May 24	Los Angeles
Bishop Alemany High School	May 30	Mission Hills
Assumption	September 20	Ventura
Bishop Amat High School	October 11	La Puente
St. Paul High School	October 25	Santa Fe Springs

1960

Christ the King	March 6	Los Angeles
St. Brendan	May 15	Los Angeles
Fermin Lasuen High School	May 22	San Pedro
Christ the King	September 11	Oxnard
St. Genevieve High School	October 16	Panorama City

1961

Alverno Heights Academy	January 15	Sierra Madre
Our Lady of Guadalupe	January 22	Rosehill
St. Cecilia	February 12	Los Angeles
St. Brigid	February 12	Los Angeles
Bishop Garcia Diego High School	March 5	Santa Barbara
St. Ignatius	March 5	Los Angeles
Marymount College	April 15	Palos Verdes
Marymount High School	April 22	Santa Barbara
Louisville Academy	April 30	Woodland Hills
St. Ferdinand	May 28	San Fernando
St. Joseph	December 23	Carpinteria

1962

Our Lady Help of Christians	January 21	Los Angeles
Cornelia Connelly	February 10	Anaheim
Crespi High School	March 11	Encino
Chaminade Preparatory	April 1	Canoga Park
St. Lawrence	September 30	Los Angeles

1963

St. John Military Academy	March 3	Chatsworth
Pater Noster High School	April 21	Los Angeles

1964

St. Lucy Priory High School	February 2	Glendora
St. Polycarp	April 19	Stanton
St. Callistus	April 21	Garden Grove
St. Irenaeus	April 26	Cypress
St. Linus	May 31	Norwalk
Maryknoll	September 6	Los Angeles
Verbum Dei High School	November 29	Los Angeles
Marywood High School	December 5	Orange

1965

St. John the Evangelist	January 17	Los Angeles
Holy Trinity	January 31	Los Angeles
St. Elizabeth	March 21	Altadena
St. Mary Seminary	August 29	Santa Barbara

1966

Regina Caeli High School	February 27	Compton
St. John Seminary College	June 25	Camarillo
Paraclete High School	November 6	Lancaster
St. Francis Xavier	November 12	Burbank
Daniel Murphy High School	December 4	Los Angeles

1967

Serra High School	January 22	Gardena
St. Mary Academy	February 12	Inglewood
St. Joseph High School	March 5	Lakewood
Our Lady of Fatima School	May 28	San Clemente
Holy Cross Grammar School	October 8	Los Angeles
La Reina High School	October 15	Thousand Oaks
St. Francis High School	December 3	La Canada

1968

St. Bonaventure High School	January 21	Ventura
St. Joseph High School	February 4	Santa Maria
St. Euphrasia School	March 10	Granada Hills
Rosary High School	May 19	Fullerton

1969

St. Vincent School	May 17	Santa Barbara

Appendix IV
Agencies, Commissions and Departments estabished during the Archiepiscopate of James Francis Cardinal McIntyre

Catholic Press Council - 1948

Catholic Information Center - 1948

Archbishop's Christmas Party - 1949

Department of Hospitals and Health - 1950

Archbishop's Fund for Charity - 1951

Annual Motion Picture Communions Breakfast - 1952

Vocation Department - 1952

Lay Mission Helpers - 1955

Mission Doctors Association - 1959

Chancery Archives - 1962

Department of Radio and Television - 1962

Cursillo Apostolate - 1962

Liturgical Commission (reorganized) - 1963

Ecumenical Commission - 1967

Instructional Television Department - 1967

Department of Special Services - 1967

Music Commission - 1968

Right to Life League - 1969

APPENDIX V
High School Survey
1962-1963

	SCHOOL	GRADUATES
Girls	Alverno Heights Academy	0
Coed	Bellarmine-Jefferson	110
Coed	Bishop Alemany	251
Coed	Bishop Amat	207
Girls	Bishop Conaty	212
Coed	Bishop Garcia Diego	110
Coed	Bishop Montgomery	204
Boys	Bishop Mora Salesian	172
Boys	Cantwell	112
Boys	Cathedral	132
Boys	Chaminade	26
Girls	Cornelia Connelly (Seniors '65)	0
Girls	Corvallis	71
Boys	Crespi Carmelite	84
Boys	Don Bosco Technical	115
Boys	Fermin Lasuen	86
Girls	Flintridge Sacred Heart	48
Girls	Holy Family	68
Girls	Immaculate Heart	174
Boys	Junipero Serra	148
Boys	La Salle	91
Boys	Loyola	185
Girls	Louisville (Seniors in '64)	0
Girls	Marymount, Los Angeles	57

Girls	Marymount, Palos Verdes	28
Girls	Marymount, Santa Barbara	25
Girls	Mary Star of the Sea	57
Girls	Marywood	92
Coed	Mater Dei	264
Girls	Mayfield	41
Boys	Mount Carmel	126
Girls	Notre Dame Academy	88
Boys	Notre Dame	206
Girls	Our Lady of Loretto	80
Girls	Our Lady Queen of Angels	68
Boys	Pater Noster (Seniors in '64)	0
Coed	Pius X	246
Girls	Pomona Catholic Girls	64
Boys	Pomona Catholic Boys	77
Girls	Providence	107
Girls	Ramona Convent	91
Girls	Regina Caeli (Seniors '66)	0
Girls	Sacred Heart, Los Angeles	116
Girls	Sacred Heart of Mary	78
Girls	St. Andrew	103
Coed	St. Anthony	305
Coed	St. Bernard	218
Girls	St. Catherine Academy	19
Boys	St. Francis	95
Coed	St. Genevieve	99
Boys	St. John Bosco	37
Boys	St. John Vianney	81
Girls	St. Lucy's Priory (Seniors '65)	0

Girls	St. Mary's Academy	210
Girls	St. Matthias (Seniors '64)	0
Girls	St. Michael	104
Coed	St. Monica	187
Coed	St. Paul	205
Coed	San Gabriel Mission	183
Coed	Santa Clara	114
Boys	Servite	90
Boys	Verbum Dei (Seniors '66)	0
Girls	Villa Cabrini	31
Boys	Villanova Prep	26
Total:	64 High Schools	6,624

Appendix VI
THE EPISCOPAL LINEAGE OF HIS EMINENCE JAMES FRANCIS ALOYSIUS CARDINAL McINTYRE ARCHBISHOP OF LOS ANGELES

1. *JAMES FRANCIS ALOYSIUS McINTYRE*, Titular Bishop of Cyrene and Auxiliary Bishop of New York. Consecrated 8 January 1941 in Saint Patrick's Cathedral, New York, New York, by Francis Joseph Spellman, Archbishop of New York, assisted by Stephen Joseph Donahue, Titular Bishop of Medea and Auxiliary Bishop of New York, and John Francis O'Hara, C.S C., Titular Bishop of Mylasa and Auxiliary Bishop of the Military Vicariate of the United States.

2. *FRANCIS JOSEPH SPELLMAN*, Titular Bishop of Sila and Auxiliary Bishop of Boston. Consecrated 8 September 1932 in Saint Peter' s Basilica, Rome, Vatican City, by Eugenio Cardinal Pacelli, the future Pope Pius XII, assisted by Giuseppe Pizzardo, Titular Archbishop of Nicaea and Francesco Borgongini-Duca, Titular. Archbishop of Heraclea in Europa.

3. *EUGENIO PACELLI*, Titular Archbishop of Sardi, the future Pope Pius XII. Consecrated 13 May 1917 in the Sistine Chapel, Rome, by His Holiness Pope Benedict XV, assisted by Giovanni Battista Nasalli Rocca di Corneliano, Titular Archbishop of Thebes and Agostino Zampini, O.S.A., Titular Bishop of Porphyreon and Sacristan of His Holiness.

4. *GIACOMO DELLA CHIESA*, Archbishop of Bologna, the future Pope Benedict XV. Consecrated 22 December 1907 in the Sistine Chapel, Rome, by His Holiness Pope Saint Pius X, assisted by Pietro Balestra, Archbishop of Cagliari and Teodoro Valfre di Bonzo, Archbishop of Vercelli.

5. *GIUSEPPE SARTO*, Bishop of Mantova (the future Pope St. Pius X). Consecrated 16 November 1884 in the Church of San Apollinare, Rome, by Lucido Maria Cardinal Parocchi, Vicar of Rome, assisted by Pietro Rota, Titular Archbishop of Thebes and Giovanni Maria Berengo, Archbishop of Udine.

6. **LUCIDO MARIA PAROCCHI**, Bishop of Pavia. Consecrated 5 November 1871 in the Church of Titular dei Monti, Rome, by Costantino Cardinal Patrizi, Bishop of Ostia and of Velletri, assisted by Pietro Villanova Castellacci, Titular Archbishop of Petra and Salvatore Nobili Vitelleschi, Titular Archbishop of Seleucia.

7. **COSTANTINO PATRIZI**, Titular Archbishop of Philippi. Consecrated 21 December 1828 in the Church of Santa Caterina da Siena, Rome, by Carlo Cardinal Odescalchi, Prefect of the Sacred Congregation of Bishops and Regulars, assisted by Lorenzo Mattei, Titular Patriarch of Antioch and Paolo Agosto Foscolo, Archbishop of Corfu.

8. **CARLO ODESCALCHI**, Cardinal Archbishop of Ferrara. Consecrated 25 May 1823 in the Basilica of the Twelve Holy Apostles, Rome, by Giulio Maria Cardinal Della Somaglia, Bishop of Ostia and of Velletci assisted by Giuseppe Della Porta Rodiani, Titular Patriarch of Constantinople and Lorenzo Mattei, Titular Patriarch of Antioch.

9. **GIULIO MARIA DELLA SOMAGLIA**, Titular Patriarch of Antioch. Consecrated 21 December 1788 in the Church of San Carlo ai Catinari, Rome, by Hyacinthe-Sigismond Cardinal Gerdil, C.R.S.P., assisted by Nicola Buschi, Titular Archbishop of Ephesus and Pierluigi Galletti, O S.B., Titular Bishop of Cyrene

10. **HYACINTHE-SIGISMOND GERDIL, C.R.S.P.**, Titular Bishop of Dibon. Consecrated 2 March 1777 in the Church of San Carlo ai Catinari, Rome, by Marcantonio Cardinal Colonna, Vicar of Rome, assisted by Orazio Mattei, Titular Archbishop of Colosse and Francesco Antonio Marcucci, Bishop of Montalto delle Marche and Vicegerent of Rome.

11. **MARCANTONIO COLONNA**, Cardinal and Titular Archbishop of Corinth. Consecrated 25 April 1762 in the Pauline Chapel of the Apostolic Palace of the Quirinal, Rome, by His Holiness Pope Clement XIII, assisted by Giovanni Francesco Cardinal Albani, Bishop of Sabina and Henry Cardinal Stuart, Duke of York, Bishop of Frascati.

12. **CARLO REZZONICO**, Cardinal Bishop of Padova (the future Pope Clement XIII). Consecrated 19 March 1743 in the Basilica of the Twelve Holy Apostles, Rome, by His Holiness Pope

Benedict XIV, assisted by Giuseppe Cardinal Accaramboni, Bishop of Frascati and Antonio Saverio Cardinal Gentili

13. *PROSPERO LAMBERTINI*, Titular Archbishop of Theodosia (the future Pope Benedict XIV) Consecrated 16 July 1724 in the Pauline Chapel of the Apostolic Palace of the Quirinal, Rome, by His Holiness Pope Benedict XIII, assisted by Giovanni Francesco Nicolai, O.F.M.Ref., Titular Archbishop of Myra and Nicola Maria Lercari, Titular Archbishop of Nazianzus.

14. *VINCENZO MARIA ORSINI*, o.p., Cardinal Archbishop of Manfredonia (the future Pope Benedict XIII). Consecrated 3 February 1675 in the Church of Saints Dominic and Sixtus, Rome, by Paluzzo (Paluzzi degli Albertoni) Cardinal Altieri, Prefect of the Sacred Congregation de Propaganda Fide, assisted by Stefano Brancaccio, Archbishop-Bishop of Viterbo e Tuscania and Costanzo Zani, O. S. B., Bishop of Imola.

15. *PALUZZI DEGLI ALBERTONI ALTIERI*, Cardinal Bishop of Montefiascone e Corneto. Consecrated 2 May 1666 in the Church of San Silvestro in Capite, Rome, by Ulderico Cardinal Carpegna, assisted by Stefano Ugolini, Titular Archbishop of Corinth and Giovanni Tommaso Pinelli, Bishop of Albenga.

16. *ULDERICO CARPEGNA*, Bishop of Gubbio. Consecrated 7 October 1630 in the Pauline Chapel of the Apostolic Palace of the Quirinal, Rome, by Luigi Cardinal Caetani, assisted by Antonio Ricciulli, Bishop emeritus of Belcastro and Viceregent of Rome, and Benedetto Landi, Bishop of Fossombrone

17. *LUIGI CAETANI*, Titular Patriarch of Antioch. Consecrated 12 June 1622 in the Basilica of Santa Maria Maggiore, Rome, by Lodovico Cardinal Ludovisi, Archbishop of Bologna, assisted by Galeazzo Sanvitale, Archbishop emeritus of Bari and Vulpiano Volpi, Archbishop emeritus of Chieti.

18. *LODOVICO LUDOVISI*, Cardinal Archbishop of Bologna. Consecrated 2 May 1621 in the private chapel of his consecrator, near Saint Peter's Basilica, Rome, by Galeazzo Sanvitale, Archbishop emeritus of Bari and Prefect of the Apostolic Palace, assisted by Cosmo de Torres, Titular Archbishop of Hadrianopolis and Òttavio Ridolfi, Bishop of Ariano.

19. ***GALEAZZO SANVITALE***, Archbishop of Bari. Consecrated 4 April 1604 in the chapel of the Apostolic Sacristy, Rome, by Girolamo Cardinal Bernerio, O.P., Bishop of Albano, assisted by Claudio Rangoni, Bishop of Piacenza and Giovanni Ambrogio Caccia, Bishop of Castro di Toscana.

20. ***GIROLAMO BERNERIO, O.P.***, Bishop of Ascoli Piceno. Consecrated 7 September 1586 in the Basilica of the Twelve Holy Apostles, Rome, by Giulio Antonio Cardinal Santoro, assisted by Giulio Masetti, Bishop of Reggio Emilia and Ottaviano Paravicini, Bishop of Alessandria.

21. ***GIULIO ANTONIO SANTORO***, Archbishop of Santa Severina. Consecrated 12 March 1566 in the Pauline Chapel of the Vatican Apostolic Palace by Scipione Cardinal Rebiba, Titular Patriarch of Constantinople, assisted by Annibale Caracciolo, Bishop of Isola and Giacomo de'Giacomelli, Bishop emeritus of Belcastro.

22. ***SCIPIONE REBIBA***, Titular Bishop of Amicle and Auxiliary of Chieti. Elected Titular Bishop of Amicle and Auxiliary to Giovanni Pietro Cardinal Carafa, Archbishop of Chieti, 16 March 1541. To date, after extensive research, no record of his consecration has been found.

This episcopal lineage is here traced through the diligent research of Charles N. Bransom, Jr.

Appendix VII
Parallel Patterns

This essay is taken from Francis J. Weber, *Readings in California Catholic History* (Los Angeles, 1967), Pp. 77-79.

FRANCISCO GARCIA DIEGO y MORENO, our *first* Ordinary, nominated to the episcopate in 1840, considered the most important accomplishment of his tenure the erection of a seminary on land adjacent to Mission Santa Ines.

JAMES FRANCIS CARDINAL MCINTYRE, our *present* Ordinary, nominated to the episcopate in 1940, considers a most important accomplishment of his tenure the erection of a seminary on land adjacent to Mission San Fernando.

JOSEPH SADOC ALEMANY y CONILL, our *second* Ordinary, was a highly respected and outspoken metropolitan archbishop at Vatican Council I.

JAMES FRANCIS CARDINAL MCINTYRE, our *present* Ordinary, is a highly respected and outspoken metropolitan archbishop at Vatican Council II.

TADEO AMAT y BRUSI, our *third* Ordinary, a recognized authority on collegial infallibility, had never set foot on California soil before his arrival as residential bishop.

JAMES FRANCIS CARDINAL MCINTYRE, our *present* Ordinary, a recognized authority on papal infallibility, had never set foot on California soil before his arrival as residential bishop.

FRANCISCO MORA y BORRELL, our *fourth* Ordinary, ordained at Santa Barbara on March 19th, lost his mother at the age of ten and was raised by an aunt.

JAMES FRANCIS CARDINAL MCINTYRE, our *present* Ordinary, installed at Los Angeles on March 19th, lost his mother at the age of ten and was raised by an aunt.

GEORGE THOMAS MONTGOMERY, our *fifth* Ordinary, first native American to govern the diocese, functioned for some years as a coadjutor arch-bishop but never succeeded the residential prelate.

JAMES FRANCIS CARDINAL MCINTYRE, our *present* Ordinary, first papal prince to govern the archdiocese, functioned for some years as a coadjutor archbishop but never succeeded the residential prelate.

THOMAS JAMES CONATY, our *sixth* Ordinary, fifty-four years old at the time of his episcopal appointment, was known for his championship of Catholic education through his position as Rector of The Catholic University of America.

JOHN JOSEPH CANTWELL, our *seventh* Ordinary, named archbishop in 1936 was Vicar General of a large archdiocese before coming to Los Angeles.

JAMES FRANCIS CARDINAL MCINTYRE, our *present* Ordinary, fifty-four years old at the time of his episcopal appointment, is known for his championship of Catholic education through his erection of 206 schools.

JAMES FRANCIS CARDINAL MCINTYRE, our *present* Ordinary, named domestic prelate in 1936, was Vicar General of a large archdiocese before coming to Los Angeles.

Appendix VIII
Honors and Awards

In his position as Archbishop of Los Angeles, James Francis Cardinal McIntyre received hundreds of citations, awards, commendations and resolutions over the years, most of which are safely filed away in the Archival Center at Mission Hills, California. Among the more noteworthy of those honors are:

Principality of Monaco - Medal of Saint Devote (1956)

Republic of Mexico - Rose of Tepeyac (1960)

Republic of Italy - Knighthood of the Grand Cross of the Order of Merit (1961)

Republic of Spain - Grand Cross of the Order of Isabel la Catolica (1968)

****

Order of Alhambra - Lifetime Achievement (1960)

Los Angeles Memorial Coliseum - Plaque unveiled (1966)

Boy Scouts of America - Silver Bear Award (1966)

American Jewish Committee - Star of David (1970)

Community Service Award - United Way (1966)

Salesian Boys Club - *Padrino* of the Year (1970)

Admiral of the Texas Navy

INDEX

SCHOOLS